Administering
SAP™ R/3

MM-Materials Management Module

Administering
SAP™ R/3

MM-Materials Management Module

ASAP World Consultancy
Jonathan Blain and Bernard Dodd
with Helen Boardman
and Peter Chapman

Contributions by
Philip Vaughan
Ian Henderson

Administering SAP R/3 MM-Materials Management Module

Library of Congress Catalog No.: 97-69807

ISBN: 0-7897-1502-3

00 99 98   6 5 4 3 2 1

Interpretation of the printing code: the rightmost double-digit number is the year of the book's printing; the rightmost single-digit number, the number of the book's printing. For example, a printing code of 98-1 shows that the first printing of the book occurred in 1998.

Screen reproductions in this book were created using Collage Plus from Inner Media, Inc., Hollis, NH.

Contents at a Glance

Introduction   Focusing on Materials Management   1

I | Using the SAP R/3 Materials Management Application

1   Implementing Integrated Materials Management   9
2   Understanding Materials Purchasing   33
3   Understanding Material Requirements Planning   61
4   Understanding Inventory and Warehouse Management   129

II | Knowing How Materials Management Fits into SAP R/3

5   Integrating MM   171
6   Understanding the SAP R/3 Business Engineer   205
7   Analyzing Materials Information   289
8   Utilizing Reports and Interfaces   313
9   Understanding Network Computing   343
10   MM Education and Training   367

| Appendix

A   MM—A Consultant's Perspective   385

Index   391

Table of Contents

Focusing on Materials Management   1

In This Book   2

Scope of This Book   2

What Will Be Gained from This Book   3

Introducing the SAP Corporation   4

History   5

Markets for SAP Products   5

From Here...   6

I Using the SAP R/3 Materials Management Application

1 Implementing Integrated Materials Management   9

Commercial Fundamentals   10

The MM Flow of Events and Processes   11

The Departments of Business   11
  Head Office   12
  Subsidiary Companies   12
  Plant   12
  Material   12

The Accounting Operations for Materials Receipt   13
  Goods Receipt   13
  Transactions   13
  Chart of Accounts   13
  Material Valuation   13

Reviewing the Terminology of Materials Management   14
  Maintaining Basic Data   14
  Materials Requirements Planning   16
  Purchasing   16
  Inventory Management   19

Material Valuation   19
Invoice Verification   20
Warehouse Management   20
Special Functions   21
ABC Analysis   21

Using the SAP R/3 Basis System   22

The Interface Between System and User   22
  Ergonomic Design   22
  Sessions or Modes   23

The Transaction Concept   24
  Automatic Documentation of Transactions   24
  Manual Document Entry   26

Using Standard Components Controlled by Tables   27
  The Role of Tables in Standard Business Software   28

SAP R/3 Business Applications   28

CA-Cross Application   28

Trends in Marketing SAP R/3   29
  Accelerated SAP   29
  Components as Separate Managed Objects   29
  Industry Solutions and the Vertical Market Initiative   29

Price List Module Components of MM   30
  MM-BD Master Data   30
  PP-MRP Material Requirements Planning   30
  MM-PUR Purchasing   31
  MM-IS Purchasing Information System   31
  MM-WM Warehouse Management   31
  MM-IM Inventory Management   31
  MM-IV Invoice Verification   32

From Here...   32

2 Understanding Materials Purchasing 33

Procurement by Exception   34

Using Materials Master Records   36
Materials Master Record Attributes   37
Customizing Your MM-Materials Management Module   37
Alterations to Materials Masters   38

Material Types   38
The Control Functions of a Material Type   39
Batches   40
Special Stocks   40

Purchasing Info Records   41
The Data Environment of a Purchasing Info Record   41
Purchasing Info Record Structure   42
Creating Purchasing Info Records   42
Central Control Function   43

Bills of Material (BOM)   43
BOM Header   43
BOM Items   43
Types of Bills of Material   44
Using Bills of Material   44

Procurement Procedures   45
Pricing Conditions as Data Structures   46
Price Determination   46
Maintaining Conditions   47

The Vendor Data Concept   47
Once-Only Vendors   48
User Departments   49
The Structure of Vendor Master Records   49
Account Groups   50

Managing Sources of Supply   50
Choosing a Vendor for a Specific Material   50
Automatic Vendor Evaluation   51

Applying Subcriteria   52
Displaying Automatic Vendor Evaluations   52
Vendor Net Price Simulation   52
Alternative Vendor Pricing Plans   53

Using MM to Control Purchasing Operations   53
Purchasing Documents   54
Purchasing Document Structure   54
Purchase Requisition   54
Generating a Purchase Requisition   54
Sources of Supply   55

Allocation of Purchase Requisitions   55
Purchase Requisition Release Strategies   55
Buyer-Generated Purchase Requisitions   55

The Request for Quotation Procedure   56

Generating a Purchase Order   56
Using References to Minimize Data Entry Work   56
Referencing a Purchase Requisition   56
Automatic Generation of Purchasing Documents   57
Buyer Options for Creating Purchase Orders   57
Single and Multiple Account Assignment   57

Establishing Outline Purchase Agreements   58
Types of Contracts   58
Scheduling Agreements   58

Profiting from Purchasing Reports   59
Analyzing Purchasing Documents   59
Standard Analyses of Purchase Order Values   60

From Here...   60

3 Understanding Material Requirements Planning 61

The Business Logic of Materials Controlling 62

Controlling Functions Available in SAP R/3 62

Reviewing the Financial Management Concepts 63

The SAP R/3 FI-Financial Accounting Modules 63
  Checking the Data 64
  Two Primary Functions of the General Ledger 66
  Special General Ledger Transactions 66
  Year-End Closing 67
  International Taxation 67
  Standard Taxation Functions 67
  Intercompany Accounting 68
  Paying for Intercompany Purchases 69
  Vendor Payments to an Alternative Recipient 69
  Intercompany Payments 69
  Language Differences 69
  Currency 70
  Currencies in Transactions 70
  Currency Exchange Differences 71

Understanding the CO-Controlling Application 71

Business Planning and Control 72
  Alternative Cost Accounting Methods 72
  Progressive Implementation of Cost and Profit Controlling 72
  The Controlling Area Concept 73

Integrating Financial Accounting with Controlling 75
  The Value-Adding Process and the Role of Cost Objects 76
  Integrated Planning and Decision Support 76

Reporting in CO-Controlling 77
Integrating CO-Controlling with R/3 Applications 78

Cost Element Accounting Principles 78
  Cost Element Parameters 79
  Accruals 80
  Calculating Price Variances 80
  Reporting in Cost Element Accounting 80

CO-CCA Cost Center Accounting 81
  Actual Costing 81

Cost Distribution Within CO-CCA 82
  Assessment 83
  Surcharge Calculation 83
  Cost Center Planning Procedures 83

CO-ABC Activity-Based Cost Accounting 85
  Activity Types and Allocation Bases 85
  Activity Planning and the Flow of Activities 86
  Simulation and the Reconciliation of Activities 86
  Activity-Based Cost Planning 87
  Political Prices 87
  Indirect Allocation of Costs to Non-Measurable Activities 88
  Cost Center Variances 88
  Charging Variances 89
  Alternative Activity Rates in Parallel 90
  Activities and Services Costing 90
  Planning and Simulating the Subprocesses 91
  Using Process Cost Rates 91

CO-OPA Order and Project Accounting 92
  Order Data Formats 93
  Status Management of Orders 93
  Order Classification by Content 94
  Order Planning 94
  Unit Costing 95
  Open Items 95
  Actual Cost Accounting Transactions 96

Settlement of Orders   97
Settlement Rules   97
Order Summary Evaluations   98
Capital Spending Orders   99

Integration of CO-OPA with FI-AA Asset Accounting   99

Product Cost Accounting   100
Costing Requirements of Different Types of Companies   101
Quantity Structures   101
Product Costing Techniques   102
The Cost Object as an Account Assignment Device   104
Results from Costing a Cost Object   105
Valuation Methods   106
Input Valuation   106
Analysis and Reporting in Product Cost Accounting   107
Planning and Simulation from Unit Costing   107

CO-PA Profitability Analysis   108
Cost of Sales Accounting Using Standard Costs (Interim Reports)   109
Fixed Cost Absorption Accounting   109

The SAP R/3 Organizational Structure   110

The Routes of Control Data Flow   111

Revenue Element Accounting   112
Posting Revenue Data   112
Estimate Revenue Elements   113

Calculating Profitability   114
Business Segments   114
Key Figures   115

Sales, Revenue, and Profit Planning   116

CO-PCA Profit Center Accounting   116
Ledger-Based Period Accounting at the Profit Center Level   116
Ledger-Based Period Accounting Profitability Reports   117

Material Requirements Planning   118
Defining Material   118
Material Type   119
Material Group   119

Net Change Planning   119

Consumption-Based Planning   119

Reorder Point Planning   120
Delivery Time   120
Safety Stock   120

Forecast-Based Planning   120

Net Requirements Calculation   121

Controlling Your MRP   121
Automatic Replenishment   121
Inventory Management and Automatic Reorder Point Planning   121
Storage Location MRP   122
Automatic Steps of the MRP Planning Run   122
Continuous Inventory Management   122

Quota Arrangements   123

Bill of Materials Explosion   123

Lot-Sizing Procedures   123
Static Lot-Sizing   124
Periodic Lot-Sizing   124
Optimum Lot-Sizing   124
Additional Restrictions on Lot Size   124

Interpreting the MRP Results   125
MRP List   125
Stock and Requirements List   125
Display Formats for MRP Results   125
MRP Run Exception Reporting   125

Using Material Forecasting Models   126
Constant Consumption Model   126
Forecast Trend Model   126
Seasonal Fluctuation Model   126
Seasonal Trend Model   127
Monitoring the Validity of a Forecast Model   127
Reprocessing a Forecast   127

From Here...   127

4 Understanding Inventory and Warehouse Management   129

Understanding the Benefits and the Mechanisms of Inventory Management   130
Managing Material Stocks by Quantity   131
Managing Material Stocks by Value   131

The Goods Movement Control Concept   132
Goods Receipts for Purchase Orders   132
Automatic Notification to Procurement   133
Material Planning   134
Goods Issues   134

Transfer Postings Within Your Company   135
One-Step Stock Transfer   136
Two-Step Stock Transfer   136
Stock Transfer Reservations   136
Goods Movements for Consumption in Production Orders   136
Quality Inspection Stock   137

Managing Batch Data   137
Data Structure   137
Batch Determination in Goods Movement   138

Managing Special Stocks of Material   138
Vendor Special Stock   138
Customer Special Stock   138

Stock Taking by Physical Inventory   138

Inventory Functionality   139
Physical Inventory Sampling   139
Defining Inventory Procedures for Inventory Types   140
Inventory Analysis and Display   141

Inventory Controlling Performance Measures   141

Restricting the Scope of Inventory Analysis   142
Limiting by Material Numbers   142
ABC Analysis   142

Limiting by Material Types   142
Period of Analysis   142

Quality Management with ISO 9000   142

Comprehensive QM Functions   143

Central Functions Used by the QM Module   143

Internal QM Functions   144
Quality Planning   144
Quality Inspection Management   144
Quality Control   145

Integrating QM   145
QM in Materials Procurement   145
Goods Receipt Inspection Procedures   146
QM in Production   147
Displaying Production Control Charts   148
QM in Sales and Distribution   148

Using Catalogs in QM   148

Inspection Planning   149
Inspection Instruction   149
Documenting the Usage Decision   150
QMIS (Quality Management Information System)   150

Using MM to Value Your Materials   150
Using Valuation Structures   151
Controlling the Criteria for Valuation   152
Valuation Accounting Procedures   153
Lowest Value Determination   156
Valuation Perspectives   156

Posting Results of Lowest Value Determination   157
Goods Receipt Posting Procedure   157

Using MM to Manage Your Warehouse   158
Warehouse Number   159
Storage Type   159
Storage Bin   159
Storage Section   159
Storage Bin Type   159

Using Transfer Requirement Documents   159
  Goods Receipt   160
  Goods Issue   161
  Picking Goods for a Delivery Note or Transfer Order   161
  Posting Changes and Stock Transfers   161
  Transfer Confirmation Option   161
  Informing Inventory Management of Differences   162
  Automation of Transfer Order Processing   162

Search Strategies in Warehouse Management   162
  Storage Type Search   162
  Storage Section Search   162
  Bin Type Search   162
  Storage Bin Search   163

Stock Placement Strategies in Warehouse Management   163

Stock Removal Strategies in Warehouse Management   163
  FIFO   164
  LIFO   164
  Combining Partial Quantities   164
  According to Quantity   164
  Assigning the Strategy   164
  Splitting Large Delivery Units   164
  Storage Unit Management   164
  Storage Unit Functions   165

MM Special Functions   165
  Consignment Material Processing   165
  Special Stocks of Consignment Material   166
  Material Movements   166
  Subcontracting   166
  Vendor Special Stocks   167
  Goods Receipt from a Subcontractor   167
  Physical Stock Transfers by Stock Transport Orders   167

Decentralized Warehouse Management   168

From Here...   168

II Knowing How Materials Management Fits into SAP R/3

5 Integrating MM   171

Relating MM to Your Accounting and Other Modules   172

Materials Invoice Verification   172

Entering a Materials Invoice That References a Purchase Order   173
  Finding a Materials Reference   173
  Multiple Order References   173
  Accessing Related Information   174

Discovering an Incorrect Invoice   174
  Overwriting Each Variance   174
  Defining Tolerances   174
  Automatic Invoice Blocking and Reasons   175

Releasing a Blocked Invoice   175
  Canceling Individual Blocking Reasons   175
  Adjusting the Date for Terms of Payment   175
  Blocking Reason Is No Longer Valid   175
  Automatic Blocking Release   175

Accounting Functions Available for Materials Invoice Processing   175
  Release Transactions for Blocked Invoices   175
  Posting an Invoice Receipt   176
  Entering Invoices with Reference to a Goods Receipt   176
  Entering Invoices That Have No Order Reference   176
  Adjusting Items Before Posting an Invoice   177

Document Simulation by Preliminary Document Entry   177
  Automatic Creation of Tax Items   177
  Cash Discounts at Invoice Posting   178
  Standard Terms of Payment   178
  Methods of Clearing a Cash Discount   178

Procedures Used with Materials Invoice Verification 178
    Entering Invoices in Foreign Currency 179
    Assigning a Material Invoice to Different Accounts 179
    Incurring Additional Costs After a Transaction Is Cleared 179
    Canceling an Invoice Receipt by a Credit Memo 179
    Handling Down Payments 179
    Making Text Notes During Invoice Verification 180

Materials Delivery Cost Accounting 180
    Planned Delivery Costs in the Purchase Order 180
    Entering Unplanned Delivery Costs 181

Open Finance 181

Using the Relationship Between MM and PP-Production Planning 182
    Work Centers 182
    Routings 182

Allocating Materials to Routings 183

Customer-Driven Production 183

Electronic Commerce Partner Applications 184
    R/3 PP-CBP Constraint-Based Planner 184
    Networked Workflow 184
    Workflow Templates 185

Business Partner Networking 185

European Monetary Union Component 185

Product Data Management Component 186

Web-Enabled SAP Business Workflow 186

Integrating MM with SD-Sales and Distribution 186

SD-MD Master Data 188
    Account Groups 189
    Contact Person 189
    Carrier and Supplier 189
    Relationship to the HR-Human Resources Records 189
    Relationship to the MM-Materials Management Masters 190
    Bill of Materials 192
    Material Status 192
    Stock and Inventory Inquiries 192
    Customer Material Info Records 192
    Types of Business Transactions 193
    Partners and Personnel 195
    Customers, Prospects, and Contacts 195
    Competitors and Their Products 196
    Sales Activities and Promotions 196

SD-SHP Shipping 197
    The Shipping Work Lists 197
    Managing the Delivery of an Item 198
    Picking 199
    Links to the MM-WM Warehouse Management System 200
    The Formalities of Goods Issue 200
    Decentralized Shipping 201
    Processing Complaints 202

Integrating MM with HR-Human Resources 202

From Here... 203

6 Understanding the SAP R/3 Business Engineer 205

How MM-Materials Management Uses the Structure of Your Plant 206
    Defining the Client 206
    Defining the Company Code 207
    Defining the Purchasing Organization 207
    Defining the Purchasing Group 207
    Defining the Plant 208
    Defining the Storage Location 208

A Database in Common 208

Departmental Access to Centralized Materials Master Records 209

SAP R/3 Data Structure Policy 209
General Data at Company Code Level 209
MRP and Purchasing Data at Plant Level 210
Data at Storage Location Level 211
Control Functions of Material Types 211
Using Industry Sectors 212
Material Units of Measurement 212
European Article Numbers 212
Storage Area 212
Quants 213
Batches and Special Stocks 213
Maintaining Materials Data Records 213

Vendor Masters 213

Understanding a Semantic Model 214
Interpreting Semantic Models 214
Diagrams as Models 215

The R/3 Reference Model 216
The Data Object Structure of the R/3 System 216
An Enterprise Model for Reference 217
Customizing the Reference Model 217

The Concept of an Event-Driven Process Chain 217
Three Basic Design Principles 218
The Evolution of Information Models 218
Event-Driven Process Chain Objects 220

Stimulus-Response Theory and Event-Driven Process Chain Methods 221
S-R Chains 222
Responses by the System to Events 222

Understanding an Entity-Relationship Model 223
Semantic Data Modeling Concepts 223
Displaying the Relationship Between Entities 226
Data Architecture 228
SAP-EDM Enterprise Data Model 229

Exploring the Enterprise Data Model 232
The Data Attributes of an Event 232
Event Attribute One 232
Event Attribute Two 233
Event Attribute Three 233
The Data Attributes of a Function 234
Function Attribute One 234
Function Attribute Two 234
Function Attribute Three 235
The Data Attributes of a Process 236
Process Attribute One 236
Process Attribute Two 237

EDM Documentation Components 238

Business Aspects of the Materials Architecture Area 238

Structured Information for an Entity Type 238
Specialization Types 239
Standard Specialization (1) 239
Standard Specialization (2) 240
Standard Specialization (3) 240

Relationships Between Entity Types 240
Relationship (1) 240
Relationship (2) 241
Relationship (3) 241
Relationship (4) 241
Relationship (5) 241

Other Features of EDM Documentation 242
Starred Name Client* 242
Time Dependency Annotation 242

How to Interpret the EDM Documentation 242
Dividing the Data Model for Clarity 242
Displaying an EDM 243

Area Architecture 243
An Ordering Principle for Entity
Types 244
Connections Between Areas 244

Processes in a Data Model 245
Typing 245
Events 245
Event-Driven Process Chains 246
Entity Types as Significant Events 246

Existence Dependency of Entity
Types 246

Architectural Areas with Entity Types of
Low Existence Dependency 246
Person 247
Hazardous Material 247
Material 247
Storage Area 247
Plant 247
Material Valuation Area 247
Material Valuation Type 247
Purchase Order Acceptance/Fulfillment
Confirmation Structure 248
Vendor Evaluation Criteria 248
Condition Rule 248
Purchasing Organization 248
Sales and Distribution Organization
248
Legal/Logistic Area 248
Logistics Information Structure 248
Task 248
Fixed Asset 249
Asset Valuation Chart 249
Account Determination 249
Payment Rule 249
Business Year Division 249
Time 249
Language 249
Currency 250
Unit Of Measurement 250
Business Partner 250
Business Partner Structure 250
Cost Accounting Area 250
Business Area 250
Company Code 251

Client 251
Cost Origin 251
Cost Type 251
Account Structure 252
Ledger Updating Rule 252
Ledger 252

Architectural Areas with Entity Types of
Higher Existence Dependency 252
Material Requirement 252
Production Order 253
Warehouse Stock 253
Plant Stock 253
Transaction Figure—Material 253
Purchase Requisition 253
Vendor Inquiry 254
Vendor Quotation 254
Purchase Order 254
Purchasing Outline Agreement 254
Procurement Information 254
Condition 255
Customer Order 255
Sales 255
Transaction Figures—Logistic 255
Transaction Figure—Fixed Asset 255
Transaction Figure—Cost Type 255
Transaction Figures—Finance 256

Architectural Areas with Entity Types of
Highest Existence Dependency 256
Shipping 256
Stock Movement 256
Goods Receipt 256
Goods Issue 256
Creditor Invoice 256
Creditor Payment 257
Inventory 257
Price Change 257
Cost Settlement 257
Purchase Order History 257
Posting 257

Using an Entity-Relationship Model 258

Entity Relationships in Purchasing 258

Materials Grouping for Storage 259

Units of Measurement   259

Business Partners   260

Plant Material   260

Viewing an Information Model   260

The Formal Graphics of EPC Modeling   262
Event   262
Function   264
Logical Operators   264
Control Flow   265
Process Pointer   265
Organizational Unit   266
Information or Material or Resource Object   266
Information or Material Flow   266
Resource or Organizational Unit Assignment   267

Combining Events and Functions   267
Two Events May Trigger a Function   267
A Function May Generate Two Events   269
An Event May Trigger More Than One Function   270
Two Functions May Generate the Same Event   271

Process View   273
Lean Event-Driven Process Chains   273
Event-Driven Process Chain Example   273
Choosing Key Events   276

Information Flow View   276

Data View   277

Function View   279
Function View Level 0   279
Function View Level 1   279
Function View Level 2   279
Function View Level 3   279

Organization View   279

The Concept of a Business Framework   280
Open Architecture   281
Mapping Business Logic   282

A Structure of Business Engineering Tools   282
The BEW Business Engineering Workbench   282
Runtime and Development Environments   283
Elements of the Development Environment   284
Object Browsers and Navigation   284
ABAP/4 Processor   284
The Framework of Multi-Tier Client-Server Architecture   285
Network-Centered Computing with Objects   286

Customizing to Fit Your Company   286
Configured, Inspected, and Tested Before Installation   287
Dynamic and Continuous Business Reengineering   287
Recommended for all R/3 Implementations   287
Tools to Update the Data Objects   287
Configure to Order   287
Continuous Customization   287

From Here...   288

7 Analyzing Materials Information   289

Purchasing Analysis Options   290
Analysis of Purchasing Documents   290
Discerning Trends   290
Analysis of Materials Accounting   291
Vendor Performance Analysis   291

Components of the Logistics Information System   291
Standard Information Structures   292

Standard Analytical Reports   293
  Totals   293
  ABC Analysis   293
  R/3 Classification   294
  Dual Classification   294
  Ranking Lists   294
  Planned and Actual Comparison   294
  Using a Comparison Period   295
  Net Order Value Frequency Analysis   295
  Forecasting   295

Preparing the Analysis Sequence   295

Information Systems Requirements   295
  High Volumes of Transactions   295
  Current Period Queries   296
  Predictable Reports   296
  Anticipating Analysis Requirements   296
  Diverse Patterns of Demand   296

Analysis for Inventory Controlling   296

Optimization in Inventory Controlling   297
  Meaningful Performance Measures   297
  Objects to Analyze   298

Standard Analysis for Inventory Controlling   298
  Scoping the Inventory Analysis   298
  Building a Set of Items for Analysis   299

Total Analysis of the Materials   299

Ranking List Analysis   299

Displaying Analysis Results   300

User-Specific Analysis   300
  Unique Report Design   300
  Interactive Analysis   300

Drill-Down Analysis Path   301
  Displaying Graph Data   301
  Displaying Info Table Data   301

Exploring the Logistics Information System   302
  The Components of the R/3 Integrated Logistics System   303
  Computer Integrated Manufacturing   304
  Engineering Change Management   304

Maintaining the Logistics Information System   305
  Exception Reporting   305
  Triggered Reporting   305
  Separate LIS Database   305
  Sources of Data for the LIS   306
  Updating the LIS Database   306

LIS Information Structures   306
  Reporting Objects   306
  Reporting Periods   307
  Predefined Performance Measures   307
  User-Defined Performance Measures   307

Using the LIS Standard Functions   308
  Standard Reporting from the LIS   308
  Reporting Pathways   308

Filtering Tactics   309
  LIS Predefined Analyses   309
  LIS Presentation Graphics   309
  LIS Report Writer Functionality   310
  Critical Performance Early Warnings   310

LIS Planning Functions   310

From Here...   312

8 Utilizing Reports and Interfaces   313

Using Reports   314
  Creating Custom Reports   314

Using Interfaces   334
  Direct Input   335
  Source Database   335

Creating the Upload File   335
Configuring for the Upload   336
Batch Input   337
Implementing BDC Processing   340

From Here...   342

9 Understanding Network Computing   343

The Attractions of Business on the
Internet   344
Electronic Commerce in Supply Chain
Improvement   345
Tracking Materials   345
Manufacturer Part Number Manage-
ment   346
Customer Electronic Commerce with
R/3   346
Electronic Data Interchange   346

Components for Internet and Intranet
Use   347
Browsers   347
Web Servers   347
Internet Transaction Server   348
SAP Automation   348
Internet Application Components   348
Business Application Programming In-
terfaces   348
Customer-Driven Production by
IAC   349
Online Facilities   349
Electronic Commerce and Secu-
rity   349
SAP R/3 Year 2000 Compliance   350
Certification Tests   350
Date Change Across Data Inter-
faces   351
Continuous Process Improvement Capa-
bilities   351
Developments in Application Inter-
faces   351
Engineering Change Management   351
Internet Transaction Server   351
Thin Clients   352

SAP R/3 Release 3.1 Java User Interface   352
PP-CBP Constraint-Based Planner   353

Self-Service Applications   353
EARS (European Administration Re-
sources System)   354
Automating Marketing and Sales Force
Administration   354

Using Push Technology   354
Trends in Consumer-Led Supply Chain
Technology   355

SAP R/3 Business Objects   355
Using the Business Object Reposi-
tory   356
Structure of the Object Repository   356

SAP R/3 Business Workflow   358
Requirements for Extended Document
Management   358
Product Data Management   359
PDM Workflow Template   360

Networked Workflow   360
Executing Workflow Templates   360
Configuring R/3 with Specialized Sub-
systems   361

Supply Chain in Context   361
Forecasting Business Configura-
tions   362
Automated Transportation Develop-
ments   363
Developing the Controlling Role of the
Customer   365

From Here...   365

10 MM Education and Training   367

Managing Change   368
Understanding the Challenges   368
Knowing the Key Points of Prin-
ciple   368
Realizing the Impact on Business   369

Structuring a Program   371
Using SAP Courses   371
Designing In-house Courses   372
Managing Expectations   374

Developing Detailed Education and Training Plans 375

Scope of Education and Training 377

MM Module Education and Training Planning Example 378

MM Training from a Consultant's Perspective 378
Utilizing Technical Skills 379
Utilizing Application Skills 379
Utilizing Management Skills 379
Utilizing Change-Management Skills 379

From Here... 380

Appendix

A MM—A Consultant's Perspective 385

Implementing Successfully 386

Consumption-Based Planning 387

Purchasing 387

Inventory Management 388

Valuation and Account Assignment 389

Warehouse Management 389

Invoice Verification 389

From Here... 390

Index 391

Credits

SENIOR VICE PRESIDENT OF PUBLISHING
Richard K. Swadley

PUBLISHER
Joseph B. Wikert

GENERAL MANAGER
Joe Muldoon

DIRECTOR OF SOFTWARE AND USER SERVICES
Cheryl D. Willoughby

MANAGER OF PUBLISHING OPERATIONS
Linda H. Buehler

EXECUTIVE EDITOR
Bryan Gambrel

EDITORIAL SERVICES DIRECTOR
Lisa Wilson

MANAGING EDITOR
Patrick Kanouse

INDEXING MANAGER
Johnna VanHoose

ACQUISITIONS EDITOR
Tracy Dunkelberger

PRODUCT DIRECTOR
Nancy Warner

PRODUCTION EDITOR
Mitzi Foster

COORDINATOR OF EDITORIAL SERVICES
Charlotte Clapp

WEBMASTER
Thomas H. Bennett

PRODUCT MARKETING MANAGER
Kourtnaye Sturgeon

TECHNICAL EDITOR
Nam Huynh

SOFTWARE SPECIALIST
David Garratt

ACQUISITIONS COORDINATOR
Carmen Krikorian

SOFTWARE RELATIONS MANAGER
Susan D. Gallagher

EDITORIAL ASSISTANTS
Jennifer L. Chisholm
Wendy Layton

BOOK DESIGNER
Ruth Harvey

COVER DESIGNER
Dan Armstrong

PRODUCTION TEAM
Jeanne Clark
Ian Smith

INDEXER
Bruce Clingaman

Composed in *Century Old Style* and *ITC Franklin Gothic* by Que Corporation.

I dedicate this book to my dear wife, Jennifer, and our beautiful daughter, Kezia, who was born October 3, 1996, and to my parents, David and Neva Blain, who have been so supportive.

—Jonathan Blain

About the Authors

ASAP World Consultancy is an international SAP consulting company and is part of the ASAP International Group. It is in the business of selling high-quality products and services relating to SAP and other enterprise applications, computing systems, and implementations. The company specializes in Enterprise Transformation Management delivering integrated business solutions. ASAP World Consultancy is part of the global ASAP Group whose activities include the following:

- Introductory SAP Courses for Corporate Clients Globally
- SAP Implementation Consultancy
- SAP Permanent Temporary and Contract Recruitment
- Business Process Re-engineering, Renewal, Change Management, and Transformation Consultancy
- SAP Human Issues Consultancy
- SAP Internal and External Communications Consultancy
- SAP Project and Resource Planning Consultancy
- SAP Skills Transfer to Your Employees
- SAP Education and Training
- SAP System Testing Consultancy and Resourcing
- SAP Documentation Consultancy
- SAP Procurement Consultancy
- SAP Access and Security Consultancy
- Hardware and Installation Consultancy
- Development of SAP Complementary Solutions
- SAP Market Research
- SAP Product and Services Acquisitions, Mergers, and Joint Ventures

ASAP World Consultancy operates all over the world. The company is known for the following:

- Accelerated Skills Transfer
- Maximising Retained Value
- Transformation Management
- ASAP World Consultancy Implementation Methodology
- ASAP Institute

The company prides itself on the quality of its people. It uses a combination of its own employees, sovereigns, and associates, who bring a wealth of experience and skills to meet the needs of its customers.

ASAP has a commitment to quality and is focused on meeting the business objectives of its clients through a number of highly specialized divisions and companies.

ASAP World Consultancy can be contacted at the following address:

ASAP World Consultancy

ASAP House

P.O. Box 4463

Henley on Thames

Oxfordshire

RG9 6YN

UK

Tel: +44 (0)1491 414411

Fax: +44 (0)1491 414412

E-mail: **enquiry@asap-consultancy.co.uk**

Author Comments: **info@asap-consultancy.co.uk**

Web site: **http://www.asap-consultancy.co.uk/**

ASAP 24-Hour Virtual Office, New York, USA

Voice Mail: (212) 253-4180; Fax: (212) 253-4180

See the advertisements at the back of this book for more details.

Jonathan Blain is the founder of the ASAP group of companies. He has been working with SAP products since 1991. He has a strong business background, having spent 10 years in the oil industry working in a variety of different roles in the downstream sector for the Mobil Corporation. He worked as an analyst during the systems build stage on one of the world's largest international SAP projects and later as a senior implementation analyst during the implementation. He has specialist knowledge of large-scale SAP implementations, project management, human issues, planning, communications, security, training, documentation, and SAP recruitment. He has benefited from professional business training with the Henley Management College and other institutions.

As a management consultant, he has specialized in matching corporate business strategies to IT strategies. He has a special interest in business engineering and the effective management of change when implementing large-scale IT systems.

Coming from a business rather than a systems background, he is focused on providing business solutions. He believes that the implementation of SAP can improve the way that companies do business and that, provided common sense and logical thinking are applied, SAP implementations need not be daunting.

Jonathan is a keen yachtsman and is the vice-chairman of the Yacht Owners Association in the UK. He has been instrumental in the development of the *Hy-Tech Sprint* yacht, a revolutionary 43-foot light displacement, water-ballasted ocean cruiser.

Bernard Dodd, after graduating in psychology at Aberdeen University, built and directed an industrial training research unit over a period of nine years at the Department of Psychology, University of Sheffield. Two years with an international business consultancy lead to an open competition direct entry to the specialist Civil Service where he served the Royal Navy for 17 years to become the senior psychological advisor to the Second Sea Lord.

Since 1990, he has specialized in technical interviewing of experts and the writing of system documentation and user handbooks for the computer-intensive industries.

Helen Boardman has 15 years experience in education and training. Her technology focus has been centered on desktop technologies and UNIX-based workstations and networking. She has worked in sales and marketing roles and conducted courses in business communication. Helen holds a masters degree in Educational Management, covering personnel issues, computer-based training, and the role of education in change management, and has conducted research into assessment and appraisal techniques. For the last nine years, she has provided research and documentation support to an enterprise application, executive reporting, and an SAP consultancy. She is currently carrying out research into SAP training in order to provide a user-friendly guide to both users and consultants. The question of accelerating skills transfer in the rapidly changing workplace is the focus of her research towards a doctorate.

Peter Chapman has been working with systems for over 14 years and SAP since 1994. While earning his first degree in business, he worked with a team from CSC and the Australian Navy programming a real-time military simulation in Ada. Subsequently, he worked for Andersen Consulting among others and completed a masters degree in Cognitive Science at Edinburgh University. His ambition is to develop an information system that models the human brain's storage mechanisms, and he has been working on an alternative data storage algorithm for many years. While freelancing as an ABAP programmer, he is completing a C++ prototype that uses dynamically evolving structures to represent a user's conceptual understanding of data being stored.

Ian Henderson trained as a production engineer with Rolls Royce Aeroengines and has had over 25 years experience of working with enterprise application systems around the world. During the last three years, he helped established a successful consultancy business in the SAP market. He is a founder of the ASAP International Group.

Philip Vaughan worked for many years as a senior logistics executive with BASF. He has five years experience project managing and consulting with SAP and has an expert knowledge of MM and PP.

Acknowledgments

In writing this book, we have benefited from the help and support of many people. There would not be space here to acknowledge everyone. They have each given their time and effort freely to make this book thorough, accurate, and useful to the readers. Equally, there are many companies who have given us much of their valuable time and shared their thoughts and opinions.

Our heartfelt thanks go to everyone who has helped. The writing of this book has been a team effort, and just praise should go to each and every team member.

Tech Support

If you need assistance with the information in this book or with a CD/disk accompanying the book, please access Macmillan Computer Publishing's online Knowledge Base at **http://www.superlibrary.com/general/support**. If you do not find the answer to your questions on our Web site, you may contact Macmillan Technical Support by phone at **317/581-3833** or via e-mail at **support@mcp.com**.

Also be sure to visit Que's Web resource center for all the latest information, enhancements, errata, downloads, and more. It's located at **http://www.quecorp.com/**.

Orders, Catalogs, and Customer Service

To order other Que or Macmillan Computer Publishing books, catalogs, or products, please contact our Customer Service Department at **800/428-5331** or fax us at **800/835-3202** (International Fax: 317/228-4400). Or visit our online bookstore at **http://www.mcp.com/**.

Focusing on Materials Management

In this chapter

- In This Book
- Scope of This Book
- What Will Be Gained from This Book
- Introducing the SAP Corporation
- History
- Markets for SAP Products
- From Here…

Have you ever regretted the cost and waste of having unwanted items in store? Have you had to compromise on quality and profitability because the available item was not quite suitable for the purpose? If so, you will appreciate why materials, parts, and consumables of all kinds really should be managed with the utmost care. SAP R/3 has been able to focus on material resource management and evolve a suite of standard business programs that can save money, space, time, and waste. This book demonstrates what can be done. This will allow you, the reader, to see how the benefits could be realized in your own company and in your own community of material consumers. This application is going to be used to conserve all kinds of scarce resources in commercial and public sector endeavors.

In This Book

The following items will be covered:

- Getting up-to-speed on professional materials management thinking.
- Understanding how SAP programs work and why they are reliable, adaptable, and efficient.
- Using the SAP R/3 Business Engineer to build your specific system from standard software.
- Finding how your materials can be managed in the best possible way through the MM-Materials Management application.
- Getting to the heart of the Enterprise Data Model, which will carry your materials information and your expertise.
- Tracking the details of purchasing and pricing.
- Getting to know the automatic materials management processes and using them for profit.
- Making sure that the whole of your enterprise is in touch with your materials management system.

Scope of This Book

Many companies hold stock. On the inventory are raw materials, partly finished goods, finished goods, technical documents, user manuals, patents, office supplies, and so on. This book concentrates on how you can use SAP's standard software to manage all these different types of materials, so as to satisfy both your customers and your shareholders by having ready on time what you need, but not to hold expensive stocks of material that is unlikely to be used.

Other books in the series focus on related aspects of your business. However, this book does give you basic understanding of the accounting and production environment within which materials management takes place.

Sections in This Book

This book is arranged in groups of chapters:

- Chapter 1, "Implementing Integrated Materials Management," introduces the principles of managing materials using the SAP R/3 MM-Materials Management application.
- Chapter 2, "Understanding Materials Purchasing," shows how better purchasing decisions can be made.
- Chapter 3, "Understanding Material Requirements Planning," extends the concepts of planning and control to the forecasting of materials requirements.
- Chapter 4, "Understanding Inventory and Warehouse Management," details the MM facilities for looking after your stock.
- Chapter 5, "Integrating MM," explores the connections between materials management and the manufacturing and sales functions.
- Chapter 6, "Understanding the SAP R/3 Business Engineer," sets out the many ways in which SAP R/3 is provided with tools to make best use of its functionality.
- Chapter 7, "Analyzing Materials Information," demonstrates how to use the SAP R/3 facilities for collating and interpreting materials data.
- Chapter 8, "Utilizing Reports and Interfaces," gives valuable advice on how to get the best from an integrated materials system.
- Chapter 9, "Understanding Network Computing," shows how the materials management application can be part of a network.
- Chapter 10, "MM Education and Training," points the way to a career in materials management.
- The Appendix is an overview, "MM—A Consultant's Perspective."

What Will Be Gained from This Book

There are two divisions of expertise carried by the book. One is a matter of how the material stuff of business can and should be planned, purchased, warehoused, inspected, and valued. The other is a mapping of the many ways in which materials databases and other management systems can be deployed on a worldwide basis without the loss of efficiency.

Whichever realm of knowledge is salient to your career, perhaps both, you will find it useful to exercise your understanding by challenging the assertions and testing out the information presented.

Intended Readers

You may be a reader with a background in SAP computing who is seeking to specialize in materials management, or you may be a materials specialist who would like to know if SAP standard business programs can match up to the sophistication of materials management systems designed purely for that function.

Introducing the SAP Corporation

SAP was founded in 1972 and has grown to become the fifth largest independent software company:

- Used by over 6000 companies
- Used in over 50 countries
- More than 9000 sites worldwide
- 31% share of the worldwide client/server enterprise application software market
- User numbers growing by 50% annually
- SAP R/3 sales rising by 70% annually

Product Overview

The SAP system is comprised of a number of fully integrated modules, which cover virtually every aspect of business management. Materials markets and customer expectations are putting continual pressures on organizations to improve the performance of their systems. While many software companies have looked at sensitive areas of business and developed systems to support those areas, SAP has looked toward the whole business. It offers a unique system that supports nearly all areas of business on a global scale. SAP offers you a choice. You can replace your independent systems with one single modular system, or you can install the SAP R/3 Basis with one or more applications. Each module performs a different function, but is designed to work with the other modules. It is fully integrated. You can also use the wide range of interface arrangements to link to your independent systems.

There are two main groups of products:

- SAP R/2 for mainframe installations
- SAP R/3 for multiple-tier client/server configurations, which may include SAP R/2 mainframe installations

SAP is a German company but operates through subsidiaries, affiliates, and partner companies all over the world.

The Executive Board

- Dietmar Hopp, Chairman SAP AG
  Sales & Consulting, Administration
  Germany, Middle East

- Prof. Dr. H. C. Hasso Plattner, Vice Chairman, SAP AG
  and Chairman, SAP America Inc.
  Basis Development, Technology & Marketing
  North and South America, South Africa, Australia, Japan

- Dr. H.C. Klaus Tschira
  Human Resources & Development

- Prof. Henning Kagermann
  Accounting & Controlling Development
  Europe

- Dr. Peter Zencke
  Logistics Development
  Asia Pacific Area

The Name

The name SAP stands for Systems, Applications, Products in Data Processing.

Corporate Headquarters

SAP Aktiengesellschaft
SAP AG
Neurottstraáe 16
D-6909 Walldorf
Germany
06227 34-0

History

SAP was founded in 1972 by five ex-IBM engineers who had acquired the rights to a real-time finance and material management system that they had designed for ICI.

The SAP R/2 product is mainframe-based. Its growth made it the leading IBM mainframe product in Germany, with good overseas sales. In 1995, it was estimated that by the year 2000, there would be over 1000 R/2 installations, most of them large.

In 1992, SAP launched its R/3 system, which runs in a client/server environment. This product has seen simply phenomenal growth. From a zero base in 1992, there are in 1997 over 9,000 R/3 installations with an estimated 1,000,000 users. This compares with approximately 1,700 mainframe-based R/2 installations.

Markets for SAP Products

SAP markets its products all over the world to almost every industry, as well as government, educational institutions, and hospitals.

You can find SAP implementations in all of the following industrial sectors:

- Raw Materials, Mining, and Agriculture
- Oil and Gas
- Chemical
- Pharmaceutical

- Building Materials, Clay, and Glass
- Building and Heavy Construction
- Primary Metal, Metal Products, and Steel
- Industrial and Commercial Machinery
- Automotive
- Ship, Aerospace, and Train Construction
- Transportation Services and Tourism
- Electronic/Optic and Communication Equipment
- Wood and Paper
- Furniture
- Consumer Packaged Goods–Food
- Consumer Packaged Goods–Nonfood
- Clothing and Textiles
- Retail and Wholesale
- Communication Services and Media
- Storage, Distribution, and Shipping
- Utilities
- Financial Services, Banks, and Insurance
- Government, Public Administration, and Services
- Museums and Associations
- Health Care and Hospitals
- Education Institutions and Research
- Consulting and Software

From Here...

Many SAP products are mentioned in this book, and it may be useful to use some of them as stepping stones through it.

- How can MM reduce the cost of materials?

  See Chapter 2, "Understanding Materials Purchasing."
- How does SAP R/3 work?

  See Chapter 6, "Understanding the SAP R/3 Business Engineer."
- Where is the art of data processing for materials management going over the next few years?

  See Chapter 9, "Understanding Network Computing."

Using the SAP R/3 Materials Management Application

1 Implementing Integrated Materials Management   9

2 Understanding Materials Purchasing   33

3 Understanding Material Requirements Planning   61

4 Understanding Inventory and Warehouse Management   129

Implementing Integrated Materials Management

In this chapter

- How do I work out what materials will be needed and when?

- Will the system help purchase the things we will need?

- Holding too much stock is costly; holding too little is risky. How can MM help?

- There may be several warehouses holding my materials, and some things are held in more than one warehouse. Can MM handle this?

- What happens to invoices?

- There may be a great deal of money tied up in materials in the warehouses and in process of being manufactured into the final products. Can MM reduce the exposure?

The ideas underlying materials management are simple but the application of them to a complex manufacturing or sales organization is not. You want to have the right material objects in the right place at the right time. This means buying them at a favorable price and arranging for them to be delivered just in time for your manufacturing or sales processes to add value before they are shipped to the customer.

There can be no doubt that materials management has to be central to every company. How can anything work if the proper tools, materials, components, energy, and documentation are not available when they are needed? Just count the cost of trying to work with the wrong resources and the effect on the customer of supplying something he has not ordered!

The purpose of the MM-Materials Management module is to provide detailed support for the day-to-day activities of every type of business that entails the consumption of materials, including energy and services. The word "material" is given the widest connotation.

Commercial Fundamentals

Imagine you receive a sum of money that corresponds to an outstanding invoice both in the amount and in the customer identification. The items referenced can be traced to a purchase order from this customer, and the specifications of the goods received tally with the goods ordered. Your warehouse has records of dispatching the very same goods and also of receiving them from the supplier.

There have been several business processes running in this scenario:

- Invoice Verification
- Inventory Management
- Warehouse Management

Should the need arise, you could also conduct a Material Valuation to assess the financial assets represented by your Inventory.

Yet your warehouse itself and the equipment used there are assets with a value, which your accountant will want to bring into Fixed Asset Management.

If your materials require protection from the elements, from each other, or from inherent aging processes, which require them to be used in rotation and before a "Sell By" date, then there has to be a Quality Management system in place to see that these controls are working properly.

How commodious your warehouse facilities have to be and the quantities of materials to be held in them are determined by the processes of Material Requirement Planning (MRP). This function, in turn, has to receive information from Sales and Distribution about available goods and from Production Planning about the goods anticipated on the basis of orders and forward planning.

The MM Flow of Events and Processes

Although it may be rare for a material to pass smoothly and exactly along the procurement process path, it is useful to trace this route because it does touch upon the processes that make business sense and that do follow a logical sequence.

Requirements for a material are calculated on the basis of MRP results, which also take account of stocks available.

If a requirement is detected, then:

- Determine source of supply by selecting a vendor
- Create and process orders for the material
- Monitor the orders
- Receive the goods to the warehouse
- Verify the accuracy and validity of the invoice against the order

The Departments of Business

Your company may have different titles for the departments; indeed, your company may have no separate departments at all. But the SAP system will assume that your organization is deployed over various levels of responsibility and that you will simply not use all the levels available in the software if you do not need them. This is a matter that is established during customizing when the standard software is fitted to your specific situation.

Business processing depends on assigning data to data objects that can be identified in the database when the time comes to retrieve the information. Today's date is held in a computer location, which every business process can find when necessary by reference to the data entity label or identification code associated with it. This code marks it as a particular data entity.

The logic of business data objects is akin to the operation of a mold or pattern. The master can be used to create as many copies as are required. If you have a master data object, a date and time stamp, for example, you can carry out some process to generate copies or instances in which the information stored is a specific time and date plus a label that shows what is being time stamped.

SAP systems rely on an enterprise data model that includes all the master patterns needed to generate instances of all the data items needed in your business.

These masters are identified as entity types, which are numbered. For example, details of a particular material are recorded on a master record, which has the format copied from entity type 1027.

If you know the entity type, you can work out what all the fields mean when you examine a data object. If you do not know the entity type of a data object, you cannot interpret the information held there. In practice, of course, your user terminal will work out what everything means and simply tabulate your information with correct labels and titles on the display.

Head Office

A corporate headquarters is a legal entity that is responsible for the financial documents that show the viability of the corporation. If there is only one company, then the head office function has to be conducted there and the address of the head office will be the same as the address of the company. Apart from the production of the financial documents, the balance sheet, and profit-and-loss statement, the head office has no legal obligation to house any of the departments, nor need it manage any of them in detail. In SAP systems, the head office is identified as the Client or Client*. Any document in the system can be traced to only one Client. Data entity 1001 is reserved for Client*.

Subsidiary Companies

If an enterprise has a head office, a purchasing organization, and a sales office, then the Client could be financially responsible for two subsidiary companies: one purchasing and the other sales. Each of these subsidiaries would be assigned a company code in an SAP system if they each produced their own balance sheet and profit-and-loss statement. The company code is held in a data entity of type 2037.

Plant

In order to do work, a company has to occupy space. This space is classified as "plant." A specific plant will, therefore, belong to a particular company code that will be apparent in an SAP database because the identification code of the plant will include the company code and the client code. Plant is entity type 1003, and each plant storage area will be recorded as data in entity type 1004.

Material

If any goods are used to do work, either as part of the product or as resources consumed in carrying out the work, these items will be classified as material. Raw materials, partly-finished goods, and parts of assemblies are all types of material. The SAP system also regards documents, such as plans or patents, as material that must be inventoried.

Material Classification   Entity 1015 specifies the type of material and entity 1021 indicates the industry sector with which it is associated. 6020 is the division entity and 5386 the entity that could place the material in the catalog of hazardous material.

Plant Stock   Material that is held in the plant ready to take part in production or for direct sales is classified as plant stock. All stock has to be associated with a specific plant, and the same material held in different plants will be treated as separate stocks. The same stock may be held in different storage areas, perhaps because it is important not to mix production or delivery batches. Entity 5122 identifies the storage area and 5362 is for plant stock that is not inventoried by storage area. Batch information is stored in records of entity type 5123, which will include a "time stamp," which is a record of the time and date as printed on many documents.

One of the reasons for having a formal set of data records to hold materials information is to enable you to find anything that is on your inventory. Another reason is to be able to identify the ownership and value of a storage location containing material.

The Accounting Operations for Materials Receipt

The tracking of the value of material as it passes through a company is accomplished by a series of processes, which are formally enacted by the SAP software according to strict rules. These rules serve to support the GAAP, generally accepted accounting procedures. The standard transaction posting process generates an audit trail of SAP documents that cannot be altered subsequently. Entity 2107 signifies the general ledger and 2006 is a general ledger finance account transaction figure, also time stamped.

Goods Receipt

The entities for goods receipt are 5132 for the quantity, 2040 for the value, and 5126 for each item on the receipt.

Transactions

There will be a company code, entity 2037, on the goods receipt value, and a time reference, because this value must appear on the balance sheet and profit-and-lost statement of the company for a specific financial accounting period.

Chart of Accounts

The chart of accounts, entity type 2001, will include reference to a chart of account item, entity type 2002. There will be a number of finance accounts, entity type 2012. One of these will be associated with a specific company code to generate an instantiation of entity type 2005, which is a company code finance account.

Material Valuation

The receipt of the goods will affect the stock of the relevant materials and there will be consequent effects on the material valuation of the stock. Entity type 5507 signifies that the data comprises the details for a material valuation transaction figure.

Reviewing the Terminology of Materials Management

The ideas that have been found to be useful in manual methods of managing materials must find their counterparts in a software system that is designed for the same processes.

There are nine main divisions of work into which the tasks of materials management can be allocated:

- Maintaining Basic Data
- Materials Requirements Planning
- Purchasing
- Inventory Management
- Material Valuation
- Invoice Verification
- Warehouse Management
- Special Functions
- Information System Access

Each of the main types of work will use specialized terminology that will reappear as the names of SAP software functions and documents. Entity types are available for all these business objects.

Maintaining Basic Data

The complexities of material inventories, their raw materials, assemblies, documents, and so on, demand an extensive set of data objects to store the verbal and numerical information that your company will need at the various stages of business. The data has to be entered and kept up-to-date. Its meaning is interpreted from the entity type of the data object used to store it. Much of the standardized terminology of materials management is about the names of data structures.

Account Assignment Category A key on a transaction document indicates whether or not each item is to be assigned to an auxiliary account such as a cost center. This key determines which additional data is required for the item, for example, the account number of the cost center.

Account Group A key that can be used as part of account assignment when posting to G/L accounts in financial accounting.

Alternative Unit of Measure Defined in the SAP R/3 System in addition to the base unit of measure. Examples of alternative units of measure are:

- Order Unit (Purchasing)
- Sales Unit
- Unit of Issue

Base Unit of Measure   Unit of measure in which the stock of a material is kept. The system converts all quantities entered in other units into the base unit.

Consumable Material   Procured material or service that is settled on a value basis via cost element accounts or asset accounts.

There are consumption materials:

- Without a material master record
- With a material master record without inventory management
- Without a material master record with inventory management on a quantity basis only

Cost Center   Unit within a company distinguished by area of responsibility, location, or accounting method.

Issuing Plant   The plant from which the materials are withdrawn for a stock transfer.

Material   Term for all objects processed in materials management. A material master record is usually created for each material in the SAP System and each material is assigned a material number.

Material Group   Grouping together of several materials with the same characteristics.

Material Master   All the materials used in a company and their data are contained in the material master records.

Material Type   An indicator that subdivides materials into different groups. For example: raw materials, semi-finished materials, finished materials, and operating supplies. The material type determines the material's procurement type and controls the following:

- Screen sequence control
- Field selection
- Type of number assignment in material master maintenance
- Type of inventory management
- Account determination

Order Price Unit   Alternative unit of measure that can be used by the purchasing department for ordering purposes. The order price unit allows you to express the order price in a unit that differs from the order unit.

Order Unit   Unit of measure that permits a material to be ordered (by purchasing) in a unit that differs from the base unit defined for the material.

Organizational Level   Hierarchy level on which certain data in the material master record is entered. Examples of organizational levels include company code, plant, and storage location levels.

Procurement Type   Classification that determines whether a material is produced in-house, whether it is procured externally, or whether both are possible.

Unit of Issue   Unit of measure that expresses the quantity of materials issued from the warehouse. The unit of issue allows you to record material usage or consumption, stock transfers, transfer postings, and physical inventories in a unit of measure other than the stock-keeping unit.

Unit of Measure   Unit that allows you to determine the dimension or quantity of a material. The SAP system contains several units of measure, including: base unit of measure, unit of entry, unit of issue, order unit, and sales unit.

Materials Requirements Planning

The consumption histories of the various materials and their predicted consumption estimates have to be used to prepare a plan for purchasing and warehousing suitable stock. Although there are various strategies for arriving at such plans, the MM application is able to work with any combination of them. The materials controller may also enter values directly when none of the pre-programmed strategies is appropriate.

Forecast   Estimation of the future values of a time series. In SAP MM, a forecast is carried out on the basis of a first-order exponential smoothing procedure.

Forecast Model   States the most obvious structure of a time series of material requirements. The following standard forecast models are available: constant model, trend model, seasonal model, and seasonal trend model.

Procurement Lead Time   Time it takes for the ordered material to be available in stock after the purchase order has been released.

Requirement Tracking Number   Identification number that facilitates the monitoring of the procurement of required materials or services. This number can relate to a requisition note (requisition document or requirement slip) that was not generated in the MM system.

Purchasing

Although the technical terms of the purchasing processes are easily understood, they do signify the standard name for the entity type in which specific data is stored. Each entity will be processed only in the standard ways that have been programmed in the application.

Date Required   Date in a reservation when the material is to be withdrawn from the warehouse.

Delivery Costs   Costs that are incurred by the order in addition to pure material costs include:

- Freight costs
- Duty costs
- Miscellaneous delivery costs, including packaging

Delivery Date   Date when goods are delivered or a service is rendered.

Delivery Schedule   Time plan for successive delivery of parts of the total quantity of a material, which are agreed upon in an item of a scheduling agreement. You can specify the exact delivery time in the delivery schedule.

Effective Price   Price calculated taking all existing price conditions into account, such as taxes, delivery costs, discounts, and miscellaneous provisions.

External Procurement   Procurement from an external supplier of raw materials, operating supplies, trading goods or services for the organizational units within a company that requires these items.

Final Delivery   Last goods receipt of a particular material with reference to an order item. No further deliveries are expected for this item. The order item is regarded as closed.

One-Time Vendor   Term for a vendor master record used for processing transactions involving miscellaneous vendors that are not part of a customer's regular suppliers. If an RFQ or PO is sent to a one-time vendor, you must enter the one-time vendor's address manually.

Order Price History   Series of prices representing the purchase prices charged by a vendor for a material or service over a certain period extending up to the present.

Price Comparison List   Method for comparing prices in quotations. The price comparison list also directly compares a quotation with the minimum, average, or maximum price on an item-by-item basis.

Pricing Conditions   Terms of payment negotiated with a vendor, such as surcharges or discounts. Pricing conditions determine, for example, how the system calculates the net price.

Purchase Order   Request to a vendor to supply certain materials or perform certain services. A purchase order contains general data including terms of delivery and terms of payment, and one or more items with details such as material description, order quantity, delivery date, and price.

Purchase Requisition   Request or instruction to the purchasing department to procure a certain quantity of a material or service on or by a certain date.

Purchasing Document   Instrument used by the purchasing department to procure a material or services. The standard SAP R/3 System includes the following purchasing documents: purchase requisition, RFQ request for quotation, purchase order, contract, and scheduling agreement.

Purchasing Document Type   Identifier that allows a distinction to be made between the various forms of a document category. It determines, for example, the relevant number range and the fields for maintenance.

Purchasing Document Category   Identifier for the classification of purchasing documents. Purchasing document categories include the following: requests for quotation (RFQs), purchase requisitions, purchase orders, contracts, and scheduling agreements. Purchasing document categories can be subdivided into purchasing document types.

Purchasing Group   Key for a buyer or group of buyers responsible for certain purchasing activities. A purchasing group is internally responsible for the procurement of a material or class of materials, and, as a rule, the principal channel for a company's dealings with its vendors.

Purchasing Info Record   Source of information for the purchasing department about a certain material–vendor relationship. The purchasing info record contains the following data: general data, quotation data, and order data. The purchasing info record permits the purchasing department to obtain the following information: which materials a certain vendor has submitted a quotation for or supplied to date and which vendors have quoted prices for or supplied a certain material.

Purchasing Organization   Organizational unit that negotiates general conditions of purchase for several plants.

Purchasing Value Key   Key defining the valid reminder days and tolerance limits applicable to the material (in the material master record) for the purchasing department. The purchasing value key serves as an input aid.

Quantity Contract   Contract in which the purchase quantity of goods or services is agreed upon. In order to create a quantity contract you must enter the agreed quantity.

Quota Arrangement   Method for dividing the total requirements for a material among certain sources of supply by allocating quotas to each source. The quota specifies which portion of the requirement should be procured from a given source of supply. The system uses the quota to propose a source in requisitions and purchase orders.

Rejection Letter   Communication informing an external supplier that its quotation (bid) submitted has not been accepted.

Release Point   Person, department, or other organizational unit of a company that must release (that is, approve) the items in a purchase requisition before the ordering process can be initiated. Several release points can be specified by a release strategy.

Release Strategy   Term used in purchase requisition processing. The release strategy specifies which release points must approve the items of a purchase requisition and in which order. A certain release strategy can, for example, be specified for all purchase requisitions whose value exceeds a certain amount.

Scheduling Agreement   Type of outline agreement. A scheduling agreement is a long-term agreement between a vendor and a customer that involves the subsequent creation and regular update of schedules for the delivery of the materials specified in the line items of the agreement.

Source List Specifies the allowed (and/or not allowed) sources of supply for a material in a plant. It also indicates the period for which the source is valid. The source list of material is composed of source list records, each of which identifies a possible source of supply for the material.

Source of Supply Procurement option for a material. A source of supply can be an external source (vendor) or an internal source (for example, a company's own plant). The preferred source at any one time can be determined by the system on the basis of quota arrangements, source list records, outline agreements, or info records that have been defined for the material.

Value Contract Contract in which the purchase of goods or services is agreed up to a certain total value. The goods to be released against the contract are specified in contract release orders. Criterion for the performance of a value contract is its agreed total value.

Vendor External source from whom materials or services can be procured.

Volume-Based Rebate Cumulative, period-end discount granted by a vendor to a customer, usually based on the volume of business done with the customer within a specified period. The volume-based rebate is defined with the help of condition records.

Inventory Management

Area of logistics that includes the following tasks: management (recording and tracking) of stocks of a material on both a quantity and value basis; planning, entering, and documenting all stock movements including goods receipts, goods issues, stock transfers, and transfer postings; and physical inventory (stocktaking).

Goods Receipt Term in inventory management that refers to the acceptance of goods from a company. Goods receipts are documents posted with or without reference to a purchase order.

Goods Receipt Blocked Stock Quantity of a material delivered or supplied by a vendor that has been received subject to conditional acceptance and that has not yet been placed in final storage. Goods receipt blocked stock is not yet regarded as part of the receiving company's own stock, but is taken into account in the purchase order history.

Storage Location Organizational unit that allows the differentiation of material stocks within a plant.

Material Valuation

Determination of the material stock value. Valuation-relevant data for a material include: valuation price, valuation class, valuation procedure by standard price, or moving average price. A business can be seen as a process chain in which value is added or subtracted according to the commercial significance of what is accomplished. A scarce material may acquire value simply by being held in stock until the market price rises. Information may enjoy the same transformation in value, although this may be more difficult to evaluate.

Price Control Indicator that determines the material valuation procedure. In the standard SAP System there are two procedures: standard price valuation and moving average price valuation.

Price Unit Unit that the valuation price refers to in the material master record.

Valuation Area Organizational level on which stocks of a material are managed based on value. The valuation area is either a plant, several plants in a company code, or all plants in a company code.

Valuation Category Criterion for the separate valuation of different stocks of a material. Reasons for "split valuation" include: quality, batch, or degree of purity.

Invoice Verification

Term that encompasses the entering and checking of vendor invoices. Vendor invoices are compared with the purchase order and goods receipt. They are checked in three ways: content, price, and quantity. Payment for goods or services usually waits on the receipt of an invoice from the supplier that tallies with the purchase order in all respects. The details of the materials or services received have to be located and matched with the relevant order items before tests for correct quantities, specifications, and prices can begin.

Exchange Rate Relationship between two currencies. This rate is used to translate an amount into another currency.

Gross Price Price that does not include discounts or surcharges, freight charges, and administration costs.

Net Price Price including all vendor surcharges and discounts.

Warehouse Management

Materials can lose part of their value if they are not properly stored. They can effectively lose all of their value if they cannot be located when they are required for manufacturing or dispatch. The material handling equipment in a warehouse may be highly specialized and varied. This may well entail careful scheduling of stock movements so that the handling plant can be used efficiently.

Stock Materials management term for part of a company's current assets. It refers to the quantities of raw materials, operating supplies, semi-finished products, finished products, and trading goods in the company's stores/warehouse.

Stock Material Material that is always kept in stock (for example, a raw material). A stock material has a material master record and is managed on a value basis in a material stock account.

Special Functions

The MM application includes a range of functions that are variants of standard processes. The normal accounting procedures may not be followed, and there may be special documents created.

Consignment   Form of business in which a vendor maintains a stock of material at a customer (purchaser) location. The vendor retains ownership of the materials until they are withdrawn from the consignment stores. Payment for consignment stock is only required when the material is withdrawn. For this reason, the vendor is informed of withdrawals of consignment stocks on a regular basis.

Consignment Material   Goods from one or more vendors handed over to a company for storage or sale on a consignment basis and that are stored in this company's storage facilities. Consignment material is not transferred to the company's valuated stock until it is withdrawn. As a result of such withdrawals, the company incurs a liability toward the vendor. Such liabilities are settled at certain intervals.

Consignment Stock   Stock made available by the vendor that is stored on the purchaser's premises, but remains the vendor's property until withdrawn from stores or transferred to the purchaser's own valuated stock.

Multiple Account Assignment   Term for account assignment of an order item to several accounts. The distribution of the costs can be carried out on the basis of percentages, quantity, or amount.

Order   Describes a task to be carried out within a company. Some companies would refer to this as an internal order or a works order. The order specifies which task is to be carried out, when the task is to be carried out, what is needed to carry out the task, and how the order costs are to be settled.

ABC Analysis

Analysis that classifies the materials in a company by their consumption value is conducted by multiplying current price by quantity. Each material in the analysis is given an ABC Indicator that provides information about the consumption value of the material. The following consumption values are

- A: important part/high consumption value
- B: less important part/medium consumption value
- C: relatively unimportant part/low consumption value

Using the SAP R/3 Basis System

The SAP R/3 Basis System is the core of R/3 that is delivered with every installation. It comprises what amounts to the operating system for the SAP standard business process software plus a number of additional components designed to help you design and install an implementation that fits precisely to the business you wish to be running when it goes live.

The Interface Between System and User

An interface is defined strictly as a description of a set of possible uses of an object, such as a database held on a third-party system. Specifically, an interface describes a set of potential requests in which an object can meaningfully participate. You can ask a database for certain types of information as long as you make your request in the query language that the database can recognize. The design of the screens and the logic underlying their reactions to the entries of the user are consistent across applications and hardware.

The concept of a user interface is copied from communications theory. You could say that a user interface is really a kind of list of all the things you could do with it. If you put in the correct signal as a command, you can expect the interface to make sense of it and set a sequence of business processes that will produce the results you are expecting. For the majority of occasions you will not need to know what these individual processes are, although you may like to be told if any of the sequence is being delayed, for example, by hold-ups in communicating with a database system that may be in a distant location.

A user interface is not able to do anything sensible if you give it a signal that is not part of its repertoire. If you have a voice interface on your computer, you may be able to train it to recognize your voice when you speak correctly. If your computer does not have a voice interface, it will take no notice of what you say to it.

This is perhaps a silly example, but it does illustrate the difficulty of having a complex system. The user interface to control this complexity has to be complicated to a similar degree. If you have 10 functions, you could have 10 buttons to select them. If you have thousands of functions, you need a better arrangement.

Ergonomic Design

The idea underlying the design of the user interface is to implement the best ergonomic practice. You could define ergonomics as the art of arranging working environments so that people make as few errors as possible and suffer no undue fatigue or repetitive strain injuries. This means setting up displays and entry devices that are attractive and informative. It should be pretty obvious how to work the system. Your designers should arrange for the users to do things in ways that come easily and seem natural. There should be a provision to streamline repetitive tasks if they cannot be automated altogether.

The SAPGUI A GUI is a Graphical User Interface. In simple terms, you can see your texts and data set out in tables or pictures and you can select at least some of these items with your cursor. Whether you move your cursor with a mouse or a keyboard command makes no difference. The SAPGUI is designed to give the user an ergonomic and attractive means of controlling and using business software by offering the possibility of pointing to the items of interest. You may highlight a particular text or numerical field and then use special function keys to elicit additional information touching on that item. You could highlight a part number, for instance, and then ask for a list of where this part was used throughout your company. Another option would be to discover its price.

Understanding the Dynpro In the SAP System, a dynpro is a dynamic program that controls the screen. In particular, a dynpro manages all the actions that take place when you click your mouse, press a function key, or type in some data. There will be validation work to be done and perhaps other processing logic built into the dynpro so that it is able to control exactly one dialog step. The dynpro is atomic, which means it does all its work or none.

Sessions or Modes

When you press keys or click a mouse to choose an item on a screen, you will probably begin a session. If you have chosen incorrectly, the session will begin with an error dialog, which will continue until you have made a valid entry. If the entry was recognized as a command for the system to do something, the screen will change to let you know that something is happening. If that something is going on too long for you to wait, you can open another session at the same time. The screen will show you a fresh window for your other session. You now have two modes running at the same time. You could have up to six, each in its own window.

When any of your modes is ready for you to do something, its window will let you know. By using several modes, you can get more work done in the same amount of time. You can arrange them on your screen and minimize those you do not wish to monitor.

Using the R/3 Session Manager If your terminal presentation device, your "front end," is being executed in Windows 95 or Window NT, you can make use of the R/3 Session Manager, which is automatically generated from the Business Engineering Workbench (BEW).

The sessions available to run on your GUI are presented as lists of icons to set up various types of menu according to the type of work you are doing and your authorization level.

A typical session manager display will include the following panels or frames, which will contain the active icons. Sessions currently running will be highlighted:

- Tabs for pages for Logon and the main groups of applications
- Buttons for user-specific, company, SAP standard, document, and help menus
- Application Bar items for such areas as office, logistics, accounting, tools, and information catalog
- Application browser frames for each of the active applications
- User-specific list of functions
- Session list of currently active modes with the top window highlighted

Any of the items in a display generated by the R/3 Sessions Manager can be dragged and dropped into any of the user lists, such as the user-specific list and the session list. This possibility is referred to as a "pin board" function.

The Transaction Concept

A business transaction is an exchange between one part of a system and another. The production plant, for example, will take delivery of some material from a warehouse in exchange for a delivery receipt. The warehouse will be able to use the delivery receipt to reconcile the stock of material on the inventory. Meanwhile, the accounting department will have noted that the valuable material has passed from the warehouse to the production plant. It will post some financial transactions to record this exchange of value for material.

When a user is working at a terminal, a transaction with the system is not finished until the system is satisfied that the entry of information has been correct. The system will record the transaction automatically as a document that will remain in the system as proof of who entered the information and when exactly this occurred.

If the transaction concerned a purchase order, for example, the details of that order will have been written on the document by the system wherever possible. The user will have selected a supplier already on the database, so the details can be entered by the system, and so on.

Automatic Documentation of Transactions

A transaction of posting to any account will not succeed unless debits equal credits. The entries for such a posting will not be accepted unless they pass the validation tests applied in the dynpro step of the dialog routine running at the point of data entry.

This successful posting to an account as a result of the transaction is regarded by SAP as a self-contained and coherent unit of data. It constitutes a meaningful business act. Information has to be given to the SAP System, and the system will have checked for all the errors that could be detected at this stage of the business process. It makes sense to mark this off as a task element and the Generally Accepted Accounting Principles (GAAP) commend the practice of leaving evidence of every accounting task element.

The Document Principle

The unit is defined as an SAP Document because evidence of this posting event and the details of the transaction can be displayed in a standard document format. No posting can take place without leaving an SAP Document ready to be used in the audit and in any processing or posting to control or analysis accounts.

A transaction of entry, checking, and posting data can take place directly with the FI-Financial Accounting system, where the results will include posting to the GL-General Ledger and its sub-ledgers. A transaction can also direct data to other SAP applications. An example would be to enter data from original documents such as goods receipt notes and packing lists.

Before a transaction can be successfully completed, the mandatory SAP Document has to be created. This will occur only after strict validation of the entries. Uniform data structures have to be used. The transaction has to obey clear-cut rules about posting. The SAP Document will identify the rules in use for each line item.

A data object is a cluster of data items recorded as fields. Each field is allowed a maximum size and type of content according to the defined data domain that has been assigned to it. A field will not be allowed to accept any value or other content unless it is in accord with this domain definition.

An SAP Document is a data object, and must comply with the standard rules of SAP objects.

SAP Document Header Fields

On your SAPGUI, an SAP Document will be displayed first in overview format and then in more detail, depending on which line item has been selected.

The header of an SAP Document overview will always include organizational data and full identification of the document, as follows:

- Document number
- Company code
- Fiscal year
- Document date
- Intercompany number
- Reference document
- Debit/credit total
- Currency

SAP Document Line Item Detail Fields

The body of an SAP Document will be displayed in overview with one line of column titles and one or more line items to carry summary details of the entries.

Further details of each line item can be accessed using overlay windows at the display terminal, as follows:

- General ledger account
- Company code
- Intercompany number
- Currency
- Transaction amount
- Debit/credit
- Tax amount
- Tax code
- Business area
- Cost center
- Order identification
- Project identification

- Asset identification
- Material code
- Personnel number
- Allocation code
- Reference document identification
- Document header text
- Document type (transaction type, journal type)
- Posting key (debit or credit, what type of account this line item is allowed to be posted to)

Manual Document Entry

If you have to enter manually an invoice, for example, that has not been posted automatically, SAP R/3 will provide all possible help. You can enter and post a check received and match the payment to specific open items in the customer account, all in one operation.

The successful posting of a transaction does not occur until the necessary data is recorded as an SAP Document and is complete and error-free. You can set aside a transaction document before it is ready for posting, in which case the system will validate any information you have already entered and report to you any discrepancies.

The SAP Document has to end up with a document header showing posting date, document date, document reference number, and currency key. The body of the document will contain one or more line items that will show the amount and identify the product and the terms of payment. The system will generate certain line items such as tax entries, cash discount, and exchange rate differences, as applicable.

You can set up helping routines and use standard data entry functions such as the following:

- Recalling a previous screen for copying and editing
- Retaining data for individual users for several transactions
- Adapting a copy of a data-entry screen so that it is better suited to a set of transactions that you are expecting
- Searching for an account number by using matchcodes to narrow the search

An SAP Document that records a previous transaction can be copied to act as a sample or model to be edited. This sample can be a regular document that has been set aside, perhaps as an incomplete transaction document. The posting date and new values may have to be entered, by you or by the system, before posting.

Recurring Entries   If you are expecting to have to make a series of entries where the amounts are always the same, you can set up a recurring entry. Monthly service fees would be an example.

A recurring entry is a set of data that will not be used until the due dates. Until then, the entries will not update account balances.

You will have to specify the first and last dates and the frequency or time interval between. The system will automatically post the required transaction on each of the due dates.

The Set Concept   The logical concept of a set is used in the FI-GLX Extended General Ledger for reporting, planning, and ledger processing.

A set refers to a data structure and its relationships with other data structures.

A set of numbers can be defined, where the numbers are the identification codes of bank accounts, for example.

A list of cost centers can specify a set.

The actual members of a set may not be known until the set definition is called into use. The "top three operating divisions for gaining new customers in the current month" is a set definition of this kind.

The definition of a set can include relationships between specific firms or companies in a group, not necessarily at the same level. They can be specified by their individual company codes.

A set can comprise any collection of data objects that meet the logical criteria forming the definition for membership of that set.

Specific business functions can call on a set definition stored for use later. Assessment and distribution often take place under the control of sets.

Materials management uses the set concept through its use of material types that may be supplemented by using logical connectives to build set definitions that can be stored for use accessing information from materials masters.

Using Standard Components Controlled by Tables

SAP software is designed to be installed without fundamental modification. All SAP R/3 modules and applications can be integrated with each other and will work perfectly using their default settings. You can choose which applications and modules to install.

In order to make your installation work exactly in the way you want it to carry out your business processing, you must arrange for each function to be set up with the details of how it is to be integrated. This information is held in tables in the functions, which are the only parts of the software to which the user has access. The process of adjusting how a standard business program is to operate is referred to as "customizing." You are not allowed to interfere with the fundamental logic and programming of SAP business software.

The Role of Tables in Standard Business Software

A table is a collection of data fields arranged in rows and columns, not all of which need be visible on the screen at the same time. Because each data field will have a specified length expressed as the number of characters it will hold, the length of a row in a table will equal the sum of the number of characters in each field in the row. Each field in a column will have the same number of character spaces. However, a screen field may not be as large as a data field. If you are typing into a screen field, the characters will move to the left when you get near the end of the field. You can continue entering characters until the underlying data field is full.

Tables are used throughout the SAP systems to present data that fits into a rectangular pattern of rows and columns. A list of part numbers, their names, and their prices would fit nicely in a table of three columns' width and it could have as many rows as there were different parts.

You could ask for the table to be sorted so that the most expensive parts came first, or you can have the list arranged in order of the part number. Your screen will seldom be big enough to let you see the whole table, so you have to have some way of selecting which items to look at.

SAP R/3 Business Applications

The SAP R/3 System comprises the "R/3 Basis," a body of software code in which all the core applications are integrated. Not all the applications in the Basis need be configured in your specific installation. There are many additional applications that can be installed and configured as required. The word "Basis" usually refers to the standard R/3 facilities that are always available no matter what other components have been configured.

The core applications are as follows:

- FI-Financial Accounting
- CO-Controlling
- HR-Human Resources
- PP-Production Planning

Any combination of these core applications may be integrated with any of the supporting applications.

CA-Cross Application

The R/3 Cross Application area comprises a set of modules that can be used throughout the R/3 system and its integrated applications:

- CA-BPT Business Process Technology
- CA-DM Document Management
- CA-CL Classification
- CA-CAD CAD Integration

R/3 Release 3.0 includes cross application components available in earlier releases and additional integrative modules, which are coded without the "CA" prefix:

- SAPoffice
- SAP Business Workflow
- R/3 Business Engineering Workbench, which includes the R/3 Reference Model and the R/3 Implementation Model
- R/3 Business Navigator, which includes the R/3 Process Model, the R/3 Data Model, and the R/3 Customizing system
- R/3 Analyzer, which is available online with the R/3 system or as a stand-alone PC-based system and is used to access the R/3 Reference Model

Two additional SAP products should be mentioned in the context of cross-application modules:

- OSS-Online Service System
- CCMS-Computing Center Management System

Trends in Marketing SAP R/3

The high demand for enterprise application software, even in medium and small companies has given rise to a range of variations in the way SAP R/3 is delivered.

Accelerated SAP

Accelerated SAP (ASAP) is a version of R/3 that is largely pre-configured before delivery. It is aimed at the small and medium-sized companies with the particular objective of having a rapid implementation.

Components as Separate Managed Objects

The aim of the SAP Componentisation project is to rebuild R/3 so that the various modules can be installed, maintained, and updated separately. In the language of object-oriented programming, the SAP R/3 modules are to be offered as "managed objects" that can be serviced as independent units.

Industry Solutions and the Vertical Market Initiative

A number of implementations of SAP R/3 have been delivered in a pre-configured state with some of the customizing processes already carried out. These versions of R/3 are known as Industry Solutions and may take the vertical market initiative, which aims to provide a complete business data processing system running at all levels of your company and across all departments. An Industry Solution is a version of the standard R/3 system, which may include some or all of the components of any of the R/3 applications, according to the sector of industry for which it has been designed.

Industry Solution Configurations of SAP R/3 have been developed for the following sectors:

- Automotive Industry
- Banking
- Chemical
- Education and Training
- Health Care
- Investment Management
- Pharmaceutical
- Real Estate
- Sales and Distribution
- Transportation
- Aviation
- Consumer Products
- Construction
- Engineering
- Insurance
- Oil and Gas
- Public Sector
- Retail
- Telecommunications
- Utilities

Price List Module Components of MM

The components of each SAP application are identified as price list items. Some of them may not be needed in your particular company. Many companies will wish to implement the materials purchasing and materials requirements planning components because of the potential benefits of tight control of these processes offered by MM. Inventory and warehouse management are often of special interest to industry sectors where health and safety requirements dictate a close control of material origins and batch histories such as the food and medical sectors. The aviation industry is an example where assemblies and parts are closely monitored and tracked by their serial numbers. From a financial accounting point of view, the invoice verification and material valuation modules provide a fine-tuned control window on these essential processes.

MM-BD Master Data

The basic or master data component is essential because it includes the materials masters and their entity type definitions, which you can use without modification in many implementations. The following price list components constitute the master data module:

- R35100 Material master record
- R35110 Vendor master record (Purchasing functions)
- R35120 Classification
- R35130 Document management

PP-MRP Material Requirements Planning

The requirements planning component is not essential to the functioning of the materials management application.

- R37200 Forecast
- R37210 Consumption-based planning

MM-PUR Purchasing

The purchasing functions provided in the SD-Sales and Distribution application are able to provide standard purchasing support, but there will be no particular support for specialized materials management operations.

- R35200 Basic purchasing functions
- R35210 Contracts/delivery scheduling agreements
- R35220 Quota arrangement
- R35250 Subcontract order processing

MM-IS Purchasing Information System

If your business seldom uses a vendor more than once or twice, or if you always use the same vendors, then the purchasing information system and vendor evaluation functions need not be configured.

- R35230 Vendor evaluation
- R35240 Purchasing information system

MM-WM Warehouse Management

The simpler your warehouse complex, the less need you would have for the warehouse management component. However, if some of your materials have to be tracked, for hygiene or safety reasons, for example, then you may wish to maintain thorough batch histories and records of how your stock was finally disposed.

- R35300 WM basic functions
- R35350 WM basic functions
- R35370 Storage unit management
- R35371 Storage unit management

MM-IM Inventory Management

The inventory functions are usually installed by companies that hold complex stock or items of high value.

- R35400 Goods receipt
- R35410 Inventory management
- R35420 Physical inventory
- R35440 Inventory controlling

MM-IV Invoice Verification

The SD-Sales and Distribution application includes the basic software, but the extensive control and security functions of the invoice verification component are preferred for materials management in most companies.

■ R35500 Invoice verification basic functions

■ R35510 Balance sheet valuation procedure

From Here...

■ How do I put together the various components?

See Chapter 6, "Understanding the SAP R/3 Business Engineer."

■ How is information about a material transmitted to the production departments?

See Chapter 5, "Integrating MM."

CHAPTER 2

Understanding Materials Purchasing

In this chapter

- How automatic purchasing can be set up using data already in your system
- How systematic record-keeping can keep track of vendor performance
- How the materials you need to purchase can be identified from bills of materials
- How the data for purchasing is stored for automatic retrieval during purchasing
- How stored rules and conditions can be used to create precise purchasing arrangements
- How potential sources of supply can be assessed using vendor net price simulation

Some would claim that the heart of an enterprise is in the buying department. There are ways of unblocking the arteries. The approach of the SAP R/3 system is based on using master records of every data object of interest to your company. In the materials purchasing area, the records of interest will be materials you need in your manufacturing or logistic functions, and the vendors who can or could supply you. When the time comes to place an order or purchasing contract, you will want to be sure that you have the best set of candidate vendors to receive your invitation to tender.

A potential vendor has to pass three tests:

- Can the vendor supply the goods to specification?
- Does the vendor have a good record in delivery and quality?
- Is the price right?

MM-MP, Materials Purchasing is a software module that specializes in managing the application of these criteria to vendors and your transactions with them.

Procurement by Exception

Is it a realistic objective to go for automatic procurement? What would be the advantages? What would it entail?

You must have planning of material requirements, even if it's only on the back of an envelope. Even if you operate an opportunistic buying department that acquires discounted stock and then looks for ways of disposing of it profitably, you will still have to plan when and where you are going to warehouse it.

By chance or as the result of hard research, you will have some potential vendors in mind. You may have been able to negotiate an outline agreement with some of them for the things you know you will need.

You will have your preferences in the delicate matter of choosing which suppliers to favor with your orders. Reliability of delivery, constant and predictable quality, price, and rapid response to emergency order are all factors that you could possibly bring into the decisions of who to choose.

How could all this kind of hard-headed business thinking be handed over to a computer?

MRP (Material Requirements Planning) is the name for a function carried out somewhere in your company. You may have a department with this name. You can certainly call on a module of this name if you have installed and configured SAP R/3 MM-Materials Management.

Two streams of data feed MRP. Quantities, timetables, and specifications of materials needed to meet production and delivery schedules will have been generated as a result of customer or work orders already on your books. The second stream of information upon which intelligent MRP feeds will be the forecast requirements for which you have no more than planning data at best. These are the ideas arising from prudent guesswork as to what your company will need in the way of materials and services from the current period out into the "planning horizon."

Some element of your planning data may arise, not as the result of prudence, but in the form of higher management aspirations. They have a tendency to set targets to please the shareholders and hopefully motivate the workforce.

So you could perhaps tell yourself that MRP took into account the following three factors:

- What is needed to complete firm orders
- What will probably be needed, judging by prudent and sensible forecasting
- What might be needed if production targets are to be met

What you might like to do is plan and purchase an excess of some materials just in case there is a shift in the market requirements that your company could exploit if it had these items in stock. Statisticians would mutter words such as "probabilistic risk-taking." Others would recognize this as gambling.

What you can do in business gambling is tell yourself honestly what your costs and profits are. You can conduct profitability analysis, and there is an SAP R/3 component with this very title.

However you compute your profits, you will need to store data about the costs. If you are holding stocks just in case an opportunity arises, then you should know what these warehouse facilities are costing and how they might be more (or less) profitably utilized in some other way.

Your "might-come-in-handy" stock of materials begins with a price that you paid for it. As you hold it in contingency stock, the market price of this quantity will probably vary. So at each accounting period, which could be daily or hourly, you could have the material valued. And there is an SAP R/3 component called Material Valuation.

In summary, it seems that a set of data about vendors could support an efficient purchase pricing operation, a materials requirements planning function could factor in forecasts and orders, and a contingency stock manager could be supported by at least firm computations of the financial risks being run. MRP could link to purchasing, and interventions could be limited to fine tuning the forecasting rules and conditions. Contingency stocks could be maintained by a combination of purchasing conditions and interventions by the buyers or whomever had the authority to gamble in this way.

The makings of a system for procurement planning by exception are available. The standard SAP business process software is perfectly capable of setting up the commercial operations such as requesting quotations, ordering, receiving, and settling. Again the exceptions to standard conditions need be the only occasions where, of necessity, there has to be an intervention.

Speed of response would be one advantage to be claimed by procurement by exception. Offline data processing could make best use of computing resources, and human operators carrying out repetitive procurement functions would seldom be needed.

A potential disadvantage of automatic buying is that it would be easy to overlook the fact that the decisions were being taken by a set of rules and logical conditions. These may include elements that no longer stand up to business logic. Suppose you had a rule that said you should always buy at the lowest price. It also would be prudent to have an additional condition that forced your procurement system to seek a range of quotations, perhaps across a geographical or business region, so that you did not create a shortage of alternative suppliers by always buying from the one, probably large, source that was able to offer the lowest price.

If you opt for procurement by exception and automated paperwork, you should employ some canny managers who know how the data processing system works and where it should be fine tuned to keep up with wise business logic. They should have knowledge of the vendor data models and conditions so that they can fine tune the system.

Using Materials Master Records

To implement an integrated system of production planning and materials management, you must have a shared database wherein anyone in your company can find out all there is to know about any material passing through the plant, providing he or she has the necessary authorization. Everyone must use the same rules and data structures when they enter data about part numbers and descriptions of these parts. All finished products and semi-finished products must be subject to exactly the same information discipline, and so must all raw materials.

The SAP R/3 System will expect you to use a system based on the organizational structure you defined during Customizing, but the system is flexible, and you can construct whatever arrangement best suits your company.

Access to your vendor master records can be controlled using the standard authorization checks. The vendor masters can be maintained in the user departments on a decentralized basis, or centrally at the company code level.

For example, you will probably want to maintain data at the company code level if it is to be used throughout the company. Accuracy and uniformity are ensured by this arrangement, but there is also a very compelling additional benefit: if you wish to change any detail—a change of address of the expert on this material, or a change of raw material specification, for example— you have only to alter the material master at the company code level for the new information to be immediately in place on every screen that needs it.

Material requirements planning data is kept at the plant level, where it is needed on a moment-to-moment basis. Purchasing data will be needed at the plant level to maintain the inventory and anticipate potential shortfalls in the materials used in production. The economical batch size is an example of a purchasing data element that can be used to minimize the costs of production.

Stock data, product details and quantities, quality inspection reports, and so on are maintained at the storage location level, because they can be planned into the production process with full cognizance of the inventory, handling, and transport implications. These may affect which storage location is chosen as the source.

Materials Master Record Attributes

When your SAP R/3 MM System is installed it will include a full set of master records. These masters are in the form of entity types that can be copied and filled with specific data. You may wish to edit the format of some of the data fields and perhaps their names or titles, which will appear on the graphical display of the users. And, of course, you will need to enter the specific details of the materials needed in your company. The system is delivered with tools to help you make all the adjustments necessary to have your implementation correctly running your business as soon as possible. For your convenience, the data fields are grouped into clusters called "attributes."

A typical materials master record will have data attributes as follows:

- General data such as material number, description, units of measure, and technical data
- Plant-specific data such as material requirements planning type, planned delivery time, purchasing group, and batch indicator
- Evaluation data such as evaluation price, evaluation procedure, and evaluation quantity
- Warehouse management data such as unit of measure, palletization instructions, and directions to place in or remove from stock
- Sales-specific data such as delivering plant and sales texts

Any of these data clusters can be further subdivided. For example, the plant-specific data might be extended to include the following types of data:

- Storage location data such as the permitted period of storage, the individual stockfield, or storage area within a storage location where the material is kept
- Forecast data for this material
- Consumption data for this material

Customizing Your MM-Materials Management Module

The R/3 system includes a Customizing component as standard. It allows the implementers of the R/3 system and its applications to select the functions that are relevant to the client company from the full array of SAP standard business programs. The Customizing component requires the implementers to select or enter all the details that will appear when the standard programs are in use.

The format of a materials master record is defined by a template. This is suggested by the system when you have identified your requirements by selections from the materials management sections of the Customizing menu.

At this time you can also specify how long you want your material numbers to be, and the format to be used to separate such data elements as the company code and the purchasing organization identifier.

You will probably prefer to have each user department see only those elements of the material master that it needs, according to the type of transaction it undertakes. The system will prompt you to identify the user departments during customizing.

Alterations to Materials Masters

Materials masters can be maintained and corrected centrally or in each user department, where the relevant information is at hand. The records will still be held under the company code, so other departments may use them.

It is a standard feature of the SAP R/3 System and its application modules that every transaction effecting a change in the master data records will be recorded in a log compiling the change management history for this record. The date and reference of the update will be recorded on the master.

There are several security levels to protect a master from unauthorized access. You may be prevented from looking at a data object or from changing it. You may also be prevented from creating new data objects by copying a master or generating one from the beginning. It may be the case that certain masters can be maintained only by named employees, or by members of a named department.

Material Types

In accordance with the concept of building data objects that can be used and understood throughout your enterprise, the Materials Management application identifies groups of data records that are likely to be needed together or that will probably have to be treated in a particular way. For example, if your inventory includes dangerous materials, you will want your system to be able to tell you who the specialist experts are who could advise you if you had a query about storing or handling these materials. The concept of material type might be used in this sort of context.

The type to which you assign each material is a matter that you decide according to the custom and practice in your company. For example, you may establish the following material types:

- Raw materials
- Semi-finished products
- Finished products
- Services
- Trading goods
- Internally owned empty containers or transit rigs
- Externally owned containers

The Control Functions of a Material Type

The consequences of assigning one of your materials to a particular material type will include a variety of constraints and restrictions that will make the system easier to use and less likely to generate errors. For example, the material type master record may contain data elements that control the following activities in relation to each of the materials assigned this material type:

- Which user departments can maintain the material, in the sense of making alterations to the data in the material master records
- The procurement type of this material
- How the FI-Financial Accounting module will assign a stock account automatically
- Whether the financial values or the quantities of the material on inventory are updated, or both

The materials management system will offer you a choice of all the standard material types, to which you can add your own by establishing new material type master records and specifying how you want the system to respond.

Industry Sector   If your company, or one or more of the companies in your group, has to deal with a material that must be treated differently according to some criteria that you specify for your own convenience, the concept of an industry sector can be applied.

In the material master there will be a data element that can hold an industry sector indicator, which can then be consulted in order to control how this material is used. For instance, you may wish to differentiate between products sold directly to the public and those going to other manufacturers to be incorporated into their products. The industry sector could be used to identify where the transaction processing methods should be adjusted for the different customers. The same industry sector can be used to identify important differences in how you deal with different types of vendors supplying your company with goods and services. It may be convenient to define some industry sectors purely on the basis of one data element, such as the unit of measure (for example, European pallets, bags, or truck-loads).

Standard Units of Measure   The management of material can take place using the individual piece as the atom or smallest indivisible entity. On the other hand, some materials have to be handled in groups defined by their packaging or their containers to be manipulated by the transport equipment.

If your company has a variety of units of measure for the same material, you can define conversion factors to be applied to the base unit. These factors can work either way. The system can be set to compute the size and weight of a single piece from a pallet that had been weighed and carried a specified number of base units; or the system could use a factor to compute the size of a quantity of base units, assuming that they were to be packed on the standard pallets, and so on. These calculations can be defined for each material individually.

Alternative Units of Measure   Your inventory is managed in the base unit of measure for each material. However, you may also wish to define alternative units of measure for the convenience of particular user departments. For example, your base unit of some component may be a piece. Your purchasing organization may order them in the pallet load; your sales organization may offer them in crate loads; your production facilities may order them in boxes; and your costing operations may deal with them as individual pieces.

During customizing you will be invited to select or enter the names of your units of measure and to provide conversion factors that your MM system will use to convert between the base units of measure and the alternative units.

Batches

Stocks of each material are managed at the level of the storage location so that you can always tell the difference between stocks of the same material held in different storage locations. You might operate a policy of using the nearest source of stock first, for instance, if your warehouses are distributed over a wide geographical area. Your stock can be further subdivided for management purposes.

A batch is a partial stock of material that should be managed separately from other partial stocks of the same material. This partial stock will usually be given a batch number and other documented characteristics, such as the day it was produced and the quality inspection report.

A batch or lot may be distinguished as a production lot because it was all made from the same constituents in the same production campaign. This tracking of lots can be a legal requirement—in the food processing industry, for instance—or it may be a recognition that, although the circumstances of production may not be entirely controllable, the quality of the material can be monitored and this information can be related to the individual batch while it remains in the plant. The weather and the composition of the raw materials are two factors that can affect a production process. Knowing the identity of a batch and the laboratory analysis to which it has been subject can be very important when it is time to use the lot in further production processes or when it is to be sold to a customer.

A batch may also be identified because the quantities of materials in it arrived together from the delivery route. A delivery lot may have been subjected to influences during its transportation that could be important for its users. If one item from a delivery lot is found to be unusual, then the other items from the same delivery may have to be set aside for a quality control inspection.

Special Stocks

A batch or a single item can be assigned as a special stock for a number of reasons that you may wish to redefine during customizing. The standard special stock definitions fall into the following groups:

- Vendor special stocks—Materials that arrive on consignment from a particular vendor, and for which there may be a deferred payment arrangement whereby the user of these special stocks does not pay for them until they are used.

- Customer special stocks—Containers or other transportation equipment that still belong to your company but are temporarily with your customer because they have been used to hold your products. The customer may have to incur a special charge if this packing material is not returned before the due date.

- Event-related stocks—Materials that have been ordered specifically because they will be needed for a planned event (for instance, the building of a make-to-order product for which the customer has placed a firm order).

Purchasing Info Records

One of the ways to add extra value to the materials processes of your company is to keep track of the performance of your vendors and other suppliers of your materials and services.

If you want to find out which vendors have supplied a particular material in the past, or which materials can be obtained from a specific vendor, you should look in the purchasing info records. These are master records containing information on the relationships between vendors and the materials and services they have to offer and have supplied in the past.

There are two types of purchasing info record, depending on whether it is known for certain that a vendor can supply a specific material. A previous satisfactory delivery from that vendor of exactly the right material would be a starting point. A current quotation based on a detailed material specification would also be helpful. Failing such evidence, the purchasing info record may comprise information that is perhaps no more than merely encouraging. What may have been established by previous buyers or researchers is that the vendor in question can supply materials of the same materials group, not necessarily all of them, not necessarily the specific material required.

If this vendor has quoted for this material, then your database will include a material master record associated with the vendor. The purchasing info record will relate the material master record to the correct vendor master record.

If the material you require belongs to a material group, such as stock steel, and one of your vendors has quoted for or supplied stocks of this material group in the past, then the purchasing info master record will tell you that this vendor is a possible supplier. The relationship established by the purchasing info record is between a vendor master and a material group master. This vendor can supply some materials of this material group.

The Data Environment of a Purchasing Info Record

If you have located a particular purchasing info record, you can use it to gain access to the rest of the data environment for that material. The following types of information will be available to you by pointing to the appropriate parts of the of the screen and using the special function keys:

- The ID number of the most recent purchase order involving the vendor on the purchasing info record
- How much of this material has been ordered from this vendor to date
- Current and future prices and purchasing conditions

- The identification numbers of the most recent purchase orders to any other vendors that included one or more of the materials on the purchasing info record, which will help you compare prices and packaging requirements
- Descriptive text concerning the material, which is normally printed on the purchase order
- Other ordering statistics regarding this material or this vendor
- The price history of this material as ordered or quoted by different vendors
- The numerical rating assigned to this vendor by the vendor evaluation system

Purchasing Info Record Structure

The header of the purchasing info record contains general information that will be relevant to all organizational levels. These levels will carry the data applicable to the individual purchasing organizations or plants that will make use of the material when it arrives.

By using this structured level approach, the purchasing info record can show where there are different purchasing conditions for the different purchasing organizations in the company. If you as a purchaser identify a material of interest, and if you have the necessary authorization, you will be shown the relevant purchasing info records.

This is the sort of information you would expect to find:

- Certificate of inspection data
- Texts to be used on purchase orders
- Reminders
- Unit of measure
- Purchasing conditions
- Purchase order history
- Assignment to stock or consumable material

Any of the data fields on a purchasing info record can be used as a search specification to retrieve all the info records that have the same data field value or a logical or mathematical function of it. For example, you can seek all info records that concern a specific material type or all info records that do not.

Creating Purchasing Info Records

A purchasing info record is created or changed automatically when any of the following events occur:

- A quotation is entered
- A purchase order is entered
- A long-term purchasing agreement is created

It is also possible to create or edit a purchasing info record manually by copying and editing a master or an existing record. The system will ensure that your copy is given a unique ID code.

Central Control Function

The process of creating a purchase order will automatically cause the system to look for purchasing info records that might be relevant. If one is found, the system copies the data into the new purchase order for your approval.

By this means, the important information, such as the price and the vendor details, can be determined centrally and maintained there for use by all who need it. It will appear without error on the purchasing documents, no matter who is doing the purchasing.

Bills of Material (BOM)

A bill of material (BOM) is a description of what makes up a product in terms of its constituents. The concept is central to production planning and control. It is used to describe the structure of products that occur in the main types of manufacturing:

- Repetitive manufacturing
- Manufacturing with variants
- Process manufacturing
- Make-to-order manufacturing

The structure of a bill of material is adopted from the PP-Production Planning application master, which requires a header and one or more items to be documented.

BOM Header

The header of a BOM will indicate whether it is released for production in its current form. This occurs as part of the status management procedure.

You have to assign a BOM to one or more plants and define the period of time over which it will be valid.

BOM Items

A bill of material item is a description of a component of the assembly. Any number of items can be in the bill of materials; and any combination of item categories is permitted.

The categories of item may be used in the BOM item list and as subitems, by-products, or scrap as follows:

- Stock Item—Stock items are components kept in stock.
- Nonstock Item—Data on nonstock items can be maintained in the bill of material where it can be accessed by the Purchasing module of MM.
- Variable-sized Item—The quantity to be used is calculated automatically from the sizes or dimensions entered in the purchase order.
- Document Item—A bill of material may include one or more document items such as drawings and safety instructions.

Part

I

Ch

2

■ Text Item—A text item can store all types of text, which will then be accessible by any user of the BOM.

■ Subitem—A subitem can be of any complexity and takes the form of one or more BOM items. It is used to describe components in more detail. For example, a subitem may refer to the installation point of the assembly, which is described by the BOM.

■ By-products and Scrap—A bill of material may represent scrap by a negative component quantity. A by-product may be identified as a separate material component, which is also assigned a negative quantity. These negative quantities are taken into account in material requirements planning and in product costing.

Types of Bills of Material

The Production Planning format of a bill of material is available to all industry sectors and may also be used to maintain bills of material for sales orders, projects, equipment, and documents. The open structure of a bill of material allows you to convert and extend a simple BOM to generate a variant BOM, a multiple BOM, or a customer-order BOM. There are five different forms of bill of material that are based on a uniform structure and are accessed from a standard user interface:

■ Simple BOM—One rigidly-defined bill of material is assigned to one material.

■ Variant BOM—A variant BOM can be used to represent several similar materials.

■ Multiple BOM—A multiple BOM refers to products that are made using different production processes and from different components or different relative quantities of components.

■ One-time or Customer-order BOM—In make-to-order production you may create a one-time bill of material in response to a specific sales order.

■ Configurable BOM—The items of a configurable bill of material are identified and sequenced on the basis of logical links. This arrangement is ideal for complex variant product structures. In continuous flow production, the bill of material may have to take account of the processes being used and the results of earlier processing or analysis of raw materials.

Using Bills of Material

The different departments in your company will use the bills of material in different ways. To facilitate this, you can mark some or all of the BOM items as relevant to specific departments. The user can then work with a subset of the items selected according to their relevance marking. For example, you may mark the items for their relevance to Engineering and Design, Production, or Product Costing.

Another option is to create a separate bill of material for each department.

Maintaining Bills of Material As an open structure document, the bill of material is amenable to creation and maintenance from a full range of interfaces. If your implementation has been configured to do so, you can use the BOM management functions in your MM application. With computer-assisted design installed you can use the CAD dialog interface to copy, edit, and update bills of material.

Where several materials have similar components, you can use a copy function and edit to incorporate the differences.

Assembling Bills of Material with R/3 Classification   The R/3 Classification System can be fully integrated with your BOM maintenance functions so that you can use it to identify suitable materials quickly as you create a bill of material.

BOM Display and Drill-Down   Displaying and printing BOM data is amenable to user control so that you can ask for presentation of data in a variety of forms:

- Level-by-level
- Multilevel
- Summarized
- Single-level where-used lists
- Multilevel where-used lists

If you are viewing BOM data in graphical form, you can freely navigate between the points of the display and thereby access the data selectively.

Using Engineering Change Management on Bills of Materials   You may wish to update many of your bills of materials when prices and components change. The integrated engineering change management functions can be used to carry out mass changes and to track the complete change history of a BOM.

Procurement Procedures

If you need something, you look for a source. If you are trying to conserve your resources, you will look for the cheapest source. If you are looking toward long-term profitability, then you may want to go for a combination of reasonable price and reliability of delivery for as long as you think you will need to use the source.

Because you will have been in business for some time, your purchasing departments will know about some suppliers and about their performance in delivery and quality. You may wish to look around for additional vendors of the materials you need. Then you will want to put the possible sources in some sort of rank order so you may make a choice.

Vendor selection will be followed by purchase order or production order processing with a stage of monitoring to approve the allocation of financial or production resources.

Your goods will arrive and need checking and storage. The invoice will arrive and also need checking. The accounts and the inventory will have to be updated.

At any stage in this procurement sequence, you may discover important facts about the materials you have purchased and the vendors who supplied them. You will want to record these facts and store them in a place where they will be easily noticed by anyone intending to make additional purchases of these materials or from these vendors.

One of the important documents is the purchasing info record, which is maintained separately for each material. The data held in this record is used to set up the processes for selecting vendors for each material on the basis of predetermined rules and decision logic referred to as "conditions."

Pricing Conditions as Data Structures

The SAP R/3 System includes a mechanism for establishing conditions in the form of condition master records. They can refer to any subject-matter domain or any SAP R/3 application. The logical interpretation of a condition is illustrated by the if-then format:

- If X is true, then Y becomes true.
- If the sales quantity is equal to or greater than the first price break, then the order attracts a discount of three percent.

The conditions that are most commonly met in materials management are provided by the system in predefined standard form. You can also add to this list by creating your own conditions.

The main use of conditions is in specific price determination based on the following types of considerations:

- Discounts
- Surcharges by percentage and absolute amounts
- Delivery costs
- Cash discounts for prompt payment
- Taxes

Price Determination

The user can define the sequence in which price determination conditions are applied during the pricing process. The system will propose a set of default values in the purchasing document, which you can amend and supplement with additional charges.

Each purchasing organization in a company can have its own pricing procedure. And each vendor or vendor group can be assigned an individual pricing procedure.

The pricing of purchase orders takes place automatically on the basis of the conditions established in the price determination master records.

The conditions set out in purchase info records are master conditions to be applied to all purchase orders issued to that vendor. If there is a purchasing contract in force with a vendor, the master conditions will be stored in the contract document.

Starting with the master pricing conditions, there are various factors that may have to be taken into account before the final price is determined:

- The purchasing organization
- Whether the individual vendor is subject to specific pricing conditions or modifications of the master conditions
- Whether the invoicing party differs from the actual supplier of the materials or services
- Whether certain items are subject to special conditions on the basis of, for example, the material, the material group, the material type, or the plant
- Whether there is a contract item involved that attracts special conditions

Maintaining Conditions

When a record is changed in the purchasing master conditions, the alterations are promulgated automatically through all the purchase orders and contracts in which they are used.

By this means, you can quickly simulate the effects of any changes in a vendor's price strategy. If a vendor is prepared to offer your company a global discount using a percentage or absolute discount on all purchase orders you have placed, this will affect your prices. By how much, you can find out by making a temporary alteration in the master purchasing conditions for this vendor. The effect can be displayed by viewing, for example, a listing of all your purchase orders for this vendor and comparing the total under the new and the old purchasing conditions.

Limits on Manual Changes to Conditions   Default prices are calculated from the pricing conditions for each material and for each vendor, taking into account the quantities and any other factors allowed for in the master purchasing records. But buyers may wish to make manual alterations to these master records. Limitations on the manual alteration of default prices can be specified by the purchasing manager and these will be stored in the central purchasing conditions master records. The purchasing manager can specify upper and lower limits on the adjustments that are allowed to be made by buyers at the various levels of authorization. These limits can be defined in percentage terms and as absolute amounts.

Validity of Master Pricing Conditions   A set of pricing conditions stored in a master record is given a validity defined by a starting date and a validity period.

If the starting date is in the future, the purchasing conditions will not be applied until that date. When the validity period is reached, the new base prices, discounts, and surcharges will be automatically used in price determination, unless the purchasing manager authorizes anything different.

The Vendor Data Concept

The fundamental method of entering vendor data is by using an existing master record as a reference or model to be copied and modified to correspond to the data that has to be stored. Each copy of a master record will be assigned a unique number by the system.

If you change any master record, or any copy of one, you can be sure that the system will have logged this event. You can look back over the history of such changes for any record you select.

There are provisions for attaching texts to master records for whatever purpose is applicable to your company:

- Addresses of vendor warehouses, technical support, shipping contractor, and recipient of returnable packing
- Purchasing agreements
- Conditions of delivery
- Terms of payment
- Regulations for storage and shipment

The standard display facilities enable you to select a specific vendor master or set of masters by any of a wide range of methods. For example, you can locate a record by entering its number, or you can select a group of records on the basis of match codes, which are suggested during customizing and which you can alter to suit your requirements.

When you find what you need, you can "drill down" to see all the data associated with the vendor of interest.

The main purchasing functions served by the set of vendor master records are:

- Requests for quotations
- Processing quotations
- Ordering

The main financial accounting activities supported by the vendor masters are:

- Data entry during processing
- Verification of invoices from the vendors
- Payment of invoices to the vendors

Both of these groups of activities call upon the same common set of vendor masters when processing transactions.

Once-Only Vendors

The system offers a master record, specified as an entity type, which can be used to store the basic transaction data for all vendors who are not expected to supply your materials or services on a recurring basis.

User Departments

As an example, the purchasing department needs the vendor information for ordering and checking deliveries, but the financial department is also interested in the vendors because payments have to be effected. The sales function may also have an interest if the vendors are also to be customers. Each of these different user departments in your company will have a particular set of data fields in the vendor records that they need. These are formally recorded as "views." The system provides for these views by a series of tables in which each user department can specify which data elements of the vendor master records are to be accessed for their particular operations. Not everyone has to look at everything.

The Structure of Vendor Master Records

The level of the organizational structure at which the master records of a vendor are stored will depend on who normally uses that vendor. Your purchasing organization will be assigned the general data and the accounting data will be held at the company code level. If you have buyer groups, they may specialize in only some of your vendors or only some of your materials.

Each vendor master will have the same data structure, which will be adjusted to suit your company during customizing. The attributes of this data object will include such data clusters as:

- General data, such as the address and details of the communication channels to be used for e-mail and fax
- Purchasing data concerning prices and delivery, together with the conditions and agreements made with this particular vendor
- The accounting data, which will include details of the vendor's bank for direct payment and any agreed arrangements for payment; this data will be managed and maintained at the company code level

When an invoice or a purchasing transaction is being verified, the idea is to check the details of the vendor that are needed on this particular document and any calculations or authorization restrictions.

The vendor company may have a complex structure in which its sales organization is separate from the parent company. The vendor head office may bill you for goods supplied by the sales department, for example. So it may happen that the vendor master record has attributes or clusters of data fields to manage the monthly debits and credits, and an attribute for purchasing data concerning the purchasing organization, such as the currency to be used on orders and the defined trading conditions that specify how intercompany transactions are to be conducted. And there will also be data attributes for the accounting information under the company code, such as control account identification, terms of payment, and bank details.

Account Groups

Vendor accounts are assigned to account groups on the basis of their similarity according to criteria that you define during customizing. One group is for one-time vendors, about whom you will not wish to store more data than needed to complete the current transaction because you do not expect to use them again. The structure of their master records will be truncated as soon as you identify them as one-time or once-only vendors by assigning them to this account group.

The system will also suggest specific master data structures for account groups confined to banking connections or head office business, and so on. You can adjust the account group master data structures to suit your company.

Vendor accounting data is managed at the company code level and includes such information as the vendor's bank identification and details of payment transactions. The main effect of assigning a vendor to an account group is to allow the system to filter out data fields that are not required for transactions with members of that group, so they do not appear on your screen when you are doing business with them. For example, if you are building a purchase order, you do not normally need to process the screens that deal with bank data. Each vendor account group is allocated a specific range of vendor master record numbers. You can tell which vendor account group you are dealing with by looking at the vendor account number. If the company code appears, you also will know that this record is maintained at the company code level. In general, the concept of vendor is used to represent a source from which material can be procured. The nature of this material as a tangible object or in the form of a service, and how it is bought and handled are matters documented in the material master records.

Managing Sources of Supply

An experienced buyer may be able to make a wise choice of sources from the vendors and any internal production plant or storage location that has material available to meet his requirements. However, it may be difficult to build this experience in a changing market and with a changing labor force made up of people who share many tasks rather than specialize in one. If this scenario is even remotely like parts of your organization, the automatic vendor evaluation function should be given serious attention.

Choosing a Vendor for a Specific Material

The buyer needs a list of sources for each of the materials and services of interest to his purchasing group within the purchasing organization. This list is usually maintained manually because there are frequent changes in the details, and sometimes new entries as fresh vendors come into the market and the products of the purchasing company undergo development and, thus, require new sources of materials.

The source list for a material can also be maintained automatically by the following techniques:

- Adopting an existing source list as a first proposal for manual editing
- Copying from outline purchase agreements that refer to this material
- Copying from purchasing info records that have been used to generate purchase orders in the past

Using a Source List   The source list data maintenance functions provide facilities to assign dates and time periods to sources so that they are used only during the periods defined. They are not allowed to supply goods "out of season."

Part

I

Ch

2

The source list is compiled as needed from source list records, one for each source for each material in the plant. A source can be identified in various ways:

- A fixed source will be the preferred source over a specified period of time.
- An effective source will be noted as equivalent to a fixed source for the moment of time for which the source list is being compiled.
- A source can be marked as blocked over a time period or until the block is removed.

The source list effectively provides suggestions, which can be checked manually or automatically against purchase requisitions or purchase orders to ascertain how reliable the delivery and quality might be.

The source list records can be maintained manually if there is a shortage of data to be used to evaluate automatically the reliability of the vendors.

Using a Quota Arrangement   A quota system can be set up by which two or more vendors or internal sources share the requirement. The time-dependent condition can be applied in conjunction with the quota system. This is taken into the calculation when a choice of sources is being evaluated automatically.

Automatic Vendor Evaluation

Every vendor for a particular material, including internal providers, is awarded a score out of 100 by the vendor evaluation system. The main criteria used by the system are as follows:

- Price
- Quality
- Delivery
- Service

Up to 99 main criteria can be defined by the user, and the contribution of each of them to the total score can be weighted so as to emphasize the factors that your company feels to be most important. The scoring is automatic once you have decided which criteria to use.

Applying Subcriteria

The system provides five subcriteria for each main criterion. The user can define up to 20 sub-criteria.

The scores for subcriteria can be calculated in different ways according to the type of data or other input that can be made available, as follows:

- Automatic calculation uses data that already exists in the system.
- Semiautomatic calculation relies on values entered by the buyers, from which the system then calculates the score for the subcriterion.
- Manual input occurs when a buyer enters a vendor's score for a subcriterion and cuts out any assessment of other data for this part of the evaluation.

Buyers can be allowed the option of manual entry or one of the varieties of automatic evaluation, according to the importance of the material or the other attributes of the pool of possible suppliers.

If any change is made to the data or the formulas used by the vendor evaluation system, a log entry is made and the event is recorded.

Displaying Automatic Vendor Evaluations

The system allows a wide flexibility in how the results of vendor evaluations are displayed. You can have a rank ordering of all vendors on the basis of all their scores on the materials they supply, or you can call for a rank ordering of suppliers for a specific material or service.

You can, for example, compare prices during the procurement process or automate the vendor selection or order creation processes. You have the choice of setting up automatic processing by default or have the system display any proposed transaction for your approval before posting it. The Vendor Evaluation component enables you to find the best vendors using criteria of your choice. You also have the option of requiring purchasing documents to be part of a release and approval procedure before they can be further processed. Purchasing activities are approved by authorized members of staff by electronic signature. You can send purchase orders or forecast delivery schedules to the vendors either on paper or electronically (by EDI, for example). The purchase order history allows you to monitor the status of your order and track deliveries or invoices already received.

Vendor Net Price Simulation

The buyers for the materials and services you need will want to know who are the best suppliers.

The vendor net price simulation is a standard function that can operate with any order quantities and other order data. It will take into account any incidental costs of delivery. If there is a cash discount for prompt payment, it will factor this into the simulated price. In the same way, the system will recognize if there are any price breaks applicable because of the quantity required or the expected total price of the order, or if part of the order would qualify for such special purchasing conditions.

The purchasing info record system can be used to set up different simulations, as in the following examples:

- Comparing the prices of various vendors for a material or material group
- Comparing the sales conditions of various vendors for a material or material group
- Allowing for any prompt payment cash discounts
- Showing the vendor's prices for all his materials
- Taking account of the effects of crossing the vendor's price breaks for total price and quantity, using the appropriate timetable of validity periods and conditions
- Reviewing the net price of a range of vendors for various order quantities and other order data, such as delivery times and conditions attached to late deliveries

Alternative Vendor Pricing Plans

The system can be asked to determine the best source on the basis of the quantity required, the date required, and the vendor net price. And it can do this for any number of plan versions that you have set up to explore the shape of the purchasing decision environment. The flexible display functions will present the results in graphical form should you so wish. You can drill down through this information to see what you need to know.

And because the order information will include the date by which delivery is required, the system can check that the net price has been computed using conditions that will be valid at that time.

Using MM to Control Purchasing Operations

The aim of the MM-PUR Purchasing component is to be able to automate the purchasing function of your company as much as possible to leave the buyer only the exceptional circumstances to deal with.

Almost all the data needed to create a purchase order should be in the system already. It should be copied automatically to reduce errors and speed up the task.

A purchase order may start life as a purchase requisition originating in one of the user departments, or it may be created as a result of material requirements planning.

A source of supply of the material or service has to be identified by the system, by the user who needs the material, or by the purchasing department, perhaps after soliciting quotations from a number of potential suppliers.

The most common method of generating a purchase order is by copying one prepared for a previous purchase and updating it as necessary.

Part
I
Ch
2

Purchasing Documents

The traditional paper documents associated with purchasing in a large organization have been reengineered to take advantage of the benefits of a fully integrated system in which almost all of the information required to complete them can be found in the master records of the system, where they are kept up-to-date.

The following documents are used in purchasing:

- Purchase requisition
- Request for quotation
- Quotation
- Purchase order
- Contract
- Delivery scheduling agreement

Purchasing Document Structure

The header of a purchasing document contains the document number and the details of the vendor. The remainder of the document comprises one or more items referring to specific materials or services to be procured and the quantities required.

Each item in a document can refer to one or more supplements. For example, an item in a purchasing document could refer to a supplement that detailed the order history of this item from this supplier.

Purchase Requisition

A requisition is a request for a service to be rendered by another department; in the case of a purchase requisition, the request is for the purchasing department to procure a certain quantity of a material or service and have it delivered to the originator by a specified date.

The purchasing organization responds to the requisition by going through a series of steps to determine a source of supply, perhaps after a request for quotation submitted to several potential suppliers. When the purchase requisition has been checked and a supplier chosen, the requisition is released to be converted to a purchase order, which is checked again and released to the vendor for purchasing action, with the obligation to pay for it when the time comes.

Generating a Purchase Requisition

There are two ways to create a purchase requisition:

- Use a reference document as a model and edit a copy of it on behalf of the requesting department
- Have the purchase requisition generated automatically by the material requirements planning process

Sources of Supply

If the system is aware of a suitable source of supply, it will use it automatically to create a purchase requisition. The following sources of supply will be recognized and used to generate the purchasing document if they are relevant:

- A fixed vendor as specified in the material master record
- An outline purchase agreement that has a validity period, which includes the required delivery date
- A purchasing info record that identifies a possible vendor of the material or service required

In this context, an internal source of supply, such as a manufacturing plant in an associated company, can be regarded as a vendor.

Allocation of Purchase Requisitions

Your company may have a list of approved suppliers for each of the materials you use in your business. You may have a specialized buying section responsible for a particular type of material.

If no approved sources can be identified, a list of possible suppliers has to be created in order to be able to distribute a request for quotation document.

Purchase Requisition Release Strategies

Whether or not a purchase requisition is approved for release as a purchase order depends on the conditions imposed by the release strategy, which usually takes the form of a chain of release points. These release points are the individuals or the organizational units assigned the responsibility of approving requisitions once they have been assigned a particular release strategy.

The release strategy is assigned automatically when the purchase requisition is entered. The strategy chosen will depend on such factors as the value of the requisition and the material type of the requested items.

Buyer-Generated Purchase Requisitions

Given a list of the items awaiting purchasing action, the buyers may well generate the purchase requisitions that fall into their areas of responsibility, because they will know where to obtain the particular materials.

Part

I

Ch

2

The Request for Quotation Procedure

When a request for quotation to a vendor elicits a quotation, it will be returned in the form of a list of the vendor's prices for the material, together with the purchase conditions and perhaps some additional information. This data is entered on the original request for quotation document, which thereby becomes a store of all the information necessary to make an informed choice among the vendors who have responded to the request for quotation.

When all the quotations have be entered, the buyers can access the price comparison list and use it to have the system conduct a comparative analysis of the quoted prices and conditions, with a view to determining the most favorable quotation.

The analysis data can then be automatically stored in a purchasing info record and the unsuccessful bidders automatically sent rejection letters.

Generating a Purchase Order

The aim of the automated purchase order component is to reduce the time taken to process purchase orders and minimize the chances of an error. The method is to use data already in the system as far as possible.

Using References to Minimize Data Entry Work

The buyer can elect to use any of the following methods of finding an existing document to provide the data for a new purchase order:

- Select from a list of current requisitions.
- Select from a list of previous purchase orders.
- Call up an existing longer-term buying contract for this material and create a release order for the required amount of material to be delivered on the date specified, which will cause the texts, prices, and conditions to be copied automatically from the contract to the release order.

Referencing a Purchase Requisition

The purchasing info record performs some of the functions of a contract, in that it contains details of the vendor's prices and conditions for specific materials. When you create a purchase order, you may initiate the creation of a purchasing info record or the updating of one that exists already.

When you have called up a purchasing info record as a reference for a purchase order, it is only necessary for you to enter the material number, the order quantity, and the delivery date required.

Automatic Generation of Purchasing Documents

The place most often used to begin generating purchasing documents is the purchase order item overview screen, which will display the most important information you will need, whether you are creating a new purchase order, a request for quotation, or a delivery schedule. The information you can highlight and copy from this screen is as follows:

- Material number
- Purchase order quantity
- Purchase order price
- Plant
- Storage location

Buyer Options for Creating Purchase Orders

The buyer will be offered a range of options to progress the creation of the purchasing document:

- Vendor known—The preferred choice if the buyer knows perfectly well who will be the supplier.

- Vendor unknown—This will cause the system to try to find suitable vendors on the basis of the purchase order items that have been entered up to that point in the creation of the purchase order. The buyer may have to allocate particular orders among the proposed vendors if there is more than one suggested by the system.

- Allocated purchase requisitions exist—A reminder to the buyer that he or she can call up a list of all the purchase requisitions that have been placed with sources of supply from the purchasing group to which the buyer belongs. From this historical data the buyer can choose a vendor, if one is suitable, and the system will copy the relevant data to the new purchase order.

Single and Multiple Account Assignment

The account to which the amount is to be posted when the goods are delivered has to be determined during the creation of the purchase order. The user has to select the type or name of the account, and the system will carry out an internal check and propose an account number that will be entered on the purchase order if it is accepted.

Several accounts may have to be posted when the goods ordered by a purchase order are delivered. The net order value can be apportioned on a percentage basis or in terms of specified amounts to any number of individual cost objects, such as projects or cost centers.

The allocation of a net order value to cost objects and the posting of the value to an account in the FI-Financial Accounting system are initiated by data copied automatically from purchase requisitions or contracts and replicated on any other documents that are generated using them as references.

Establishing Outline Purchase Agreements

If your company frequently uses the same supplier for one or more materials or services, each subject to specified conditions that are likely to remain essentially the same for a period of time, it may be useful to set out a purchase agreement in outline form. This outline purchase agreement will have a period of validity during which the conditions of the agreement will remain valid, and it will have a limit set to the quantity or value of the goods that can be supplied under this agreement during this period of validity.

The agreement is in outline form because it does not make any reference to the date required or the actual quantity or value of the material or service that is to be delivered. This information has to be supplied by a subsequent issue of a release order or a delivery schedule, which will refer to the outline purchase agreement so as to be able to define the conditions and other details of the contract to supply.

Types of Contracts

There are many terms used to refer to an outline purchase agreement. This discussion treats all of these names as equivalent to an outline purchase agreement:

- Blanket order
- Blanket contract
- Period contract
- Bulk contract
- Master agreement
- Master contract

The contract to which an outline purchase agreement is the preliminary, and which is the source of data for generating documents, may be a value contract or a quantity contract, according to the manner in which the upper limit is defined. The value or quantity specified in the outline purchase agreement will be the limit for the period of validity.

Scheduling Agreements

In many industries, the price of materials may be much affected by the uncertainties of supply and demand. Your company may wish to introduce a degree of stabilization into such a situation by setting up an arrangement for a schedule of material deliveries over a defined period of validity, during which the prices and conditions are to be kept constant.

The scheduling agreement will usually specify a total or target quantity for the period and a particular type of vendor scheduling of the constituent deliveries. Each material or service in the agreement may well have its own vendor schedule. The details of the schedule within the validity period will be regularly updated as the requirements of the purchasing company become known.

Vendor Delivery Schedules   The vendor undertaking to supply according to a schedule does not receive a purchase order or a release order. Once the scheduling agreement validity period has begun, the vendor works to a vendor delivery schedule, which is regularly updated.

Each line of the vendor delivery schedule represents an individual delivery shipment consisting of a specified quantity of the particular material, delivered to a precise storage or holding location in your plant on a particular date, and perhaps also at a particular time on that date if you are operating in a just-in-time "KANBAN" environment.

Benefits of Vendor Delivery Scheduling   Where vendor scheduling agreements are in place for all the component parts that go to make up a product assembly, the company can take advantage of a wide range of favorable effects that may add considerable value to its products and give it a competitive edge over rivals.

A vendor delivery schedule can reduce the processing time and the amount of paper or electronic transmissions entailed by the equivalent series of individual purchase orders or release orders.

The production at a plant can take place with the minimum of waiting stock, perhaps none.

The vendor need not hold up shipments in order to amass the quantity needed for a large delivery because the order is dispatched to the schedule. From the vendor's point of view, the schedule gives a steadier basis on which to plan production.

Profiting from Purchasing Reports

Purchasing managers have to keep track of all their purchase orders and all their purchasing organizations. They must also be continually aware of their vendor population and newcomers to it that they have not yet used.

If there are trends in the requirements of their own company, they must notice them in time to plan their purchasing schedules.

Analyzing Purchasing Documents

The following inquiries can be answered by calling for the relevant report:

- Which purchase orders were placed with a certain vendor over a specific period?
- Which purchase orders have been processed as far as delivery?
- Has this vendor delivered all or only part of this purchase order?
- Does this vendor have a good record for delivering on time?
- How many orders from this vendor have been received and found to be invoiced correctly?
- What is the average value of purchase orders handled by this purchasing organization or this buyer group?
- What are the total values of orders placed by each of the purchasing organizations in this company?

Standard Analyses of Purchase Order Values

The standard SAP R/3 analysis functions are available to be applied to the historical data to be found in the purchase orders and the associated purchasing documents, as in the following examples.

Totals Totals analysis will let you see the number and total value of existing purchase orders.

ABC Analysis ABC analysis shows the distribution of vendors across three groups, defined as (A) vendors that account for the highest value of material purchases, (B) vendors accounting for an average value of purchases, and (C) vendors from which the value of purchases is lowest.

Using a Comparison Period Analysis by comparison with a reference period is designed to show how a composite value has changed over time or across data objects, such as a comparison between this period last year and the current period for the total value purchased by each of the purchasing organizations in the company.

Net Order Value Frequency Analysis Frequency analysis shows which order values occur most often in each purchasing organization and can be used, for example, to negotiate a better discount, based on an immediate discount for large orders rather than an end-of-year volume rebate.

Purchasing Analysis Display Options The large volume of purchase documents and master records to be found in most systems running the MM-Materials Management module necessitates a powerful yet flexible suite of functions to display to the user just what is wanted for the immediate purpose, and to leave out what is not wanted. The following search specifications are typical of the needs of the purchasing management departments; many of them are, or could be, initiated by special function keys:

- List all purchase orders issued by this particular purchasing group during this specific time period
- List the requisitions for this material from any or all of a specified group of vendors
- List all archived purchasing info records for this material for this plant
- Display the purchase order history of the selected item

From Here...

- How does MM support MRP?

  See Chapter 3, "Understanding Material Requirements Planning."

- How are the materials components used in the other R/3 applications?

  See Chapter 5, "Integrating MM."

- How is my company going to know how to set up a complex system such as SAP R/3 Materials Management?

  See Chapter 6, "Understanding the SAP R/3 Business Engineer."

Understanding Material Requirements Planning

In this chapter

- How the SAP R/3 FI-Financial Accounting application is connected to the CO-Controlling application
- How the CO-Controlling modules relate to your MM-Materials Management modules
- How to make use of the integrated systems to support planning, costing, and control
- How to plan material requirements and use forecasting models

Materials are assets. They have a value that could compute on the basis of the prices you paid for them, or on the prices they might fetch if you were to sell them in the current market. Materials are also resources in the sense of being able to take part in activities that increase the profitability of your enterprise. You could sell them at a profit by using them in manufacturing or some other value-adding activity.

The art of financial controlling is to plan and monitor such activities to further the objectives of your enterprise.

The Business Logic of Materials Controlling

The purpose of setting up a financial controlling operation is to utilize the data collected by the financial accounting systems. Your accountant keeps track of your debts and payments, and also of your incomes.

Your controller studies all these documents to work out which parts of your company are wasting time and money, and which parts are generating profits. The controller tries to tell your management how to do better next time.

If many of your accounting and controlling functions are carried out by data processing, then your accountant and your controller will do their work by monitoring the automatic functions they have authorized. They will have some targets, some plans, against which to judge the actual performance of your various departments.

The SAP R/3 CO-Controlling application is the part of the core R/3 functionality that specializes in computing the planned values for the significant variables in your enterprise. A simple controller might set targets in the form of planned sales volumes for each month by assigning the sales volumes for last year equally to the 12 months of the year. A more subtle controller might make allowances for the number of manufacturing days in each month according to the works calendar that shows shut-downs for holidays and maintenance.

If you had a materials controller, the planning operation could be even more subtle. You could buy in extra materials when the prices were favorable and warehouse them until they are needed. But you would be advised to check with your financial controller in case the cost of the extra warehousing should prove to be more than the savings you might make by favorable purchasing. This is the realm of profitability analysis.

Controlling Functions Available in SAP R/3

Your material controller will probably be most interested in the techniques used to record the costs of materials in such a way that they can be settled on accounting data objects where they will be available for analysis.

Suppose a particular material comes in a special packaging for protection. It is processed and sold as part of a complicated product, an assembly. Shall the cost of the packaging be counted as an overhead cost, part of the cost of the raw material, or shall it be settled in some other way?

When the time comes to analyze the profitability of manufacturing this assembly, how will the special packaging be taken into account? Suppose the material could have been delivered in larger consignments using different packaging. Would the whole manufacturing process have been more profitable?

What you want your controlling processes to do is to record significant data, analyze it, set out reasonable forecasts, and inform management. In relatively stable situations, you might decide that management would be satisfied if the only reporting that took place would be in the form of reliable and timely early warning of values or trends that were apparently deviating from the planned targets.

Reviewing the Financial Management Concepts

Some of the financial ideas important in the materials management context are as follows:

- The General Ledger is where the information is accumulated for the balance sheet and profit-and-loss statement.
- The Personal Accounts in the General Ledger are Accounts Receivable and Accounts Payable.
- Financial Controlling is the process of planning the value flows in an organization and then recording the actual values for comparison with the plan.

The SAP product module FI-Financial Accounting comprises a number of components. They may be installed and configured in various combinations to suit the individual company.

The SAP R/3 FI-Financial Accounting Modules

The FI-Financial Accounting components are titled as follows:

- FI-GL General Ledger
- FI-AR Accounts Receivable
- FI-AP Accounts Payable
- FI-AA Asset Accounting
- FI-LC Consolidation

The computer can be made to be good at what it does only if it is endowed with impeccable behavior. As much as possible, it must be incorruptible. Entry errors may occur that are not detected at the time. In such instances, it must be possible to trace the origin of the error, make corrections to the accounting, and perhaps take steps to make this type of error less likely in the future, or at least have it detected at the time. The SAP System takes this moral stand very seriously. Each time a transaction takes place between SAP and the outside world, an SAP Document is created and stamped with the date and time. The terminal device signs the document, and the user is obliged to leave his or her identification there too. From this moment of formal entry launching the transaction, there is no further opportunity to annotate or adjust anything illegally. The time-stamped SAP Document recording the entry event will be locked. Therefore, it is best if it is checked before it is launched, and it would be very helpful to append any annotations or explanatory remarks at this stage. There will always be a choice of standard annotations to cope with most eventualities, plus the possibility of entering free text by way of explanation.

If the transaction is legal but in error, then a correcting transaction must be enacted. This too will leave its mark on the audit trail by generating an SAP Document.

Accruals are an essential part of modern online accounting. Costs and charges—possibly profits as well—are linked to the time period and cost or profit center to which they belong, rather than to any general fund. The aim is to reveal the true value to the company of whatever activity is using its resources.

Checking the Data

Checks are made at every stage where an automatic assessment can be made as to whether the information coming in is reasonable. Do the figures balance? Is this transaction legal? Has this decision-maker been authorized to make this choice?

SAP standard business software is built around the aim of providing continuous measurement of the profitability of everything that is going on. Each business function will be recording how often it is used and how long it takes to do its work. And this kind of performance information will be available to illuminate any scrutiny of how resources are being utilized.

This sophistication in accounting performance measurement, provided as standard in the SAP Systems, is additional to the Generally Accepted Accounting Principles (GAAP); but it may well make a very significant difference to the figures on the profit and loss account.

The ideal accounting system will be able to re-create an unbroken audit trail from each and every transaction to the balance sheet and profit and loss account of the company. The auditor should be able to point to any number on the financial documents of the company and ask to see how it was computed, right back to the documents that came from the outside world to carry the information that found its way into the computer.

SAP FI-Financial Accounting can always deliver an unbroken audit trail, because every external and internal transaction creates a record in the form of an SAP document, which can be called to substantiate the audit and prove the credentials of the company's accounts.

And upon this foundation it is possible to demonstrate just how the system is complying with the GAAP tenets as applied to computerized accounting systems. The GAAP requirements arise from a set of statutory regulations, decrees, and ordinances that embody the experience of the accounting professions and serve as the basis upon which each nation may develop additional accounting traditions and requirements.

FI-AP Accounts Payable and FI-AR Accounts Receivable are sub-ledgers of the FI-GL General Ledger and completely integrated with it. They are sometimes referred to as the Personal Subledgers because they contain information that is associated with customers and vendors and might be subject to rules or customs of privacy and nondisclosure.

The balance sheet has a Receivables Account in which line items in customer accounts are subtotaled or totaled. The Payables Account in the General Ledger subtotals or totals the line items from the vendor accounts.

Each customer transaction updates the balance of the Receivables Account in the General Ledger and each vendor transaction updates the balance of the Payables Account in the General Ledger.

MM-Materials Management has sub-ledgers and balance sheet accounts, which are integrated with the General Ledger in the same way as Payables and Receivables.

For each of these transactions in the sub-ledgers and the FI-General Ledger an SAP Document is created, which can be used to keep track of any element of the transaction details recorded in it. If you wanted to retrieve transactions for analysis, you could find them by any of the data elements, such as:

- Material code number
- Asset number
- Personnel identification number of the data entry clerk, buyer, or salesperson

The FI-General Ledger module also offers some of the facilities of an extended general ledger, even if the SAP Extended General Ledger system has not been installed. The extended facilities allow you to enter cost data such as cost center, cost unit, and project identification with each transaction.

After each transaction, because the General Ledger will have been updated, you can display or print lists of updates to the balance sheet and profit-and-loss statement. You can also print or display balance sheet reports and any other report of the financial system. The list of where a specific material had been used in sales or manufacturing might be of interest.

Assets may attract the attention of controllers because of automatic reports of their ratios, depreciation, capitalized cost, and net book value. Inventory transactions, invoices, and personnel expenses are other examples of aspects of a business that can be made available to controllers, because the SAP System has the unbreakable habit of capturing all transactions from all system components in the form of SAP Documents that can be collated and analyzed into whatever informative structure is logically feasible.

The logical qualification is an obvious reminder that data that have not been entered into the SAP System at some stage or other cannot take part in subsequent analysis.

If, however, the necessary primary data are in the system, then automatic profit and loss information can be computed. Overheads can be monitored and attributed to such headings as cost center and order settlement. Product cost accounting can shed light on the costs of ongoing jobs. Technical and commercial projects can be monitored, controlled, and brought into the plans. Profitability analysis will be possible on the basis of cost of sales and period accounting.

At any time it is possible to clear individual line items in business transactions and effect a reconciliation of separate controlling units with the General Ledger.

Two Primary Functions of the General Ledger

The FI-GL General Ledger component recognizes that there are two main reasons for asking for reports from a general ledger: The shareholders want to know if the company is financially sound, and the managers want to know how the year has turned out.

Monitoring Financial Health   Shareholders may be very interested in the financial statements required by law: the balance sheet and the profit-and-loss statement. These two financial documents are the basis of external accounting because they reveal the financial health of a company.

The profit and loss computations depend on closing the accounts in the general ledger at the end of the financial year. One of the primary functions of the general ledger is to allow this year-end closing to take place in an orderly manner.

Reviewing the Results for the Year   The other primary function of the general ledger is financial accounting for the current fiscal year.

The function of collecting and recording data from transactions is one part of financial accounting. Posting data and effecting reconciliation on a continuous basis make up the other part.

The SAP System creates a document for each transaction that can be used for a flexible reporting and analysis system, with the ability to establish a valid audit trail using these recorded transaction documents.

Reconciliation is effected at the transaction level before an entry is posted, but there has to be a closing of the reconciliation accounts at the end of the month and then at the end of the year. A facility exists in R/3 to call up daily or monthly reports at any time.

Special General Ledger Transactions

The accounts in the special general ledger are reconciliation accounts for special sub-ledger transactions that do not directly involve sales or purchases and may not be balanced with the Receivables and Payables. The special general ledger indicator is a single character code to distinguish these transactions from sales to customers or purchases from vendors. The following transaction types are examples of special general ledger transactions:

- Acquisitions
- Dispositions
- Depreciation
- Transfers
- Down payments
- Bills of exchange
- Monthly payroll
- Period closing entries

Year-End Closing

The law for closing a fiscal year requires entries to closing accounts for the balance sheet and profit-and-loss statement. The SAP FI System ensures that year-end closing entries are transferred from sub-ledgers such as:

- Accounts Receivable
- Accounts Payable
- Fixed Assets

Provision is also made for closing entries manually and individually. You can close a fiscal year at any time. The flexible online reporting system will offer separate formats of the financial documents for tax authorities, stockholders, legal consolidation of associated companies, and so on.

International Taxation

The SAP System is international. The taxation functions you commonly need have been programmed as standard business functions with tables of parameters available for customization to the organization and to the specific operational features required.

When you use the SAP System, you will have signified the country where your company is located, and if prompted, the country where your vendor or customer is located. The system will adopt the taxation regimes appropriate to each of these countries.

The system calculates tax or adjusts it automatically. When you enter the transaction you cause the system to create the SAP document containing all the details. Then it immediately posts the taxes as it updates the accounts. The required tax reports are generated automatically.

Standard Taxation Functions

The FI-Financial Accounting module includes the following standard international taxation functions:

- Taxes on sales and purchases
- Bills of exchange tax
- Tax base for tax calculation
- Definitions of all required tax rates
- Methods for the determination of due dates for tax payment
- Tax calculation procedures
- Tax base for cash discount
- Dependent taxes as surcharges or deductions
- European Community acquisition tax
- Division into deductible and nondeductible taxes

Part

I

Ch

3

Withholding tax can be programmed to suit your requirements. The process makes use of the following functions:

- Tax base
- Definition of all required tax rates
- Flagging of all vendors effected
- Determination of due dates for tax payments

The system verifies withholding tax when you enter a vendor invoice and payment. You do not have to check the tax entries later. The necessary reports are prepared automatically.

Although the system will adopt the appropriate standard tax regime as soon as you have indicated the country, you can adjust parameters to meet your specific tax requirements. For instance, you may have to make adjustments to the standard procedure because of a change in the national taxation regulations, or because you are working in a country that does not exactly follow any of the standard tax regimes programmed into the system.

Country-specific tax requirements are notified in the SAP INT International component, and may have been used to customize your particular implementation.

Intercompany Accounting

A group comprising two or more individual companies will have an organizational structure designed to facilitate day-to-day operations. For example, each company may buy material and manage a warehouse. Each may run a sales and distribution division. To increase the complexity of the organization somewhat, suppose there is also a head office, which functions as a separate company.

The head office, as a company, may have oversight of two other companies. Each of these business units will incur expenses and probably enjoy revenue.

For the sake of business convenience, it may well happen that two or even three of these units will combine to make a purchase, perhaps at a discount because of the size of the order. One payment to the vendor will be made against one invoice.

Again for good business reasons, the units may join forces to provide a service to a customer. For example, Purchasing may provide the material goods, and Distribution may look after their delivery. Again, one payment from the customer will be made against one invoice.

If each of these business units is managed as an individual company, all intercompany transactions within the group and with customers and vendors must obey the rules of intercompany accounting. In particular, transactions must leave records that will allow intercompany business to be legally audited to give a true picture of the group as a whole and of the individual companies when it comes to drawing up the financial documents.

With modern online computerized accounting systems, the balance sheets and the profit-and-loss statements of the group and each individual company will be readily available at any time.

The principles of intercompany accounting are applied when your company is part of a group; they also apply when your customer or your vendor is part of another group.

The SAP accounting system uses methods that support intercompany transactions and complies with GAAP.

Paying for Intercompany Purchases

Several companies in a group may purchase from the same vendor. You can pay for the purchase by making a single payment, with the vendor account number being the same in the vendor master record in each company in the group. One company has to keep a central bank account to be used to pay on behalf of the other companies.

Vendor Payments to an Alternative Recipient

Your supplier may not have to deal with its payments due. For example, it may have a head office that will receive payment. You can record in its master data the account number of this alternative recipient. The system will then process return transfers and other vendor payment business through the banks to the alternative recipient.

If you do post vendor invoices to an affiliate, you have to record in the master data of the branch vendor a group-wide company account number that will be used during consolidation to eliminate the invoices that would otherwise appear twice in the company accounts. The system will be able to look at the transaction documents bearing this group-wide company account number and identify any entries that are replicated because the payment was made to an affiliate that was not the original vendor.

Intercompany Payments

One vendor may have supplied several company codes in the same group. The payment system can make one payment and then settle the intercompany accounts by calculating and posting receivables and payables between company codes.

The transaction needs you to define one of the company codes and enter it as a normal paying company. The system will assign the document a unique intercompany identification number, which will be used to ensure that the other members of the company code group will pay their shares.

Language Differences

R/3 is an international system. The names of all general ledger accounts can be translated if the language key is entered together with the name of the account in the target language. This process can be repeated for all languages in the group. By this means you might add or modify general ledger account names in the language of the holding company, and later log in and call for the account balances in the language of your log-in profile.

In a listing of the charts of accounts, each chart will be annotated to show the main language and all the alternatives available.

Currency

The following operational currencies have been defined and their codes are assigned to each function by default (you can alter the default settings):

- Local currency is also the reporting currency for the company code.
- Document currency is that specified for entry on SAP documents.
- Group currency is an alternative to document currency for group reporting.
- Updating currency is defined for posting debits and credits to the general ledger in parallel with the local currency.
- Credit limit currency is that which has been chosen to maintain the credit limit.
- Ledger currency is an alternative to the updating currency for that ledger.

Additional currency assignments are available in the SAP Foreign Exchange Management component.

Currencies in Transactions

Each company code has a local currency for reporting. The system records amounts in this local currency and also in a currency that has been specified as the document currency, which will be used on all documents in addition to the local currency.

You can enter documents in any currency.

You have two options for converting currencies:

- Enter an exchange rate when you enter the transaction document.
- The system translates between document and local currencies by referring to a table of daily exchange rates that is either updated manually or maintained automatically by a link to a separate database.

The system can be customized in various ways, which include:

- A specific user is obliged to enter amounts in a particular currency, which can be the local currency or the document currency.
- A specific user can be permitted to enter amounts in either local or document currency.

Whatever the customizing arrangements, the system will display amounts in both local and document currencies. It will round off minor differences, using rules established for this purpose. These differences can occur when several line items are converted and then added in both currencies.

Customer monthly debits and credits are kept by the system only in local currency. The reconciliation account for the Accounts Receivable sub-ledger is kept in local currency and in all the other currencies that have been posted.

Currency Exchange Differences

A line item can be expressed in a currency other than the local or document currency. You can enter payments to clear such foreign currency line items using either local or document currency.

The payment expressed in the document currency will have been converted from the local currency at an exchange rate adopted by the system according to the rules laid down for assigning the daily exchange rate. If this rate has changed from the rate prevailing when the invoice was written, the payment amount may not match the open item amount. In such cases, the system will automatically calculate and post an exchange difference entry to a separate account established for this purpose.

Understanding the CO-Controlling Application

The SAP R/3 System includes the CO-Controlling system as an integral part. The concept of business controlling includes the planning of values such as costs and revenues, which will appear in the financial documents. The performance of the company has to be monitored and reported in relation to these planned values. Advice and information to management should be the outcomes.

The implementation of the CO-Controlling system will entail specifying the details of which quantities and values are to be subject to planning and, therefore, to the subsequent monitoring and reporting functions.

The following components comprise the SAP CO-Controlling module, which is an integrated system for overhead cost controlling:

- CO-CCA Cost Center Accounting
- CO-ABC Activity-Based Cost Accounting
- CO-OPA Order and Project Accounting
- CO-PA Profitability Analysis
- CO-PCA Profit Center Accounting

The FI-GLX Extended General Ledger uses accounts that are based on a range of sub-ledgers that allow overhead cost analyses from different points of view. For example, accounts may focus on cost centers, product costs, or activities. These facilities are provided by using the SAP CO-Controlling system as an internal accounting system.

The implementation of a controlling function in an organization is carried out in an SAP R/3 System in the following phases:

- Defining the structure of the organization in terms of units that can be controlled
- Setting up information flows that can monitor the performance of the controllable units
- Running the controlling system through cycles of the controlling tasks, which are repeated at a frequency suited to the type of business process

Business Planning and Control

In accord with the basic divide-and-measure approach to business control, it is useful to differentiate the operational controlling systems from the functional controlling systems.

The operational controlling systems are provided with SAP R/3 components to support the four operational tasks:

- Capital investment controlling, which transfers activities to be capitalized and used to calculate depreciation and operating profits
- Financial controlling, which monitors and plans scheduled payments from projects and orders
- Funds controlling, which sees to the procurement, use, and creation of funds in all areas
- Cost and profit controlling, which monitors the costs of all company activities

Alternative Cost Accounting Methods

The SAP R/3 standard business functions provide all the functionality needed to support most modern cost accounting systems.

The main differences between costing concepts arise in connection with the scope of the costs they include and the structure of these costs with respect to the organization structure. There are variations in the use of standard versus actual costs, and in the allocation of costs directly to the products or services, in contrast to allocating them to overhead. Methods may also differ in the relationships between cost center activities, such as in the use of primary costs, cost components, and secondary cost breakdown.

The following cost accounting methods can be accommodated in the SAP R/3 System:

- Actual costing
- Static and flexible normal costing
- Static and flexible standard costing
- Variable direct costing
- Activities and services costing
- Functional costing

You may wish to take a step-by-step approach to the implementation of cost control by, for example, using actual costing and collecting the primary expenses in the cost centers by allocation and perhaps later, automatically by direct posting.

Progressive Implementation of Cost and Profit Controlling

The modular structure of SAP R/3 applications is designed to allow you to move progressively according to the developments and requirements of your company. The application modules are discussed in a sequence, which is in accord with this concept of progressive implementation.

Cost element accounting is a standard approach, which is integral to the R/3 system. Functions are predefined to create and maintain cost element master data and calculate imputed cost elements. The R/3 system can mediate the importing and incorporation of posting data from external systems. There is full reporting on cost elements. Individual business transactions are structured, recorded, assigned, and reported using the FI-GL General Ledger profit-and-loss account structure.

CO-CCA Cost Center Accounting has to plan, monitor, control, and settle all business activities and responsibilities. It has functions to create and maintain cost center master data and to accept or modify definitions of statistical ratios. Cost center postings and transfers have their specialized functions, as have distribution, assessment, and allocation between cost centers. Primary cost elements can be used in the planning functions for cost centers. The user can define the screen and printed report layout formats from the cost center reporting system. Planning functional dependencies and the detailed planning of cost centers are supported by the CO-CCA Cost Center Accounting component.

CO-ABC Activity-Based Cost Accounting is used to cost the internal flow of activities with functions to plan, evaluate, and allocate.

CO-OPA Order and Project Accounting is specialized in the tasks of planning, monitoring, and settling the activities, services, and processes that take place as the result of internal orders and projects.

CO-PA Profitability Analysis is required in order to report on complex sales organizations and complex product hierarchies. In SAP R/3, results analysis is conducted using the cost-of-sales approach or by period accounting.

The Controlling Area Concept

The starting point and method of navigating through the details of a controlling system are a structure made up of units and links. This structure is stored in the SAP R/3 System, and can be inspected in various ways, including a graphical representation. The structure may be the same topological network as the management structure, each level of managers being responsible to more senior managers on the level above. Traditional organizations in business tend to have a pyramid structure rising to the owner on the pinnacle. Government and military organizations are notorious for having very tall pyramids. Modern, small companies in the high-tech domain are notorious for having very flat structures, very few layers of management and a boss who is ready to speak to anyone at almost any time.

The logical justification for any type of structure is based on the demands placed on it by external circumstances and by the need for the owner to exert some control over it.

The controlling area of the owner is perhaps the managing director or the chief executive officer. This person has a controlling area of the whole company. The department heads have controlling areas defined by the territory of their departments; or perhaps their controlling areas are better specified by the activities for which they are responsible.

The SAP R/3 module CO-Controlling holds master data on the controlling areas that you have decided to establish for your company. These may correspond exactly with the departments that exist already, but if you are looking for a method of adding value to information and material as they pass through your company, it would be prudent at least to consider other ways of setting up controlling areas.

What you will be looking for are profit centers that can be controlled on the basis of the measured profit they contribute to the company. One or more of these profit centers will constitute an area of responsibility that will be a proper subject for the application of controlling-area discipline.

The conceptual tools of area controlling include the following:

- Cost center. This is defined as a place in which costs are incurred. It may be a unit within a company, distinguished by area of responsibility, location, or accounting method.

- Order. This is used as an instrument for planning and controlling costs. In a business environment, it will be a document. In the SAP environment, it will be an SAP Document, which has a standard set of constituent parts and is subjected to strict internal control by the computer system so that it can take part in the legal requirements of an audit trail.

- Project. The defining characteristic of a project is the fact that it has to achieve a certain result in a specified time without exceeding the budget allocated to it. There are many types of project: capital-spending, research and development, engineer-to-order manufacturing, investment program, data processing, and customer project, for example.

- Cost object. Whatever work is undertaken, whether planning, controlling, informing, and so on, there are features that can be used to focus the computation of costs. The cost object need not be a real object, and it needn't really engage in any activity that would consume resources or generate revenue. The cost object is a convenient conceptual destination that can appear in the accounts with accrued costs or revenues.

- Market or business segment structure. The control of a business may be improved if information is collected about part of it—for example, the sale of certain products in a specified market area over a range of accounting periods. Another example of a segment would be the value of the raw materials in each of the possible locations where the capacity for additional production could take place.

In logical terms, a controlling area is defined as a set of accounting units within an organization that all use the same cost accounting configuration. Normally, the controlling area is coextensive with the company code, which usually stands for an individual company in a corporate structure. For cross-company cost accounting, one controlling area may be assigned to cover the areas of responsibility of more than one company code.

These conceptual tools have been efficiently programmed into the SAP standard business processes in the most useful of forms, the generic form, which you can customize to fit your particular circumstance. For example, you can record in the master data how you want to define the business segments and how you want to select which cost objects to monitor. And you can say how orders and projects will be assigned to cost centers.

The CO-Controlling module will accept your requirements and deliver a flexible controlling system that fits your company.

Integrating Financial Accounting with Controlling

At the heart of every accounting system is the general ledger, and the SAP System is no exception. The FI-Financial Accounting module serves the FI-GL General Ledger.

The common chart of accounts contains all the accounts available to a company. Every company, and, therefore, every unit identified by a company code, must be assigned to the common chart of accounts.

The concept of the controlling area is integral to the internal controlling functions. Each controlling area is assigned to the common chart of accounts. This ensures that every transaction in each area is posted to an account in the common chart of accounts, and will, therefore, be reconciled and take part in the financial accounting that provides the balance sheet and profit-and-loss accounts required by law.

Part
I
Ch
3

The CO-Controlling system uses the FI-GL General Ledger accounts directly. In particular, it uses the FI-GL General Ledger profit-and-loss accounts as primary cost and revenue elements.

With certain exceptions, the CO-Controlling system needs no separate reconciliation with the FI-GL General Ledger and its sub-ledger accounting systems. The exceptions arise if you use the special feature of CO-Controlling that manages imputed costs or accruals. CO-Controlling allows you to create imputed costs at a level of detail other than that used in financial accounting: You can record costs that have no equivalent, or have an equivalent with a different value, in the accounts of financial accounting. These intentional differences can be reconciled and cleared by using the CO-Controlling functions provided for this purpose.

Secondary cost elements are maintained by CO-Controlling in addition to the primary accounts of the FI-GL General Ledger. This constitutes a two-level system of accounts: Each level records accounting data using a different degree of detail.

However, the extra details maintained by CO-Controlling in the secondary cost elements are integrated with the FI-GL General Ledger accounts by means of the controlling areas, which are represented in the common chart of accounts. In accordance with GAAP (Generally Accepted Accounting Principles), it is possible to trace any transaction posted on the general ledger down through the controlling area and then to the cost center, which will be holding all the details of the cost elements that were used to compute it.

The value flow in the sub-ledgers of the FI-GL General Ledger is always reconciled via special reconciliation accounts. You can always analyze data into summaries using these accounts, which will give you such reports as monthly debits and credits, account balances, and so on, and you can inspect individual business transactions. With this kind of functionality, you can substantiate any of the values shown in your trial balance.

If you have installed and configured an SAP application such as CO-Controlling, you will have an additional and parallel way of looking at the value flows in your organization. But because the system is fully integrated, you will know that the values and value flows revealed by the external accounting documents, the balance sheet and the profit-and-loss statement are fully reconciled with the value flows that are uncovered by your parallel internal accounting system, implemented using the standard business functions of the SAP CO-Controlling module.

You will have a fresh way of looking at how the values change by doing business.

The Value-Adding Process and the Role of Cost Objects

In simple terms, a cost object is something that incurs costs: two of them cost twice as much; 10 of them cost 10 times as much.

A particular cost object can be declared to be in a market segment by entering it in the master record of that segment.

This cost object could also be identified in the processes of inventory accounting.

A cost center will be charged overhead, because that is where the costs originated. Overhead posted to that cost center will then be transferred to the cost objects that are the responsibility of that cost center. The proportion of the overhead allocated will be according to the quantities of cost objects, or by some other rule. In this way, the cost object has to bear a share of the overhead.

Revenues and sales deductions are reported in the relevant market segments and profit centers.

You can use period accounting at profit center level, incorporating changes to the inventory in the period. You can also use cost-of-sales accounting at the market segment level.

The cost object method enables an accurate system of accounting that will help you control the value-adding business processes of your company.

Integrated Planning and Decision Support

One of the important decisions to be made is often the product mix. You want to make sure that you optimize the contribution of each product line to the profit margin. Your methods will include tentative variations in the planned production costs, which the system will develop through the work flows of your organization to arrive at the planned values in each of the areas of interest. You can display any combination of planned values for any cost object or set of objects, right up to the planned figures for the entire company.

This is integrated planning, and it depends on the following functions that are programmed in the CO-Controlling system:

- Planned assessment, distribution, and accruals of imputed costs
- Planned allocation of internal activities
- Planned assessment of costs on orders and projects

These functions cannot succeed unless you have provided the data or told the system how to find them. The system will support you in this preparation by guiding you through the essential tasks and performing the necessary calculations automatically wherever possible:

- Planning of cost centers
- Planning of internal orders and projects
- Determining standard costs of products for stock production and for unit costing of customer orders
- Planning contribution margins and profits in sales management

Again, the system needs information to help you in the development of your plans, and CO-Controlling will provide the programs to support the following preliminaries:

- Creating the activity plan using the activities for each work center and cost center
- Integrating detailed planned sales quantities for the individual reference objects, including assigned costs and revenue
- Developing automatic standard cost estimates based on bills of materials and routings

Part

I

Ch

3

Reporting in CO-Controlling

The SAP EIS Executive Information System and the reporting facilities of CO-Controlling are fully integrated. You may have access to the Logistics Information System, which is part of the EIS. Within SAP R/3, the reporting facilities are highly flexible. Reports are easy to define for *ad hoc* purposes and to maintain as needs change. The content and format are virtually unlimited, and can be differentiated by user groups.

Reports can be stored, recalled, and processed by the SAP graphics presentation component.

Online navigation facilities make it easy for you to switch between report formats without losing the focus of your inquiry. For example, you can select an item on a list and use the function keys to call up a more detailed report on the item selected.

Reports designed in the CO-Controlling module are applicable to all its components.

Standard predefined reports are available for the following purposes:

- Comparing actual values with the planned entries
- Comparing the performance of different cost objects, such as cost centers, orders, and projects
- Assembling balance lists and balances of activities
- Inspecting individual line items

You can select a cost center and call up all the settlement objects linked to it. You can also trace the costs on each object back to the individual business transactions that caused them. This is named the drill-down process.

Integrating CO-Controlling with R/3 Applications

All the information in all the R/3 applications that have been installed and configured is available directly. Any of the information outputs of the system, from the annual sales and production plan to the individual planning steps and down to the planning and processing details of individual orders, may be called upon by the CO-Controlling system.

For example, standard business functions are available for the following tasks:

■ Using bills of materials and routings to prepare cost estimates for products and orders

■ Updating a costing as production progresses by transferring times and material valuations automatically as they become available

■ Evaluating quantities used of supplies and raw materials

■ Evaluating semi-finished and finished products in stock

■ Using cost-of-sales accounting to provide an ongoing analysis of profitability based on invoiced sales quantities

The success of a controlling function depends on the integration of planned and actual data at all stages and levels of the production process.

Cost centers can be given time factors for each of their activities by applying the methods of activity-based cost accounting. For example, the HR-Human Resources Management application can transfer the planned personnel costs to the FI-Financial Accounting and CO-Controlling modules. The actual, confirmed, monthly personnel costs are updated simultaneously in both FI-Financial Accounting and the cost accounting components in CO-Controlling.

The personnel data used for salaries and wage payments are the same as the data used to allocate personnel costs to orders and projects; HR-Human Resources provides both.

Cost Element Accounting Principles

A cost element is a classification code. It is a mandatory data field on transactions that involve costs arising in a company code. It is used to label and differentiate the following types of cost:

■ Direct cost elements for goods and services procured externally

■ Indirect (internal activity) cost elements

There may be several cost element types, based on a classification of cost elements by uses or origin, for example:

■ Material cost element

■ Settlement cost elements for orders

■ Cost elements for internal cost allocations

A cost element is also used to maintain a collection of information, in particular, the transaction documents that bear the code of the cost element and that have been selected, for example, for a specific accounting period.

Direct cost elements are maintained in the FI-GL General Ledger master records. Indirect cost elements have no counterpart in the financial accounts, and are maintained exclusively in cost accounting.

The cost element concept ensures that each business transaction posted under a particular cost element in the CO-Controlling system is properly assigned to the relevant cost centers, orders, projects, cost objects, and so on.

Each material issue in MM-Materials Management, each invoice recorded in SD-Sales and Distribution, each external invoice in SD-IV Invoice Verification—each of these flows via the FI-GL General Ledger account to the appropriate cost or profit object.

The expense accounts of the FI-GL General Ledger chart of accounts are automatically adopted by the CO-Controlling system as primary cost elements. Additional primary cost elements have to be added to the financial chart of accounts to accommodate accruals and imputed costs. The aim is to ensure that all the costs incurred in a particular accounting period and documented in the CO-Controlling system are properly reconciled with the general ledger. The method of establishing a default coding block cost element is also used to support this aim.

Secondary cost elements are created and managed only in CO-Controlling. They represent value flows such as:

- Internal cost allocation
- Surcharge allocation
- Settlement transactions

Cost Element Parameters

The CO-Controlling system carries an extensive set of standard cost elements that you can adopt and edit for your own installation. There is a matchcode search facility to locate the one you want on the basis of a specific name or label that you have assigned. The matchcode search may also include values such as order number ranges and dates that you define so as to narrow the field of your search. You can block out those you are unlikely to need.

The standard cost elements will begin with certain parameters established, for example:

- Default coding block element assignment to the balance sheet accounts
- Whether quantities are recorded
- How costs are displayed in reports

The system will log any changes you make to the cost element masters.

A cost element group is a technical term for a set of cost elements used in conjunction with select records and to define lines and columns in reports. They can be used for planning purposes. There are no constraints on how you combine and arrange cost elements into cost element groups. You can display the cost element groups in the form of a tree diagram.

Part

I

Ch

3

Accruals

The accounting period most useful when controlling a business is seldom the same period used for financial accounting. To effect a reconciliation, it is necessary to use accruals that assign imputed costs to the financial accounting periods and under an account heading that indicates their cause. There are three methods: percentage, plan/actual, and target/actual.

Percentage Method   If the cost elements are known, you can build up a database from which to calculate the imputed costs for each financial period by allocating a percentage to each period. And you can do this for both planned data and actual costs—by period and by cause.

Plan/Actual Method   If no relevant historical values or quantities are available to enter into your base cost elements, you can make a plan or estimate of them across the relevant time periods and by cause. Then you can have the system post the planned values as imputed costs and later make an adjustment when the actual cost data become available.

Target/Actual Method   If you expect your costs to be directly related to the operating output, then you can use the techniques of activity-based cost accounting to arrive at target values, which the system will post as imputed costs to the relevant financial accounting periods and causes. Again, you must have the system make an adjustment when the actual values can be obtained.

There are other ways of accounting for imputed costs that entail simultaneous posting of accrued costs to both FI-Financial Accounting and CO-Controlling. Alternatively, you can establish imputed cost objects, which can be reconciliation cost centers or reconciliation orders.

Calculating Price Variances

The CO-Controlling system can calculate the influence of price fluctuations for each posting transaction. The difference will be displayed as a variance in the SAP Document recording the transaction.

The SAP MM-Materials Management application can provide the difference between the standard price of a material and the moving average price.

Differences can also be computed between the actual cost to the cost center, and the value posted to it from FI-Financial Accounting as a percentage share of the actual value distributed across a number of cost centers.

Reporting in Cost Element Accounting

The flexible SAP R/3 reporting system allows you to analyze cost elements from any point of view:

- By individual cost elements, cost element groups, or subgroups
- By other cost objects, such as cost centers, orders, and projects

CO-CCA Cost Center Accounting

A cost center is a place in which costs are incurred because at least one activity originates there. It need not correspond to a real place in the geographical sense; it may be a functional unit that makes business sense. If one person does two different types of work, you might find it helpful to place one type in one cost center and the rest in another. The cost center is a unit within a company distinguished by area of responsibility, location or special accounting method, and by activity-related aspects.

All cost centers have to belong to a controlling area. If there is more than one FI-Financial Accounting company in the area, then you also have to say which cost center belongs to which company by assigning a company code to the master record for each cost center.

Each cost center has a defined validity period, and all changes to the master record will be related to this validity period. You decide when cost center changes are to take effect.

The cost center master record will indicate by parameters which functions can be active:

- Will the cost center master record accept planning data?
- Is posting allowed to this cost center?
- Will the cost center maintain open items?
- Can quantities be entered on the cost center master record?
- What blocking logic applies?
- What is the type of this cost center?
- What is the cost center currency? This defaults to the area currency, but can be changed.

The values you assign to these parameters are matters to be decided during customizing when you have to decide whether the structure of your data system will be a faithful replica of the way you do business now, or a design for the way you would like to be doing business when your system is fully operational.

The cost center concept allows transaction data to be validated against cost center masters as soon as they are established, even if CO-CCA Cost Center Accounting is still being implemented.

Cost centers may be grouped in alternative configurations that may be changed at any time. The transaction data itself is always assigned to the relevant cost center. Alternative cost center groups may correspond to organizational or functional distinctions related to decision-making, departmental, or controlling requirements.

Actual Costing

When primary costs are entered, you specify a cost center as the destination in the cost accounting system. SAP R/3 will automatically create an SAP Document to record the transaction and post it to the appropriate sub-ledger of the FI-GL General Ledger. At the same time, CO-Controlling will cause a second copy to be made for itself. Thus, CO-Controlling can be self-contained, yet the audit trail is still intact.

Part
I

Ch
3

The following SAP applications are fully integrated with CO-CCA Cost Center Accounting, and may act as feeder systems sending actual cost data to it:

- FI-Financial Accounting
- FI-AM Asset Management
- MM-Materials Management
- PP-Production Planning
- HR-Human Resources Management
- SD-Sales and Distribution

The data from these feeder systems can be used in calculating statistical ratios for the purpose of internal cost allocation and ratio analysis. The data can be formed into groups and used in the same way as cost elements and cost centers.

External data from non-SAP Systems may be automatically transferred through SAP standard interfaces, and there is a flexible and supportive interface for the manual input of data. Every transaction is recorded in the standard form of a CO document, which is additional to the standard SAP Document created by every transaction.

Costs are transferred between cost centers, but the original cost element data remain unchanged. CO-CCA Cost Center Accounting sponsors two types of distribution of costs:

- Periodic transfer of primary cost totals from FI-Financial Accounting to a temporary clearing cost center in CO-Controlling
- Distribution of primary and secondary costs within CO-Controlling

Cost Distribution Within CO-CCA

The distribution method of CO-CCA Cost Center Accounting is totally flexible and under your control.

The sender is a cost center that has access to rules for distributing the cost elements to the receivers, which are also cost centers. You have control over the allocation structures, so distribution is made to suit the needs of your company. The identity of the sender is preserved in all distribution postings, and the system keeps a log of all the relevant data.

You can simulate distribution to test out the effects of the rules before you post the values. The variety of available distribution rules is illustrated by the following examples:

- Fixed specific amounts, or values calculated at the time and based on shared portions or percentages
- Actual data or planned data
- Allocation across a pattern of cost centers that is determined at the time by the system

Generally, it is advisable to group sender and receiver cost centers in the same controlling area so as to give them identical distribution rules, because you can then combine distribution rules. For example, you could allocate, say, 70 percent of a cost arising from sales evenly to the cost centers for individual sales representatives and split 20 percent between the central sales organizations in proportion to the number of sales representatives working to them. This example illustrates that you do not have to distribute all the costs: The sender cost center still has 10 percent.

The effects of a distribution can be seen immediately by calling for a standard online report available through the special functions keys. And you can repeat the distribution procedures at any time.

Assessment

The processing logic is similar for assessment and distribution. The cost center sending cost data is credited with the total of the accounts that have been assigned to it, and the receiver cost center is debited using special cost elements that signify that the transaction is part of an assessment procedure.

By looking at the appropriate secondary cost elements, you can analyze the results of the assessment.

Surcharge Calculation

A cost allocation method that is additional to assessment and that is available in CO-Controlling is to use the surcharge calculation function. This calculates a supplement, usually as percentage, that is used to apply overhead in absorption costing—for example, when a service receiver is charged for overhead incurred by the service provider on an individual business transaction basis.

You can call on CO-CCA Cost Center Accounting to calculate a surcharge at a percentage rate based on one or more cost elements. The system will simultaneously credit and debit the relevant cost centers with the calculated surcharge, which will be posted under a predefined surcharge cost element.

Cost Center Planning Procedures

The purpose of cost center planning is to anticipate the volume of costs for a particular period at each of the cost centers you have identified in your company. You can plan for one fiscal year ahead, or for several. You can have the year divided into parts, up to 365 in number, or you can use a rolling system of planning.

Within your overall period of choice, the fiscal year perhaps, the system will reallocate any planned values according to your selection from the predefined distribution keys, to which you may add your own.

One of the things you have to decide is the planning level. The planning level defines the cost center where you set out your plan. If the plan is to be applied across the entire enterprise, then the planning level will be the SAP Client that will subsume all subordinate companies. If the plan is for a single subsidiary, then the level will be Company Code and this code will appear on all master records associated with this plan.

The plan will specify details such as:

- Quantity-based activities
- Value-based primary and secondary cost elements
- Statistical ratios

When you have settled on the planning level, the system will provide you with detailed planning support in the form of standard texts for documenting the plan and formulas for calculating all the standard statistical ratios. The SAP product costing system will be able to supply information to your plan in the form of quantity and value details of particular cost elements.

Although you can change and correct the cost center plan at any time by repeating individual sections of the overall planning sequence, you can also block your plan, version by version, to prevent any changes. You can also use the standard R/3 authorization functions to control changes to your plan.

It may be the case that your cost center plan contains a planned value for a particular cost element that should really be subjected to more detailed attention. The system allows you to define individual items to separate what you regard as the important factors that should be subjected to detailed planning. The following influencing factors illustrate the concept:

- A material may be subject to wide fluctuations in cost due to an unstable market. Your plan could specify the code number of this material, and the SAP MM-Materials Management application would keep your plan up-to-date by posting the current price of this material to your plan.
- Some cost centers in your plan may be sensitive to employee-related wages and salaries. You could have this influencing factor evaluated using price tables and cost rates, by employee group or by individual employee, if necessary.
- Some cost centers may be sensitive to the costs associated with individual activities and external services. You might well highlight these as influencing factors to be actively and automatically taken into your plan.
- There may be risks or overheads that ought to attract surcharges at some cost centers. These can be factored into your plan.

SAP standard business functions are also available to support the concept of having cost centers working to a cost center budget.

CO-ABC Activity-Based Cost Accounting

In cost accounting terms, an activity is a process that can be counted and that attracts costs. In business terms, a production process is achieved by a network of activities. If you want to find out the cost of a process, you have to know the activities and the quantities of work done by each.

The purpose of the CO-ABC Activity-Based Cost Accounting component of the SAP R/3 CO-Controlling module is to help you plan, monitor, and settle activity types in the accounts of cost centers.

Activity types serve as allocation bases and are used as cost drivers to determine and send incurred costs to receivers.

The CO-ABC Activity-Based Cost Accounting system allows you to develop fully integrated activity costing in a controlled, step-by-step fashion. There is an inevitable logical sequence:

1. Define the activity types that are of interest to your company because they add value, attract costs, or both.
2. Specify how each activity type will be measured and the units to be used.
3. Create a plan using your activity types and their quantities.
4. Extend the plan to include the costs that are dependent on activities and the rates to be applied.
5. Allocate, or set up rules to allocate, activity costs for both planned and actual data.
6. Pre-distribute the fixed costs and attach a value to each of the activity types that are not amenable to measurement.
7. Determine the variances over the period and allocate them to activities or cost centers.

Activity Types and Allocation Bases

The measurement of productivity has to start with a measurement, or at least a quantitative assessment of activity. In a production cost center, there will be measurements of time required, number, weight, or volume of each product, units finished and semi-finished. The service cost centers will have records of jobs, hours worked by each skilled trade, and energy and materials used.

Sales and administrative tasks are also becoming subject to measurement of a nominal kind, where something that can be counted, such as the number of calls made, is used as an index of activity; each call entails an amount of work that can be assessed and evaluated, at least in average terms. Data on an activity will typically, depending on the type, include information on the planned activity quantity, the capacity, and the output quantity. Activities may be assigned to activity groups, so you can carry out some operations on all the members of the group simultaneously. This might be useful as you change your controlling task from planning to allocation, to determination of cost rates, and so on. There is no limit in CO-Controlling to the number and scope of the activity groups you use.

The master record of an activity group will contain parameters that you can use to define how the group is handled. There are parameters to define settlement cost elements to be used in the direct allocation of planned and actual values. You can flag particular activities as statistical, which will ensure that the system adopts a standard procedure for calculations according to the needs of the moment, including assessment, distribution, and computing ratios for use in reporting.

Activity Planning and the Flow of Activities

For each cost center, you have to arrive at a planned value for each activity. And you must reconcile this amount of activity with the amount of activity planned in the Logistics system. The system will assist you with this.

The CO-ABC Activity-Based Cost Accounting module differentiates three types of planning:

- Planning statistical ratios
- Planning activity quantities
- Planning primary and secondary cost elements

A statistical ratio in planning can be simply a number for each posting period, or it can be a cumulative number computed for each period on the basis of data. If the cost center produces activities that are quantified, the planned or actual quantity of output can be the basis for planning the primary and secondary cost elements, because the output quantity of the cost center can be converted to values.

Given the input of primary and secondary costs to a cost center and the output in terms of evaluated quantities of activities, you can have the system compute the efficiency of the cost center in each of its activities.

The same method is used to plan the activities to be produced and consumed in the flow of internal activities.

You then have the basis for planning secondary costs.

Simulation and the Reconciliation of Activities

The logistics plan and the controlling plan may be inconsistent. Bottlenecks and idle production capacity may be foreseen.

Interactive activity analysis allows you to look at several activities at once to see which will have spare capacity and which are destined to be subjected to demands that are beyond their capacity. You may be able to affect a displacement of work or resources, or replace one activity with another. The system will immediately simulate the cost effects of your tentative change of plan, which you can confirm when you are satisfied, or store as a separate version of the plan.

Starting at any cost center, you can command a display of the activity types received from or sent to an adjacent cost center level. This allows you to trace the functional dependencies between individual activity types.

Activity-Based Cost Planning

Each activity type and each cost center can be given as many cost elements as necessary. You can enter the planned cost elements as values, or as values to be computed at the time on the basis of quantities and the rates prevailing. The cost element can be given a planned overall value or a planned quantity.

Both procedures can be carried out as full or marginal costs and can direct a split into fixed and variable components. The system provides formulas, formal specifications, texts, and report characteristics.

The CO-Controlling system distributes the planned values for the variable primary cost elements for the year. You can see the effects on costs of any fluctuations in planned activity levels. You can call for the fixed costs to be distributed using standard rules or your own rules.

The internal exchange of activities also causes secondary costs to be incurred. These are computed by taking the amounts of the allocated activity quantities and valuing them at the appropriate standard rates defined in the sender cost centers. The receivers of internal activity costs will include the following:

Part

I

Ch

3

- Cost centers
- Orders for cost centers that are overhead cost orders
- Production orders for semi-finished and finished products
- Capital spending orders for fixed assets
- Sales orders or sales cost objects

Having planned values for internal orders, you may wish to allocate the planned costs to the receiver cost centers. The original producing cost centers will retain the information.

Political Prices

Standard prices and standard rates at which cost centers activities should be charged are among the important results to come out of any planning exercise. The total cost is divided by the total quantity in each case.

You may be in a business that prefers not to use the actual or historical standard price computed as an average based on total cost and total quantity.

You may have to set rates that are determined by political factors rather than by computation. You have to enter political rates manually. You can then use them to evaluate planned and actual quantities. The system thus retains an accurate representation of internal activity cost flows and cost allocations, even if the rates are not the strictly determined product of formal business planning.

Indirect Allocation of Costs to Non-Measurable Activities

The system has indirect cost allocation functions that you can use to allocate costs accurately to the objects which caused them. You may be able to apply standard methods if you can derive an index of activity that can serve as a quantity to which you can apply a rate. But the indirect allocation functions are available for those times when the most reasonable method is to assess costs and allocate them to their causes.

Cost Center Variances

Variance analysis is a method of monitoring business activity. A variance is defined as the computed difference between actual costs and planned costs, using the following formula:

Actual Cost = Planned Cost +/− Variance

Variances can be calculated at any level:

- Cost center
- Cost element
- Activity type

The following are four variance factors that explain why actual costs can differ from planned costs:

- Price variance, caused by differences between the actual and the planned prices of the goods and services used.
- Usage variance, arising from uneconomical working practices in the production process.
- Volume variance, which occurs when the planned volume is not reached or if it is exceeded, giving rise to the fixed costs being under- or overabsorbed by the actual volume of product.
- Cost center over- or underabsorption of fixed costs as a result of using different standard rates in the plan from those applied in the posting of actual activities, the so-called political rates; the same effects may occur if the cost center plans have not been reconciled.

The total of these variances for all cost elements and activity types within a cost center provides the overall variance for that cost center.

For each combination of cost element and activity type on each cost center, the CO-ABC Activity-Based Cost Accounting system maintains a value structure for controlling. Each of these values is split into fixed parts and variable parts:

- Planned costs
- Target costs
- Variance types
- Actual costs
- Planned/actual usage

You can have the variances calculated and included as part of the cost components. The formulas follow:

Actual Cost = Planned Cost +/– Cost Variance

Actual Price = Planned Price +/– Price Variance

Target Costs = Actual Volume × Planned Rates

Usage Variance = (Actual Costs – Target Costs) × Price Variance

Volume Variance = Target Costs × Actual Activity divided by Planned Price

Over-/Under-Absorption = (Target Costs – Allocated Costs) × Volume Variance

Charging Variances

The CO-Controlling system evaluates each activity by applying the planned rate to the activity quantity. If you have the historical variances, or your system can get them for you, there is the possibility of using them in a fresh version of your plan. Similarly, if you have some way of anticipating future variances, or if you want to conduct a what-if simulation exercise, then again, you can create a fresh plan version.

You may want to use anticipated variances in the cost allocation process. In order to represent accurately the value flow in your company, it is essential to allocate cost center variances periodically. You can specify whether to use historical, standard, or anticipated variances for the subsequent charging process, and in this way, transfer all variances directly to your profitability analysis system.

An alternative approach is to pass on usage variances to the receivers but keep as a charge on the producing cost center the variances resulting from too little output. They will go to the profitability analysis system from there.

You can charge variances periodically to the following types of receiver:

- Individual cost centers
- Internal orders or projects
- Production orders, and then to the finished and semi-finished product inventory
- Cost objects in profitability analysis
- Fixed assets

If you arrange for actual variances to be charged to cost objects in CO-PA Profitability Analysis, you will be on the way toward the creation of the detailed cost structures that are necessary to a system of contribution margin accounting.

Variances are posted under the CO-ABC Activity-Based Cost Accounting system using the rules and procedures of direct cost allocation. The system specifies the allocation cost element by its identification code and by whether the value is fixed or variable on either sender or receiver object. It also ensures that identical variance types are in use.

Part

I

Ch

3

The effect of all these procedures is to accurately allocate all actual costs to the precise area of the company where they were caused. This serves both the legal requirement of external accounting, and the need for comprehensive internal reporting as a basis for controlling the company.

Alternative Activity Rates in Parallel

The method described previously can be regarded as an imputed allocation approach: Cost centers accrue costs because of the activities they undertake and the overheads they enjoy.

The CO-Controlling system will also operate a system of parallel activity rates that can provide a family of alternative evaluations relevant to various accounting purposes.

At the cost element level, you can put together a portfolio of costs to be included in an alternative activity rate for each cost element. If these rates are used when calculating internal activity flows, you will be able to produce cost estimates conforming to all legal and tax regulations for which your portfolio is correct.

These calculations lead to the derivation of the balance sheet and profitability analysis. You can compare costs of sales and total costs of production, both estimated and as they appear in the external financial documents—the balance sheet and profit-and-loss statement.

Activities and Services Costing

By looking more and more closely at the way they produce their goods and services, companies have been able to make extensive improvements. The need is for a system of structured overhead costing.

The first thing to do is to identify and define the cost drivers—the allocation bases that influence how activity costs are allocated to the cost centers that generate them.

The cost driver is a subprocess that can be measured for individual cost center activities. For example:

- Number of purchase order items successfully processed
- Number of quotation items
- Delivery items in sales
- Dunning operations employed to hasten overdue payments and payment differences handled

Subprocesses are grouped together into primary processes that can be addressed by the product costing system to determine the costs of administrative and service activities.

You will discover what each subprocess costs. You are on the way to an activity-based profitability analysis.

Planning and Simulating the Subprocesses

The basic disciplines of activity-based accounting have to be applied to ensure that the activities at a cost center are integrated with the accounting and controlling systems. However, there is a further level of detail to be considered if activities are to be analyzed into their constituent subprocesses.

A business process can be represented by a chain of activities and products or a network of such chains. In the SAP R/3 System, this chain or network is managed by a process sequence structure, which may be of any complexity.

The process sequence structure can be used to simulate the flow of material through a sequence of activities that create perhaps a series of semi-finished products and that terminate with the finished product.

The SAP PP-Production Planning module is specialized in this work.

For the purpose of analyzing overhead activities and services, the CO-ABC Activity-Based Cost Accounting module provides full supporting functions.

The system of costing based on a process sequence structure requires that all the processes and subprocesses be quantified in terms of quantity and value flow, so that analysis and reporting can occur to a level of detail that will yield a balance of activities to document the ways in which the activity level of the parent cost center exerts influence on the costs of the primary processes and their subprocesses. How do support costs alter when business gets better or worse?

Using Process Cost Rates

The purpose of applying the methods of activity-based costing to the detailed processes and subprocesses of a production company is to compute process cost rates. How much does it cost to put one invoice item through the office? How much to move one pallet from production to warehouse?

If you have process cost rates at this level of detail, you can take a standard costing based on a bill of materials and routings, for example, and cost each of the processes entailed. Or you can have the SAP System do it for you.

If you have these process cost rates for all the subprocesses in each activity type, you can transfer the process costs from CO-CCA Cost Center Accounting directly to CO-PA Profitability Analysis.

Because you have the process costs associated with each activity embraced by CO-CCA Cost Center Accounting, you can have these process costs included in the value flow patterns that are identified by both Product Costing and Period Costing.

CO-OPA Order and Project Accounting

The purpose of the CO-OPA Order and Project Accounting module is to analyze and settle the costs arising from internal orders and projects.

The purpose of internal orders is to monitor costs to assist in decision making and to manage the allocation and settlement of activity costs to target objects, including FI-GL General Ledger accounts. Projects may also be used for these purposes. Complex projects are more properly the province of the SAP R/3 PS-Project System.

Internal orders are usually defined for a particular task, event, or internal change measure that has to be planned, monitored and settled in great detail. These orders are distinguished by their origin and by the time allocated for their completion. They vary in their settlement arrangements and in how they appear in the reporting functions.

SAP R/3 classifies internal orders as follows:

- Production-related orders used in Logistics
- Sales orders used in SD-Sales and Distribution
- Internal orders used in CO-Controlling

Although the internal orders of the Logistics modules and the SD-Sales and Distribution component serve mainly to monitor resources used and sales achieved, they also document estimated costs, actual costs, and revenues. In the PP-Production Planning and Control modules, the order has the job of annexing information on the latest estimate of costs until the actual costs replace them when the order is complete.

Sales orders that document costs and revenues are accessed by the CO-PA Profitability Analysis system. They also carry the information needed by CO-Controlling and PP-Production Planning and Control, for example. The orders for processing and settling internal costs usually support the integration of different business systems with the ways the particular company likes to do business and settle the costs.

Internal orders in CO-Controlling are differentiated by the following characteristics:

- Whether logistical, controlling, or settlement in main function
- Content of the order, such as product or project
- Whether an individual order or a standing order
- The significance of the values on the order, such as plan costs, actual costs, or variances
- Settlement receiver for the order, such as fixed asset account, cost center, cost object, project, stock, business segment, sales order, or FI-GL General Ledger account

It is an important feature of the CO-OPA Order and Project Accounting component that you can assign the relevant costs on each of the orders and projects to the various receivers, split by period and allocated accurately by cause. They can be used for both overhead cost controlling and production controlling.

If you wish to have an internal exercise that is a simple single-level project, used only in the CO-Controlling system, you will be invited to specify how you want to monitor it and settle the costs incurred.

Order Data Formats

The master data record for an order comprises the order number and the parameters for controlling the business and technical system functions that will deal with it. You will have been authorized to use a certain range of order numbers; otherwise, the system will assign the number.

The order master will bear control data to signify the transaction groups in which it can take part. For example, an order type Planning will allow the entry for planning purposes only of information such as primary costs and overhead costs.

The order master will also include parameter fields to organize overhead components and to control the settlement functions. Some orders will have the function of monitoring all open purchase orders, for example; others are intended for the detailed settlement of individual cost items.

This system of order parameters set into the master records enables you to establish a suite of order types that can be used to nominate the manner in which each order will direct the value flow in your company along the lines already defined by your organizational structure and the way in which your company has chosen to group its business functions.

Status Management of Orders

The status of an order is the stage it has reached in its life cycle. The SAP CO-OPA Order and Project Accounting system is particularly flexible in the way that it allows you to decide what should happen at each stage and, indeed, through which stages a particular type of order should proceed on its way to completion. For example, you can choose where to have the system plan primary or secondary costs for each order.

The typical status sequence for an order will encounter the following stages:

- Order opened, basic data identified
- Planning primary and secondary costs
- Released for posting
- Execution
- Technical completion
- Accounting completion

Some of these business functions can be allowed to operate across more than one status. Planning information can be allowed to be added to an order while it is being executed, for example.

Order Classification by Content

Because they are treated differently, orders are classified by their content and controlling objectives into various types.

Job orders collect and analyze the planned and actual costs for a commodity or operational event that is not going to be capitalized, such as minor repairs or staff training. These orders will be settled on the objects that caused them, by means of the periodic cost center accounting procedures.

Capital spending orders on the fixed assets produced in-house and on maintenance costs serve to manage the planning and allocation of costs over the lifetime of the order, which can be an open order.

Production orders are used to set up costing sheets by gathering primary costs from FI-Financial Accounting and secondary costs from overhead assessment. Activity costs come from internal allocation. Issues of raw materials and semi-finished materials are notified from MM-Materials Management. Production orders in Logistics use bills of materials, routings and cost centers. They are fully integrated into the overall capacity planning and monitoring functions.

Sales orders can have posted to them any type of cost and revenue item taken directly from SD-Sales and Distribution. These can be transferred directly to the appropriate business segments in CO-PA Profitability Analysis.

An individual order is typically unique and of long duration. The quantity structures are seldom fully known at the start, so planning is carried out in stages. Where an individual order entails multilevel production processing and a complex web of activities, partial orders may be created. The SAP R/3 Project System is specialized for this kind of work in make-to-order production.

Standing orders are used when cost centers have to be split into smaller activity units, such as small repairs, minor maintenance, or individual vehicles in a company fleet.

Statistical orders are used to receive additional account assignments for the purpose of summarizing, sorting, and displaying cost objects according to specific criteria. The amount posted appears under the original cost element heading on the appropriate account, and again on the statistical order. Revenues can also be collated by a statistical order.

Order Planning

You can plan the overall value of an order. You can also plan according to the cost elements and activity types, either on the specific order, or by transferring the values from a unit you have already costed. The following cost elements and activity types are amenable to planning on orders:

- Primary costs by cost element or cost element group, in values or in quantities to which the system will apply cost rates at the time
- Cost center activities as the secondary costs, planned down to the level of individual operations, if necessary

■ Overhead, planned using the overhead application functions

■ Statistical ratios, to be used to form business ratios when reporting

Distribution keys provide a choice between planning orders on a yearly basis with a standard distribution across months, and planning for each month separately. Order groups may be assembled for overhead calculation, planning, and reporting.

The functionality and screens used in CO-CCA Cost Center Accounting are available to give planning views of your flexible combinations of planning objects and planning content. For example, you may call for planning views on all or any of the following situations:

■ Many cost elements on a single order

■ Many cost element groups on a single order

■ Many cost elements on an order group

■ Many cost element groups on an order group

Whatever planning steps you take, you can store in the system a choice of standard explanatory texts with additional information to document your decisions.

If the order takes a long time to execute, the assumptions on which the plan was built may become outdated. Each plan is noted as a new version whenever you change something, so that subsequent analysis will arrive at an accurate picture.

If a plan has already been released and changes have to be made, you can have the system document the entry of the modified order plan and the changes made to it, in the form of a copy of the plan line items which have been altered.

Unit Costing

You may have a cost element plan that is too global for certain requirements. Perhaps you want to assign only some of the costs, for example, to an order. You can create the order using cost elements and have the system make out a unit cost plan later, when the actual values or quantities are transferred to the order.

Open Items

If you want to place a reservation on a certain quantity of material, or if you still have a commitment to pay for an external service on a specific order, then you enter an open item. In the display, open items will appear as values and quantities under the appropriate cost element heading in the correct fiscal year and in the period that includes the planned supply date.

Open items can arise through purchasing in the MM-Materials Management system. If the invoice has been received, the open item can be evaluated from the actual prices; if not, the anticipated price has to be used. Delivery costs are displayed separately so they can be evaluated in the appropriate currency for the place where each cost element was incurred.

Material reservation in MM-IM Materials Management, Inventory Management will create an open item which will be evaluated at the carrying price.

You can also generate an open item manually in the form of a funds reservation.

As you reduce an open item, the system will help you manage it using the original currency. Analysis and posting can take place under the system rules for foreign currency and its exchange.

The aim is to replace each open item on an order with the corresponding actual costs. If an open item concerns external services, the system will reduce the purchase order by value, using the invoiced amount whether full or partial. The system will identify any price differences by account and by order.

If an open item is a goods purchase order, as soon as the goods are received, the system will automatically reduce the quantity and the value for the open purchase item. If the invoice is received before the goods, the system will adjust the open purchase order by adopting the invoice value in place of the purchase order value. Should any amounts on the invoice or on the services received remain unsettled, the order will stay open until they are finally cleared completely.

The order number and the posting details are retained when an order progresses from one business transaction to the next. The system can thus document the purchase order history, which enables you to trace a partial delivery or a partial invoice to the purchase order and then back to the original purchase requisition.

Open item management illustrates the close integration of Logistics and Accounting in the SAP System.

Actual Cost Accounting Transactions

Every SAP transaction generates an SAP Document. If the document contains a posting to an order number, the CO-OPA Order and Project Accounting system will charge the amount to the order under the relevant cost element heading and with that order number. You can trace the history of origin of each line item throughout the lifetime of the order.

Activities must take place so that production orders, maintenance orders, and job orders may be fulfilled. These activities will be the responsibility of one or more cost centers. And for each of these activities, the responsible cost center will demand payment in the form of an internal cost allocation.

The CO-Controlling system will evaluate the activity quantity at the appropriate rate. At the same time, there will be line items created to document the flow of value from the producing sender objects to the receiving objects. These will take the form of a credit to the sending cost center and a debit to the receiving order. This is the process of direct internal cost allocation.

If the activity is not amenable to quantification—if you cannot say exactly how much of the item is needed for the order—you have to use indirect cost allocation, in which a periodic total is shared in some way between the receiving cost centers or orders.

Overhead is a charge that should be allocated as accurately as possible to the items that have to share its burden. This distribution is discussed in the section on CO-CCA Cost Center Accounting.

Settlement of Orders

Order settlement is the process of passing costs from the originating order to other cost objects. There are two groups of these target objects: internal postings within CO-Controlling, and external postings to the accounts managed by FI-Financial Accounting and other applications.

Internal postings settle orders automatically using CO-CEA Cost Element Accounting. This component creates the necessary credit and debit line items, to any of the following objects:

- Cost centers
- Internal orders
- Projects
- Business segments
- Sales orders

Orders may be settled by postings to external objects using the following functions:

- FI-AA Asset Accounting, for assets under construction or capitalized assets.
- MM-Materials Management, which settles any product manufactured in-house to inventory under the material number for a warehouse.
- FI-Financial Accounting can settle orders to the appropriate FI-GL General Ledger account.

Settlement Rules

Each order master includes a data element that determines the settlement rule to be applied to that order. The rule includes the following control parameters:

- Period of validity for the settlement rule.
- Target object or objects to which the costs are to be sent—for example, if part of the costs of the order will be capitalized and the rest distributed between certain cost centers.
- The cost element or elements under which the order value is to be credited—using cost element groups results in a debit to the receiver under each element.
- Settlement of costs to a cost element within the CO-Controlling system.

The settlement rule may be a defined debit to the receiver. Several receivers may be targeted in proportions calculated from equivalence numbers or percentages. Absolute amounts may be settled, or costs may be based on quantity and the system will use the rate current when the settlement is performed.

Part
I

Ch
3

If the order includes information on a suitable target object for settlement, such as a responsible cost center or related project identification, the system will operate a default distribution rule generated on the basis of this information.

Orders that allocate costs to cost centers tend to be settled periodically; capital spending orders will be settled at period-end after the project has been completed.

Orders to be settled can be grouped according to the following criteria:

- Order type
- Date when settlement is to be performed
- Receiver of the settlement
- Corporate or company code
- Settlement to internal or external accounting system

You can create a settlement simulation list in the CO-OPA Order and Project Accounting system using the allocation groups to check that the orders are both correct and complete. When the simulation is correct, you can use the list to execute the settlement. You can reverse a settlement made previously, and repeat it at any time.

The system calculates the total settlement and the individual amounts debited to each receiver in the controlling area currency, from which you can convert if necessary. The settlement function differentiates debiting an order with full costs and debiting only direct costs. You may have previously distributed fixed costs in CO-CCA Cost Center Accounting, in which case this is allowed for in the value flow.

The order reporting system will show you the settlement history, which comprises the dates and details of the amounts already settled, any reversals performed, and the balance remaining on the order.

Order Summary Evaluations

If you want to compare two or more orders in detail, you may find it helpful to have the system classify orders using a hierarchy. The CO-Controlling system will allow you to put any criterion at the top of your hierarchy and any other criteria at each level below. You might ask these sorts of question:

- How do the various companies in this group compare across these functions: repairs, advertising special campaigns, and so on?
- How do the various companies in this group compare, for all departments, all production orders?

These criteria together create a hierarchy over which the system can collate the data, in this example for all production orders. The SAP R/3 flexible reporting functions allow you to view this data at any of these levels of your hierarchy, and to switch readily from one viewpoint to another.

In fact, the system offers a complete system of order reporting from line item up to order, cost center, controlling area, and company. The online reporting techniques allow you to take any summary and "drill down" to the details of the order items that contribute to it.

Capital Spending Orders

The main objective of a capital spending order is to monitor the costs of producing assets and commodities in-house.

Maintenance projects can be controlled and accounted in the same way.

The distinguishing feature of the SAP module CO-OPA Order and Project Accounting is its ability to settle in detail the actual costs according to rules individual to each item. The following must be specified:

- The target object(s) defined as one or more fixed assets in FI-AA Asset Management
- The date of the settlement
- The scope of the costs to be settled
- The settlement cost element heading
- The supplementary information

In addition to this ability to settle capital spending orders in precise detail, the system has the following important capabilities:

- Planning is available for all resources and costs required, in quantity and value.
- Charges can be computed from prices at the time, with imputed allocations of overhead and actual costs.
- Open items for purchase requisitions, purchase orders, and material reservations are closely monitored.
- Display is possible of all cash-related procedures, such as down payment requests and down payments.
- Concurrent evaluation and analysis of order reports can be performed.

Integration of CO-OPA with FI-AA Asset Accounting

If you are managing fixed assets such as buildings and machines, the settlement of capital spending orders is of crucial importance. The SAP R/3 System offers detailed settlement rules and a close integration with the FI-AA Asset Accounting component to yield the following advantages:

- Settlement of costs to the appropriate balance sheet accounts under the heading of Assets Under Construction while the capital spending order is ongoing
- Order-based display of special depreciations for Assets Under Construction

Part
I

Ch
3

■ Recognition of subsidies, grants, and down payments

■ Settlement of partial orders over a hierarchy of orders

Because all costs are based on unified posting and settlement rules in the SAP R/3 System, you can allocate costs from orders and projects to the various target objects using the same rules, or rules you have specified separately. You can keep track of complex overhead costs with maintenance and capital spending orders; the chance to take effective action in good time will be yours.

Costs and deadlines on orders and projects that take a long time to complete have to recognize the financial facts of life: Money is not always available when you need it. Financial and liquidity planning need to know what costs are expected on the orders and projects. It helps to have some idea of how the costs are likely to be incurred in detail over the first few accounting periods and, in broader terms, up to the date of completion.

A cost schedule is a plan extending the length of an order or project showing the values expected to be allocated to costs. The schedule has a key date. Until this date is known and entered on the plan, the forecast of costs has to be moved ahead to the best estimated date.

The SAP R/3 System provides support in the following ways:

■ The system will automatically determine the tasks from the planned start and finish dates for the order.

■ Cost distribution across the schedule can be suited to the specific order.

■ Graphical representations of the data model are readily available online and in print.

The following manipulations of the cost schedules and the task plans are automatically available:

■ Shifting the start date, retaining the duration

■ Compressing the duration, retaining the finish date

■ Expanding the duration

If you have carried out cost element planning or created a unit costing for the order, the system can use this information to develop a cost schedule.

Product Cost Accounting

The purpose of product cost accounting is to determine the unit cost of whatever product units your company does business in. These units are referred to as cost objects, with one cost object for each product or each distribution package for each product.

The context is a technical production system that is customized to a particular company; the outcome is a company-specific costing system that integrates the flow of cost information from its origins.

There is a core technical discipline based on the principle that costs should be accurately allocated to the processes that incur them. And there are several costing systems that embody this principle in the particular circumstances of a certain type of business.

Product cost accounting addresses two types of costing:

- Production Order Costing
- Inventory Costing

Four types of cost object controlling are differentiated, because they offer different benefits according to the type of business they are located in:

- Make-to-Stock Production
- Process Manufacturing
- Make-to-Order Production
- Plant Construction

All of these types of product cost accounting are supported by the CO-Controlling module by the flexible use of cost objects.

Costing Requirements of Different Types of Companies

Modern controlling methods have developed to support technical manufacturing processes and service industries. The methods have to match the needs of the individual company. The SAP approach is to establish a core of standard business functions that can be controlled by the implementer through the medium of parameters, so as to yield a customized system finely tuned to the requirements of the different classes of user in the specific company.

Manufacturers require a costing system that shows where and by how much their manufacturing processes add value to their raw materials. They differ in their style of manufacturing according to whether they make to a production order, or make to replace stock on their inventory. Their processes differ over a range, from discrete one-off production, to repetitive production, to continuous flow production.

Trading companies need a method of costing to enable them to apply overhead and surcharges to the cost prices of their goods, which they often have to keep to set or agreed-upon final selling prices.

Service companies are tending to adopt the principles of process costing, which revolves around the concept of cost drivers—in this case, service activities. They need to be able to define, measure, plan, and pass on costs incurred by their cost drivers, service calls, and other activities.

Quantity Structures

The manufacturing industry has a polished costing method based on routings taken by work units and bills of materials. They need to know what processes the product has to undergo, the costs of materials and resources, and the quantities. This is referred to as the quantity structure for this product. If you have this information, you can begin to cost the product by assembling the costing components.

Make-to-Order   In the make-to-order company, the customer order sets off costing. As each order is unique, there may be a shortage of routings and bills of materials that can be applied without editing. Yet it is of the utmost importance to be able to arrive quickly at a cost prediction for this one-off product, so as to be able to issue a quotation and take part in competitive bidding for the work. An effective costing system for this sort of company would have to give this approach to one-off bidding a high priority, for on its speed and accuracy all future business may depend.

Make-to-Stock   Those manufacturers who make to stock will apply standard bills of materials and routings about which they may well have copious actual data. Products and orders can be costed from this database.

Continuous Flow   Where the manufacturing process is continuous, it is probably not amenable to much in the way of variation. It will probably only work at its best if the rate of flow is within narrow limits. Nevertheless, the contribution of the various cost components to the cost of the finished product will not be without interest for the management and shareholders. It will be important to understand how and why costs vary if the flow rate and quality are allowed to move out of the normal operating ranges. This might happen because of variations in the raw materials or in the environmental conditions at the manufacturing plant.

Product Costing Techniques

A costing system uses a set of costing objects, which are the different products, production and other orders, resources, and so on. The only qualification for a costing object is that it can be allocated costs that mean something when they are totaled under that costing object. The costing objects can be conceptual or tangible, organizational or geographical.

The pivotal concept in costing is the structure of cost drivers—cost objects onto which the actual costs are settled according to how they were incurred. SAP R/3 CO-Controlling provides a range of model structures on which you can base a structure specific to the needs of your company.

There are three types of costing values that might be settled on a cost structure:

- Planned values
- Target values
- Actual costs

There are two ways of applying cost data to arrive at a specific costing:

- Allocate the full costing to the cost objects.
- Allocate only the variable costs to the cost objects, and apply overhead or surcharge.

An integrated costing system has to have at least the following capabilities:

- Calculate alternative cost plans using different versions and timings.
- Control the activities and the value added by each operation.
- Settle actual costs, according to how they occurred, on a specific cost structure.

Unit Costing   If your company makes unique products only to customer orders, you will need unit costing. You have very little choice but to cost each individual order by deciding which unitary components you will have to put together; and you will have to find out what other costs will be incurred as you do so.

The relevant database is a set of reference unit cost estimates. CO-PC Product Cost Accounting will help you locate which elements you need, and you can transfer them in blocks to the relevant quotes and sales order items or to the cost accounting objects which will be orders and projects.

This will build the planned costs of the quote, which can be compared to the actual costs as the order proceeds toward completion. Materials will be consumed, and these materials will all have their quantities or values assigned to the accounts under the correct cost element headings as data are collected on the activities that consume them. Overhead will be applied, and charges for external activities will add to the cost.

The sales order will be documented with a continuous comparison between planned and actual costs for the whole of its life. From this data, a simultaneous calculation of contribution margin can be carried out and the results recorded on the sales order document.

Part
I
Ch
3

Order Costing   In make-to-stock production, it is useful to combine order and unit costing methods, because order lots and batches of product are usually produced in response to production orders.

Different cost estimates are prepared as alternative versions that take part in simultaneous costing, so as to ensure exact control of the actual costs incurred by the relevant cost elements, sender cost centers and their activities, materials used, and so on.

Settlement of some or all of the costs to stock and automatic calculation to support inventory control over finished and semi-finished products are supported by the system. The value of stocks of unfinished goods and work in process can be calculated automatically.

Process manufacturing includes production processes that have a step-by-step structure and those that entail a cyclic input of materials.

Continuous flow production is characterized by long processing runs of a single basic material.

The control document for continuous flow processing is the period production order. Comparisons are made between target and actual costs, planned output for a period and actual output, including cost usages from backflushing surplus material or summarized confirmations of production. The costs are charged to individual cost elements of the production structure in relation to the quantities produced.

Backflushing occurs in the chemical industry, for instance, where some of the output can be returned to the process as semi-finished product. There may be by-products and co-products with alternative uses to the main product, and some product may bypass some of the production stages in the process cycle. The production order will document these variations.

Trading companies need a costing system that can provide accurate valuations of the costs and the prices, taking into account the individual costing and pricing structures that prevail in the type of business and under the market conditions at the time of valuation. The basic method is to apply overhead to cost prices. Costing the overhead allows you to apply the overhead according to cost elements, or indeed, in relation to overhead you have already calculated. The system will allow you to use different levels of sales prices, such as net sales price or gross sales price, to compute additional overhead or surcharge, such as discounts or cash discounts. These factors differ in wholesaling and retailing.

Service companies use the functions and elements of process costing. The service operations have to be defined in terms of individual activities that can be measured. If these activities can each be measured, then they can be subject to planning. When the work is done, the actual amount of each activity component can be entered in quantitative terms; the measured activity is the cost driver. This allows the valuation process to cost each activity using predetermined rates, and thus allocate the costs to the service cost structure under the appropriate cost element headings. From this point on, the flexible reporting system of SAP R/3 can be used to collate the information and present it for the benefit of the decision-makers in your company.

The Cost Object as an Account Assignment Device

A cost object exists for SAP R/3 if there is a master record for it. The function of a cost object is to control the allocation, analysis, and settlement of costs that are related to the object it represents. It may relate directly to a production unit; it may be an organizational structure component that is useful in reporting value flows. In essence, a cost object is an identification number and a set of master record data fields that can be accessed in connection with that number.

Unit costs of all cost objects are the basis for arriving at all costing values.

The cost object could be an entity which is quite independent of any particular SAP application—a convenient peg on which to hang information relevant to the specific costing procedures of your company.

A cost object may collect the costs of two or more other cost objects. This constitutes a cost object hierarchy, which can branch down any number of layers and extend to any number of cost objects on each level. Most cost structures will be in the form of cost object hierarchies of an inverted tree shape if plotted, for instance, through the SAP R/3 online reporting system using the graphical interface.

If you run projects or production lines, you might find it informative to have certain cost information gathered by cost objects, in parallel to the normal product costing. One way of achieving this is to define unique cost objects for each project or production line of interest.

Should your installation have other SAP modules installed and configured, you will find it convenient to make use of the cost objects from these applications to define your own unique cost objects by copying some or all of the data structures from these predefined SAP cost objects. For example, these cost object types are used in the following application modules:

- PS-Project System network, project item
- CO-Controlling internal order

- SD-Sales and Distribution sales order
- MM-Materials Management material number
- PP-Production Planning production order, routing
- PM-Plant Maintenance maintenance order

If you have the unit costs for all your cost objects, you can display inventory costings and call for profitability analyses using the full set of fixed and variable costs. You can make use of any combination of the costing systems current in your company.

The SAP R/3 System carries the definitions, in the form of master data, for all the cost object controlling functions of the SAP integrated system. Any transaction that bears data relevant to costing will be processed according to these definitions.

Results from Costing a Cost Object

Costing results are stored by version so that different methods and different periods may be compared. Each assembly is itemized in a costing created from a cost object. The data used can be planned or actual, and can be as valuations or as quantities to which standard rates can be applied by the system at the time. The results of a costing comprise information on each of 40 cost components for each cost object, itemized for each assembly, and the whole is replicated for each version of the costing structure, if required.

Legal analysis demands that the origins of cost estimates be identifiable. This, in turn, requires that details must be kept for the cost origins of all the contributors to the values recorded as the cost object components. A cost origin has to be a document which identifies a transaction by such means as:

- The vendor number for external procurement and the provision of external activities
- The operation number, the identification of the sender cost center, and the activity type for each internal activity
- The material number or material group code if there were stock movements or the consumption of goods
- The cost center for charging overhead

The SAP R/3 System running CO-PC Product Cost Accounting can carry out the following procedures using cost origins to associate posted movements with cost elements:

- Conduct valuation using individual cost structures or cost rates.
- Assign costs to standard cost elements.
- Establish the costing basis for overhead.
- Accept planning and account assignment directives at any level of the costing structures.
- Prepare reports at any analysis level to display planned or actual resource-usage variances.

Valuation Methods

The following costing systems are available in the CO-Controlling module of the SAP R/3 System and may be used in any combination:

- Unit costing
- Product costing
- Production order costing
- Cost object controlling for make-to-stock production
- Cost object controlling for process manufacturing
- Cost object controlling for make-to-order production
- Cost object controlling for plant construction

The valuation of input factors and the presentation of this data for costing analysis are carried out by a uniform valuation method across all costing systems. The source of the data differentiates the methods, insofar as there have to be different methods for costing when technical quantities are involved, such as when using bills of materials and routings. Variations also occur when existing cost estimates have to be copied or referenced. Manual entry of cost estimates is supported, and the R/3 system will offer suggested default values wherever possible for editing as necessary.

The valuation process extends to the following calculations:

- Planned input quantities with planned allocation rates and planned prices
- Actual input quantities with standard prices and standard activity prices
- Actual input quantities with actual prices and actual activity prices
- Partial or total output quantities
- Scrap quantities
- Order-specific cost settlement according to the quantities delivered
- Calculation of all types of variance
- Profitability analyses to different layout formats

Input Valuation

Input quantities can be evaluated by any of a range of methods. The method chosen is recorded as the valuation variant. These variants are listed below:

- Standard prices, current prices, future or previous
- Moving average prices
- Tax-based and commercial or "political" prices
- Standard activity prices
- Actual activity prices
- Applying variances on standard or actual prices adjusted to match changes in planning or historical amounts

In the service sector it is possible to have the system split the costs into fixed and variable components, which allows you to carry out marginal and absorption costing in parallel. Any point of view of output may be taken for the purpose of evaluating services rendered.

By having the required functionality available online, SAP R/3 is able to offer a modern control system covering products and the analysis of results. The following outcomes are supported:

- The cost of goods manufactured and the cost of goods sold are displayed on efficient and informative cost structures that are understandable from a business point of view and accurate from a product cost accounting perspective.

- The company can see the effects on the financial accounts and year-end closing of using different valuation techniques, so choices can be made on the basis of correct information.

- Not all the divisions of a corporate group have to use the same valuation methods, but can use the ones most suitable for them.

- Detailed costing records can be made available for each alternative or parallel valuation of variances between planned and actual costs for each business segment.

- The costing methods throughout the group are not necessarily dependent on the costing documentation requirements of the logistics operations.

Analysis and Reporting in Product Cost Accounting

The structure of a report can be made to suit your requirements. The standard system contains many predefined standard reports which you can modify and extend, often in the online mode. Both the format and the data are under your control.

Orders can be grouped by order type, for instance, and then line items selected on the basis of their connection to a specific cost object. Summaries and graphical representations are available at all stages of analysis and reporting.

Cost objects may be compared and the variances computed using any dimensions for comparison: between orders, between periods, between similar cost objects, between cost objects of quite different kinds.

Planning and Simulation from Unit Costing

You can apply unit costing irrespective of the status of an order, because it is based on a quantity structure that you have defined manually. These are some of the uses of a comprehensive system of unit costing:

- Price determination
- Costing to make quotes and bids
- Costing to support the processing of orders
- Planning of costs and resources to prepare order and project cost estimates

- Making sample cost estimates for new or existing products using an existing estimate as a reference model to be edited and updated

- Defining sales prices for sales orders

- Preparing, planning, controlling, and settling investments by means of orders and projects

- Preparing cost estimates for base planning objects, which can range from a single-level assembly to a multilevel structure that includes other base planning objects. A base planning object may also be an instrument for integrating information from other, non-SAP, applications.

You can display the costing information before, during, and after production or project activities, and before, during, and after sales activities.

In the activities of sales and distribution, you can use unit costing to good advantage in two ways:

- To transfer unit cost estimates at any time to reference objects such as orders, projects and sales orders

- To cost and check quickly the feasibility of extra sales orders, or alternative or modified product components or characteristics, and any changes in the activities involved

CO-PA Profitability Analysis

CO-PCA Profit Center Accounting is closely associated with CO-PA Profitability Analysis.

There is an important distinction to be made between the following aspects of profitability analysis:

- Profitability Analysis is the periodic analysis of the profit and loss made by the strategic units or by the entire company.

- Cost of Sales Accounting is also a form of profitability analysis. It is used in the management of market-oriented activities.

They both call on the same costing information, but treat it in different ways. Sales managers need to be able to estimate profits in the short term by using interim reports—based on standard values and imputed costs derived from standard manufacturing costs with cash discounts and rebates—because the actual data are not available at the time the billing document has to be issued. Periodic profitability analysis can wait for the actual values to be collated.

The SAP R/3 CO-PA Profitability Analysis component is designed to make available the full range of analyses covering the following requirements:

- Current sales data valued with standard costs and prices at the level of the individual product and for individual customers

- Calculation of actual cost variances for summarized business segments on a periodic basis

- Proportional assignment of fixed costs in order to measure net profit at the divisional level
- Application of period profit center accounting in situations where there are large fluctuations in stock levels

Both the periodic profit-and-loss statement and the interim sales report have to be able to provide the answers to similar questions, even though their answers may take different forms:

- What is the relationship between gross sales and net sales revenue?
- How were the sales deductions calculated for each market segment?
- What was the profit on this specific order?
- Which products or market segments are showing the greatest increases in sales revenue?
- Which products or market segments are making the highest contribution margin?
- What are the shifts, if any, between the main business segments?
- What are the planned contribution margins for each product?

The Cost of Sales Accounting method using standard costs to produce interim reports, allowing you to look at any market segment immediately, without waiting for the actual data to arrive.

Cost of Sales Accounting Using Standard Costs (Interim Reports)

The market-driven needs of sales management dictate the requirement to be able to estimate profits in the short term by using interim reports based on standard values and imputed costs. These interim values are derived from standard manufacturing costs with cash discounts and rebates because the actual data are not available at the time the billing document has to be issued.

When the actual data arrive, the interim reports are usually reconciled with them on a period basis to yield the Cost of Sales Accounting Using Actual Costs (reconciled reports). Because of the lag in time, these reports are not so useful for managing the sales activities; their function is more to document and summarize.

Fixed Cost Absorption Accounting

Profitability accounting requires that profit and loss be calculated on the basis of both full costs and marginal costs using contribution margin accounting.

The actual costs can be assigned to the business segments en masse or in proportion to sales. Therefore the fixed costs can be absorbed across several levels of the organization for each period.

When costs are assigned to user-defined business segments, they have usually been gathered from one or more cost centers. However, costs may have been assigned to orders so that they can be collected from the customers; these costs can also be taken into account. Direct costs can be assigned to any level of a business segment.

Part

I

Ch

3

The SAP R/3 Organizational Structure

The structure of an organization from an accounting point of view has to be formally defined if it is to be used by a computing system. SAP R/3 defines a multilevel structure in terms of nested classifications, which are known collectively as the EDM Enterprise Data Model. The model is outlined below:

- **Client** is a name attached to a data set that cannot overlap any other client data set. For example, TEST and TRAINING could be clients with separate data sets. SAP R/3 will work with only one client at a time.

- **Company Code** is the identification number of an independent accounting unit that can generate its own financial statements. It is a legal requirement that a group that operates in several countries must establish a separate company code unit for each country.

- **Business Area** is a subdivision of a company code that further subdivides the figures posted to the general ledger of the parent company code, but has to be reconciled with it. The business area is not an independent business unit, although it will manage the transaction information and the financial results shown in the company code balance sheet and the profit-and-loss statement, insofar as they concern its own business area.

- **Controlling Area** takes into cost accounting both the accounting units, such as company codes and business areas, and the logistics units, such as plant and sales organization. A controlling area may embrace several company codes, provided they all share a common chart of accounts.

- **Operating Concern** is a unit used in CO-PA Profitability Analysis to focus on the market and sales of a business, in order to set off costs against revenue. An operating concern can embrace several controlling areas, provided they all use the same chart of accounts. The operating concern can also be selective in its zone of interest by defining specific segments of the market—in terms, for example, of a product range for a certain customer group in a sales area.

- **Profit Center** is a subsection of the business that is responsible for its own profit or loss. It must be assigned to only one controlling area.

Under the CO-Controlling system, any profit-related activity, such as sales or the internal exchange of goods and services, will be documented in at least one of the controlling cost objects, such as orders, materials, assets, and cost centers. Each of these cost objects must be assigned to the corresponding profit center.

In order to calculate a result from profitability analysis, all profit-related activities are copied to CO-PCA Profit Center Accounting, where they can be associated with their profit centers.

The Routes of Control Data Flow

CO-Controlling uses transaction data from the FI-GL General Ledger accounts to maintain its own set of records. Overhead costs are posted to one of the cost centers according to their source of origin. The CO-Controlling system uses additional postings to assign the direct costs to other cost objects, such as orders, processes, other cost objects, and business segments.

The overhead costs that have been posted to the cost centers according to their origins are also reassigned by allocation rules to the other assignment objects, according to their usage of the overhead.

CO-Controlling shares out both direct costs and overhead costs among the assignment objects according to their usage, and also allocates the values to other cost objects for the purpose of control and analysis.

Revenue and sales deductions are posted directly to the relevant business segment or profit center. The cost objects either remain in inventory or are posted through to profitability analysis.

You can thus carry out period accounting at profit center level, taking into account changes in inventory. And you can call for cost of sales accounting in each business segment.

CO-Controlling operates a system which is parallel to the FI-Financial Accounting system, but separate from it. You can display a business-oriented profit-and-loss analysis, because all the data objects that have a bearing on the computation of value added are represented in the analysis and can therefore be scrutinized down to the details of the individual transactions from which the data are drawn. The cost data are allocated according to rules which are under your control—there need be no obscurity as to how to interpret the analysis reports.

Customer quotations and sales orders give rise to the information which CO-PA Profitability Analysis needs:

- Billing documents
- Sales quantities
- Revenues
- Sales deductions

Goods that are issued, received or manufactured give rise to the information that goes, for example, into the calculation of:

- Manufacturing costs
- Standard costs
- Moving average price
- Transfer prices

External activities carried out by contractors, for example, are either posted directly to CO-PA Profitability Analysis from FI-Financial Accounting, or they are settled from the orders and projects, which also input to CO-PA Profitability Analysis.

Analysis for separate business segments can be affected, because cost and revenue data can be posted directly to a business segment, just as they can be posted to any cost center. Any of the following systems can carry out direct postings automatically:

- FI-Financial Accounting
- CO-Controlling
- SD-Sales and Distribution

By contrast, a profit center is not a separate account assignment object. The values held by it are derived from the master data assignments of the cost objects in the CO-Controlling system. Posting these values to a profit center occurs automatically in the background under the supervision of the CO-PCA Profit Center Accounting standard business functions.

Revenue Element Accounting

Generally Accepted Accounting Principles (GAAP) require that the values recorded in the accounts of a company shall be in a permanent state of reconciliation. In order to comply with this requirement, an online accounting system has to maintain a journal, a set of account balances and all the documents to support them. SAP R/3 meets these conditions and, in some respects, exceeds them.

Posting Revenue Data

In particular, revenue data transferred to CO-PA Profitability Analysis can be reconciled with the posted revenue in FI-Financial Accounting.

The SD-Sales and Distribution system posts revenue data originating in the invoiced sales orders to the relevant FI-GL General Ledger accounts for revenue accounting. These accounts have to be specified in the common chart of accounts belonging to the company code. This chart will define the usual revenue accounts that have been structured to suit the company code, and there will be accounts that contain sales deductions, return deliveries, rebates, credit memos, and any other noted financial instruments used by that company code.

To allow reconciliation between the two systems, the revenue elements defined in FI-Financial Accounting must be in accord with the revenue elements used by the CO-PA Profitability Analysis system. This shared set of revenue elements must reflect not only the financial accounting structure of the chart of accounts, but also the structures that have been developed in order to facilitate a sensitive and timely mechanism for cost controlling and profitability analysis.

The billing data from the SD-Sales and Distribution system, or from an individual user interface, have to be directed simultaneously toward two accounting processes:

- FI-Financial Accounting has to identify the destination in terms of the revenue accounts of the chart of accounts.

- CO-PA Profitability Analysis has to identify the destination in terms of the revenue elements of that system, which are usually derived from the revenue account structure that appears in the chart of accounts.

In company codes where the sources of revenue are not readily matched to the revenue elements of the CO-PA Profitability Analysis system, it is usual to use the facilities of the FI-GLX Extended General Ledger to associate the revenue sources with the appropriate items chosen from the lists of origins that are recognized by this component. The additional subdivisions of revenue accounts supported by the FI-GLX Extended General Ledger remain reconciled with the FI-GL General Ledger revenue accounts. The advantage of calling on the extra analysis information available through the FI-GLX Extended General Ledger is that it enables accurate reconciliation with the revenue elements of the CO-PA Profitability Analysis component.

Estimate Revenue Elements

It may well happen that the billing data transferred to CO-PA Profitability Analysis is not accurate. Revenue elements may have to be estimated. For example, a sales deduction could be estimated as, say, 10 percent of domestic sales revenue on the grounds that previous analysis would support this as a reasonable prediction.

The benefit is that the CO-PA Profitability Analysis system can provide a complete and up-to-date estimate of gross and net revenues as soon as the billing takes place.

Such estimated sales deductions are usually posted and transferred to FI-Financial Accounting, where they can be balanced with the actual sales deductions when they become available. If necessary, the CO-PA Profitability Analysis system will then adjust the calculation for future estimates.

A typical report structure for an estimated revenue element would include the following display fields:

- Gross revenue
- Freight and packing
- Discount
- Estimate rebate or cash discount
- Estimate warranty
- Net revenue

Calculating Profitability

Profitability is calculated for a business segment. The SAP R/3 System is supplied with a set of criteria from which the definition of a business segment can be assembled. The most commonly used criteria are provided as lists of proposals which may be adopted or ignored when you set up your own CO-PA Profitability Analysis system. You can define unique criteria to suit your own circumstances.

Business Segments

These are some of the ways you can specify how you want to define the business segments to be used in your company code:

- From the customer masters, define some customer groups on the basis of their shared location, line of business, value of past transactions, and so on.
- From the material masters, define a range of products that will comprise a business segment.
- From the required business classification code that you have defined for entry on each sales order, select certain values to comprise a business segment.

Data that will be used to specify criteria can be taken from any of the integrated SAP applications. Complex criteria can be built up using the objects that appear only in the CO-Controlling module or only in the CO-PA Profitability Analysis system itself.

Criteria may be combined across dimensions and levels to make a business segment specification that will give you the profitability analysis for exactly what it is that you want to take a look at. For example:

Segment A is defined as any transaction that involves any member of Customer Group CG1 that is in Industry I6 and deals with any product in Product Group P4 and has been authorized by Sales Consultant SC26. And it might be that Sales Consultant SC26 is defined as any member of Department G who has been temporarily assigned to Department S and is working from Office O7.

In summary, a business segment is a portion of your business that you have defined in terms of products, customers, activities, and organization, combined in any way you want.

Unlike cost centers and order data structures, for example, the business segments do not have to exist in the form of master records. When a segment is needed, the transaction data is assembled according to the definition of the segment. When a document is automatically transferred from another integrated application, SD-Sales and Distribution, for example, all the information about the customer and the products that is needed to meet the criteria for the business segments is copied from the relevant customer and product master records to the sales order or the billing document. When this data is transferred to the CO-PA Profitability Analysis system, the remaining criteria for building the business segment are applied to determine where the item is posted in the CO-PA Profitability Analysis system.

Manual entry of line items is supported, together with the use of planned values. In these circumstances, the CO-PA Profitability Analysis system will derive the information necessary to place the entries or planning date in the appropriate business segments.

A business segment is an account assignment object to which an entry may be posted, provided all the segment criteria are met by valid data in the entry. This proviso ensures that subsequent analysis will be possible, using different sub-selections from the business segment criteria if necessary.

Key Figures

The R/3 CO-PA Profitability Analysis system uses the concept of key figures to define the lowest level at which it is possible to display the quantities, revenue, sales deductions and costs when you are carrying out a contribution margin calculation for a business segment. The system will offer lists of commonly used key figures as proposals for you to adopt or supplement by key figures of your own specification.

These key figures can be set at any level of detail. Revenue, for example, could be displayed across a revenue element structure comprising revenue from external customers and from partner companies. Revenue alterations, such as credit memos and rebates, and sales deductions can be displayed as separate revenue elements.

Costs are stored as value fields, the details depending on the specific SAP R/3 applications which have been installed and configured. For example, the following costs could be displayed in the CO-PA Profitability Analysis system:

- From CO-PC Product Cost Accounting, the manufacturing costs from product cost estimates
- From CO-OPA Order and Project Accounting, the manufacturing costs, or the cost of the goods sold as documented on sales orders
- From CO-OPA Order and Project Accounting or from the SAP R/3 PS-Project System, the manufacturing costs or the cost of purchases, as documented by projects
- From CO-OPA Order and Project Accounting, or from the SAP R/3 PS-Project System, the costs of overhead projects or orders
- From PP-Production Planning, the variances from production orders
- From CO-CCA Cost Center Accounting, the fixed costs
- From CO-CCA Cost Center Accounting, the variances
- From FI-Financial Accounting, the direct postings
- From CO-PA Profitability Analysis, the estimated costs

Sales, Revenue, and Profit Planning

The planning of sales quantities, revenue, and profit in the context of corporate planning is the exclusive province of the SAP R/3 CO-PA Profitability Analysis system. The business segment is the focus of this planning.

The possibilities of business segment planning include the following:

- Planning the sales quantity for a business segment
- Using the planned sales quantity and the values available to the system for revenue, discounts, rebates, and so on, to compute the planned gross revenue and planned net revenue
- Transferring the planned costs, such as manufacturing cost and cost center overheads, from the CO-Controlling system, and calculating the planned profit for a business segment
- Planning all fixed cost allocations at different levels of the segment

The CO-PA Profitability Analysis system allows you to plan sales quantity data for any number of business segments, defined as you wish. So there is no need to specify a permanent level at which planned values and quantities will be entered. Each business can operate sales and profit planning in the most informative way. And the SAP R/3 graphical interface is available to assist you.

CO-PCA Profit Center Accounting

A profit center is not an independent account assignment object. It derives its information from existing account assignment objects. The master record of each account assignment object includes a field that identifies the responsible profit center. The profit center is defined by an organizational master record in the system, and can therefore store descriptive information, in particular, the criteria that define which account assignment objects it is responsible for.

Profit centers can be summarized and their results combined on any number of hierarchical levels and across different hierarchies.

The profit center is a way of looking at a particular selection of transaction data assigned to various accounts to see how it affects the operating profit of that portion of the business the profit center represents.

Ledger-Based Period Accounting at the Profit Center Level

Profit centers allow you to collate all profit-related posting information under the divisions of your organizational structure.

Every posting is saved simultaneously as a line item and totals are recorded in the FI-GLX Financial Accounting Extended General Ledger.

As a consequence, CO-PCA Profit Center Accounting is functionally separate from the cost-of-sales accounting used in CO-PA Profitability Analysis.

When you place an original account assignment object in the domain of a profit center, you are setting up separate data flows under control of the posting rules that will be obeyed by the CO-PCA Profit Center Accounting system. Transaction data are transferred in real time. When it comes into existence in the FI-Financial Accounting system, the CO-Controlling system will set up a copy in parallel, and the CO-PCA Profit Center Accounting system will reflect this copy.

Primary cost information will be reflected from:

- Cost centers
- Orders
- Projects
- Product planning orders

Secondary costs may be reflected in profit centers as a result of:

- Cost allocation
- Cost assessment
- Cost distribution
- Transfer postings
- Order settlement
- Accruals
- Surcharges

Revenues can appear in profit centers as the result of:

- Direct account assignment from FI-Financial Accounting
- Billing documents via the interface with SD-Sales and Distribution

Values attributable to changes in inventory and work in process can also be reflected in profit centers.

Ledger-Based Period Accounting Profitability Reports

The line item of a period accounting profitability report represents an FI-GL General Ledger account number and its name. The line items can be selected and organized by hierarchies of profit centers.

There is continuous reconciliation at the company code level between the FI-Financial Accounting system and the CO-PCA Profit Center Accounting system. Thus, the inputs to each profit center can be any combination of the following sources of information:

- Customer orders and projects
- Cost objects
- Fixed assets

Part
I
Ch
3

- Materials management
- Internal orders and projects
- Manufacturing orders
- Cost centers

The benefits of this integrated system include the following insights:

- The flow of the value of goods from one profit center to another is displayed, having eliminated internal transactions.
- The profitability report reveals the origins of all profit-relevant data.

This chapter has reminded you of the mechanisms of financial accounting and controlling as they are applied by SAP R/3 throughout all its applications. If, in your company, the high cost of materials and the complexities of keeping track of them are where really big improvements in productivity are to be engendered, then the MM-Materials Management module will be the focus of your attention.

Material Requirements Planning

MRP, Material Requirements Planning, is based on a simple idea: Make sure you have what you will need, ready to use, before you begin. We all know that MRP done well can be a very profitable process because we have suffered when it is not.

MRP uses some words which have slightly different connotations from their meanings in everyday language.

Defining Material

All objects processed in materials management can be classified as materials. A material master record is usually created for each material in the SAP System and each material is assigned a material number. Tangible goods, objects, gases, powders, even documents are all materials. Intangible goods classified as materials include services, rights, and patents.

A material is bought, sold, consumed, or manufactured during production. It is a prime object of business activity.

Some organizations will also classify persons along with materials.

Material Master   All the materials used in a company and their data are stored in the format of the material master.

Assembly   An assembly is an inventoried material that comprises two or more material items that are themselves inventoried. An assembly may have a Bill of Material that specifies its constituents.

Material Type

It is useful to have an indicator that subdivides materials according to the way they are used, such as raw materials, semi-finished materials, operating supplies. The material type can also determine the user screen sequence, the numbering in the material master records, the type of inventory management, and the accounts to which transactions are posted.

Material Group

A list which comprises one or more materials with the same characteristics can be named and classified as a material group.

Net Change Planning

Net change planning is conducted by calculating the net requirements of those materials whose stock or planned requirements have changed during the day or other planning interval. Calculations take place only for those materials and services that have attracted planning changes, or that have been used or supplemented in the planning period. If one of your stocks is increased or decreased, then a net change has taken place and planning action is called for. In addition, if your planners have approved a change in your forecast requirements for a material, then action is also called for.

MRP, Material Requirements Planning, is a generic term for the activities involved in creating a production schedule or procurement plan for the materials in a plant, company, or company group. There are several variants on the idea of trying to purchase no more and yet no less than what you will need: and some of these variants entail taking different kinds of business risk.

The material requirements planning run usually applies the net change planning procedure, in which the only materials to be subject to planning are those whose stocks have changed during the working day. In some industries, the "planning horizon" may be defined as shorter than a day so that the MRP Materials Requirements Planning controller can have a tighter control. If the planned requirements have also changed, there will have to be a corresponding alteration in the purchasing proposal.

Your material requirements planner can also be given information about important parts or assemblies, and warnings of exceptional situations.

Consumption-Based Planning

There is a simple and easy-to-use planning method used in companies that do not have their own production plant. It works on the assumption that stock that has been promised by a planned order is no longer available to promise (ATP) and should be replaced by initiating a materials planning procedure which will lead to a purchase order proposal and eventually to replenishment of the stock.

There are two procedures for consumption-based planning:

- Reorder point planning
- Forecast-based planning

Reorder Point Planning

You can set up a method of planning in which a purchase order is created if the available stock of a material falls below the reorder level. This reorder point planning does not respond directly to changes in planned requirements, although you can set the safety stock at values large enough to cope with anticipated demand.

The reorder point is also known as the reorder level. If the warehouse stock of a material falls below the reorder level, the system automatically creates a purchase order proposal, unless the purchasing department has already created a purchase order for the required quantity.

Delivery Time

To replenish stock takes time. Therefore, the reorder point will have to be calculated on some assumption about how the remaining stock might be used while awaiting a delivery. The expected average consumption would be a reasonable value to use in lieu of anything better.

Previous consumption values over a comparable period under similar trading conditions would be a refinement, and a knowledge of future requirements would complement the picture.

Safety Stock

Prudence would counsel you to add a little safety stock in case the delivery of your materials is held up for any reason. If your are producing in-house, you may also use the concept of safety stock to be added to your inventory of finished or semi-finished materials so that you can cope with unexpected orders. The amount of safety stock you wish to hold will be affected by the risks to your profitability that a failure to complete an order might entail. Are you operating under penalty clauses? Will your future be affected by a failure to deliver on time?

Forecast-Based Planning

You can arrange automatic reorder point planning procedure so that the forecast requirements are taken into account.

This method uses a forecast value or forecast quantity of stock rather than a stock reorder level as the starting point for the plan to replenish the inventory.

The material requirements planning controller will carry out a material requirements forecast at regular intervals for each material needed over the period. For this purpose, the period can be defined as a day, week, month, posting period, or split periods within these. The planning horizon can be set in terms of the number of planning periods to be included in the calculations.

The basis for the forecast calculation will include provisions for safety stock and assessment of the historical consumption data.

As material is reserved to be withdrawn from the warehouse in each planning period, the forecast requirement for that period is reduced by the corresponding amount. The remainder of the original forecast requirement for the period is then entered for the material requirements planning run and will be entered on a purchase order. Stock that was planned and has been used will not be reordered because purchase orders for the planned values will have been created already.

Net Requirements Calculation

The calculation of net requirements compares the forecast quantities of each material for each period with the quantities that are expected to be available. Some of this stock may be in the warehouse now, and some of it may be scheduled for delivery in time to meet the requirement. Your net requirements function will check that every forecast requirement for material is covered, either by an available warehouse stock, available to promise, or by scheduled receipts which have been generated as a result of planning by the purchasing department.

If a deficit is foreseen, a purchase order proposal is generated by the net requirements function.

Controlling Your MRP

The key parameters for each material on your inventory and in your anticipated requirements are the reorder point quantity and the safety stock quantity. These values can be entered manually for single materials or for material types or material groups based on criteria you have defined. Alternatively, these key parameters can be suggested to the materials controller by the system on the basis of past data and extrapolation rules which you have specified for this purpose. The controller can, of course, adjust these purchase order proposals before releasing them as purchase orders.

Automatic Replenishment

In the context of materials management, the main function of material requirements planning is to monitor stocks and automatically generate purchase order proposals to be forwarded to the purchasing department. Checks are made that your purchasing organization has not already created a purchase order for the quantity required.

Inventory Management and Automatic Reorder Point Planning

If your material is of high value, because individual pieces are of high value, or because you hold a large stock of them, it will be important for you to keep stock levels low in order to avoid having capital invested in your inventory that could be working elsewhere. However, you need to balance this cash consideration against the risk of being unable to meet a delivery schedule because you have run out of stock. Clearly, you need to know how long it takes each supplier to replenish your stocks and how reliable he or she is in meeting deadlines. You may also need to collect data on how many sub-standard items or low quality batches are to be expected in consignments from each of your vendors.

The way you anticipate your requirements is important. Can you do better than order on the basis of average consumption? Is your demand seasonal? Can you plan from your order book? Is your purchasing organization able to choose when to order so as to take advantage of buying material at favorable prices or from favorable sources, even though they may be unreliable?

Storage Location MRP

You may have some storage locations that you prefer to manage separately from the rest of the plant. You can identify these to the MM application and the MRP will be conducted as a separate operation for these locations.

Material requirements planning is normally carried out at the plant level, so all the stock available in the plant is recognized by the materials planning run, whatever its storage location. However, you can also carry out material requirements planning runs at the level of individual storage locations, or at the plant level, with certain storage locations excluded according to your instructions.

Automatic Steps of the MRP Planning Run

The MRP list is compiled by carrying out a series of steps:

- Net requirements calculation
- Lot size calculation
- Scheduling
- Purchase order proposal creation
- Exception message creation

The controller can adjust the material reservations and the purchase order proposals by interacting with the displayed values of the MRP results. Individual materials can be replanned online immediately.

Continuous Inventory Management

You could have your MM system operate automatically to reorder stock in the light of evidence it has collected regarding consumption and delivery, and to have it take account of any purchasing decisions your buyers have researched.

The inventory management function ensures that every time a material is taken from the warehouse, the stock level is checked to see if it has fallen below the reorder level. If this is the situation, then an entry is made in the material requirements planning file so as to generate a purchase order on the next material requirements planning run.

Quota Arrangements

You may take some of your supplies from several vendors, each of which operates its own delivery schedule. You can have the system take this into consideration automatically by specifying quotas across vendors, across schedules, or both. This restriction will be built-in automatically at the stage of the material requirements planning run, using the specification you have established.

Bill of Materials Explosion

If the materials on your inventory are units or bulk materials that can be counted or measured, the quantities required can be set out in the purchase order documents. Similarly, your inventory will be carried out in the base units appropriate for each material. But if some of your materials are assemblies, your MRP may have to be more complex.

In essence, a bill of material is a document of which the header carries information about the period of validity and the status of the document, together with the plant or plants to which it is assigned because the assembly will be manufactured, assembled, or warehoused there. The items on a BOM refer to the components of the assembly.

If your plant handles assemblies which are never purchased or dispatched as separate components, then you will probably not need bills of material for them. But if you buy in components, or if you sell any components separately, then you will need to know what is in the bills of material for the assemblies in which they take part.

Your MM system will unwrap a bill of material and determine the components. And, if any of these components is itself an assembly, then it too will be unwrapped. And so on. The process can be exponential in the rate at which it adds to the material items required. Therefore, it is referred to as a Bill of Materials Explosion.

Lot-Sizing Procedures

When a material requirements shortage is anticipated as the consequence of a planning run, the lot size for reordering is taken from the material master record, where it has been specified by the material requirements planning controller. The way it is determined and used depends on the choice of lot-sizing procedure.

The SAP R/3 System supports an extensive set of lot-sizing procedures, to which you can add user-specific procedures as required. There are three basic procedures: static lot-sizing, periodic lot-sizing, and optimum lot-sizing.

Part

I

Ch

3

Static Lot-Sizing

The lot size is calculated from the quantity specifications in the material master record. There are three criteria which can be used:

- Lot-for-lot order quantity
- Fixed lot size
- Replenish up to the maximum stock level

Periodic Lot-Sizing

The size of the lot to be reordered can be determined from the requirement quantities of one or more planning periods added together to form a purchase order proposal. There is a choice of time period over which the requirements are to be totaled:

- Daily lot size
- Weekly lot size
- Monthly lot size
- Lot size based on flexible period lengths within the accounting periods
- Freely definable periods according to a planning calendar used to determine lot size

Optimum Lot-Sizing

The cost of a large lot of material may yield a low unit cost, but there will be associated costs independent of lot size, plus storage costs which are usually related to lot size. There are several methods of working out an optimum ratio between the lot size and the independent and storage costs. SAP R/3 supports the following optimization procedures:

- Part period balancing
- Least unit cost procedure
- Dynamic lot-size creation
- Groff reorder procedure

Additional Restrictions on Lot Size

The material master records will allow you to impose additional restrictions on the reorder lot size. The following types of restriction are supported:

- Minimum lot size causes the system to round up the quantity reordered to meet the minimum lot size.
- Maximum lot size ensures that the system will not group together period requirements that will generate a quantity larger than the maximum lot size.
- Rounding adjustment specifies that the lot size shall be rounded up or down so as to arrive at an exact multiple of the order unit to obviate the need to split a packaging unit, for example, or to ensure that the delivery transportation vehicle will be used efficiently.

Interpreting the MRP Results

The job of a material requirements planning run is to generate a purchase order proposal if a requirements shortage is detected.

MRP List

An MRP list can be limited by the MRP controller who sets up parameters to filter out or include only the materials or stock situations of interest. The list search specification can be stored for subsequent use.

The MRP list shows the stock situation and the requirements as they were at the time of the last MRP planning run. These runs will typically take place overnight or at other times of relatively light system demand.

Online and printed versions of the MRP list are available on demand from your user terminal.

Stock and Requirements List

The stock and requirements list corresponds in content to the MRP list. It does, however, offer additional information which might affect materials activities. For example, goods receipts and goods issues will be shown if they have occurred since the last MRP run. The controller will thus have an up-to-date picture of the availability of all materials.

Display Formats for MRP Results

The following display formats are available for the material requirements planning results, and you can readily change from one to another:

- Days
- Weeks
- Months
- According to posting period
- According to the planning calendar
- According to the user-defined flexible period split

MRP Run Exception Reporting

During a material requirements planning run, the system will generate exception messages to alert the controller if any of the following events occur:

- Scheduling delay
- Rescheduling and cancellations
- A material stock level falling below the safety stock level

The controller may decide to group exception messages so that they can be displayed together. This is done by specifying the structure in an exception group master record. By this means, the material controller can set up the system so that it provides early warning of any situation that has been defined in the exception group master records.

Using Material Forecasting Models

A material forecast is used to determine requirements and to compute the safety stock and reorder level for individual materials. The data processing is normally carried out in batch mode, but analysis for a single material may be conducted online. The material forecast depends on historical data, and its validity will therefore depend on the accuracy of this data. The other crucial assumption is that material consumption patterns can be discerned in the data that are likely to continue into the future.

To represent a pattern of material consumption, the system has available a choice of four basic models, from which it will choose the best fit automatically if you do not want to impose a choice of your own.

Constant Consumption Model

This forecast model computes a single value which best fits the varying consumption values for the material as recorded in the historical data; it represents the average value, slightly refined, if you wish, to play down the effects of occasional very high or very low values by finding the "central tendency" of the data.

This model makes no allowance for any shift in the central tendency and so could prompt you into holding stocks which are progressively too high or too low if indeed your requirements are changing. On the other hand, if your needs are erratic and, in detail, unpredictable, it may be a very reasonable choice to assume that your company's profitability would be best served if you used the historical consumption average for each material as the basis for reordering it.

Forecast Trend Model

If your consumption of a material is steady or erratic, but if the central tendency is to steadily increase or decrease, then the best prediction you can make would be to assume that the trend will continue. Your consumption graph of a material would be a straight line sloping up or down against the axis of time period. Your forecast would be placed on the same straight line.

Seasonal Fluctuation Model

Shrewd observation or arithmetic computation might suggest that some of your material requirements vary with the months or even weeks of the year. If there is a regular pattern which repeats itself every year, with the peaks and troughs occurring at the same time of year and reaching to about the same value at each cycle of the pattern, then your MM system would be able to discern this by calculation. You could then continue this pattern as a forecast consumption for future planning periods.

Seasonal Trend Model

If your system finds that the data for a material contains a repeating pattern that is also subject to an upwards or downwards trend, then this sloping pattern can be used as your forecast for the material.

If the system has found which model best fits the historical data, or if you have told the system which model to apply, the chosen model can be used to predict the value or quantity of material likely to be required at any time in the future. The assumption is that the pattern discerned in the data, or mandated by the material requirements planning controller, will continue to be applicable. You have to assume that there will be no discontinuity in the pattern of consumption of this material. For example, if a significant group of your customers take to buying out of season and stockpiling, you may have to reconsider which forecast model to apply. Should you use a seasonal trend model that is phase-shifted to allow for the stockpiling?

The only real comfort offered by the system in this matter is its ability to recalculate the parameters of the models at any time, and rebuild its forecasts using the latest data available.

Monitoring the Validity of a Forecast Model

Your system will have chosen a forecast model for each of the materials you have chosen to index your consumption and, hence, your materials requirements. As actual consumption data arrives, the validity of the model can be assessed by computing the difference between the forecast amounts and the actual consumption.

You can arrange for an exception message to be generated if the forecast proves to be wrong by an amount that you have specified. And you can have the system reassess whether a different forecast model would have been a better choice. In all these calculations, the system will automatically calculate all the points necessary to plot the forecast as a curve or straight line about which the actual consumption data, or the known requirements planned, can be plotted. You can set up conditions to warn your controller if the spread of the data points starts to increase significantly.

Reprocessing a Forecast

If the automatic exception messages generated during an MRP forecast run suggest the need for a revision of the forecast, the data in them can be used to reprocess the result.

From Here...

- How easy is it to actually find out about stock items?

  See Chapter 7, "Analyzing Materials Information."

- What are the options for finding out what is available already in stock?

  See Chapter 4, "Understanding Inventory and Warehouse Management."

- Can materials be ordered over the Internet?

  See Chapter 9, "Understanding Network Computing."

Understanding Inventory and Warehouse Management

In this chapter

- How to find a place for everything and keep everything in its place
- Automating stock placement and retrieval
- Planning and executing integrated quality control over materials

Knowing what you have in stock and where you can find it when you need it is valuable business knowledge. To be able to place a monetary value on it is a legal requirement. To use it according to strategies that are in the best interest of your company makes good business sense.

Understanding the Benefits and the Mechanisms of Inventory Management

The inventory is both a list and a physical collection of material items. Inventory management entails the planning and control of material stocks by quantity and value. It has also come to include the planning, data entry, and documentation of all goods movements to, from, and within the storage locations in the warehouses used by the company. Warehouse management can be regarded as an essential supporting function that has the job of making sure that the decisions taken by the inventory management system are carried out as effectively and efficiently as possible.

Two aspects of your stock deserve special attention: quality and value. The quality of your stock will eventually have a profound effect on your reputation and hence your sales. The value of your stock will depend on the quantities, the prices, the quality, and the market value of the goods and services that you produce using this stock.

The sales of goods and services depend on many factors, but if your company holds stock, however briefly, then the profitability of these sales will be likely to be affected by the efficiency with which you control your inventory. There are several potential errors in business:

- Run out of stock when the goods you need are in short supply
- Run out of stock when the goods you need are going up in price
- Hold stock that is not likely to be needed before the next chance you will have of replenishing your reserves
- Hold stock that costs more than the current price on the market

You may also consider that a missed opportunity is an error:

- Fail to buy extra stock of materials you will need when they are low in price
- Fail to sell surplus stock when the sale price is favorable
- Fail to "corner the market" by overstocking when you suspect that a rival will be seriously inconvenienced by running short of this material

A more subtle kind of error concerns the profitability of your inventory management activities:

- Is the value added by stock holding significantly more than the costs of warehousing?
- What kind of network of warehouses would make most profitable use of the available transport facilities?

- Should some of your customers be given better service based, for example, on better inventory management by your company?

- Are you spending too much or too little on quality control over the materials as they pass through your business processes?

- What are your losses in terms of spoiled materials or thefts, and how much does this cost?

You could regard all these questions as matters of common business logic—putting effort where it will yield best returns and contribute to the viability of your endeavor. What the SAP R/3 Materials Management application offers is the computer mechanisms to execute efficiently and reliably any management decisions you make. If you decide to run your inventory with a small surplus, then the MM system will keep on doing this automatically for you until you decide otherwise. If you want to keep a close watch on the high-value items, then MM will again keep up this vigilance for you once you have established the parameters to control automatic procedures.

Managing Material Stocks by Quantity

Almost every company will want to manage inventory in terms of the amounts of materials or numbers of parts and assemblies. In the SAP R/3 System, any transaction that will cause a change of stock is entered in real time, and the consequent update of the stock situation will take place immediately. The effect is to give the user an overview that is always current of the stock level of any material. You must know if you have an item available to promise (ATP). Anyone else in the company who is thinking of placing some kind of reservation on this stock will immediately know whether it is available or not. And the material requirements planning file will receive an entry for this material if the reorder level has been reached.

Part
I
Ch
4

Managing Material Stocks by Value

The SAP R/3 MM System automatically keeps track of value in your inventory of materials.

When you post a movement of goods, the value of this stock is also updated. A chain of consequent postings will occur:

- There will be an automatic posting of the value change to the GI-General Ledger account in the FI-Financial Accounting module.

- Line items will be created for the account assignments needed in the CO-Controlling module, such as cost centers, orders, projects, and assets.

- The system will work out the amounts to be posted using the actual quantity of material to be moved, which you have to enter, and the value of this amount of material, which it computes using the data in the order and the master records for this material.

It is also possible to post goods receipts for which the prices have not been ascertained. The values will be calculated subsequently when the invoices are received and entered.

The Goods Movement Control Concept

If the system is to keep track of the quantities and values of your materials, it has to be alerted if any movement of material occurs, whether from one storage location to another, or by delivery to a customer.

Each movement of material causes the system to create a document recording the amounts and values, as well as the time and date of the movement. This serves as a proof that the goods were dispatched. When they arrive at their destination, the entry of their goods receipt will complete the proof of the movement.

The planning of anticipated inventory movements can be affected by using reservations identifying the material that has been allocated to a particular customer or production order, or perhaps assigned to some kind of special stock.

The physical movement of the stock within the warehouse can be controlled by means of printed goods receipts and goods issue slips, which can carry the appropriate bar code to speed data entry.

There are several standard methods available in the system that will support the comparison of the physical stocks with the book inventory balances:

- Periodic inventory
- Continuous inventory
- Sample-based inventory

These methods can be supplemented by installing and configuring the MM-WM Warehouse Management module, which will allow the detailed oversight and control of warehouses with complex systems of storage bins and storage areas.

Goods Receipts for Purchase Orders

When goods are delivered that have been ordered by a purchase order, the system will locate this purchase order document and propose default data from it to form the goods receipt documentation. If there has been no over-delivery or under-delivery, the goods receipt is documented on the purchase order, which can then be given an updated status. The goods receipt data is used to update both the purchase order and the vendor valuation record.

If the purchase order carries no goods receipt annotation to confirm delivery by the required delivery date, the purchasing department can begin the reminder procedure. Because the goods receipt data is recorded on the purchase order, there can be a follow-up of the purchase order history to judge how reliable the vendor has been with respect to delivery dates and the correctness of the quantities and specification of the goods or services supplied.

When the vendor invoice arrives and is entered, the system again refers to the purchase order to verify that the material and the quantity are in accordance with what was ordered.

When the purchase order and the invoice have been shown to be in agreement, the system can value the goods receipt by applying the price to the quantity.

The system will allow you to enter goods receipts for several purchase orders in one transaction.

Contingencies in Goods Receipts for Purchase Orders   If it is the case that a delivery note has arrived with no reference to a purchase order, the user can look up the possible purchase orders under the material code number or the vendor number.

The entry of a purchase order number will cause the system to display a collective entry screen showing all the open purchase order items separately. The scope of this display can be the plant under the user's company code or all plants in the group.

If there is still no reconciliation of the delivery note or goods receipt with an open purchase order, the user can ask to see detailed information about the order item and make notes against the item in the document by selecting a standard short text or by using free-form text from a word processing system.

You may have to enter a goods receipt using a different unit of measure from that given in the purchase order. The system will tolerate this and effect a conversion. The storage location and the quality inspection indicator will default to the values in the purchase order item, and these can be overridden by manual entries. The delivery costs determined by the planning procedures will also be transferred automatically. If there are tolerances allowed for under-delivery or over-delivery, these will be checked automatically.

One purchase order item can be distributed to several storage locations by creating several goods receipt items, one for each of the separate destinations. For example, a partial quantity can be posted to quality inspection and the remainder to goods receipt blocked stock, where it will remain until a favorable quality inspection report allows it to be released for production.

Goods Receipt to Consumption   Some goods are destined for immediate consumption rather than storage. In such cases, the system will pick up the account assignment from the purchase order data. The account may be a cost center or order, for example. Even if such just-in-time purchases are to be allocated to several control accounts, this can be done by the system when the delivery has occurred and the goods receipt has been entered.

Automatic Notification to Procurement

The person in the procurement department who deals with purchase orders that go directly to consumption will be notified of the arrival of the goods by an automatic letter via the SAPmail system as soon as the goods have been accepted.

Material Planning

A material that is going to be required in the future will obviously have to be subject to planning. A quantity and, therefore, a provisional value will be computed for each of the planning periods that stretch away from the current period to the planning horizon. The planning department will have decided, on the basis of past data or orders for products that are already on the books, that a certain requirement for this material will exist for each of the planning periods.

A wise purchasing department will have chosen a vendor and set up the purchase order, the outline purchasing agreement, or the contract, which will make it very likely that the required material will arrive at the production line on the due date, and perhaps at the due time of day, ready to be incorporated in the product. The existence in the system of a purchase order or other type of commitment or reservation can be used by the planning department to review the materials planning situation and check that the stocks in hand or on order are likely to meet the actual and the forecast requirements.

Reservations   A reservation is an instrument for making sure that this material is moved from stock to consumption at the correct moment. It assumes that the stock will be on inventory to enable this to happen, and it assumes that no other production order or customer order has already been promised this quantity of this material.

Dynamic Availability Checking   The system will automatically check that the material mentioned in a material reservation has not already been assigned elsewhere. If it is free and, therefore, available to promise (ATP), the system will show this amount of stock under the heading of reserved stock for this material. The quantity of stock available for other purposes will be reduced by the same amount, so that "double-booking" of the material does not occur.

The following data will be included in the entry to initiate a reservation:

- Material number
- Batch number (if applicable)
- Planned quantity
- Scheduled delivery date
- Intended use of the reserved material, such as the production or customer order number for which it is to be reserved

When the reserved material is approved for release to production or another destiny, the actual quantity will be substituted for the planned quantity in the calculation of the costs and values.

Goods Issues

When goods are removed from a warehouse, there has to be a posting to keep track of the quantity and value of the material withdrawn. This will trigger the posting of a reduction in the quantity and value of the warehouse stock of this material.

Planned and Unplanned Withdrawals   Every transaction concerning a withdrawal from a warehouse can be treated as a planned withdrawal or an unplanned withdrawal. The consumption statistics will show them separately because a planned withdrawal will be balanced against the quantities planned whereas the unplanned withdrawal will have to be set against the stock margin allowed in the forecast or simply replenished by a new purchase order.

Intelligent Data Entry   If you begin to create a goods issue for material that has been reserved, the system will assume that you need the quantity stated in the material reservation and that you will want to post the withdrawal to the account assigned in that document also.

Before you can complete the goods issue, the destination of the withdrawn material has to be stated in the ship-to party field. This location will be printed on the withdrawal slip.

Storage Location Display   If you are running a complex warehouse system under the MM-WM Warehouse Management component, the system can show you all the storage locations holding the type of goods you require. If you cannot see what you require, then you must initiate a purchase order or a reservation of the materials if they are already on order.

Batch Management Displays   If the materials are shipped and inspected in batches, the batch identification will be part of the reservation procedure. There can be rules for the utilization of batches, for example, to ensure that they are used in arrival-date order.

Transfer Postings Within Your Company

A quantity or "quant" of material can be moved from one storage location to another, or it can be designated for a specific purpose without being physically moved, or it can be moved and designated.

A simple system is for the goods to be received to a warehouse and then withdrawn to be sold or to be consumed by the production processes. The arrangements are slightly more complex if there is more than one warehouse and more than one production plant.

Some or all of these cost centers can belong to different parts of the enterprise and have their own company code. This signifies that they are legally obliged to publish their own separate financial documents in the form of the balance sheet and profit-and-loss statement. For example, a production facility may be assigned a different company code from the sales and distribution department. Material may be produced in one and sold to the other.

With a complex storage arrangement, and the need to maintain separate accounts for each company code, the materials management function has to be subtle.

If some material stock is transferred from one warehouse to another, and if these warehouses belong to different company codes, the financial accounting systems of both company codes have to be coordinated to reflect the fact that something of value has moved from one to the other.

Part

I

Ch

4

One-Step Stock Transfer

A transfer of stock in one step entails two posting operations in the transaction, as follows:

- Withdraw the stock from the warehouse and credit the sender.
- Deliver the stock and debit the receiver.

If your delivery processes take a long time, or if you have to keep a continuous watch on the value flows between the parts of your organization—for insurance purposes, for instance—then you may wish to hold a separate accounting record for goods that are not available because they have been withdrawn from storage, yet they are not in the hands of the receiving organization.

Two-Step Stock Transfer

An interim receiver account may have to be introduced with a title such as "transfer stock" if the stock is going to spend a long time in transit, as in the following example:

- Withdraw the stock from the warehouse and credit the sender.
- Assign the stock as transfer stock and debit the transfer stock account.
- Transport the stock to the new location.
- Release the stock from the "transfer stock" status and credit the transfer stock account.
- Deliver the stock and debit the receiver.

The important feature of the transfer stock is that it is not unrestricted stock. It cannot be used until it is received in the storage location and in the accounts of the receiving cost object, such as the production plant, for instance.

Stock Transfer Reservations

The classic example of transfer stock would be the goods in a cargo vessel on the high seas. The stock has value, but it cannot be used until it is delivered. However, quantities of the stock can be reserved for specific orders and also traded on the commodities market. By these types of operation, value may be added to or taken away from the stock while it is still in the status of being transfer stock.

Goods Movements for Consumption in Production Orders

Raw materials, semi-finished materials, assemblies, and components for production are received into the warehouse and their receipt is posted in inventory management. Any of these components that have been planned for production will have been automatically reserved for consumption by the production process on a specific date. Unforeseen circumstances may arise, necessitating the withdrawal from the warehouse of components that were not part of the reservation because they did not figure in the plan. Nevertheless, if they are used for the purpose of completing a customer order or a production order, they have to be costed along with the planned materials and documented on the order.

Bulk Materials for Production Orders   When the order being completed is a production order using bulk materials, the quantity needed may not be known exactly until the completion confirmation document for the production order has been posted. It is at this stage that the adjustment of inventory will be confirmed by supplying the actual quantities in place of the planned estimates.

Other Products   Many processes give rise to by-products, co-products, and waste materials. The difference between these types of product is in their cost consequences. Some yield sales revenue, while some incur costs of disposal. The quantities and sometimes the values can be planned and recognized in the accounting procedures.

Quality Inspection Stock

The processes of inventory management make provision for the temporary or permanent absence of part of the stock for the purpose of quality inspection. A partial delivery quantity, perhaps a selection of batches or a sample of items taken from them, becomes a transfer batch, which is transferred immediately to stock in quality inspection.

If the quality is acceptable, the remainder of the stock in quality inspection is transferred to unrestricted-use stock, where it can be reserved against future orders or withdrawn to consumption when required.

The quality inspection may also take place after the material has been received into the warehouse and planned for issue. In such cases, it would be transferred to quality inspection stock on its way to the consumption location.

Managing Batch Data

Certain materials have to be permanently associated with the batch identification they received when first manufactured and inspected. Pharmaceutical products and some foodstuffs fall into this category.

Even if the material can be repackaged, it may still have to be managed in conjunction with batch numbers.

Data Structure

The system will maintain a unique batch number master record, on which the data pertaining to that batch will be stored, such as:

- Country of origin
- Date of goods receipt
- Storage location and conditions of storage
- Batch quantity, weight, and dimensions
- Shelf-life expiration date
- Status as warehouse stock or quality inspection stock

Batch Determination in Goods Movement

The use of a material that is managed in batches will be scheduled on a batch number basis so that the material will be selected for withdrawal in order of its date of manufacture, although it is possible to enter a different priority manually or choose batches from a list.

All movements of the material must identify the batches by number.

Managing Special Stocks of Material

The essential characteristic of a special stock of a material is that it is owned by a company or a person different from the owner of the storage location in which it is on inventory. For example, your company may be renting storage space from another company. Your stock will be listed on that company's inventory as special stock. Conversely, you may have special stock on your inventory because it is owned outside your organization. The point is that special stock has to be managed separately for each vendor, customer, or sales order.

Two types of special stock are recognized by the system and managed separately:

- Vendor special stock
- Customer special stock

Vendor Special Stock

There are three types of special stock held on behalf of a vendor:

- Consignment material belonging to the vendor but stored on your premises
- Returnable packaging material belonging to the vendor but stored on your premises
- Material provided by you to the vendor, who is a contractor or subcontractor to you

Customer Special Stock

There are three types of special stock held on behalf of a customer:

- Consignment material that is yours but is still at the customer's location, awaiting your decision as to its disposal
- Your returnable packaging material that is at the customer's location
- Sales order stock that has not been settled and is, therefore, still owned by you

A data entry for special stock movements has to include the identification of the vendor, the customer, or the sales order.

Stock Taking by Physical Inventory

It is a legal requirement that every company perform a physical check of the inventory at least once in the course of a business year. If you have a client enterprise with several company codes representing subsidiaries, then each of them is required to conduct an inventory. SAP R/3 standard business programs are available to carry out the following physical inventory procedures:

- Periodic inventory
- Continuous inventory
- Inventory sampling

The scope of inventory procedures include the following types of material:

- Unrestricted-use stock
- Stock in quality inspection
- Special stock

Inventory Functionality

There are many functions to support the taking of a physical inventory:

- Physical inventory documents can be created.
- Warehouse inventory lists can be printed.
- A block can be placed on stock movements of materials being inventoried.
- Data entry of the results of physically counting the stock is automatically related to the entries on the physical inventory documents.
- Differences between the physical inventory and the book inventory are presented in list format.
- Differences are posted using the items of the physical inventory documents for reference.
- Large differences prompt the creation of documents to support a recount of the discrepant items.

Every physical inventory is recorded for each material and retained indefinitely, so that the history of any stock item can be traced over any number of years for which data has been collected.

Physical Inventory Sampling

When a warehouse contains a very large number of stock management units, it is possible to manage them and conduct a physical inventory of them on the basis of samples. Because the relationship between the sampled items and the rest of the warehouse can be determined automatically, it is possible to infer the full warehouse inventory from the results of physically counting the selected sample.

The goods receipts and issues at the warehouse can be managed using the same technique.

Defining Inventory Procedures for Inventory Types

The legal requirement for conducting a physical inventory is that every storage bin should be checked at least once each fiscal year for quantity and the identity of the material it contains.

The SAP R/3 System allows you to define the physical inventory procedure individually for each storage type. This facility allows you to take account of any special technical or organizational factors concerning the materials or the storage arrangements that should be documented in conjunction with the inventory. The following inventory procedures are provided as standard programs that can be controlled by parameters established during customizing:

- Annual inventory count
- Continuous inventory
- Continuous inventory during stock placement
- Continuous inventory based on zero stock check
- Inventory based on sampling procedure

Marking Bins with an Inventory Indicator   When a storage bin has been inventoried, the corresponding storage bin master record is updated with an inventory indicator showing the date on which an inventory procedure was used on it.

This indicator also serves as legal proof that the physical inventory was carried out.

Posting Differences Automatically   If any difference is detected between the recorded inventory and the physical inventory, the details are posted automatically to an interim storage area record for differences. The MM-IM Inventory Management component has access to this interim storage record, and the inventory manager can authorize the clearing of these differences by difference postings to the appropriate stock accounts.

Automatic Bin Inventory History   A history log is automatically maintained by the system to document the inventory history of every storage bin over a very long time period. This can be accessed in dialog mode.

System Inventory Record   The task of conducting the annual physical inventory is assisted by the system inventory records that are automatically generated when required, and by their associated functions, as follows:

- Printed warehouse inventory list
- Entry functions to post the counting results to the corresponding warehouse inventory list items
- Initiation of a recount if serious discrepancies are detected
- Investigation support to establish the reasons for discrepancies
- Clearing of differences with the semi-automatic creation of explanatory documents

Wherever possible, the SAP R/3 System uses standard text phrases that can be identified by code number and, therefore, stored without wasting space. They are expanded as normal text in the language of the user when needed for display or printing. One application of this technique is to have the system suggest a standard explanation or comment that might be appropriate in a note or annotation. The user may permit the automatic annotation to be added by default, or may require that automatic comment texts be suggested but not posted in the document until they have been approved and perhaps edited by an authorized user.

Inventory Analysis and Display

Stock levels vary as a function of demand and supply. The stock that is available to promise at any particular moment will depend on the activities of several departments. Materials requirements planning, purchasing, sales, and production all affect stock, and may do so in a very uneven manner as their separate requirements and reservations are posted to the materials management system. Reordering is controlled by parameters such as lot size, safety stock, and order quantities. The purpose of inventory analysis is to check that these parameters are optimum for each material on your inventory.

In practice, especially if you have a large number of materials, it may make sense to use sampling inventory techniques.

The results you will be looking for will be in the form of ranking lists of stocks according to various performance measures. You may wish to compare different stock performance measures using a classification display and perhaps a graphical presentation to emphasize the critical features and trends.

You will be particularly interested to know any materials that have a high capital lockup because you have invested financial resources in them that cannot be used elsewhere. You will want to know of cases of inefficient amounts of stock or excess coverage. Dead stock that is no longer used may deserve to be pruned from your inventory.

Inventory Controlling Performance Measures

The MM-IC Inventory Controlling component of the MM application can compile six performance measures for each inventoried material:

- Consumption value using ABC analysis
- Stock value
- Dead stock
- Range of coverage using forecast consumption
- Slow-moving items
- Inventory turnover

By studying these performance measures you can arrive at a judgment as to the effectiveness of the controlling parameters such as safety stock and lot size that are in current use. Standard drill-down facilities enable you to inspect the performance measures in depth so that you can determine which adjustments to make.

Every analysis of inventory can be carried out at any organizational level. A total analysis classifies all materials of an area and gives you an overview. Ranking list analysis gives results that you can filter by specifying threshold limits to the data you wish to scrutinize.

The following data objects are standard for analysis:

- All plants, cumulative
- Sales organization
- Purchasing organization
- Plant

Restricting the Scope of Inventory Analysis

You can selectively restrict the materials that will be used to provide data for either Totals Analysis or Ranking Lists scrutiny.

Limiting by Material Numbers

You can enter a list of material numbers, which may include ranges of numbers, to be selected for analysis or excluded from it.

ABC Analysis

Using boundary limits of your choice, you can have the data classified as A, B, or C, according to the placing of the source of the data in a rank ordering. For example, you could classify A materials as those in the top 5 percent for value, B materials as the next 30 percent, and C materials for the remainder. Then you could ask if the high value A materials had a different range of coverage to the lower value B, and so on.

Limiting by Material Types

If you have assigned your materials to types such as semi-finished materials, operating supplies, and so on, you can specify this type as a means of selecting the materials you wish to analyze.

Period of Analysis

You can use any period for an analysis by specifying the start and finish dates or by choosing one of the standard units of time such as month or financial year.

Quality Management with ISO 9000

The International Standards Organization 9000 series of standards have the goal of improving the practice of quality management throughout industry. In particular, ISO 9000 requires a shift of emphasis, and therefore resources, from the traditional activities of post-production inspection and the rectification of defects, following the concept that the entire production process should be the subject of quality management.

The workloads of quality-relevant activities should map onto the Planning, Production, and Usage phases of manufacturing.

The Planning phase contains the following:

- Market research
- Design
- Testing
- Production planning

The Production phase contains the following:

- Procurement
- Production
- Final inspection
- Warehousing

The Usage phase contains the following:

- Shipping
- Maintenance
- Disposal

Comprehensive QM Functions

The SAP R/3 quality functions are not separated as a CAQ (Computer-Aided Quality) system. They are fully integrated with the R/3 applications and, as such, constitute a CIQ (Computer-Integrated Quality) system.

The activities necessary for personnel quality management are integral to the HR (Human Resources) application. The CO (Controlling) modules plan and manage the costs of assessing and controlling the quality of all resources. Test equipment monitoring for quality purposes is part of the PM (Plant Maintenance) application.

Within the Logistics application, the quality management components support quality planning, quality inspection, and quality control. These functions are applied to procurement, product verification, quality documentation, and corrective action.

Central Functions Used by the QM Module

The central service functions available for all data processing are naturally available to ensure that quality management activities acquire the computing resources they need for processing and archiving quality data. They are as follows:

- The standard R/3 central document management function is used to control quality documents and maintain them in central archives.

- Engineering change management is applied automatically to material masters and ensures that records are kept of any changes to bills of material, master recipes, routings, and inspection plans.

- Material specifications and batch definitions are organized by the R/3 classification system.

- Inspection data can be evaluated and summarized using tools available in the Logistics Information System.

- Quality-related costs can be recorded, settled, and analyzed using the standard controlling functions.

- Graphics tools and interfaces to specialized presentation servers can be used to enhance the presentation and interpretation of quality data.

- Inspections and other quality activities can be scheduled using the Workflow component.

The combined effect of these functions is to provide the user with a flexible method of inspecting the plans and results of quality control tasks. The costs are available, so the profitability of the quality control activities can be assessed in so far as the benefits and failures of quality control operations are recorded in the accounts.

Internal QM Functions

The functions regarded as internal to the quality management module are those that do not directly interact with the processes or data belonging to other modules.

Quality Planning

Separate master data records are maintained for quality planning and inspection planning. Material specifications may be stored specifically for quality management purposes. Inspection plans may be stored and used as required for different QM purposes.

Quality Inspection Management

The QM data may be used to trigger inspections, choose an inspection plan, calculate the appropriate samples, and then process the results.

Shop papers for inspection actions and results may be printed automatically.

Results can be recorded automatically and the defects recorded. The decisions about whether batches shall be used can be automated and the follow-up actions initiated.

Quality Control

The QM module provides facilities for taking sampling decisions dynamically on the basis of sampling result histories. Stocks that have been consistently of high quality may not be sampled as extensively as materials with a history of unpredictable variation.

Inspection results can be summarized as inspection scores, which reflect the quality of the inspection lots.

Notifications about quality problems or trends in quality can be set for automatic distribution if the situation warrants it.

The workflow system can be arranged to take quality notifications and adjust the sequence of operations according to pre-arranged condition rules.

The QMIS (Quality Management Information System) can be primed to collate inspection data and problem data.

Integrating QM

An inspection lot is a group of data records arising from the carrying out of an inspection on a sample of material.

The functions of an inspection lot are

- Document the fact that an event has occurred that should be the occasion for an inspection, such as the arrival of some goods
- Record the status or progress of the inspection process
- Collect all the data concerning the inspection, such as the inspection specification, the results, and the decisions taken regarding usage of the materials

The triggering event that initiates an inspection does not usually arise in the quality department. Other departments will set aside inspection lots for the attention of QM.

QM in Materials Procurement

In accord with the recommendations of ISO 9000, every step of the procurement process should be subject to quality management disciplines. The idea is to do whatever can best raise and maintain quality within the constraints of commercial profitability.

Inquiry QM   Perhaps an inquiry to a vendor can be made more effective by appending a copy of the delivery terms for the material, which may have been defined by the quality department. The purchasing agent may have to be told that the material will not be accepted until it has been released by the quality department. If a particular vendor has failed to keep within the delivery conditions, the quality department can block inquiries to this vendor, block purchase orders, or block goods receipts for specific materials.

Vendor Selection QM   A standard function of the MM materials management application is to inform the buyers of the delivery reliability and price history of each of the vendors under consideration. This information can be presented as a summary in the form of a vendor quality score that is automatically updated from the latest history records.

Purchasing QM   When your purchasing department is seeking an important or valuable material, it may be the practice for the quality department to insist that the vendor is released, as a token of approval, before the purchase order is issued. A particular vendor may only be released under conditions that limit the supply to a particular period of time or to a specified quantity.

These restrictions will be issued with the purchase order and become part of the technical delivery terms and the currently valid quality management agreement. The vendor may be obliged to include a quality certificate with the delivery.

Inspection at the Vendor's Premises   Although goods are normally inspected when they are received, it is possible to create the inspection lot records for materials that have been inspected before they arrive at your plant. EDI, Electronic Data Interchange, is one of the preferred techniques for acquiring inspection data from external sources. SAPmail can also serve the same function.

Goods Receipt Inspection Procedures

The goods receipt is both a document and an event that usually triggers an inspection.

Quality Certificates   One of the first inspection actions is to check whether a quality certificate from the vendor is required as part of the delivery terms. A certificate may cover the entire goods receipt, or it may be necessary for the vendor to supply a separate certificate for each purchase order item or for each batch.

Posting to Inspection Stock   The default arrangement is for the entire delivery of a material on a goods receipt to be posted to inspection stock so that it is classified as "not available." None of the materials management functions can touch the inspection stock until it is released. The materials requirements planning activities will have made an allowance for the delay between goods receipt and release from inspection stock status.

At this time the system creates the inspection lot record, which is subsequently used to gather and store the inspection data and usage decisions.

Planning the Details of the Inspection   In most instances, a suitable inspection plan and sampling procedure will be available in the system. The plan will be chosen according to the material type and any other factors that may have been mandated on the grounds of such factors as the value of the material or the consistency of the quality of the supply.

The inspection plan will specify which attributes of the material are to be inspected, and how many determinations of quality are to be made for each attribute. For instance, the weight of a lot may be taken only once, but some of the physical characteristics may need to be sampled in several places to prove whether the lot is uniform.

Instructions for drawing samples or carrying out other inspection procedures can be printed as soon as the inspection plan has been selected.

Usage   When the inspection lot data has been collected and processed to determine quality, the quantity of the lot that has proved to be acceptable is released by posting it to unrestricted-use stock. If some of the delivery is not accepted, it can be posted as special stock.

This usage decision process ends the control exercised by the quality department over the inspection lot. However, the results of the inspection are posted to update the lot quality record and the inspection lot quality score is applied in the vendor evaluation process.

Updating the Supply Relationship   After each inspection, all quality information relating to the material can be updated, and so can the vendor evaluation. It may happen that the vendor has proved to be reliable in the quality of the material and in meeting the delivery terms in all respects. According to the conditions you have programmed, your system may allow this vendor to be updated from a prototype delivery status to a production delivery relationship.

You can determine how you want to name and use the status indicators of the supply relationship. For example:

- Prototype supply
- Preliminary series
- Production series

You can set the inspection plan choice so that the sampling and other procedures are appropriate to the status of the supply relationship of the vendors.

If the inspection found defects, your system can notify the vendor by an automatic letter or some other quality notification configured for these occasions.

QM in Production

Integrated planning, process controlling, and inspection is the technique of creating process routings that meet the needs of all three disciplines.

For example, test equipment is often assigned as an instance of production resources and tools (PRT) rather than as a quality control resource.

When a production order is created, an inspection lot record is set up at the same time so that all the inspection specification and record keeping shall be associated with this production order. If circumstances arising during manufacturing affect the quantity, for example, then the changes will be copied to the inspection lot records.

Similarly, it is possible to link the confirmation of inspection results with the confirmation of production operations in the PP Production Planning application. By this means, the event of a successful inspection result is combined with the confirmation that a process is complete to generate the more significant event that signals that the process has not only come to an end, but also that the product of this process has passed inspection.

The PP application supports complicated production runs, and the QM functions can integrate with them to match this complexity.

Displaying Production Control Charts

A control chart displays how the quality of a production process is changing, with time or with quantity. The following formats are standard:

- Mean value of each of a series of samples with the acceptance tolerances shown graphically
- Mean value chart without tolerances, known as a "Shewhart Chart"
- Standard deviation chart, which shows how far the samples deviate from the central tendency of the results

You can arrange for the system to issue warnings if the inspection results go outside limits you have set. You may also refer to the variability of previous deliveries.

A process capability index is a display of mean inspection values and their variances compared with limits you have previously defined.

QM in Sales and Distribution

An inspection of goods is triggered by the posting of a delivery note, which is the way that your system knows that a delivery has arrived. The delivery note causes the creation of an inspection lot set of records that are then released. This release declares to the users that there is a delivery for which no inspection results have been posted. There is an inspection lot with no quality data.

If you have configured your system to interpret them, you may be able to read your vendor's quality certificates. You may have created your own forms using SAPscript and obliged your vendors to use them to communicate with your goods receipt department.

Using Catalogs in QM

A catalog is a data structure formed from elements known as codes. These codes can be associated as code groups. The codes and code groups can be accompanied by explanatory text in one or more of the SAP-supported languages.

If you want to say something about a material, you can probably say it using terms taken from the list of standard codes. For example, the following terms are standard codes:

- Accepted
- Rejected

After inspection, every delivery of a material should have one or the other of these two codes in the delivery master record.

Which codes you want to use will depend on the nature of your business. You could probably create a set of terms, one for each of the different types of defect that you might find in your goods receipts. And you could probably group these defect names according to the type of defect, such as dimensions wrong, color wrong, finish poor, wrapping damaged, and so on.

If you now put all your codes on the screen in the form of menus, you could ask your inspectors to write their reports, perhaps entirely, by selecting defect groups and particular terms from these groups.

Over time, your inspectors could amass a collection of these reports, which your system could easily sort and filter using the standard terms as search criteria. Then you could ask for reports to answer questions such as "How many assemblies were delivered with the wrong color?"

This system of using multi-choice menus instead of free text is referred to as a catalog because you can publish a book in which all the items are arranged and sorted according to a uniform system of characteristics. There is no doubt about the meaning of any term in a catalog.

By talking to your experienced inspectors at the time you are configuring your materials management application you can compile a catalog of your materials and the defects you wish to be subject to quality management. From the data processing point of view, this catalog will establish the key words or terms that will always be used to report defects. And for each of these catalog terms your system can have a standard sequence of actions that can be initiated as soon as the defect is discovered.

Inspection Planning

An inspection plan is held as a master data record and called into action by routing during production and by other events such as goods receipt. The inspection plan documents the following elements:

- The inspection operations to be performed
- The characteristics to be examined at each of the inspection operations
- The test equipment to be used

The inspection plan is associated with the current quality level of the material and the outcome will be one or more inspection instructions.

Inspection Instruction

An inspection instruction is a printed or electronic document addressed to an inspector who applies it to a specific inspection lot. The lot inspection instruction defines the scope of the inspection that has to be carried out for each inspection characteristic that has been planned for this inspection lot.

An inspection instruction is technically attached to a particular inspection lot, and is valid on no other lot. However, the inspection plan that was used in defining an inspection instruction can be assigned to more than one lot. The following arrangements are supported:

- An inspection plan is assigned to a specific material.
- An inspection plan is assigned to several materials.
- An inspection plan is assigned to one or more vendors.
- An inspection plan is assigned to one or more customers.

Documenting the Usage Decision

When an inspector has examined an inspection lot and recorded the data required in the inspection instruction, the material is assigned a usage. Some materials have to be documented after every inspection. The other possibilities may be determined according to the material type or as a result of a specific decision by the inspector. Some of these results are as follows:

- The study of the inspection characteristics did not get to the end of the procedure.
- One or more of the inspection characteristics failed to come up to standard in the inspection lot, but the lot was accepted.
- All the inspection characteristics were up to standard in the inspection lot, but the lot was rejected.

An inspection sample may not all be tested if the results are very good and the vendor is a reliable source of high quality material. Some of the characteristics may be taken as satisfactory on the grounds that the attributes actually tested showed no defects.

You can imagine circumstances where a marginal set of inspection results is deliberately overlooked because the material is required in production where allowances can be made to cope with the sub-standard material.

These are deviations from the inspection instruction and have to be documented by the inspector.

If a usage decision is reversed subsequently, the normal process of documenting changes will record the fact and the reasons for the change of usage assignment.

QMIS (Quality Management Information System)

The QM module supports the analysis of stored quality data using predefined SAP R/3 reports and by offering a database from which the user may draw quality information to create customized reports. The module also services the LIS (Logistics Information System) by providing the QMIS (Quality Management Information System).

Using MM to Value Your Materials

The standard approach of the SAP System is to assign values automatically to materials on an ongoing basis. The data is stored in material master records and can be adjusted manually.

When it is necessary to value materials for balance sheet purposes, the system offers the last-in-first-out (LIFO) evaluation procedure, to which the lowest value determination procedure can be applied.

The process of calculating the worth of material stock is titled "valuation" if the result is expressed in terms of monetary value. Of course, some material may be tactically or strategically more valuable to your company than its nominal value might suggest. How the monetary value of a stock of material is computed will depend on the valuation class to which it has been assigned and the valuation procedure in use for materials in this class.

Using Valuation Structures

The scope of a valuation exercise can be controlled by choosing company code or plant to specify the level of the separate valuation areas.

If the valuation area is company code, all the stocks in each company code area are valuated on the same basis, and the results are accumulated over the company code.

If the valuation area is a plant, each plant in the company will have its stocks valuated separately.

Valuation Classes   Materials with similar characteristics can be grouped together to form a valuation class. The FI-GL General Ledger stock account to which the valuation will be posted will depend on the valuation classes assigned to it.

Valuation Categories   Different sets of material valuation criteria can be associated with particular valuation categories. For example, you may wish to use different valuation criteria because the material may have a net value that is partially dependent on where it has come from, the amount of work that has already been done on it, and, perhaps, the taxes or surcharges it has attracted.

The following are examples of valuation categories:

- Procurement
- Origin
- Status

The valuation category system can also be used to represent differences in the condition or makeup of a material. A material stock can be split into separate lots for valuation purposes according to a valuation category scheme based on factors such as:

- Quality
- Batch purity
- Batch quality control results, such as the variance in the critical dimensions
- Batch specification
- Batch history

Valuation Types   Valuation types are nominal values specified for each valuation category. You may decide that your stock of a particular material should be valuated according to the formula specified for each of the valuation types to which it could be assigned. You can specify a different valuation formula for each country of origin, for example, according to the following set of valuation types belonging to the material valuation category Origin:

- Domestic, which may be the country of the plant or the company code
- European community
- USA
- Other country

The lists of possible valuation types and valuation classes are matters that depend on your company's requirements as established during customizing.

Controlling the Criteria for Valuation

Your purchasing organization will be using a price control procedure during its dealings with vendors. This may be a useful source of data upon which to compute a value for a stock of your materials.

The price control strategy in force may be used to determine how a material stock is to be valued:

- Standard pricing requires all the stock of a material to be valued at the same standard price, regardless of the costs of any fresh postings to the inventory.
- Moving average pricing computes the price to be used to value the entire stock of a material by averaging the prices of all postings held in the inventory at the moment when the computation is carried out.

In addition, each material can be selected individually or on the basis of membership of a material group to be subject to last-in-first-out (LIFO) valuation. It can also be allocated to a LIFO pool, and valued in this context.

Stock Valuation Changes   The transactions that can be expected to alter the material stock quantities and stock values include those posted in connection with the following events:

- Goods receipts
- Transfer posting
- Goods issues
- Invoices
- Detection of stock differences between book inventory and physical inventory results

The amounts arising from these transactions will depend on the price control strategy in operation for each material involved.

Valuation Accounting Procedures

The basic valuation procedure entails applying prices to inventory and posting the total to the general ledger. The goal is to have the inventory situation continuously monitored by the system so that reports can be generated at any time. The choice of price control method for a material affects the posting procedure at goods receipt and invoice receipt level.

Standard price control technique uses prices derived from historical data, with various adjustments made to arrive at values that can be used throughout the planning period. All inventory postings are carried out using the standard prices for the materials. If there are variances between the standard price and the amounts charged on invoices or goods receipts, these differences are posted to price difference accounts. These differences provide a method of monitoring price changes and comparing them with the moving average prices, which are displayed for each material in order to provide a comparison.

Moving average price control technique requires that all goods receipts are posted with the goods receipt actual values, rather than standard prices. These acquisition prices are used to update the material master records automatically. There are very few circumstances in which a price variance can arise. This might occur if there are stock shortages. Manual changes to the acquisition price can be effected in the material master, but these are seldom necessary.

Delivery Costs   A purchase order can include an entry for the delivery costs, which will be the planned delivery costs. These will also be entered automatically in a goods receipt posting. These planned delivery costs can be assigned for posting to a freight clearing account or perhaps to a customs clearing account.

The corresponding amount is posted as an offsetting entry to the stock account if standard pricing is in use, or to a price difference account if pricing is based on the moving average.

The delivery costs, therefore, appear either as part of a higher price used in valuating the material, or as a price difference posting.

Cash Discount   The valuation of a material can take account of the terms of payment agreed upon with the vendor and recorded in the purchase order. Your system can make a net posting for both the goods receipt and the invoice receipt to adjust for the cash discount. This discount will lower the moving average price for this material. When the invoice is paid, the cash discount clearing account will receive an offsetting entry for the amount of the cash discount.

Split Valuation   You may wish to place a different value on parts of your stock of a material, perhaps because it has come from a different country of origin, or perhaps because you are splitting your stock on the basis of batches.

Balance Sheet Valuation   When it is necessary to value an inventory for the purpose of drawing up a legal balance sheet, there are two standard computing functions available in the SAP R/3 materials management component:

- Last-in-first-out (LIFO) valuation
- Lowest value price determination

The results of these valuations are used to compute valuation adjustment postings to the FI-GL General Ledger for tax purposes and for commercial reasons concerning financial management.

Last-In-First-Out (LIFO) Valuation   If the market price of a material is rising due to inflation, the value of the company may appear to be increasing merely because the stock held in inventory is increasing in acquisition price. On the other hand, if it is assumed that the material most recently acquired—which will be at the higher price—is the first material to be taken out of the warehouse into consumption, then the value of the stock remaining will be based on the lower acquisition price of the older stock.

This lower price will be the stock valuation used for balance sheet purposes under the LIFO regime.

If there is no difference in the important attributes of the old and the new stock, either can be released to consumption. If a limited shelf life is specified, the older stock will be released first. However, for inventory purposes the valuation will apply the acquisition price of the older stock to the total quantity on inventory.

Similar materials and materials with similar functions can be aggregated into pools that are valued together. The system provides three related procedures for LIFO valuation:

- Quantity LIFO procedure
- Stock layer valuation methods
- Index LIFO procedure

Quantity LIFO Procedure   If the stock at the end of a fiscal year is greater than the stock at the end of a previous year, the system creates a layer, which is a data object. The layer data object contains the following data elements:

- Identification of the fiscal year to which it is assigned
- The material number or material pool number to which it refers
- The quantity of the material in stock at the end of the year
- The quantity of the material in stock at the end of the previous year
- The computed difference in stock of this material between the reference year and the previous year

The increase in stock of this material in the year is defined as the layer, and the value of this layer is calculated using the price for this year.

The layer defined by the stock of this material carried over from the previous year will still be on inventory, and will be valued at the price used when the inventory was valued for balance sheet purposes at the end of the previous fiscal year.

When the time comes to value the stock of this material at the end of this financial year, the quantity may be less than the previous year because the quantities issued have exceeded the quantities received. In such cases, the balance sheet valuation procedure has to decide which layer of stock is to be regarded as the source of the stock consumed; should it be the older layer or the newer?

If the LIFO procedure is in operation, valuation will start valuing the stock consumed as if the most recently acquired layer is the source, regardless of whether goods issued has actually been on the basis of batch production date, delivery batch date, or some other regime. The price of the goods consumed from inventory will be taken from the stock layer for the current year until the quantity in this layer has all been assigned to the consumption account. If yet further quantities of this stock must be considered in order to reach the quantity consumed in the year, the price will be taken from the stock layer for the previous year in accord with the last-in-first-out rule.

Stock Layer Valuation Methods   The SAP R/3 System provides various methods for valuing a stock layer of a material or material pool:

- Valuation on the basis of the current value of the moving average price maintained in the material master record.

- Price for the total year is the result of a calculation that carries out valuation on the basis of the moving average price for all goods receipts in the reporting year.

- Price for the partial year is the result of valuing the stock of each material on the basis of the moving average price for goods receipts in part of the reporting year specified in terms of the number of months, starting with the first month in the reporting year.

- Price by quantity is arrived at by applying the moving average price for each period separately, starting at the beginning of the year and stopping when the quantity of stock that has been valued is equal to the quantity recorded in the stock layer master.

The differences among these methods can be expressed as a difference in the assumptions made about the value of the stock in a layer:

- Valuation of the whole layer at the current moving average price assumes that the value of the stock has kept in step with the moving average price, and, therefore, the balance sheet should show what it is worth by applying the moving average price as it is at the time of the report, which may be some months after the end of the fiscal year being reported.

- Price for the total year valuation assigns to the whole layer the moving average price current at the end of the reporting year.

- Price for partial year valuation assumes that the most reasonable price to use for the balance sheet is the moving average taken over the beginning few months of the reporting year.

- Price by quantity valuation assumes that the balance sheet will be truest if the stock is valued by valuing a layer at the moving average price determined on a month-by-month basis, whereby it is more closely in tune with the cash flows of the company at the time.

Index LIFO Procedure   The index procedure refers to a price index for the material or material pool, and manages it by value alone. The value of a layer of a material or a material pool at the end of a fiscal year is calculated using a price index and is recorded as the base year value of the layer.

At the end of the year, the value of the pool is recalculated using the price index applied to the base year value of the previous year. If the pool includes various layers from previous years, their separate values using their own base year prices are added together. If the value of the pool is greater than the total of the values of the separate layers, a new layer is created for the reporting year, and valued by the amount of this increase. If the value of the whole pool using the current base price is less than the total of the values of the separate parts, the LIFO rule is applied, and the most recent layer is diminished in value until the pool is valued at the amount calculated on the basis of the price index applied to the base year.

Lowest Value Determination

In the custom and practice of drawing up a balance sheet, the valuation of the inventory can take place in accord with either of the following principles:

- The strict lowest value principle specifies that, where the price of a material can be determined by more than one method, the lowest value *must* be used.
- The moderate lowest value principle specifies that, where the price of a material can be determined by more than one method, the lowest value *may* be used.

For example, the value of a stock layer can be calculated on the basis of the acquisition costs of the raw materials or other components, to which you add the production costs. The alternative might be to value the layer at the price quoted on the appropriate commodity exchange or other market price listing.

The SAP R/3 System is able to support a range of procedures for automatically computing the lowest value that could be applied to stocks of material procured externally.

Valuation Perspectives

The value of stock to your company can be computed from different points of view. You could use market prices, how many working days of stock you held, or you could factor in some reflection of the extra storage costs incurred by slow-moving stocks.

Lowest Value by Market Prices   The value for a material on inventory at the end of the fiscal year can be calculated automatically by nominating the following sources of information:

- Purchase orders
- Contracts
- Purchasing info records
- Receipts of goods for purchase orders

Your procedure would note the price of each material every time it appeared in any of these documents.

Lowest Value by Range of Coverage   The range of coverage represents the time that the inventory stock of a material will last according to an estimate of its rate of consumption. The range of coverage can be based on past consumption data or on the values forecast.

The lowest value for a stock layer can be determined according to the range of coverage, calculated in months, and a percentage discount is then applied, depending on the number of months.

Lowest Value by Movement Rate   The movement rate of a material is an index of the relation between goods receipts and goods issues of the material. It is calculated as a percentage.

If a material is classed as slow-moving or non-moving, a devaluation indicator is set for it that will cause the system to apply a percentage reduction in value according to the calculation rule specified for the devaluation indicator.

Linked Valuation Procedures   The system allows you to link valuation procedures in sequence. For example, you can have the system determine the lowest price of a material according to market prices and then apply a reduction to allow for range of coverage or movement rate.

Posting Results of Lowest Value Determination

The outcome of material valuation using the lowest value determination procedure can be used to update the commercial price field and the tax field in the material master record.

Once this has been accomplished, you can call at any time for a list covering all your materials on inventory, in which the system will offer proposals on how you could effect transfer postings for the purpose of devaluing your individual stock accounts.

Goods Receipt Posting Procedure

When you post a goods receipt, the system will multiply the net order price by the quantity, and post the resulting value to the goods receipt and invoice receipt clearing account in the FI-GL General Ledger. If the price control technique in use is standard price, the quantity entered is valued at the standard price. If there is a difference between the net order price and the standard price for the order, the difference is posted to the price difference account.

When the corresponding invoice is received and entered, the goods receipt and invoice receipt clearing account is cleared—if there is no difference in the prices. Otherwise, the difference is posted to the price difference account, where it should clear the amount previously posted there when the goods were received and found by the system to be priced at a set of rates different from the standard.

If the moving average price control technique is being used, the difference is posted to the stock account, where it will contribute to the average price next time this is computed.

Using MM to Manage Your Warehouse

The MM-Warehouse Management component is designed to support the efficient and effective processing of logistic requirements within a company. In particular, the following logistics operations are provided with standard business functions:

- Manage complex warehouse structures
- Define and manage storage bins
- Manage storage types
- Create transfer orders
- Monitor stock movements
- Execute stock placement and removal strategies
- Process differences
- Manage hazardous materials
- Take inventory at the storage bin level
- Use bar codes
- Make use of warehouse reports

The MM-WM Warehouse Management system supports the processing of all movements, including goods receipts and goods issues initiated by the inventory management system, and goods issues from the sales and distribution system.

The MM-WM Warehouse Management system provides control over the movements within a warehouse, including stock transfers for replenishment orders.

Transactions in the inventory management system or in the sales and distribution system automatically trigger the Warehouse Management system to generate transfer requirements such as:

- Material movements
- Staging of materials for production orders
- Shipping of goods for sales orders

The representation of the warehouse structure in the SAP R/3 System follows the standard system of hierarchical levels stored in master records, starting with the client code, which is unique, below which there may be one or more company codes, each of which may operate one or more plants and warehouses.

Tables of logical and numerical values are provided so that you can adjust the system to make it represent the detailed structure and relationships within your configuration of warehouses and storage locations.

Warehouse Number

The physical warehouse complex is represented as a single number identifying that warehouse, and a warehouse master record on which a data structure may be stored.

Each warehouse will include various types of storage locations.

Storage Type

A storage type can be differentiated by its physical location, its technical characteristics, and its place in the organizational structure of operational units and cost centers.

A storage type is divided into sub-areas that may use different storage techniques and serve different functions or parts of the organization.

The sub-areas of a storage type will be divided into storage bins.

Storage Bin

A storage bin is the smallest part of a storage area within a storage type that can be addressed for the purpose of directing material there or withdrawing material from it. All products within a storage bin, or in a space that is treated as a storage bin, are regarded as of exactly the same type. Any one of them can be withdrawn for assignment to an order or transfer. There is no effective difference between them.

Storage Section

A storage section is a grouping of storage bins represented as a section in the system according to criteria defined by the user. You can associate them because they have certain characteristics in common. They do not necessarily have to share a location in a warehouse.

Storage Bin Type

The size of a storage bin is used to assign that bin to a storage bin type. The type is used in storage bin search to build up the quantity of material required for a transfer. Thus the bin type represents a quantity.

Using Transfer Requirement Documents

When a movement of stock has been planned in the MM-Materials Management system and needs to be executed by the MM-WM Warehouse Management system, a transfer requirement document has to be created. This can be done manually in the MM-WM Warehouse Management system, or it can be generated automatically in response to a goods movement posting in the MM-Materials Management system.

The transfer requirement can be used to plan for the following operations:

- Place goods into stock
- Remove goods from stock
- Prepare for other goods transfers by moving stock within the warehouse

The transfer requirement does not execute the stock movement. A movement will be executed only if a transfer order has been created and confirmed.

If you want to know what should be moved, and how much, the creation of a transfer requirement will provide the answers. If a movement has already been started by the confirmation of a transfer order and you try to create a transfer requirement for the same goods, you will discover whether the order was created automatically or manually, and whether an amount of the transfer has already been moved.

Stock movements are controlled by transfer orders that specify the material number, the quantity, and the storage bins from which the stock is to be removed. A transfer order is also used to release goods from quality inspection, even if no physical movement is entailed.

Goods Receipt

A typical delivery of goods to a warehouse entails the following series of tasks:

- A delivery vehicle arrives, and the supervisor has the system create a material movement document.
- The system generates a transfer requirement and a quantity posting to the goods receipt area.
- The goods are unloaded to the goods receipt area.
- The system creates a transfer order for the goods to assign them to destination storage bins, which are then reserved for these goods.
- The transfer order is printed or electronically displayed to the goods movement section.
- The goods are transferred to the storage bins reserved for them.
- The quantities in the storage bins are checked and confirmed to the system.
- The system prints the confirmation from the storage bin checking operation on the transfer order document, which is then confirmed.
- The system updates the inventory so that the goods are available for consumption or further movement.

The transfer order can support the following types of goods receipt:

- Goods receipt based on a purchase order
- Goods receipt without a reference purchase order
- Goods receipt destined for an in-house production order
- Goods receipt for a batch reserved for inspection
- Goods receipt from a customer who is returning goods that are unwanted for any reason

Goods Issue

The transfer order function can also affect goods issues for the following purposes:

- Goods issues to a cost center
- Goods issues to a project
- Staging of materials for production
- Delivery of goods to customers

Picking Goods for a Delivery Note or Transfer Order

If the SAP R/3 SD-Sales and Distribution module has been installed and configured, the MM-WM Warehouse Management system can be automatically tasked to begin the picking of goods as soon as the delivery note has been posted.

If goods are to be picked using the fixed bin picking procedure, the bin to be used will be determined from the material master, updated by goods receipts and withdrawals. If the warehouse is organized on a random basis, a transfer order will be created for each delivery item. When the transfer order is confirmed in the system, each delivery item will be updated by the quantities picked, which may not be the same as the quantities planned. In such instances, a difference is documented.

Posting Changes and Stock Transfers

If a transaction does not entail the physical movement of goods, such as the receipt of goods, their issue, or their movement from one storage location to another within the warehouse, the system will be able to offer the following choice of posting changes and stock transfer functions:

- Release stock from quality inspection
- Convert stock from consignment stock to company stock
- Effect a posting change from one batch to another
- Change a material number of a quantity of stock
- Accept the return of goods and complete the necessary processing
- Effect a posting change for a stock replenishment warehouse

Transfer Confirmation Option

Some stock movements may have to be confirmed. The system provides a confirmation function, which will execute a confirmation automatically as soon as the physical transfer has taken place. If the planned quantity is not the same as the actual quantity transferred, you can record the difference before confirming the transfer order.

If certain stock movements require confirmation, the system will not recognize any change in the relevant storage bins until the confirmation process is completed. You have to inform the system that the processing for the transfer order is finished. If only some of the transfer order items are subject to confirmation, you can register the confirmation on an individual item basis.

Informing Inventory Management of Differences

If the processing of a transfer order reveals that some of the goods were damaged during transit, or the quantities in the storage bins were insufficient or of the wrong material or batch specification, the system will have to be informed in the transfer order confirmation. This will automatically generate a difference posting to inventory management.

Automation of Transfer Order Processing

You have the facility to determine which functions can be executed automatically and which must be held up until a valid manual input has been entered.

The control functions also direct the warehouse documents to the appropriate printer or other output channel. The output can include bar codes.

Search Strategies in Warehouse Management

The method used by the system to find the storage bins to be used for the placement or withdrawal of stock is defined as a strategy. When the system has used a strategy to find a suitable set of storage bins, it will propose these for your approval or for you to change by manual entry.

The advantages of applying predefined search strategies are that the warehouse can be managed in an optimal manner for stock placements, and the system can quickly find the materials specified for stock removals.

This approach can be applied to all types of warehouse configurations and placement regimes.

Storage Type Search

You can specify that a particular material is to be stored in a specific type of storage. You can also assign classes of material to specific storage types. For example, materials of the subassembly type could be stored in high rack storage area number 1. Materials of the finished assembly type could be stored in protected area 6.

Storage Section Search

Each material can be assigned to a particular area within the storage type for that material group. For example, fast-moving items could go in the front area, slow-moving items in the back area.

Bin Type Search

Certain bin types can be assigned to specific storage unit types so that the goods placed there can be accommodated in the best possible bin type. For example, bin types can be defined as pallets, wire baskets, or warehouse floor area. Each of the bins of each type will be identified by number and, through the bin master record, by storage type and location. Restrictions on the type of materials to be stored in a bin type may also be established in the bin type master record.

Storage Bin Search

The search for a specific storage bin can be conducted using a similar strategy for both stock placement, which will be looking for unoccupied bins, and stock removal, which will be looking for bins occupied by the material required—subject to other constraints depending on the stock removal strategy being employed.

Stock Placement Strategies in Warehouse Management

Stock placement strategies can be specified to enable the system automatically to generate proposals for the placement of any stock arriving at a warehouse. Some stock placement strategies are as follows:

- Next Empty Bin—The material is placed in the next suitable empty bin.
- Fixed Bin—The material is always assigned to the same fixed bin.
- According to User Entry—The system does not make any proposal for placing the stock, but waits for the user to enter a destination.
- Addition to Stock Already in a Bin—The system finds a bin that already contains this material and attempts to place it there, unless this would exceed the capacity of the bin, in which case it automatically begins a search for another suitable bin. If no space can be found in an occupied bin, a suitable empty bin is used.
- Block Storage—Block storage is specified for materials that are to be stored in large quantities without taking up too much storage space.
- Shelf Sections—Shelf section storage is used where the storage area is able to take a different number of delivery units, depending on the size of the unit. For example, three European standard pallets can be stored in the space taken by two pallets of the size previously common in industry.

Stock Removal Strategies in Warehouse Management

The choice of stock removal strategy is constrained by the placement of the goods in storage bins according to the placement strategies. The system will know where everything is located, down to the bin identification.

There are two main stock removal strategies that can be assigned to a specific material: FIFO and LIFO. The others are explained in the following sections.

FIFO

FIFO (first-in-first-out) requires that the materials to be removed first are those that have been in the warehouse longest. They will have the earliest goods receipt date.

LIFO

LIFO (last-in-first-out) selects for first removal those goods with the most recent goods receipt date.

Combining Partial Quantities

If the system finds that a material has been placed in a storage type that includes storage areas that are not all completely full to capacity, it seeks to fulfill the transfer order by selecting a combination of full and partly full storage areas that will exactly match the quantity required. This will tend to optimize the use of storage facilities and the material-handling activities.

According to Quantity

A warehouse may contain two types of storage area for the same material: one for large delivery units containing a large quantity of the material, the other for single assemblies or small deliverable units.

Assigning the Strategy

You can define a search strategy parameter instructing the system which removal source to use on the basis of a set quantity of the material required.

Splitting Large Delivery Units

You can also arrange the splitting of large delivery units so that they could be assigned to different storage locations. This may be necessary because you cannot hold the entire delivery in any of your available locations, or you may wish to store the delivery as two or more stocks because you are going to manage them differently once they are in your warehouse.

Storage Unit Management

The storage unit management function in the MM-WM Warehouse Management component is able to maintain storage unit number records that include indicators of the type of storage unit, such as pallet, wire basket, and so on.

Under this storage unit number it is possible to group material quantities in logical units comprising a homogeneous or a mixed quantity of materials.

The storage unit number master record also stores data about the single material or combination of materials contained in the storage unit, such as:

- The material number
- The quantity of material

■ Which operations have been performed on this material

■ When this storage unit was last subjected to physical inventory

Storage Unit Functions

The following activities can be initiated from the storage unit management component:

■ Create a transfer order for one or more storage units.

■ Confirm a stock movement.

■ Add stock to existing storage units.

■ Print documents to accompany the storage unit.

One of the uses for a storage unit system is to assemble a set of constituents or component parts that are thereafter documented and marshaled to the production or sales processes as a single composite object.

MM Special Functions

The MM-Materials Management special functions comprise the following program elements:

■ Consignment material

■ Special stocks of consignment material

■ Material movements

■ Subcontracting

■ Vendor special stocks

■ Goods receipt from a subcontractor

■ Physical stock transfers by stock transport orders

The MM special functions can operate in any of the constituent components:

■ MM-MRP Material Requirements Planning

■ MM-IM Inventory Management

■ MM-IV Invoice Verification

Consignment Material Processing

If you buy material from a vendor and pay for it, this material is valued on your balance sheet. However, the vendor may have delivered to your company a stock of material that you do not have to pay for unless and until you need it. Such material is treated as consignment material, and it will not be valued on your balance sheet even though it will be on your inventory.

You may return the consignment material, or part of it, when you no longer expect to need it.

If you do withdraw for consumption a partial quantity of consignment stores, or transfer it to your own stock, the quantity you move will be valued at the vendor's defined selling price, and you will have to pay for it. Settlement of consignment material is usually effected on a monthly or quarterly basis.

Special Stocks of Consignment Material

You can manage consignment material using the normal material number, and you will be able to call on the associated data from the material master records. However, these special stocks of consignment material are managed in separate areas of the storage location, according to vendor. Purchase prices of consignment stocks withdrawn are recorded according to vendor, and a moving average price is maintained on the vendor master records for valuation purposes.

Material Movements

When a goods receipt is processed for a consignment order item or a consignment scheduling agreement, the value and quantity are posted, according to the special stock indicator, to one of the following stock master record data fields:

- Unrestricted-use stock
- General goods receipt blocked stock
- Stock in quality inspection

The same actions can be carried out on batches of consignment material if the system has been customized to apply the batch status management facility.

Consignment materials can also be withdrawn in a random sample for quality inspection.

All the movements will be posted under the control of the special stock indicator so that the pricing and valuation procedures will be alerted to the special circumstances.

There may be a contract in force stipulating that consignment stock remaining at the end of the fiscal year is to be transferred to the company's own stock. Such a transfer may be effected at other times as a periodic replenishment of company stock according to consumption or planned requirements.

Reservation of consignment stock can be effected as a method of planning the withdrawal of material to consumption or in replenishment of company stock.

Subcontracting

The subcontract order is a method of outsourcing a business process. The subcontracting function in the MM-Materials Management module offers support for the following operations:

- Placing an outside contract for production activities and services
- Providing material components to the subcontractor for the production or assembly processes

- Issuing material, such as equipment, to the subcontractor from the ordering company's own stock of plant

- Posting as goods receipts the services performed and the goods produced by the subcontractor

- Posting the consumption or usage of the issued material in the same transaction as the services and goods receipts

Vendor Special Stocks

It may be convenient to maintain a stock of your materials at the premises of a subcontractor. These will be represented in your database as vendor special stocks, because they are not available for other purposes, but still belong to your company because you engaged the subcontractor as a vendor.

If the material to be provided to a subcontractor has to be drawn from several batches, the identity of these batches is recorded in the delivery documents in case they are returned from the subcontractor or are subject to reversal because, for example, they are damaged or faulty.

Goods Receipt from a Subcontractor

When goods that have been produced or assembled by a subcontractor are received at the contracting company, the quantities of the materials supplied are valued at their valuation price taken from the material master records. The quantity and value are posted out of the stock for each material, and the quantities are included in the consumption statistics.

The value of the material received from the subcontractor is computed as the net purchase order value plus the valuation cost of the material posted out of stock for this subcontract.

If the material is managed in batches, a separate goods issue item is created for each batch from which materials have been provided to the subcontractor.

If some of the material used was already being held by the subcontractor as vendor special stock, this amount will appear as default values in the ratio of goods receipt quantity to purchase order quantity, which can be corrected by the user.

When the invoice is received from the subcontractor, the quantity of each material, which will have been already posted to consumption, can be corrected to account for any differences between the planned usage and the actual.

Physical Stock Transfers by Stock Transport Orders

You can transfer stock by means of a stock transport order if there are two or more plants in your company. The plants concerned may be production facilities or warehouses. This can make sense if the costs of transporting stock are significant and if the time in transit is considerable.

The acquisition price of this material for the receiving plant is computed as the valuation of it in the issuing plant plus the costs of delivery. If it should happen that the material is subject to moving average price control, the moving average price may change after each delivery.

The receiver plant orders the material from the issuing plant and plans the delivery costs such as packaging, freight, transport insurance, customs duty, unloading, and so on. The planned delivery costs are recorded in the specific item of the order.

The source of the material posts a goods issue referring to the stock transport order. The quantity withdrawn from stock at this issuing plant is listed as stock in transit at the receiving plant.

When the goods arrive at the receiving plant, the system is posted with the goods receipt document referring to the goods transport order. This event has the effect of reducing the quantity and value of the stock in transit account and the value of the total of the purchase orders still open at the receiving plant.

Decentralized Warehouse Management

An asynchronous program-to-program communication interface can be installed to integrate the SAP R/3 MM-WM Warehouse Management system with, for example, the SAP R/2 applications for Materials Management, Sales, and Distribution.

Stock movements in the SAP R/2 Materials Management system initiate quantity postings in the SAP R/3 MM-WM Warehouse Management system as required. Delivery orders are transmitted to a decentralized warehouse unit for shipping. When picking is completed and confirmed, the actual quantities are ready for transmitting to the SAP R/2 host computer. If the host is not available at the time, any differences on the delivery orders and any goods receipts taken from the production department are entered in the terminal of the decentralized SAP R/3 warehouse unit. When the host becomes available again, the SAP R/2 central inventory management system is updated from the SAP R/3 decentralized unit.

From Here...

- How can I decide how my materials should be documented in an SAP R/3 MM database?
  See Chapter 6, "Understanding the SAP R/3 Business Engineer."
- How do I use my computer to do more than just manage my materials?
  See Chapter 9, "Understanding Network Computing."

Knowing How Materials Management Fits into SAP R/3

5 Integrating MM   171

6 Understanding the SAP R/3 Business Engineer   205

7 Analyzing Materials Information   289

8 Utilizing Reports and Interfaces   313

9 Understanding Network Computing   343

10 MM Education and Training   367

Integrating MM

In this chapter

- What happens when you post an invoice
- How materials management relates to production
- How customer-driven production can be achieved
- How sales and distribution use materials management techniques
- How human resource management connects to materials management

A materials management system that stands alone can make your company more profitable than it would be if your goods and services were to be bought, sold, and stored in a haphazard manner. But the benefits to the profitability of your enterprise can be considerably increased if you take advantage of the links that are already formed between the materials management application and other parts of SAP R/3 that you may have installed and configured.

Relating MM to Your Accounting and Other Modules

The accounting functions of SAP R/3 are closely integrated at the software level with the functions for managing materials. In practice, the user will find that most relationships are working automatically as soon as the system goes live into production.

If you have installed and configured the relevant components, you could be working with a fully-integrated system that is comprised of the following applications:

- FI-Financial Accounting
- CO-Controlling
- FI-FA Fixed Assets Management
- MM-Materials Management

Some companies will add to this list of applications integrated with materials management by linking to their human resources system to staff the purchasing and MRP departments, for example. If your enterprise includes manufacturing, then the production planning and control applications may also be configured into the complex.

The functionality of this integrated system can be demonstrated by following the sequence of event-driven process chains that become active when you post an invoice for the purchase of some materials or services.

Materials Invoice Verification

The verification of an invoice is a standard business process that has to carry out the following tasks before your accounting department is invited to release the invoice for payment:

- Check the invoice to determine the items in it
- Check the price of each invoice item
- Check the calculations for each item

Before an invoice item can be checked, the vendor has to be identified and the details of the vendor in the invoice header have to be compared with the information in the vendor master record.

There are two obvious ways to determine the vendor:

- Look up the reference to a purchase order that should be available in the invoice
- Look up the reference to the vendor that should be available in the goods receipt

These methods are so obvious that your system will automatically use them as appropriate and suggest to you the result so that you can confirm the origin of the invoice. However, it is worthwhile to trace what happens in the two situations.

Entering a Materials Invoice That References a Purchase Order

If you are entering an invoice receipt that has a reference to a purchase order, you have only to enter or confirm the order number, and the system will propose the vendor and also the following data:

- Tax postings
- Terms of cash discount
- Individual quantities and values of each material

You can call upon any line item and correct any of the entries that have been proposed by the system.

When you post the invoice receipt, the system will send you system messages to inform you of any variances between the invoice data and the purchase order data.

Finding a Materials Reference

If you are verifying an invoice and wish to inspect the original sources, you have several options:

- Inspect the SAP Document that was generated as a result of receiving the vendor invoice as an incoming EDI (electronic document interchange)
- Inspect the SAP Document that was generated by scanning a vendor invoice using the ArchiveLink interface
- Consult the purchase order

In each case, your system will find what you need and display it on your screen without disturbing the invoice you are verifying.

The wide range of standard SAP R/3 display and data entry functions is available for use in the invoice verification process. For example, if the reference proposed automatically by the system does not appear to be the right one, you can search for an open purchase order for a specific vendor or for a particular material.

Multiple Order References

If you are trying to verify an invoice that appears to include items from several different purchase orders, you can initiate a search for all open purchase orders. Better still, you could ask for all open purchase orders that use the same vendor or that include items that correspond to the materials in the multiple order you are verifying.

Part
II

Ch
5

Accessing Related Information

If you have a query regarding an invoice presented for payment, and you are responsible for releasing this item for payment, you may have to consult widely to clear the query. For instance, the normal commercial documents will probably inform you on accounting matters such as purchase order details, order history, or vendor data, but they may not give you the information you require. The function to retrieve related information enables you to access additional information such as material specifications and handling data. You could drill down on this data and find any technical documents linked to the material master records.

Discovering an Incorrect Invoice

If you receive a system message informing you that there is some variance between the planned amounts and the actual amounts, or if you are aware of this anyway, you must write the new values over the proposed quantities and values.

Overwriting Each Variance

The following causes of variance may exist, perhaps at the same time:

- Quantity variance
- Quality variance
- Price variance
- Schedule variance
- Project budget overrun

For each discrepancy, you must make a correction before posting the invoice receipt.

Defining Tolerances

To protect your invoice verifying staff from excessive outpourings of system messages, you can define tolerances for individual variances by establishing upper and lower limits within which the system will accept the discrepancy.

The maximum amount each type or grade of user is permitted to post during invoice verification is determined during MM-Materials Management Customizing.

You are allowed to re-define tolerance limits for the individual invoice items so that you will not be subjected to unimportant system messages. If the lower limit is exceeded, you will be informed that the lower limit should be corrected. If the upper limit is exceeded, the system will allow you to post the invoice receipt document, but the line item will be marked with a blocking key code and the whole invoice will be blocked for payment.

Automatic Invoice Blocking and Reasons

When an invoice item has been found to have a discrepancy that exceeds the upper tolerance limit, the item is marked with a key indicating the reason, and the whole invoice is blocked. An item can be assigned several blocking reasons at the same time. For example, both the price and the quantity may be seriously outside the tolerance limits.

Releasing a Blocked Invoice

If you call up a list of all blocked invoices, you can deal with each one in a variety of ways.

Canceling Individual Blocking Reasons

You may decide to cancel one or more of the individual item blocking reason keys if further investigation uncovers a good reason for the discrepancy. For example, you may discover that a price variance is justified, but there is still a discrepancy in the quantity.

Adjusting the Date for Terms of Payment

You may not wish to upset the relationship with your supplier by blocking an invoice. You might decide to release the invoice for payment, perhaps after changing the date from when the terms of payment are valid, so that the financial accounting department can pay the invoice without waiting for the outcome of an investigation into the reason for the variance.

Blocking Reason Is No Longer Valid

Sometimes the reason for blocking an invoice may no longer be valid. Perhaps the shortage in delivery quantity has been made up, or perhaps the critical date in a schedule has passed.

Automatic Blocking Release

You can release an invoice yourself, or the system will automatically release all blocked invoices for which the reasons are no longer valid.

Accounting Functions Available for Materials Invoice Processing

Materials invoice verification uses the functionality of Accounts Payable Accounting from the FI-Financial Accounting application.

Release Transactions for Blocked Invoices

To release a blocked invoice receipt for payment by FI-Financial Accounting, you must enter a separate release transaction to document how you have resolved the discrepancy that caused the blocking.

Assuming that the system has accepted any variances between the purchase order and the invoice receipt, the act of posting the invoice will create a document to record the event and post the amounts to the relevant accounts, which are determined automatically. At the same time, the price history will be updated if the invoice has referred to a purchase order.

If the material in an invoice item is marked to be valued by the moving average price method, the relevant material master record will be updated at this time with the price and value of the material.

Posting an Invoice Receipt

When an invoice receipt is posted in the MM-Materials Management component, the system verifies it with the data in the purchasing and goods receipt functions, and then transmits the information to the accounting modules:

- FI-Financial Accounting
- CO-Controlling
- FI-AM Assets Management

When the invoice receipt is successfully posted, an open item is generated in the vendor account that will not be cleared until the FI-Financial Accounting component has confirmed that payment has taken place. In order to do this, the invoice receipt must reference a purchase order or goods receipt to be able to have access to the details of the materials and quantities.

Entering Invoices with Reference to a Goods Receipt

If the invoice arrives with a reference to a goods receipt, the accounts payable clerk will enter the document number for the goods receipt or the delivery slip number. The system will locate the required data and propose it for inclusion in the document that will record the receipt of the invoice. Alternatively, the user can enter the purchase order number to elicit the same information.

An individual delivery can be settled by entering the invoice receipt with a reference to the delivery note or goods receipt document.

If you enter a purchase order number during the invoice receipt entry, the system will create an invoice item for each item on the order for each goods receipt. This enables you to relate each particular goods receipt item to the order item to which it belongs.

Entering Invoices That Have No Order Reference

A bill for expenses at a hotel, for example, does not necessarily have any reference item in the system from which the details can be retrieved so that the system can propose the details for invoice receipt entry.

In such cases of purchases without purchase orders, you first create a vendor item and then create a document item corresponding to each item on the invoice you have received, so as to record all the details of the material or service for which payment will have to be made.

The resulting document can be posted to a material account, a general ledger account, or a fixed asset account, as appropriate.

Adjusting Items Before Posting an Invoice

The standard facilities for document editing allow you to adjust an invoice receipt document as many times as you need before you post it.

Document Simulation by Preliminary Document Entry

If you call for simulation of a document rather than posting, you can see the balance for the document and how the accounts would change if you were to actually post this particular invoice at this moment or at some future date.

The method of generating a simulation is to save the document as a preliminary document. This can be used if you have to interrupt invoice verification for any reason before the details are finished. You can subsequently re-open a preliminary document and continue where you left off.

A preliminary document is not posted, so there are no changes to the accounts. However, the calculations are carried out and you can see what the effects on the accounts would be if you were to go ahead and complete the transaction with a posting.

This simulation feature is useful if you have to answer questions from a business partner or check how much you may expect to pay in sales taxes, for example.

Automatic Creation of Tax Items

The system can be provided with the INT-International module, from which you can obtain automatic access to the valid deductible and non-deductible tax types for your own country and any other countries for which the module has been configured.

As the invoice receipt is entered, the tax record and the tax amount will also be entered, if they are part of the invoice. The system will check the correctness of the invoice amount, the tax record or code, and the tax amount. If there are any variances, the system will inform you via system messages, but you will still be allowed to post the invoice receipt.

If the invoice receipt does not include a tax amount, the tax can be calculated by the system using the local tax module. If the invoice items have different tax records or codes, the tax is calculated for each one separately.

When you post an invoice receipt, the appropriate tax items are created automatically.

Cash Discounts at Invoice Posting

If a cash discount is part of the agreed terms for a purchase order, you can make a net posting for the goods receipt and for the invoice receipt.

The moving average price of materials being priced on this basis will be reduced as a result of the stock posting of the relevant discount amount. An offsetting entry will be made automatically to a cash discount clearing account, where it will remain until cleared at payment.

Standard Terms of Payment

During the process of entering an invoice receipt, you can nominate the terms of payment. The standard terms of payment are expressed in the following manner, for example:

- 3-percent cash discount applies if payment is made within 10 days
- 2-percent cash discount applies if payment is made within 20 days
- Net payment is required within 30 days

The system will propose the conditions from the purchase order or suggest the standard conditions as specified in the vendor master record.

Methods of Clearing a Cash Discount

The cash discount can be cleared as a gross posting or as a net posting, as you specify.

Gross Posting   The effect of specifying clearance by gross posting is to have the system ignore any cash discount amounts until the invoice is cleared for payment, when the discount amount is posted to a separate account assigned for the purpose of recording cash discounts.

The advantage of this procedure is that the balances in the stock account and the cost accounts are not affected by the cash discount.

Net Posting   If the posting is to be cleared net, the cash discount amount is credited directly to the account to which the costs detailed on the invoice receipt are posted. The cost center, for example, will receive only the net amount from the invoice.

Excluding Items from Cash Discount   If an item on an invoice is not going to attract any cash discount for early payment, it can be so marked on the invoice receipt document and thereby excluded from any discount calculations.

Procedures Used with Materials Invoice Verification

Although the invoice verification process can be conducted automatically when everything is in order, there will be occasions when your materials supervisor will have to intervene and exercise some of the available functions directly.

Entering Invoices in Foreign Currency

It is the practice in SAP R/3 systems that invoices shall be posted only in local currency. If the user wishes to enter the invoice receipts in another currency, the system will convert the amounts to the local currency and record both in the invoice receipt document.

The method of establishing the exchange rate to use in currency conversion can be any of the following:

- A fixed exchange rate is stated on the purchase order.
- The exchange rate to be used is stored in the system.
- The exchange rate to be used is entered directly during invoice verification.

Assigning a Material Invoice to Different Accounts

Any materials not procured for stock and services must identify the accounts to which the amounts are to be assigned. An amount can be distributed to more than one account on a percentage basis or in terms of fixed amounts.

If an account has been assigned in a purchase order, that account cannot be changed if a goods receipt that has been subjected to valuation is entered during invoice verification. If the goods receipt has not been valued, the accounts payable clerk can change the account assignment.

Incurring Additional Costs After a Transaction Is Cleared

If a transaction has already been cleared and additional costs are incurred, it will be necessary to make a subsequent adjustment in the form of a debit. The adjustment is posted directly to the material or cost account, whereupon the system will automatically update the order history with respect to the value, although the quantity will remain the same.

Canceling an Invoice Receipt by a Credit Memo

If it becomes apparent after invoice verification has been completed that a credit has to be posted, the credit memo function can be called from the invoice verification program. If the system encounters a credit memo document referring to a purchase order or a goods receipt, it will be treated as a cancellation of the corresponding invoice receipt document.

Handling Down Payments

A vendor may have agreed to conditions that stipulate a down payment for all purchase orders. Alternatively, the terms for a down payment can be agreed upon with the vendor in a particular purchase order.

The down payment can be agreed upon for the order as a whole or for individual order items.

If any down payment arrangement has been agreed upon, you will receive a system message to this effect when the invoice verification function becomes aware that you are about to enter an invoice receipt for that order or for that vendor, if a standing arrangement for a down payment is in force.

Part

II

Ch

5

The down payment will have to be the subject of a separate transfer posting to a vendor account established for this purpose, where it will remain until the transaction is closed by the final payment.

Making Text Notes During Invoice Verification

The standard communication channels for internal mail are available to the invoice verification component, together with the standard interfaces to external systems. The SAP R/3 word processing system can be used to provide texts for automatic entry into an invoice receipt document or to copy parts of the invoice itself into this document.

Materials Delivery Cost Accounting

The planned delivery costs are entered in the purchase order. The actual delivery costs are included in the goods receipt posting, which will be to a freight or customs clearing account.

If the standard price control is in operation, any difference between the actual delivery costs and the planned delivery costs will be posted to the price difference account.

If the moving average price (MAP) control is being applied, the difference between planned delivery costs of the material and the actual delivery costs will be posted as an offsetting entry to the stock account of the material concerned, where it may affect the moving average acquisition price held on the material master.

Planned Delivery Costs in the Purchase Order

The delivery costs can be planned and divided into a range of delivery cost types:

- Freight costs
- Customs duty
- Insurance
- Packaging labor and materials

Each of these types can be related individually to a method of calculation. For example:

- Fixed costs per delivery
- Delivery costs proportional to the quantity
- Delivery costs proportional to the number of shipping units or transportation plant units required
- Delivery costs to be computed as a fixed percentage of the total value or weight of goods delivered

The planned delivery costs are recorded on the purchase order for each order item, and the relevant amount for planned delivery costs is posted to the material account or to the cost account when the goods receipt is entered.

At the same time, an offsetting entry is posted to a special clearing account, such as a freight clearing account.

When the invoice receipt document is being created, you can list all the delivery costs for a specific purchase order, for a particular vendor, or for a delivery note. You then can decide how you want the system to allocate the total delivery costs recorded in the invoice you have received.

When you do so, the planned delivery costs will be updated in the order history to take account of the actual delivery costs.

Entering Unplanned Delivery Costs

The first time you have any information on unplanned delivery costs may be when you catch sight of the invoice during Invoice Verification. There will have been no previous entry of planned delivery costs.

The unplanned costs have to be taken from the invoice during invoice verification and entered in the invoice receipt document. The system will automatically distribute the total delivery costs among the individual items in proportion to their contribution to the value of the entire value invoiced. You can override this proportional distribution by a series of manual entries, for which rapid data entry functions are provided where relevant.

Unplanned delivery costs are posted directly to the material account or to the appropriate cost account.

Open Finance

The essence of Open FI is the notion of a network of information sources and business processes that can be called upon in real time to generate the data that is relevant to each decision in the commercial and financial processes. With global business being conducted between complex enterprises, it is not a simple matter to determine creditworthiness, for instance. The fulsome computing resources of SAP R/3 may have to be used.

At each phase of a business process there can be activities in support that can be managed to add value to the sequence by applying information to control the process. The SAP components are designed to do this. The following sales sequence illustrates the way the components can be configured:

- Quotation, Marketing Services
- Customer Credit Control, Real Time Scoring
- Order, Monitor Export Credit Insurance
- Invoice, Factoring, Asset-Backed Securities
- Dunning Notice, Export Credit Insurance Premium Notification, Collection
- Payment, Payment history
- Asset-Backed Securities

An example of the way SAP R/3 FI is being used as a core application is in the enhanced FI-AR, Accounts Receivable component available to manage ABS, Asset-Backed Securities. Expected cash flows from orders and revenues are at the heart of short- and medium-term budgetary planning. Currency exposure cover, in the form of a micro-hedging transaction, can be effected by allocating forward exchange dealings to the order or billing document from which they originate. The Internet and intranet will change the way receivables are dealt with.

Using the Relationship Between MM and PP-Production Planning

Planning production entails working out what shall be produced and the methods of doing so within an accounting framework that recognizes the need for a company to conserve resources while adding value to the product.

Materials such as raw materials, partly-finished goods, and assemblies are among the resources used in production. The SAP R/3 System supports extensive standard business software designed to maximize the effectiveness of production planning. Materials management is clearly an essential component of an integrated production and accounting system.

Work Centers

A production process usually occurs in a clearly-defined physical place, but an SAP work center is a data object that represents the location where work is carried out on behalf of the company. The conceptual work center may be a particular machine, a job, a production line, an assembly line, or even a warehouse.

In the work center data object, the information to enable the PP-Production Planning application will be stored to carry out the following activities:

- Calculate the execution times of work performed in or by the work center.
- Determine the necessary inputs to the work center and the other work centers from which they may be obtained.
- Compute the plant, labor, and other critical capacity requirements for any of the operations that may take place in the work center.
- Calculate the costs of activities in the work center.

Routings

A routing is a data object in the PP-Production Planning application that stores all the information that pertains to a production process. A routing documents the individual manufacturing steps and the resources required for each of these steps. The quality criteria for each step are also part of the routing.

The routings are used in planning and control for the following tasks:

- Capacity calculation
- Lead time scheduling
- Production activity control
- Order processing
- Product costing

The routing describes how the work centers are linked to perform the production processes.

Allocating Materials to Routings

The SAP R/3 System allows you to set up the following relationships between materials and routings:

- One material is always assigned the same routing.
- One material can be assigned more than one routing, which allows you to have several routing versions for producing the material.
- Several materials may be allocated the same routing, which must contain at least one "switching" element that redirects the production process according to the material passing through it.

The materials management functions are fully integrated with the production planning functions and there are no particular links to be set up before they can interact.

Customer-Driven Production

The implementation of local networks based on mainframe computers and dedicated communications has a relatively long history. Client/server configurations allowed distributed computing whereby the user at a workstation or simple terminal could be connected not only to databases, but also to additional computing power to process the data. In simple terms, the concept entailed accessing a system through a terminal dedicated for this purpose. The extent and complexity of the system often is not apparent to the individual user, nor need it be in most applications.

However, there are very real limitations on the number of terminals that can be operating at the same time. SAP R/3 and R/2 are able to adjust the allocation of computing resources to the workload on a dynamic basis, and the provision of procedures to cope with equipment and communication channel malfunctions is well understood.

Apart from automated banking terminals, the direct conduct of commercial business by individual users is not yet widespread. But the SAP R/3 range of standard business software is anticipating a change.

Good logistics and access to reliable purchaser interfaces, perhaps via the Internet, can be added to a well-managed industry to add yet further value to the enterprise by responding in a timely and accurate fashion to a request.

If the connection is followed through to the production and distribution facilities, the possibility exists for the production to be responsive to the customer in various ways that will benefit the customer and allow the supplier to meet demands using fewer resources.

Electronic Commerce Partner Applications

SAP has always made use of development partners in order to accelerate the introduction of products that meet the SAP certification standards. Some of the more recent partner applications illustrate the widening range of business applications that has become apparent as the potential market is opened by the introduction of reliable network standards.

R/3 PP-CBP Constraint-Based Planner

If there are two systems that are linked by reciprocal messaging interfaces, there is the potential for conflict and circular processes in which the demand for action is passed back and forth. The R/3 PP-CBP Constraint-Based Planner carries out planning and scheduling material requirements and capacity requirements in real time. The application includes a real time Due Date Quoting capability as an option within the ATP Available to Promise server.

Intelligent planning and scheduling for global supply chain management is embedded in SAP R/3 Release 4.0. These functions operate across both inter-enterprise and intra-enterprise supply chains to give fast, advance warning of impending constraints in their supply chain plans. These potential trouble spots can be published to the relevant part of the company or network of business partners. The intelligent planner will automatically suggest ways of removing the constraints.

Networked Workflow

Standard Web browsers, Microsoft Exchange, Lotus Notes, and custom applications can use R/3 Workflow Wizards to automate workflow design and thus control the workflow via a network. Workflow status reports are made available in HTML format. The WfMC Workflow Management Coalition is an association of major software suppliers that are working toward a set of common standards. Their results include an integrated implementation, which uses 52 published Workflow Application Programming Interfaces and provides the following components:

- Session Manager
- Distribution Architect
- Reference Model
- CAT Testing
- Organization Architect
- IMG Implementation Management Guide

Workflow Templates

Workflow templates can be executed and may serve as a guide for a company's own development. The individual steps of workflow templates are pre-defined as standard tasks. They contain a task description, linkage to the application logic through business objects, and prepared linkage to the company organization structure.

The business object repository delivered in R/3 includes predefined key fields, attributes, methods, and the events associated with the business objects. Workflow definitions made from standard tasks can easily be combined and changed at any time using the graphical editor.

Workflow templates have been integrated into the IDES International Demonstration and Education System. This can "play through" the operational sequences of a sample company. The pre-configured workflow scenarios can be executed and analyzed for learning and planning purposes.

Business Partner Networking

An example of how the network can be used to improve profitability by enabling early warning information to drive an efficient system of managing receivables is illustrated by the Dun and Bradstreet "D&B Access" program. Its task is to monitor business partners on a discreet but continuous basis. The important information concerns corporate customers and business transactions carried out with them and with their affiliated companies.

The source of this information is an integrated online network of external information suppliers such as credit reporting agencies and credit sales insurance firms. The D&B database carries up-to-date information on over 17 million European companies. The information is available in 26 data elements, which can be culled selectively from the database.

European Monetary Union Component

The necessity of maintaining all financial data in Euro currency is seen by many companies as an additional burden because they will need to be able to convert from their local and accounting currencies, whether or not their country joins the European Monetary Union.

The SAP R/3 European Monetary Union (EMU) currency and conversion component is a function in the value chain that will allow customers to seamlessly convert all local currency amounts stored in the R/3 database into Euros, automatically reconciling differences caused by rounding off figures after the conversion. The new Euro functions will handle the double currency phase by enabling customers to display certain figures in either Euro or local currency, or both.

Product Data Management Component

The supply of pertinent and clear product information is regarded by many companies as an essential part of their service to their customers. Customers expect to be informed about specifications and availability before they order.

However, the task of preparing documentation is not a popular one with designers and product engineers. If professional technical authors undertake the writing, there is a difficulty in proving the accuracy of their work because the technical experts are seldom available or willing to do so in enough detail to perfect the documentation. When technical details of the product change, the documentation may lag behind. When availability changes, there may be a delay before sales support staff become aware.

SAP R/3 Product Data Management (PDM) operates with its own engineering database and it is able to integrate workflow information from engineering, manufacturing, and logistics sources. This PDM component allows customers to have ready access to product data throughout whatever business processes are needed to deliver the goods and services they require. It is possible to integrate the PDM with the SAP R/3 Global ATP Server component for "available-to-promise" order-processing transactions and decision-support activities. The ATP Server can be used across internal networks or over the Internet to check on product availability with physically distributed systems and sources around the world. The system can be used at all levels of material so that complex assemblies can be more speedily delivered.

Web-Enabled SAP Business Workflow

SAP Business Workflow offers Web-enabled workflow management on enterprise level. By extending workflow functionality over the Internet or within an enterprise intranet, customers now have an easy-to-use workflow functionality that is available 24 hours a day, from anywhere in the world.

Under the marketing concept "Business Framework," SAP Business Workflow is presented as an essential part of the integration technology allowing active process control of business processes, which may be executing in computer system environments other than SAP R/3. For example, as a customer, you could take control over certain business workflow sequences to order the particular configuration of sub-assemblies you require in a complex product. You may do this from an SAPGUI, or from any of the supported third-party desktop software components. In effect, any BAPI, Business Application Programming Interface, can trigger a predefined workflow sequence and actively control it through the SAP Business Workflow.

Integrating MM with SD-Sales and Distribution

The SAP R/3 SD-Sales and Distribution application includes the standard business programs that are needed to support all aspects of sales and distribution for almost every type of business. The emphasis of the design of the module has been on the individual person at a user interface terminal representing his or her company to the prospects and customers from whom future business will come. The module is designed to be easy-to-use, yet comprehensive in its capability to pull together, rapidly and with clarity of presentation, all the information that the customer needs to make an informed purchase and have it delivered promptly in good condition.

The design of this module puts the emphasis on using a sales strategy that is sensitive to the market.

The SD-Sales and Distribution system provides a set of master data records and a system of documented business transactions. The standard business programs of the module are organized around the following five functions:

- SD-MD Master Data
- SD-CAS Sales Support
- SD-SLS Sales
- SD-SHP Shipping
- SD-BIL Billing

Two other functions are available from the R/3 System and are used by the SD-Sales and Distribution module. They are important because they control the flow of information between the parts of a sales and distribution organization and the other SAP applications in the R/3 System. They also provide the links between the system itself and its users, wherever they might be:

- SAP EDI Electronic Data Interchange
- SD-IS Sales and Distribution Information System

Electronic Data Interchange (EDI) refers to the electronic channels of communication that, in modern business practice, have replaced the messenger systems carrying printed documents. The term "document" is used for both an electronic record and a paper one. Similarly, "printing" may in fact refer to the transmission by electronic means of information that could be printed if required.

The SD-IS Sales Information System will allow you to gain insight on all matters concerning prospecting, sales, and delivery. This system of displays and analytical processes is provided to access the master records and the transaction data in a flexible manner that allows you to conduct statistical analyses and evaluations in support of decision-making and strategic planning.

All data objects that can be associated with changes of value have to be assigned to a client and a company code so that their accounts are properly attributed in preparation for the compilation of the balance sheet and the profit and loss statement. Below the company code level, it is often useful to identify separate operational units that can function as cost collectors or profit centers.

- *Plant* can be a production facility or a group of storage locations where stocks are kept. This term is also used in the context of "transportation plant" in the SD-Sales and Distribution system. The vehicle is treated as a temporary storage location. Planning and inventory management take place at the level of the plant, and it is the focus of materials management. It can supply its material stocks to more than one sales organization.

- *Sales Organization* has a legal connotation in that it represents the unit responsible for selling and, therefore, is responsible for product liability and rights of legal recourse. All business transactions in SD-Sales and Distribution have to be processed financially within a sales organization. A sales organization can draw its materials from more than one plant.

- *Distribution Channel* defines how different materials reach the consumer directly or, for example, through a materials wholesaler.

- *Sales Division* is a subdivision of a distribution channel. The division may have been assigned only some of the total product range and there may be customer-specific agreements for each division.

- *Sales Area* defines a combination of not more than one division, distribution channel, and sales organization. Thus, if there are two divisions using the same distribution channel, each division will be considered to belong to a different sales area. An individual customer can be assigned to more than one sales area if there are differing requirements and agreements to be considered. Prices, minimum order, or delivery quantities are the sorts of factors that may have to be recognized by creating unique sales areas for them, always in the SAP R/3 structural context of a sales organization and perhaps a sales division and distribution channel as well.

- *Sales Office* is a method of representing the internal organization. It is a division under the client level.

- *Sales Group* is a further internal subdivision of the people in a particular sales office.

- *Salesperson* is the subject of a unique personnel master record.

- *Shipping Point* is a location within a plant where deliveries are processed. Each delivery is assigned to and processed by one, and only one, shipping point.

- *Loading Point* is a part of a shipping point that is able to offer a capacity to handle deliveries. There may be several similar loading points, and there may be different equipment at some loading points that make them more suitable for particular types of deliveries—forklift trucks for pallets, for example.

SD-MD Master Data

In an SAP System, information that is needed in several places or at different times is entered only once. It resides in master records where it may be kept up-to-date so that all who access it are given the most accurate and recent information available to the system.

Each master data record has a unique number, and you can arrange to confine certain ranges of these numbers to specific sales areas.

The sales department will make use of this master information in its business transactions. The following are some of the uses the sales department will find for the master data record:

- General details about business partners
- Information specific to particular customers
- Materials, including services as well as objects and assemblies

- Texts about materials and sales conditions
- Prices from cost data collected, from standard calculations, from direct entries, and from planning processes
- Surcharges and discounts
- Taxes applied according to local rules
- New product proposals to be offered during the sales processing

Account Groups

Your customer might have a complex organizational structure that prevents you from entering a simple sold-to party record for the requirement. The customer master record can be used to represent any of the following account groups:

- Sold-to party
- Ship-to party
- Bill-to party
- Payer

Each of the account groups can be assigned a specific selection from the available transaction data. Their documents will then be automatically tailor-made for them by the system. The SD-Sales and Distribution module is provided with definitions and models for the common types of customer relationships. You can also define your own account groups and specify which elements of transaction data are to be included in documents assigned to these groups.

Contact Person

All the information you need to carry out sales support is held in the contact person records that are part of the customer master. If there are several contact persons, they can be associated as equivalent or alternative contacts, or they can be assigned a key or subject name that signifies the area in which they specialize.

Carrier and Supplier

A business partner that is also a carrier and supplier would have a master record maintained in the MM-Materials Management module and also in the FI-Financial Accounting module. If the supplier is also a customer from time to time, you can enter its supplier number in its customer record in the SD-Sales and Distribution system, which will automatically create a link so that the two records always share exactly the same data in all the fields they have in common.

Relationship to the HR-Human Resources Records

If you create a personnel record, for instance, for one of your customer sales representatives, the master will be managed by the HR-Human Resources module. You will, therefore, be able to refer to a member of your staff by entering his or her personnel master record number. This will make available to you any other details about the person that you have been authorized to see.

Part
II

Ch
5

Relationship to the MM-Materials Management Masters

The products and services represented and managed by the MM-Materials Management system can also be created and referred to from the SD-Sales and Distribution module. For example, a sales representative might acquire information about a new supplier of a material that is already represented by a materials master record. The details can be posted to the MM-Materials Management system where they will be verified and incorporated into the database. If a prospective customer inquires about a material that he has not previously purchased from your company, the details available in the material masters can be used to provide up-to-date accurate information. If there is no relevant material master, the MM-Materials Management system will record this inquiry and alert the material controller.

Material Type   The material type is assigned during Customizing, and is used to associate a material with an appropriate material master data structure. This will ensure that the data fields that are not relevant to a specific type of material will be suppressed when the record is displayed on the screen.

Industry Sector   The sectors of industry that you find in your business and that should be given differential treatment in one or more aspects of SD-Sales and Distribution can be defined during Customizing. You can then make sure that products for each sector of industry are assigned the corresponding type of master data structures, which will allow the system to maintain particular information and use it to be responsive to the needs of that sector. For example, the difference between one industry sector and another may be in the matter of distribution lot size, or in the way billing takes place. In this instance, you may decide that some of your products will be sold and packaged in two or more different ways: single units for the "Retail" industry sector, and pallets for the "Wholesale" industry sector. Each sector will have a different costing and billing procedure.

There are four attributes that serve to format the material master data into clusters: general data, data specific to a particular sales area, plant-specific data, and storage location and inventory management data. The SAP term for a cluster of associated data elements is "attribute."

General Data   Any characteristic of a material that is always going to be the same is stored in the general data attribute and will be made available every time the material takes part in a transaction. For example, a specific type of steel will have a unique material number and a particular description or specification.

The units of measurement may be a function of the method of manufacture, such as a roll of spring steel, or they may be decided on the basis of the most economical unit for procuring this material, such as a pallet.

The following are examples of data that may be stored as general data because it is invariant across all sources and uses of this material:

- Material number
- Description
- Units of measure

- Weight
- Volume
- Material division, and so on

Sales Area–Specific Data   Each sales area may be supplied from a particular warehouse or manufacturing plant. Even though the material number is the same, the division of the supply between delivery plants will entail a relevant record on the material master. If, for example, the same material can be obtained from another sales area, if necessary, then the material master records should show this, even though each sales area normally uses a separate source.

The following are examples of data that may be specific to each sales area:

- Delivering plant
- Sales texts
- Units of measure
- Product hierarchy information
- Shipping data

Plant-Specific Data   Whether the supplying plant is a warehouse or a manufacturing unit, the costs of storing a material there and the Materials Requirements Planning procedures will need to be known in order to plan, cost, and schedule a sales order. This information also finds its place in the appropriate attribute of the materials master from which it can be accessed by the SD-Sales and Distribution module.

The following are examples of data that may be specific to each plant:

- MRP profile
- Production costs
- Export data

Storage Location and Inventory Management Data   A warehouse may have storage locations that are designed specifically for particular materials. If a material has to be stored in such a location, this information is stored in the material master records.

The following examples illustrate the material data that may have to be stored in the storage location and inventory management attribute:

- Temperature conditions
- No other material to be stored in the location reserved for this material
- Storage conditions, such as dust and humidity control, special handling facilities essential

Relationships to the particular sales organizations and distribution channels may affect some or all of the entries. Any particulars that have been determined by the master records of a superior level in the organizational structure will be inherited by a data object in a lower level, unless the record at the lower level carries specific instructions to the contrary. For example, a material that has to be stored in a cooled warehouse will show this requirement in its material master data record. If a particular method of packaging has been determined for a whole class of materials, any material belonging to this class will be packed in this way unless the individual material master record carries contrary instructions.

Bill of Materials

When a product is made up of several components, the details are documented in a bill of materials (BOM). If additional information is required about any of these components, a BOM explosion may be used to call in the extra documentation. If several products differ by only a few components, the technique of BOM variants may be employed.

Material Status

You can adopt the standard status indicators of the MM-Materials Management system or define indicators of your own to serve the purpose of exercising control over sales activities. For example, you may want to block the taking of orders for a batch of defective material but permit inquiries about the product in anticipation that a future batch will not be defective.

A discontinued product can be the subject of status control so that future orders will be blocked even though the product is still being shipped to satisfy existing orders.

Stock and Inventory Inquiries

Flexible display facilities permit you to assess the various plant stocks and summarize them in the form of overviews. Special stocks can be identified for different treatments. Special stock destined for only one customer would be an example.

Customer Material Info Records

If a customer needs special sales and delivery requirements that would not be met by the information stored in the customer master or the relevant material masters, you can set up a customer material info record that takes precedence over the rules established elsewhere. The info record contains the following kinds of information:

- Customer, sales organization, and distribution channel
- Your material number and description
- The customer's material number and description
- Shipping data
- Partial delivery arrangements, and so on

The system will use the customer material info record to prepare a sales proposal ready to be placed in the sales order if you approve it.

The SD-Sales and Distribution module will operate material determination and material substitution procedures if they have been established. For example, you can define a set of criteria to select a suitable material automatically. You may also have set up the criteria for a material to be substituted automatically in orders for a particular customer. The material listing and material exclusion rules are valid for a certain period of time and serve the purpose of restricting the choice of options presented by the system when preparing a sales proposal.

Types of Business Transactions

The standard version of the SD-Sales and Distribution system is able to recognize and support the most frequently used types of business transactions. You can refine or modify these functions to suit your company and create new business transaction types with the pertinent business functionality.

Inquiries and Quotations   These are standard SAP documents that are created before a sales order is taken and that are limited to a specific period of validity. They should be customized to gather information on the reasons for the inquiry and the reasons for rejection if a sales order does not arise.

By accessing one of the overview screens, you can find out whether the materials or services in the inquiry or quotation would be available on the date required. However little information is recorded as the result of an inquiry, you can use it to begin to plan a sales strategy for this potential customer. As you seek further clarification of the customer's requirements, you will be able to build a better relationship and have the results of your prospecting endeavors stored in the documents and customer master records.

Sales Orders   Even if you have not offered a quotation, you can still enter a sales order to check availability and carry out a credit limit check. You will want to carry out pricing at this stage, if you have not already done so. The required delivery date may well affect the price.

Scheduling Agreements and Contracts   This type of business transaction is an outline agreement with a customer to supply goods and services over a specified period of time. The quantities and dates are specified in the scheduling agreement.

A contract is also an outline agreement to supply goods and services in the future, but the delivery date is not specified until later, when it is published in a release order.

Rush Order   You can create a sales order and initiate a delivery at the same time. This is a rush order, which will cause the system to create the delivery for you as soon as you enter the order. It will check availability and carry out scheduling for both the order and the delivery documents at the same time.

Production to Order   If you have elected to enter this type of order, a production requirement is created to produce the material directly as a result of the customer order. When the material has reached the finished product stage, it will be treated as special stock.

The individual customer requirement is passed to material requirements planning, and the availability is checked against the customer special stock. When both the production and the external purchase order processing are completed, the appropriate inward goods movement for the customer special stock is posted. This records the fact that goods have been produced specifically for the individual customer and been assigned to his or her special stock. Delivery takes place from this stock.

Customer Consignment Stock   If you have set aside some goods that one of your customers can call upon at any time, and you have not yet been paid for these goods, they are treated as consignment goods. If you are the vendor, you still own the consignment.

The warehouse holding these consignment goods will notify the vendor if the customer picks up or is issued any of them. The vendor will charge the customer for them. If any of the consignment goods are not required by the customer, they can be returned to the vendor.

In the SD-Sales and Distribution system, customer consignment stock is managed separately by generating consignment fill-up orders for the customer, consignment issues from the stock, billing documents, and consignment pick-up documents.

Returnable Packaging   The system maintains a separate stock of returnable packaging or transportation material for each customer. This material has to be returned within a specified time period. The vendor still owns it.

The SD-Sales and Distribution system offers functions for dispatch and pickup of returnable packaging, so that you can enter it in deliveries and bill the customer for any not returned within the set time.

Complaints   If a customer complains of damage during transportation or is not satisfied with the goods or services, you can call upon special SAP R/3 functions to process these complaints.

A return is a transaction that arranges for the faulty goods to be picked up or for replacements to be delivered free of charge.

If you find that you have overcharged or undercharged a customer, you can create a credit or debit memo request document that will set in motion the appropriate financial procedure.

Third-Party Deal   If you are the contractor in a third-party deal, you will commission a third-party vendor to deliver the goods directly to the customer or to the destination specified as the customer's ship-to party. In these cases, the SD-Sales and Distribution system automatically creates purchase requisitions for the sales order that specify the delivery dates and quantities. The purchasing department, using the MM-Materials Management system, will process these purchasing requirements and create purchase orders for them. If the vendor notifies the system that the quantities or the dates have to be changed, the system will automatically correct the sales document.

The third-party vendor will send you an invoice as soon as the goods have been delivered to the customer. You can then carry out billing for the third-party deal by having the system copy the quantity delivered from the invoice document to the billing document that goes to the customer.

Stock Transfer Transactions   A requisition for stock to be transferred can be created automatically by PP-MRP Material Requirements Planning. It could also be initiated from a purchase requisition entered manually.

When such a requisition is converted to a purchase order, the plant that is to deliver the material is informed of the stock transfer requirement, and the purchase order will appear in the Delivery Due list on the SD-Sales and Distribution system display.

All the shipping functions can then be applied to the stock transfer. The FI-Financial Accounting system of the delivering plant will get a goods issue posting, and the receiving plant will be posted a goods receipt.

Cross-Company Sales   When one company needs products and services from other parts of the group, the cross-company sales function of the SD-Sales and Distribution system can be invoked. A sales organization can sell for plants in a different company code. Legally, this means that more than one company is involved in the processing of a sales order. It is necessary to apply intercompany invoicing between the company codes to adjust the value flow after the sales order has been completed.

Partners and Personnel

Because they represent your company in the market, each sales and sales support person is given a master record in the SD-Sales and Distribution system.

Sales personnel are defined as people who are documented in the HR-Human Resources system as direct employees of your company, and who also are recognized by the SD-Sales and Distribution module because of the roles they may be called upon to play in the sales and distribution activities.

Sales partners are recognized and documented in the SD-Sales and Distribution system as consultancy partners or sales agents, but they are not direct employees of your company and do not necessarily have personnel records in your HR-Human Resources system.

Customers, Prospects, and Contacts

The management of customers and sales prospects constitutes a major part of the SD-CAS Sales Support software component. The customer master record holds most of the information in the standard SAP format of attributes, which are clusters of thematically related data fields.

A customer master has records for general details as well as:

- Company organizational structure, annual sales, number of employees, status as a customer of your organization, and market areas of goods and services
- Contact persons by name and position
- Contact person details such as first name, form of salutation, birth date, marital status, buying habits, sales strategy to use, visiting hours, home address, business address, interests, and pastimes

A prospect is handled by the SD-Sales and Distribution module as a customer without a record of past purchases. The records and processing functions are the same.

Part

II

Ch

5

If you are looking for a particular contact person, you can search for the company by name or number; alternatively, you can search for the person's details, which will enable you to keep track of that person if he or she moves from one of your customers to another. You may have a very large database of potential customers on which you are keeping a watching brief and a diligent data-collecting effort.

There are no restrictions on the definition and number of attributes maintained in your master records for customers, sales prospects, and contact persons.

Competitors and Their Products

New markets and new market segments are often detected by closely observing what your competitors are doing and not doing. You can store this kind of data systematically in the SD-Sales and Distribution system.

Competitor Companies   You can use the system of master records to store data on your competitor companies, using the same structure as you use for customers but with some important additions:

- Industry classifications
- Annual sales
- Employees
- Other information about the competitor stored in a structured format that will allow you to conduct searches and compile statistical summaries

Competitive Products   You need a database that includes all the details that are important for your own products, but if you want to make a comparison, you will also need your competitors' products to be entered on the same set of master attributes. You can also have structured texts to locate critical information in ways that are susceptible to classification and search techniques.

Like your own, competitive products will be assigned to product hierarchies upon which a comparison can be based.

Sales Activities and Promotions

The outcomes of previous sales activities have to be stored in order to become an input to the design of the next sales campaign. The method used by the SD-Sales and Distribution system is to store all interactions with the potential customer population in the data structures referred to as Sales Activities. The following are examples of activities by SD-CAS Sales Support that are documented by recording the outcomes of sales activities in such records:

- Sales calls in person
- Telemarketing calls
- Brochure mailing

- Calls received from potential customers
- Presentations
- Conferences
- Promotions

The standard SD-Sales and Distribution system recognizes the following three activity types:

- Sales call
- Sales letter
- Telephone call

You may define other sales activity types to add to this list during customizing.

SD-SHP Shipping

All the data required to arrange a prompt delivery can be determined in the sales order. By having the system display all the orders due for delivery, you can manage the deadlines. Bottlenecks will be foreseen and the remedies will be at hand. The following are the main activities empowered by the SD-SHP Shipping functions:

- Monitoring the deadlines of orders due for deliveries
- Creating and processing deliveries
- Monitoring the availability of goods
- Supporting the picking operations
- Supporting packing and loading
- Managing transportation
- Creating shipping output documents and transmitting them
- Managing decentralized shipping
- Posting the goods issue document to FI-Financial Accounting at the time of delivery

The Shipping Work Lists

For every shipping point under the control of the shipping department, there can be a work list of sales orders due for delivery. How frequently these work lists are processed will be a matter to be determined by the management and operating staff—all things being equal, the sooner the better.

A shipping point is a facility that offers a separate shipping capacity. It may be one of several identical loading bays, for example, or it may have a special handling capacity such as a forklift truck that is larger than the other shipping points. The shipping point may owe its individuality to the fact that it is dedicated to the orders for one particular customer.

The appropriate shipping point is either automatically determined by the system, or entered manually during order creation. The criteria for automatic shipping point determination are as follows:

- Shipping conditions specified for the sold-to party—for example, "as soon as possible" or "normal shipping conditions"
- Loading group of the material—for example, "by crane," "by forklift truck," or "by special staff loading team"
- Delivering plant—for example, "road truck," "rail wagon," or "dedicated transporter"

Each order item has to be assigned a route. Which route is chosen will depend on the following criteria:

- The shipping conditions specified for the sold-to party
- The delivery weight of the order item
- The geographical relationship of the destination to the shipping point

Each route will impose certain restrictions in the choice of means of transport and the number and nature of the legs of the journey. If the order item has to change delivery plant en route, there will be extra costs and delays, yet to have the whole route executed in one particular means of transport may be unacceptable for other reasons. For example, it may take too long, the atmospheric pollution by the vehicle may be damaging to the reputation of your company, or the vehicle may have to make the return journey without a payload.

You can call up a list at any time to see which deliveries are scheduled to use a particular route or shipping point over a selected time interval. You may be able to effect an improvement in the planning of loading and transportation activities by a manual change to one or more of the parameters assigned by the system.

Managing the Delivery of an Item

A delivery situation is the result of taking account of the goods availability position and the agreements in place with the customer or the sold-to party concerning partial deliveries.

If the sold-to party will not accept partial deliveries, you have to see that all the items in the sales order are collected together in one delivery group that then becomes the focus. The availability check and the transfer of requirements have to be adjusted to fit the earliest delivery date possible for the delivery group.

If the sold-to party has agreed to accept partial deliveries, you can, if necessary, create several deliveries from the one sales order. This might suit the availability situation, both of goods and of shipping facilities.

It might make sense to combine several sales orders into one delivery group, if the customer has agreed to such an arrangement.

In all these procedures for effectively managing the delivery situations as and when they arise and planning to smooth their passage before the time comes, the SAP R/3 System can be allowed to act automatically by setting up the appropriate logical conditions and data elements.

Delivery Status Update The creation of a delivery document, when it is posted and proved to be valid, is the occasion for the system automatically to update the material stocks and the work list of the shipping department, where the display of delivery situation of the sales order will show the updated status key.

Shipping Output Documents When the delivery has been posted, the system will offer you a proposal to print or send by electronic mail the shipping output documents mandated during customizing.

Shipping Elements A shipping element is an item of material that is managed separately in the SD-Sales and Distribution system because it is used in shipping and is necessary for the purpose of handling and protecting the goods in transit. It may be on loan to the customer for a specified period, and a charge may be raised if it is not returned within that period. The following items can be managed as shipping elements:

- Boxes
- Cartons
- Pallets
- Trucks
- Trailers
- Supporting travel rigs

In order to protect and handle a particular delivery, it may be necessary to have the item first packed in cartons. A group of cartons, perhaps, are protected by a box, and several boxes loaded into a freight container. All these shipping elements can be treated as a hierarchy of shipping elements that is recognized by the system and specified for use for one or more types of material or one or more customers.

The shipping elements need not be specified as a hierarchical structure; they can be referenced simply as a packing list, which is also recognized by the system as a data object and can be changed under control of the procedures of change management.

Picking

A picking list, or pick list, is a document that makes sure that the goods in the warehouse arrive at the shipping point at the right moment to become part of a delivery. Clearly, only the right goods and the right quantities will do. And it is no use getting the goods to the shipping point just before the transport is due to leave if some work has to be done to prepare the goods and protect them with the specified shipping elements. If the goods need special storage conditions, picking will have to make allowances for this.

The typical sequence is as follows:

- A picking location or loading zone is automatically determined for a delivery, using data on the sales order delivery document that will indicate the shipping point and the storage conditions to be observed.

- A picking list is printed for each delivery when the delivery is created, or later. The picking list can be sent by electronic means.

- When the picking has assembled the available quantities at the picking location, the quantities are confirmed to the system. If they are insufficient but stock is available, picking is carried out again for the shortfall, using the same loading zone. If the quantities required cannot be picked to the picking zone, for whatever reason, then the delivery quantity is reduced. The system will make the appropriate adjustments to the order, shipping, and billing documents.

In some circumstances, you may have to enter the batch specification or the valuation type after picking has been completed, because only at that stage will the necessary data be accurate. For example, some process industries have to expect a variation in the makeup of the finished product, because variability in the input materials and the environmental conditions have an effect on the product.

Links to the MM-WM Warehouse Management System

If you have installed and configured the MM-WM Warehouse Management system, the initiation of picking can take place through this system.

The system maintains materials master data, which indicate the fixed storage bin or circumscribed storage area in which the material can be found during picking.

If the warehouse does not use fixed bin storage, it is treated as a random warehouse. The MM-WM Warehouse Management system makes sure that a transfer order is created for each delivery item. When the goods arrive at the picking area, the transfer order is confirmed and the system will enter the picked quantities directly into the delivery items on the delivery document.

The Formalities of Goods Issue

From the point of view of the shipping function, the business transaction is complete when the goods leave your company. In the SD-Sales and Distribution system, this event is represented by the posting of a goods issue corresponding to the delivery.

Stock values are updated in the FI-Financial Accounting module as the stock level of material is reduced by the quantity of the goods issued.

The goods issue brings to an end the delivery processing. The information on the goods issue is stored in the sales order from which the delivery was initiated. The billing due list will now show the details of the delivery, so that it can be invoiced.

Decentralized Shipping

When the SD-Sales and Distribution system has reached the point of being able to specify a delivery, it may be convenient to pass this delivery document to another system. For example, there could be several satellite systems working on a decentralized shipping basis, each receiving a subset of the deliveries due from the central system.

The following are some of the advantages recognized by those companies that adopt the decentralized shipping approach:

- Shipping processing can be carried out continuously, even when the main computing system is unavailable.
- The SD-SHP Shipping module can be used on a satellite computer in conjunction with another sales order processing system, for instance, from the SAP R/2 System.
- The system load can be distributed over various computers by relieving the main system of the shipping functions.

The net effect of decentralizing shipping in this manner is to minimize delivery times and improve customer service.

Distribution of Functions Under Decentralized Shipping   The sales order is entered on the central host computer system where the stocks are managed. The availability of the order items is checked there, and the scheduling takes place there for the shipping activities of perhaps all the satellite shipping subsystems.

When the due date arrives for a delivery, the satellite initiates the shipping activities and has the delivery data transferred from the host. Data relevant to the materials handled by the satellite will already be held there in the form of copies of the material master records.

A transfer of customer data takes place for every business transaction so that the information is up-to-date.

Picking at the satellite may be linked to a MM-WM Warehouse Management system there or in the host. As the batches and quantities are gathered to the picking location, the specifications are confirmed in the delivery document. You can add packaging and other shipping elements at the same time, together with the weights and volumes for the loading data that will appear on the shipping output documents to be generated locally.

When the delivery is completed, the goods issue for the delivery is automatically confirmed. The data is transferred back to the host, where the status of the sales order is updated.

The satellite system does not post quantities or values to the FI-Financial Accounting system; this is done centrally when the delivery confirmation is returned.

As soon as the delivery has been confirmed, the central host system will release the delivery for billing, and it will appear on the billing due list.

Part

II

Ch

5

Processing Complaints

There are two types of processing complaints: One can give rise to a credit memo, the other to a debit memo.

Returns If a customer makes a complaint about a delivery concerning the quality or the type of goods, you can pick up the goods free of charge from the customer location and generate a returns order in the sales department, which will lead to a credit memo request and eventually a credit memo posted to the customer's account in FI-Financial Accounting. The returns order will carry information about the complaint in short texts and perhaps free text, both of which can be analyzed later.

Credit Memo Requests A credit memo request may also arise in the sales department because the customer has complained about a late delivery. This request will be blocked for billing until the amount of the credit has been decided, when the request can be released, and a credit memo created. The credit memo is posted to the customer's account in the FI-Financial Accounting system.

Debit Memo Requests If a debit memo request is created in the sales department, perhaps because a customer has been undercharged, a similar procedure is followed. This time, the result is a debit memo amount, which is posted to Accounts Receivable in FI-Financial Accounting.

Integrating MM with HR-Human Resources

The following object types are used in the HR-Human Resources Enterprise Data Model:

- Organizational Unit, which is part of the R/3 Reference Model and will be assigned the name of the operating company or department that the enterprise data model is being used to represent

- Position, which is modeled from the R/3 Reference Model and named to suit the specific company with a title such as Sales Representative

- Workplace, of which there may be several assigned the same position, each able to accommodate one person

- Job, which is a set of tasks based on a specific workplace but not necessarily the only set of tasks performed there

- Task, which is a component of a job and usually comprises a fairly well-defined set of work input materials or messages for which there are appropriate work procedures

Two other object types, "Person" and "Cost Center," are used to represent the situation where a named individual is assigned to a job and is being paid to work there. The connections between the data objects in the integrated cost planning and human resource system are demonstrated by the following relationships:

- A cost center is an entity that stores the cost data of one or more organizational units. An organizational unit must be assigned to one and only one cost center.

- An organizational unit is assigned one or more positions.
- A position comprises one or more workplaces.
- A position record points to a job to be performed.
- A job record describes one or more tasks.
- A task is performed as part of the responsibilities of a position.
- A named person is assigned to a position and to one of the workplaces at which the tasks of that position may be carried on.

If you have installed and configured the Employee Substitution component from the HR-Human Resources application, you can set up your system so that a suitable person is assigned automatically to answer a query from a customer, a potential customer, or any other type of business partner.

For instance, you may have a voice-activated system that allows a caller to identify the type of service required. Your system can then identify the position appropriate to provide it. The system will then choose a qualified person and assign him or her to an available workplace that is suitable for the tasks of the position.

If you have defined the qualifications of all your staff and all your positions, and if you have in place a system for knowing who is available for work at any moment, then you can have your system assign an available and qualified person to the workplace that has been designated for dealing with the specific customer query.

From Here...

- How are the various components put together?

  See Chapter 6, "Understanding the SAP R/3 Business Engineer."
- How can you find out details about your stocks of materials?

  See Chapter 7, "Analyzing Materials Information."
- How are networked systems built?

  See Chapter 9, "Understanding Network Computing."

Understanding the SAP R/3 Business Engineer

In this chapter

- How to use the R/3 Reference Model
- How to interpret an Enterprise Data Model for materials management
- How to trace materials management activities through event-driven process chains
- How R/3 MM handles the complexities of materials transactions
- How to view an information model of your enterprise

The SAP R/3 System with its applications installed and configured is a complex but fully integrated structure of standard business software modules and components. It is perfectly possible to be a successful user of this system without knowing very much about how it works, just as it is possible to write a letter on a word processor without knowing what most of the functions are able to do.

In the case of an SAP R/3 installation, the benefits to your business increase rapidly as you learn what is available in your implementation. There are many systems and tools to teach you what the system can do. The Business Engineer is a coordinated collection of these tools presented as a support system for those who want to learn more about the SAP R/3 facilities. It will operate at the beginners level and it will continue to provide efficient support right through to the advanced programmer level.

How MM-Materials Management Uses the Structure of Your Plant

By insisting on strict adherence to a formal structure of data, no matter what the meaning of the data, no matter how complex, you can build and maintain the very large systems of databases and transactional processing routines that a modern integrated system demands.

The structure of SAP R/3 data is designed to be able to match the structure of all the configurations of head office and subsidiary operating units in the context of modern business. The standard software is not itself altered when it is implemented in your particular company—only the tables of parameters that control it so as to make it fit your specific organization and its data processing requirements.

Defining the Client

The owner of the entire SAP R/3 System is the client. For example, a corporate group could comprise a top level company with several subsidiaries. The group needs access to all the data and so this data is assigned to the client structural level. Some of the data may be stored and maintained for accuracy and timeliness at the client level because other parts of the organization may have need of it. The details of a vendor of a product used by some or all of the departments of a company would be an example of the type of data that should be stored at the client level.

The client is assigned a client code, so that a data record maintained at the group level can be recognized because this code prefixes the record number.

SAP is now using Client* to refer to the highest organizational level in the structure of an enterprise data model. This is intended to obviate confusion with the concept of client as a customer for goods or services. This discussion will assume that the Client is the highest level of the SAP structure.

The system will have only one operational client which holds the real data needed for the running of the corporate group of companies.

Training Client   A training client can be set up so that staff can carry out exercises on the system, using "for practice" data records prefixed by the training client code, but the training client will not be able to gain access to the data owned by the real client.

Testing Client   The implementing team can set up a testing client, which is used to verify that all the standard business programs are producing the designed results. Again, there will be no way of confusing the testing data and the training client data or the real client data. The testing client records will carry the testing client code, which will trigger various protective routines. You will not be able to set in motion a production facility, for example, if you are working with the testing client unless you have the required authority.

Defining the Company Code

When a corporate group is made up of one or more separate companies, each of them is legally allowed to maintain its own separate balance sheet and profit-and-loss statement. In these circumstances, the SAP R/3 System requires that the head office of the group be recognized by the client code, and each of the subsidiary companies be assigned a separate company code. This is also a GAAP Generally Agreed Accounting Practice. "Company code" is SAP shorthand for a company that is a subsidiary of the client code enterprise.

The structured data principle is applied: Data not required by an organizational unit belonging to a different part of the corporate organization can be confined to the company that uses it by storing it under its own company code. For example, the information necessary to manage the maintenance of a particular plant that one company uses may be of no interest to another part of the group. Personnel records may have to be stored at the client level, because people may be asked to move from one company code to another.

Naturally, the SAP R/3 System has provided for the situation where a set of records belonging to one company code can be copied for reference to another, and then edited to suit. You might want to do this when starting up a new company in your group.

Defining the Purchasing Organization

To keep within the law, you must assign your purchasing organization to only one company code. The purchasing organization is assigned responsibility for negotiating terms and conditions with vendors of the materials and services needed by this company code. When you buy something, it is your company that is responsible for paying for it, not your purchasing department.

Defining the Purchasing Group

Most purchasing organizations have more than one buyer. Even if there is only one person in it, this purchasing organization can be divided, for purchasing accounting convenience, into purchasing groups according to any criteria you may find helpful. Very often, there have to be specialist buyers who are knowledgeable in particular materials, and they may constitute the purchasing groups within the purchasing organization.

Defining the Plant

The SAP R/3 System recognizes a plant as a data object belonging to a specific company code. In fact, the plant need not be a production plant as such. It could be a warehouse or even part of a warehouse. What distinguishes a plant is the fact that it is the site at which value can be added by production activities or at which valuable stock can be held in an orderly fashion. There will be an inventory in which the items are identified along with their bin or other storage location. Their value is enhanced:

- If you know they are there
- If you know how to find them quickly
- If you can send the proper handling equipment to fetch them
- If you know how to take any necessary precautions for the safety of your personnel and for the safety of the materials
- If you know how to find out something about them to respond to a customer's inquiry

Defining the Storage Location

The storage location is both an actual place and a data object that SAP R/3 treats as a collective label for a set of storage bins or other units in which material is held. A single bin may be a storage location. Any number of bins can be managed together as a single storage location—in which case, the system will not be able to select material from one bin rather than another, unless special steps are taken to tell the system how to choose. This facility is provided in the MM-WM Warehouse Management component.

MM uses the structure of your plant to assign a numbering code to every item you hold there. If you know how to read this code, you can find out where any item is held, who bought it, and how its value will appear in the group accounts.

A Database in Common

The idea is simple, but the implementation may be complex. If you will need for some management or accounting purpose to tell the difference between two items, then you must have a way of attaching signals to these items: one signal for each aspect of importance. A "use by date" is a signal. "Keep refrigerated" is another signal. "Reserved for customer X" is yet another way of telling one item of material apart from another.

For some stocks, you could perhaps label every item with all the significant characteristics. A more practical proposition is to give each item an ID code and then store the rest of the information in your database.

In a modern client/server networked system, the database may be distributed and it may be served by a range of SAP and third party systems. But the principle remains paramount: The structure of data must be controlled across the whole system so that everyone can interpret the meaning of data messages. Your system has to know where to look and how to decode what it finds when it is trying to answer a query or suggest to you a suitable material for the order you are creating, for example.

Departmental Access to Centralized Materials Master Records

The material master record is replicated for each material. However, particular departments will require only some of the data elements. Purchasing will not need the same data as materials requirements planning, for example. Materials master elements can be assigned a list of the departments which are allowed to access them.

If you are in a department and select the records for this department only, you will see only the fields of the materials master which have been annotated for use by your department. You cannot see a data element unless you have permission according to your user profile which will include the code for the department in which you are working. You may be allowed no more than "Read Only" access.

SAP R/3 Data Structure Policy

The rules for data storage are standard. There may be some data elements which are not required in your implementation and these can be suppressed at the customizing stage. You may also be allowed to add elements in a controlled way within the general data structure to suit your particular requirements.

SAP R/3 includes a standard assignment system as a starting point for any customizing modifications you may require. The scheme uses the principles of data object orientation in which the successive subdivisions inherit the code numbers of the "parents" at the level above. Thus, company code items are prefixed by the code for the client because each company belongs to the Client which stands for the corporate head of the enterprise. There can only be one Client for the live production system in R/3.

General Data at Company Code Level

Each operating company in a corporation will maintain its separate financial documents, the balance sheet, and the profit-and-loss statement. When it is time to consolidate the financial performance information for the member companies, the details of the materials used and in stock will be converted to monetary values, so it does not matter if different company codes use different material data.

The following data is held at company code level:

- Material number
- Classification data
- Multilingual description
- Units of measure
- Technical data

Part
II
Ch
6

Each company can use its own material numbering and classification system provided it does not need to make many stock transfers to other companies in the group. Sister companies may decide to coordinate this data to avoid any difficulties.

MRP and Purchasing Data at Plant Level

The data objects at the plant level will be replicated for each specific plant as appropriate. Although a data structure may be copied, the details of the stock will necessarily be different in the various warehouses and other holding locations. Purchasing may well result in deliveries to a specific plant, especially if one warehouse is equipped differently from another.

Plant-Specific   This information may be different for each stock of a material held in different plants.

- MRP type
- Planned delivery time
- Purchasing group
- Batch indicator

Again, the possibility that stock is held in specialized locations and is acquired by a range of procedures requires that the materials database have the ability to record these differences and allow you to perform analyses on them.

Valuation   This information may be different for each stock of a material held in different plants.

- Valuation price
- Valuation procedure
- Valuation quantity

The value of your stock may depend on its scarcity and the costs of shipping it to your customers. Each plant can use the same valuation data, but they are not forced to do so because the MM data structure has master records to maintain different arrangements for each plant if necessary.

Warehouse Management   This information may be different for each stock of a material held in different plants.

- Unit of measure
- Palletization
- Instructions
- Place in or remove from stock indicator

Sales-Specific   This information may be different for each stock of a material held in different plants.

- Delivering plant
- Sales texts

Your materials may arrive in different vehicles or along different flow channels, and you may have your sales texts written differently according to the customers to be served by each plant.

Data at Storage Location Level

Data objects at this level inherit the plant-specific information because every storage location belongs to a particular plant.

Storage Location   This information may be different for each storage location for a particular material. The specific data about the plant will be inherited by each of the storage locations belonging to it.

- Storage period
- Stock fields

Forecast Data   This information may be different for each storage location for a particular material. The plant-specific data will be relevant because the forecasts may focus on each plant separately.

Consumption Data   This information may be different for each storage location for a particular material. The plant-specific data will be relevant because the consumption will be used to compute the forecasts.

Control Functions of Material Types

Each material in your company is assigned to a type according to how you intend to use it. SAP R/3 suggests the following material types to which you can add your own if you are prepared to create a master material type record for each:

- Raw material
- Semi-finished product
- Service
- Trading goods
- Internally owned container
- Externally owned container

By assigning each material a type, you can control how it is handled. For example:

- Which departments are permitted to maintain the material master records
- The type of procurement procedure to be used

- The stock account in financial accounting to be used in automatic account determination
- The inventory management type which will, for example, specify whether records are to be updated as quantities alone or with values as well

Using Industry Sectors

An industry sector is a branch of industry such as chemicals, marine construction, insurance, and trade. The industry sector code is used to indicate the main corporate activity of a Client. Your Client may have more than one main activity, and each could belong to a different industry sector.

You can signify how your materials are to be associated with industry sectors. SAP R/3 suggests a list of industry sectors to which you can add terms and definitions of your own.

Industry sectors can be grouped into hierarchical orders to indicate sub-sections. For example, one of your subsidiaries may sell components as trade goods to the marine construction industry and also supply the same items to your make-to-order division. You can use the industry sector classification of a material to influence the manner in which it is handled in the enterprise. You want to assign costs so that you can compare the profitability of trading some materials with their contribution to the profitability of your manufacturing orders.

Material Units of Measurement

SAP R/3 contains a set of standard units to which you can add specifications of your own.

Volume is a unit of measurement for some materials. Purchase order quantity might be more useful for others.

Entity type 1080 carries the code which is interpreted to signify which type of measurement unit is preferred for each of your materials. Some of your materials can be measured in several different units, such as boxes of twelve, pieces, pallet-loads.

A base unit of measurement is defined for each material, and there is a conversion factor to convert the net weight of the base unit to the weight of the quantity represented by each unit of measurement. The weight of the corresponding packaging is taken into account so that the shipping weight of a package can be ascertained.

European Article Numbers

To each material you can assign an EAN European Article Number that is dependent upon the unit of measurement of this material.

Storage Area

Storage area describes the arrangement of a warehouse according to organizational and spatial aspects. It can be a physical region of a warehouse or a set of locations that are treated alike.

Within a warehouse complex there can be several storage areas, such as high rack storage or block storage areas that, in turn, can consist of several storage bins.

Quants

A quant is the smallest addressable unit in a part of your warehouse. It could be defined by its dimensions or it could have barriers to limit its extent. A quant could even be a virtual unit. Perhaps your warehouse will not break open delivery units. It will count only the parcels, not the separate items they may contain. If so, then these delivery units will be your quants for this material. Storage bins are used to accommodate quants.

You may want to group some storage bins together for safety reasons.

Batches and Special Stocks

Storage location is the level at which a stock of material is managed normally. However, you may wish to assign some of this stock according to who owns it or what you are going to do with it. These batches or special stocks can be categorized:

- Consignment material from the vendor as vendor special stock
- Your containers or packaging temporarily with the customer as customer special stock
- Customer order stock for a make-to-order product, or other event-related special stock

Maintaining Materials Data Records

Changes to materials master data are recorded as change histories which show who made the alteration and when. These records can be maintained either centrally or per user department.

The standard system of authorization can be used to protect materials masters. The levels of activity are create, change, display only. Record alteration can be restricted according to department, organizational level, and by the type of transaction.

Vendor Masters

There are two groups of master records in materials management which are important in controlling costs: materials masters and vendor masters.

A "vendor" is a supplier of goods or services. During purchasing and invoice verification, the MM system can handle the various possibilities:

- Vendor is the actual supplier of the goods or services.
- Vendor is the payee for the goods or services.
- Vendor is the parent company or head office of the actual supplier, and issues invoices on their behalf.

Understanding a Semantic Model

A model is a way of representing something in a different presentation medium. The model is useful because it picks out only a few aspects of the real thing; it gives you a fresh way of looking. If you are a king and you want to have a warship built, you may find it helpful to have some miniature models built so that you can see what you will get if you decide to commission one. The model will give you an idea of what your new ship will look like—but it will not tell you how much the ship will cost, nor how long it will take to build, nor how effective it will be against the future navies of your enemies.

You could model your materials by having a set of samples of all the items you hold in stock. Your sales organization may well have a set for demonstration purposes. This set of samples could be regarded as a physical model of your inventory. However, it would not necessarily represent the quantity or the value of any of the inventory items. For this type of purpose, you need a model with more meaning—a semantic model.

A semantic model can be any form of presentation that reveals information about the thing being modeled. A rich semantic model would be able to give you lots of meaningful information; a sparse semantic model would tell you almost nothing.

A set of financial documents is a semantic model of a company that concentrates on its commercial condition and its viability as a financial concern. A site plan of a manufacturing plant is a semantic model of the physical layout of the premises. Neither of these models tells you much about the topics of the other model because they are specialized and have to select information for its relevance to their intended functions.

Interpreting Semantic Models

A semantic model is a terse logical device. It wastes no words; nor will it repeat definitions to make them easier to understand. This is why you have to know what all the symbols and drawing office conventions mean and how to interpret a site plan. This is why you have to know what the titles of the headings mean and how to read a financial statement.

On the plus side, you will find that a semantic model carries a great deal of information if you can be bothered to learn how to find it.

Of course, most business models are not like ship models. They tend to be presented in documents, although there may be a few physical models, pictures, or material samples around when the semantic model is used in public.

A common layout for a semantic model built from sentences is a list. You are intended to read the list from the top down and remember each item as you go because it may be taken for granted in a sentence further on. Figure 6.1 shows part of an enterprise model as a list of sentences.

FIG. 6.1

Part of a semantic model in sentence format.

> The client has one or more company codes.
>
> Each company code may have its own chart of account.
>
> > Therefore, any particular chart of accounts must be identified as belonging to a specific company code, which belongs to a particular client.
>
> A chart of accounts has one or more finance accounts.
>
> > Therefore, any particular chart of accounts must be identified as belonging to a specific company code, which belongs to a particular client.

This illustration of a sentence model is slightly elaborated because it includes two "therefore" sentences that are not part of the model. They are added to emphasize how you can read into a strict semantic model a great deal of procedural information.

Diagrams as Models

If you want to show a new driver how to deliver some materials, you could give him a road atlas and a list of addresses so that he could work out a route. You could draw a sketch map with lines between symbols for the places. The sketch would be a useful summary of the information in the road atlas because it would focus on the matter in hand: how to sequence the deliveries. The lines on the diagram would show the relationships between the destinations. It would be an entity-relationship model. The towns are the entities and the lines stand for the relationship of being located geographically adjacent. You might also take care to arrange your graphical model so that the long journeys are shown by long lines.

Entities and Relationships   An entity is formally defined as a part or the whole of the physical or logical universe. Thus it can be a tangible thing or a concept. In practice, a conceptual entity is not very useful unless there is an accepted definition or at least one example that can be cited as a paradigm or master model.

In business process engineering, an entity is the smallest possible collection of data that makes sense from a business point of view and that is represented in the SAP R/3 System. A date, for example, is an entity that makes sense from a business point of view because there is an accepted calendar which can be referenced by a series of numbers or alphanumeric symbols. We can interpret month, day, year. Various formats are acceptable because we know how to convert from one formulation to another. The SAP R/3 Basis software can handle these date formats automatically. For example, the date on a materials delivery can be compared with the date on the relevant delivery schedule. Your system can tell when the delivery is late because it compares two instances of the date entity—one on the delivery note, one on the delivery

Part

II

Ch

6

schedule. It determines the relationship between them. Then it decides whether the value of the time difference is within tolerance; and so the business process goes on by using the relationships between entities to control which entities to examine next. (See Figure 6.2.)

FIG. 6.2
Lateness is a relationship.

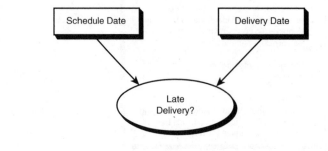

A business object is an entity, which includes certain data and procedures.

Entities linked by logical relationships that have business significance can be used to build static models of the enterprise, which in turn are portrayed in the respective computer application with its tables of specific values that were defined during customizing.

The R/3 Reference Model

The reference model is a data structure, delivered as part of SAP R/3 Basis, that contains a complete description of the R/3 system and the business functions therein. The model can be accessed in various ways and for various purposes. It can be used to simulate your business as it could be carried on if the SAP R/3 System were to be installed and configured to suit your particular circumstances. In particular, you can use the reference model to explore the relationships between the data objects that carry the important information about your inventory of materials and the vendors who supplied them.

The Data Object Structure of the R/3 System

R/3 is object-oriented. The units which the SAP standard business functions are designed to handle are data objects which can be of any complexity. For example, a data object may comprise only an identification code number for the object and one field which contains the information of interest—a part number, for instance.

Such an object is likely to be much more useful if it is permanently associated with other objects—in this instance, the name of the part in each of the SAP-supported languages, for example. The bundle of data elements comprising the part number, part name, and any other information needed about this part, is handled as a single object by the R/3 system. If you ask for this part by name or by number, the system will have available the rest of the information that goes to make up the data object. The user has control over which of the data elements shall appear on the display, but they are all there ready for immediate access.

There is no limit to the complexity of a data object because the data elements may themselves be complex objects.

A purchase order is a data object. It will include many data elements in the header, and each of the order items will represent a complex data object. When the purchase order is entered, it becomes a document which will be posted to various processes which will examine it to see if it is carrying the information which will be recognized as an event to be taken as the trigger or signal for specific processing.

Every item of information processed by the R/3 system is treated as an object. A project plan is an object. A user password is an object. An arrow on a graph is an object.

An Enterprise Model for Reference

One class of data objects that is recognized by R/3 is the enterprise model. The enterprise may be a department or the entire company, and the enterprise model is a way of specifying how the information and material moves within the organization as it does business.

In order to help you specify the material and information flows of your company in a standard manner that can be used to develop the efficiency of your business, the SAP R/3 Reference Model is provided as part of the system. It is an information model which is stored in graphical form which can be displayed using a standard symbology.

Customizing the Reference Model

The R/3 Reference Model contains all the common business process structures, linked in a totally integrated fashion which can be set to work without further adjustment. However, the standard R/3 Reference Model will probably include many functions and data structures that are not relevant to your organization. The process of Customizing is provided in the R/3 system to enable the system implementers to adjust the R/3 Reference Model until it exactly fits the needs and structure of the specific client organization.

When this match is complete, the model is referred to as an Enterprise Data Model.

The Concept of an Event-Driven Process Chain

The constituents of the R/3 Reference Model, and any Enterprise Data Models derived from it, are event-driven process chains. The graphical representation of these models is designed to show which events lead to which activities.

The designers of the SAP R/3 System found that no other method of specifying the requirements of a standard business software system was as fruitful and as easy to comprehend as the event-driven process chain. Where did the event-driven process chain come from? Why is it so useful?

Three Basic Design Principles

If you are trying to write down what goes on in a workplace, or what has to be done to get a certain result, then you will ask yourself three types of questions. You may not think about these issues at the right time, but if you omit any of them, you will discover that the work is not going as well as you expected, and that there is something missing from your job descriptions for the people involved.

What Should Be Done?   Perhaps the answer is obvious. Surely everyone knows that you should not be working at something if you do not know what has to be done. Yet there are people busy at work who have not stopped to think about the task they are tackling or the function they are supposed to be performing.

If you show someone performing the actions of a job without paying attention to what the purpose of the task is, then you may well raise a laugh. He or she is just going through the motions, without understanding.

Who Should Do Something?   If you are looking at a team of people, a department, or company, perhaps, then the second question is also an obvious one: Which member of the team should be the one to begin the task? Who is on the lookout for an occasion to set the team to work? Who is ready to notice an event of importance to the team if one should occur?

Even if you are working by yourself, the question must still be answered: Is this a job for me, or should I do nothing and let somebody else carry out the work?

If you are modeling your company, it is clearly a matter of some importance to identify which organizational unit is responsible for action in response to the significant events. And this responsibility is not just a matter of having someone to blame if something goes wrong. The organizational unit that is responsible for an activity will need to be provided with the tools, time, and energy resources to do it.

What Information Is Needed?   In order to perform a function, the responsible organizational unit needs to know what the task is. How to carry out this task will be a question of certain knowledge or skill that can be called upon, perhaps, from within the organizational unit. The necessary information for a task can be defined as an information object, a set of instructions together with the essential data, or an indication of where it can be found.

Some tasks are only performed by virtue of a human skill which is not generally available. In such cases, the critical information must include a specification of who in the company could be called upon to provide this skill or who should be tasked to enlist the aid of an outside provider.

The Evolution of Information Models

Perhaps the oldest information model is the family tree. It shows who the parents are and, therefore, who is most likely to have most power and experience. This information model is not necessarily accurate. A child may be more capable than a parent or a grandparent.

The family tree may suggest how the people are grouped into families and thus into organizational units. A structure diagram, which has a specified directionality, has arrows rather than plain lines, or has a definite up or down, before or after, which is in some way ordered. Such a structure may be drawn as a digraph, a directed graph.

The standard organization diagram is a digraph in which the ordering is from chief executive at the top to most junior worker at the bottom. Some companies may have a dozen layers of seniority; some have only two or three.

The organizational digraph may indicate who is responsible to whom. What it does not show is who does what, or how it is done.

Models of Units in an Organization   The family tree digraph leads to the organizational chart in easy stages. Groups of work people are associated as departments and represented as boxes or nodes on the digraph. Head Office is responsible for Purchasing and Sales.

The trouble with a simple organizational unit model is that it shows, by the arcs or arrows, who is in charge, but not what anyone does. In particular, there is no indication of, for example, how a sales order may cause the generation of a purchase order to replace the stock or commission work for the sales order. There is no flow of material shown, and no indication of how technical and commercial information might flow. From looking at the organization chart, you could be led to believe that all information exchanges between Purchasing and Sales must be routed via Head Office. This is almost never the situation.

Task Models   A simple task model is a cooking recipe. Take the ingredients and carry out the cooking processes. If you see this in graphical form, it would have an input block and an output block, with an arrow from input to output. One worker may perform the function of converting the input to the output. All the skill of the cook, or the expertise of the production worker, is concealed by the arrow which links the input raw materials to the finished products.

Task models can get very complicated if there are many inputs and many outputs, including the finished product, some by-products and some wastes, for example. But these task models do not usually portray the fact that a great deal of knowledge and skill is needed for the inputs to be correctly and efficiently transformed into the outputs.

Information Models   The third type of formal model to be developed has to be a supplement to the others. It concentrates on the information needed to carry out a function.

How does the worker know which materials and tools to select? Where did he acquire the skills? What is he looking at, and what is he looking for, when he is monitoring the quality of his work?

Information is a difficult concept to define. If you know that a coin has two faces, and you know that it has fallen heads up, then you have acquired one bit of information, which your computer could record as one binary digit.

The menu is the troublesome part. How can you possibly choose what to order for dinner until you know what the menu offers? If there are eight possibilities, and you choose one, then the chef will have acquired three binary digits of information from you which will be valuable to him because it means that he need not cook seven of the dishes on the menu, at least not for you.

If your R/3 system can tell whether the document is a sales order or a purchase order, then this will be information which can be used to narrow down the possibilities for subsequent action.

The concept of information is not relevant unless you know the menu. The R/3 system can recognize a large but not unlimited number of document types. You can add to this list during customizing if you are prepared to tell the system how a new type of document is to be recognized, and what actions are to be taken when one is encountered.

A gardener may know the names of hundreds of plants. She may also be able to recognize them. She could carry out the task of walking through a garden and speaking aloud the names of most of the plants. She has a considerable amount of information. However, this does not mean she is a gardener capable of cultivating any of these plants, although you would probably be near the mark if you assumed this.

The information model is good at specifying the size of the menu from which the skilled person can make a choice. The larger the possible menu of events that could occur, the greater the amount of information necessary to allocate the correct names.

Naming the parts is a good way to begin to acquire a skill, but it does not necessarily help you to do the right thing every time.

Event-Driven Process Chain Objects

If we are looking for some sort of analytical object as a standard building block for showing how a company does business, then the event-driven process chain is the prime candidate. One process may lead to another and so on down a chain which is complete only when the result is achieved. But a set of process chains that do not have precisely specified events which are their exclusive triggers are of no use. Each process chain must begin only when the specified event occurs. And, if that event does occur, then there must be no question as to whether the assigned process chain will begin or not. When the certain data elements in certain data objects are found to match the conditions laid down when defining the event that shall drive a chain, then that chain and only that chain will be initiated.

There is no limit to the complexity of an event-driven process chain because each of the processes in the chain may itself give rise to a complex data object that is able to take part in the initiation of other event-driven process chains.

Stimulus-Response Theory and Event-Driven Process Chain Methods

If you are teaching a person or an animal to do something that does not come naturally to them, something that is neither in their instinctual repertoire nor in the knowledge and skills they have learned previously, then you have to attend very carefully to the stimulus and the response.

Suppose you want the user to press key F1. You could get this to happen in several different ways:

> Take the user's finger and push the F1 key.
>
> Say to the user, "Press the F1 key."
>
> Say to the user, "Select PF1."

Have you taught the user anything useful? Perhaps the system will respond with a helpful message and the user will guess that the PF1 key may be the key to use if you need help. But not necessarily. The user may not associate what the system did with which key was pressed.

Try a different lesson. Say to the student user of the system something like this: "If you need help, and the screen is showing you a picture or other sign labeled HELP, then try pressing the key marked F1 to call the special programmed function labeled PF1."

This is not a very exciting lesson, but it does illustrate that we learn to do things, such as pressing a Help key, and we learn when this action is likely to be needed or appropriate.

For example, we could all press key F6 without difficulty. But would we all know whether that would be a good idea and would help us do what we are trying to do? The response of pressing a particular key is not much use to us if we have no idea when it should be carried out.

In the language of the psychologists, we have to associate a useful response with the stimulus for that response. If we have managed to do this on a reliable basis, we are said to have acquired an operant, a stimulus-response pair.

This may not seem very momentous—one stimulus triggering one response.

The clever part comes when we can tell the difference between stimuli that might otherwise be confused. We may have names or labels for many of the significant stimuli in our private world. Fire is a name that carries a warning. System Error 1492 is a name for something that seems to be important for the computer. What we can do if we see this on our screen is to ask somebody what to do about it. That, at least, is an appropriate response. One day we might learn a better one.

Part
II

Ch
6

Many of the errors made by people and machines occur because the response was not quite right for the stimulus situation at the time. There could be two types of fault here:

- The stimulus triggered the correct response, which was then executed badly. Right, but sloppy.
- The response was executed perfectly, but there was a subtle difference in the stimulus situation that should have triggered quite a different response. Beautiful, but inappropriate.

The essence of SAP standard process software is to make sure that all business functions are carried out absolutely without error. No matter how specialized the work of your company, if you have installed SAP R/3 software, it will be running exactly the same functions as in all the many other customer installations of SAP. All you can do is alter the way the function elements are linked together and the data stored in the data objects to which these functions refer.

Data modeling is a discipline to ensure that the structure of your data is properly formed so that the standard business software will have no trouble processing it.

Function modeling is a discipline to make sure that your SAP R/3 System does exactly what you want it to do.

S-R Chains

The stimulus-response model of the operant as a useful way of thinking about how people and machines carry out tasks can be extended to describe a sequence of actions.

The first stimulus is the signal to begin the task with the first response. As this response is carried out, it should create the stimulus situation that will trigger the next operant in the chain.

If the learning has been perfect, there will be no point where the person doing the task asks, "What do I do next?" Every action will serve as the trigger for the next. And with copious practice, the sequence will speed up and the task performer will be looking ahead and getting prepared for the steps ahead. With even more practice, the whole chain may rattle along without the performer's, paying it any conscious attention. We might say it had become instinctual. As soon as it had been given the go-ahead, the next conscious event would be the delivery of the finished result.

Responses by the System to Events

The event-driven process chain can be regarded as a sequence of actions that has been developed to provide a stable and appropriate response to the event which is its trigger. There is a simple idea here, but one which can be used to build reliable software.

Understanding an Entity-Relationship Model

If a semantic model of your enterprise is to be really useful, it must include all the entities of business significant to all the departments of your various companies. Your model must find a place for every type of master data record and every software function. Clearly an orderly classification of entities is needed. There are some special terms to be understood because they are the keys to unlocking the benefits of holding a formal data model in your SAP R/3 System.

Semantic Data Modeling Concepts

A model is a representation of something seen or understood from a particular point of view. The model filters out detail that might obscure the view or confuse the interpretation.

A model can be presented in a particular graphical or textual format, although physical models could be conceived for some circumstances. A data model shows how information is arranged in boxes or other containers such as computer records. A semantic data model attempts to attach titles or labels to the parcels of information so that the human users of such a system can understand the business significance of the information stored.

A data object in the SAP System is a region of computer storage that can be accessed by using the name of the object. Most of the names will suggest the business significance of the data held in this region.

In formal logical terminology, "things" or "parcels" are all classed as "entities."

Thus, we have reached the concept that a semantic data model of your company would have to be a picture of it seen from a point of view that distinguished, not the buildings of your plant, not the people who work in them, not your goods, nor your customers, but merely the entities that held your business data.

Entity Types as Information Objects   However, reality does impinge on semantic data modeling. The entities that hold data are assigned to entity types, and the name of an entity type tells you what the data lodging there is all about.

"Employee" is an entity type. Information about real persons will be held in a format that is specified in a master record for the Employee entity type. Perhaps the first twenty characters of an employee record is reserved for their surname or family name.

"Raw Material" is another entity type; so is "Storage area for European pallets."

These entities can be treated as information objects because they become instantiations of a master object as soon as you create a unique one for a new material or new employee, for example. Some of the data fields in the master may not contain any data because there is none. But some of the fields will be mandatory. You will have to enter the required information in order to generate the record. Both materials and people have to be given identification code numbers and names in the entity database.

Specializations of Entity Types   Some entities are part of a family. For example, "Goods issue—quantity" is the name of entity 5350. You could come upon a document that stated that a certain item existed in a specified quantity, say three pallets.

You might need to know what was supposed to happen to these three pallets.

It just so happens that entity 5350 is not allowed to be used unless there is an entry to show a specific customer or internal recipient of the goods issue. So you could determine the eventual destination of these three pallets.

But this item of goods issued could be in transit, or it could be set aside as a reservation, or you may have no information about it apart from the customer.

These various possibilities are recorded in the database as specializations. There can be various types of specializations. In the case of entity 5350 there is only one type of specialization, "Specialization type 0001 Reference object." This means that the system will annotate and differentiate between goods issue quantities according to the reference object. The scheme for entity type 5350 illustrates the use of specializations according to the objects referenced.

Specializations of type 0001 according to the Reference object based on Entity type 5350:

- Entity type 5349

  Goods issue—quantity
  - customer delivery—inward movement

- Entity type 5351

  Goods issue—quantity
  - unrelated (to any reference object)

- Entity type 5352

  Goods issue—quantity
  - customer delivery—outward movement

- Entity type 5353

  Goods issue—quantity
  - material reservation

The SAP R/3 System is delivered with an extensive scheme of entity types and specializations of various kinds. You may wish to add extra possibilities during customization if the standard scheme does not cover what you require.

Inheritance of Information   The standard SAP approach to building complex data structures is also termed "object orientation". An assembly in manufacturing is defined as a specific collection of components. One of these components will be a list of all the items that are to be included if you decide to ship the assembly. A BOM bill of materials is an example of such a list.

The concept of inheritance can be used in an informal way to denote an association between objects. The assembly inherits a list of its constituents, for example. But the importance of the object orientation rationale lies in the strict use of inheritance—and this is used in SAP data structures.

For example, your SAP R/3 System will operate with a single client code which is inherited by all documents created by it. If you have a "For training only" client code, you will find that the system never allows a training transaction to be involved with anything associated with the production client code. Training documents invariably inherit the training client code; live production documents invariably inherit the production client code.

The time and date, to give another example, is a data object that is maintained by the system. All documents automatically inherit the current time and date as they are posted. And there is nothing a user can do to the client database which will escape the automatic creation of a document to record this action.

Entity specialization is an example of inheritance.

Relationships Between Entities   The specializations of an entity type are themselves entity types. They too are master formats from which instantiations can be generated, all faithfully adhering to the data arrangements set out in the master.

For example, Entity type 5349, which is a specialization of Entity type 5350, will inherit all the characteristics of 5350. However, there will be additional characteristics that justify assigning it the status of a separate entity type. Our example illustrated that the difference, in this case, concerned the reference object to which the goods issue quantity related.

Entity type 5349 has the title, "Goods issue—quantity—customer delivery—inward movement". If you look up this entity in the materials area of the enterprise data model, you will discover that entity type 5349 is used to record a quantity of a sales materials that is being returned in connection with a customer complaint order. In fact the sales material is posted as a negative goods issue and allocated either to your own stock or to the blocked stock returns.

You will not be surprised to learn that the following are entity types:

- Sales material
- Customer complaint order—return

Entities as Complex Families   Entity type 2554 is "Transaction type".

This entity is used to classify the business or accounting transaction that took place as a result of completing a task. Thus, a sum of 1000 in the transaction currency could be posted as any of three transaction types under your client code:

- Transaction Type actual cost transfer
- Transaction Type planned cost accrual
- Transaction Type planned cost distribution

These three possibilities are coded as values which are permitted entries in the entity type 2554. If you have reason to classify a transaction according to this scheme of transaction types, the R/3 system will offer you the choice of the allowable possibilities set out in business language in the form of a menu. If your company uses different transaction types, then the list will have been rearranged as a result of the customizing process.

By selecting one of the allowed options, you cause the entity 2554 to be primed with the code value for your choice. Your transaction document will then contain a linking reference to a record where entity 2554 is the format used for storing this value.

If you need to read the result of this operation, the system will translate the value in the transaction document formatted as entity 2554. What you will see on your screen will be the understandable business text, not the code value.

By working to a strict system of entity types and allowable values, the SAP R/3 System can work quickly and store information economically. For example, the business text, "TRANSACTION TYPE planned cost accrual", is stored in the system in one place only. This is in the master record for the entity type 2554. Every time this text appears on a menu, or is printed on a document, you will know that your system has copied it from the master record. Those capitals, for instance, can be set in the master as part of the business text.

Displaying the Relationship Between Entities

To speak of families of entities is an obvious example of declaring that they are related. A graphical family tree is another possibility. The lines on a block diagram often portray relationships.

If a picture is a process diagram, it may be read as a "Do List": First you must do this task, then that, and so on.

If the picture is a workflow diagram, the arrows between the blocks may signify the start and finish relationships between tasks. Perhaps two tasks could begin at the same time; perhaps one has to be finished before the other can begin; perhaps the only relationship between them is that they must both be finished before a third task can begin. Before you go on vacation the car must be checked and the luggage packed. You can sequence these tasks how you like so long as they are completed before you set off.

Project planning relationships are often about timetables and tasks to be done. Database relationships are often about the formats of data records. One master record may be the model from which all others have to be copied so that they all use the same data objects. The software will be designed to process the master record and all copies or instantiations of it.

However, you may wish to add some fields to the master record. What you can do in these cases is to create a specialization of the master which will inherit all the master fields. Your additional data will then be processed only when your system knows how to handle the specialization.

In this example, the relationship between the original and the specialization has a direction: One is the parent of the other.

Business Relationship Types   There are several different kinds of relationships between entities in the SAP Enterprise Data Model which have been implemented in the software because they are of business significance and contribute to building robust and efficient systems.

One-to-One Cardinality   Cardinality is a property of a relationship. One-to-one is a cardinality much discussed in romantic novels. One-to-many is also discussed in such sources.

The definition of a one-to-one situation can be depicted in a table comprising two columns. If the rows contain the pairs of entities under discussion, the table suggests a one-to-one cardinality because any cell in a row is associated with one, and only one, other cell in that row.

In a secure computer environment, you will expect there to be a one-to-one relationship between identification codes and authorized users.

An obvious but important feature of one-to-one cardinality is that there is no directionality between the two entities. Either will point to the other.

One-To-Many Cardinality   A procedure that has to be performed strictly in sequence can be depicted as a block diagram in which the arrows show the sequence. In this case, the cardinality between the blocks is one-to-one. Each step is followed by one, and only one, next step.

In logic, the cardinality can be taken as the number of lines in a dependent table to which the table under consideration in principle can or must relate.

A line in a table may be related to another dependent line in a cardinality of one-to-one correspondence. Each employee identification code should be in one-to-one relationship to just one set of personal details that are correct for a real person on the payroll.

The relationship may be one-to-many if there can be several dependent lines for any referenced line. For example, there could be many satisfactory answers to a database query that asks whether a customer has an approved credit card. A potential customer may be able to prove ownership of only a few cards, perhaps none with borrowing credit.

If you see a block diagram with several arrows leaving a box you must expect to find one-to-many cardinality. What you must also expect to find is some method for you or your system to make a choice. How do you tell which path to take if there are several identical arrows?

A materials master number should refer to a unique form of raw material or semi-processed material. But there may be several batches of this material stored in different locations. To properly specify the contents of any one location you will need to establish relationships to the storage location entity, the batch number entity, the material master entity, and so on.

If your materials data have been classified and stored according to a strict enterprise data model, anyone in your company will be able to sort out the relationships between the data object entities. In fact, your SAP R/3 System can do it for you if you really have been strict about your data.

The Direction of a Relationship   The family tree expresses a set of relationships. Parents have children. Children find they have parents. You could use an arrow to indicate that the relationships had a direction.

> Parents ➡ Children
>
> Children ➡ Parents

Arrows of this type are used in the SAP documentation to show direction.

Part
II
Ch
6

The importance of the direction can be demonstrated in this example: A child can have only one pair of genetic parents. A pair of parents can have many children. The cardinality of the relationship is one-to-many in the ➡ direction and one-to-one in the ➡ direction if you accept that a pair of parents is a single entity.

Data Architecture

The network of relationships between entities in a data structure is spoken of as the data architecture because there should be a place for everything and everything should be in its place. There should be no difficulties in navigating through the data architecture.

In SAP R/3 there is a graphical display of the structure like an architectural drawing. There is a textual display like an architect's specification.

Architecture Areas　To make it easier to find your way through the complexities of an enterprise data model, even if it is of your very own organization, the various software functions and data objects recognized by the applications of your system are assigned to architecture areas.

"Material" is the name of an architecture area. So is "Hazardous material".

Structured Entity-Relationship Models　As soon as you assign entities to architecture areas, you have started to structure your model. This means you could navigate by a series of menu choices and you could operate the drill-down function at your SAPGUI to reach an entity that held the information you needed.

The graphical portrayal of the structured entity-relationship model of your enterprise will show entity types, entity relationships and entity specializations.

Degrees of Existence Dependency　The SAP Enterprise Data Model is intended to be consulted by users and software developers. It is structured accordingly.

One of the structuring concepts is the degree of existence dependency. You can interpret this concept in terms of master data and flow data.

An entity type "Plant" could be instantiated as a specific warehouse that had not been built. This item of plant could be named and costed and assigned the expenses of carrying out research, and so on. The entity type "Plant" could also be instantiated as a physical warehouse full of materials. You could say that the system knew how to handle entities of type "Plant," even if your company had no actual plant nor any plant at planning stage. In this example, the entity type "Plant" is assigned a low degree of existence dependency. This entity type exists even if there are no instances of it in your system. Your client code can own an empty set of entities of type "Plant". In fact, your SAP R/3 System will automatically associate this entity type with your client as soon as your system is configured.

By contrast of the example of "Plant," which has low existence dependency because it can be valid even when there are no instances of it, the entity type "Vendor purchase order", which is entity type 5016, cannot exist on its own.

A vendor purchase order is a purchase order that is addressed to a vendor.

The existence of an example of a valid vendor purchase order depends on there being at least one instance of each of the following entity types:

- Purchase order
- Vendor
- Time and date
- Buyer authorized for this type and value of purchase

If you do not have an instance of a "Vendor", or if you have not placed an instance of a "Purchase order", then you cannot have an instance of "Vendor purchase order".

A vendor purchase order has a high degree of dependency because its very existence depends on several other entity types having been previously instanced. In practical terms, your vendor purchase order cannot be printed unless your system can locate the relevant purchase order with its items. It also needs the address and other particulars of a suitable vendor.

Low Degree Master Data   Most of the architecture areas that have entity types of low existence dependency are referred to as master data areas. They store the rules and information that stay relatively unchanged in your system regardless of the volume of transactions taking place within it.

Higher Degree Flow Data   The architecture areas for the entity types of intermediate existence dependency carry the information formats that are relatively stable between transactions, but which may be altered as business conditions change. The day-to-day business document entity types are in this category; production order, vendor quotation, customer order, sales, and transaction figures are examples.

Highest Degree of Existence Dependency   The entity types for data that is frequently updated are stored in the architecture areas of the highest degree of existence dependency. For example, details of a material price change are dependent on the date and time data objects as well as the particulars of the material and the price change computation.

SAP-EDM Enterprise Data Model

The purpose of an enterprise data model is to make sense of and take into account how the business uses the data structures defined in the active ABAP/4 data dictionary and the Business Object Repository.

The enterprise data model is built from entity-relationship elements that portray the relevant information objects and their relationships from a business standpoint.

For example, the following relationship is between data structures seen from a data processing standpoint:

Value S = Value C + Value P.

The same relationship may admit a different interpretation when seen from a business perspective:

Profit is Sales Revenue less Costs

One view is a model for the computer to specify the calculation procedures; the other is a model of how the business can survive and flourish if the management can manipulate the values in a certain way. These examples are obviously a little sparse.

Organizational Structure in an Enterprise Data Model   The SAP R/3 general organizational units relevant to all applications are taken from the standard reference that is the R/3 Enterprise Data Model:

Client is the highest level in R/3. The data of one client may not be accessed by another client. There is often a training client and a testing client, in addition to the client code that represents your group or corporate identity and under which the SAP System runs normal business. Some data is managed at the Client level because everyone in the corporate group of companies will want to refer to exactly the same information and be certain that it has been maintained up-to-date and correct. Vendor addresses would be an example of data managed at the client level.

Company Code signifies a legal unit under the Client which produces its own financial documents, the balance sheet, and the profit-and-loss statement, and may well maintain them continuously reconciled.

Plant is an organizational unit that is seen as central to the production planning concept. A plant can be a production site, or it can be a group of storage locations that share materials. Plant is the unit for which MRP prepares plans and maintains the inventory. It is the focus of MM-Materials Management. Each plant will have been given planning and control elements such as material, inventory, operations, work centers, and so on.

The lower levels of organizational structure will tend to be specific to the application. For example, the lower levels of a warehouse data structure will reference warehouse areas and perhaps bin types and bin numbers, whereas the lowest level in a human resource personnel data structure will be an individual person.

Standard Entity Types   The following entity types are standard in the SAP-EDM function:

Organizational Unit, which is part of the R/3 Reference Model and will be assigned the name of the operating company or department that the enterprise data model is being used to represent

Position, which is modeled from the R/3 Reference Model and named to suit the specific company with a title such as "Sales Representative"

Workplace, of which there may be several assigned the same position, each able to accommodate one person

Job, which is a set of tasks based on a specific workplace but not necessarily the only set of tasks performed there

Task, which is a component of a job and usually comprises a fairly well-defined set of work input materials or messages for which there are appropriate work procedures

Two other entity types are necessarily addressed by relationships in this arena. They serve to particularize any instance of the model by naming a Person and a Cost Center. A named individual is assigned to perform a job and therefore is attached to a workplace which carries the responsibilities of a position. This position will be associated with a Cost Center such as a specific plant or department.

Relationships in an Enterprise Data Model   The data model fragment in Figure 6.3 implies the following relationships:

A named Person holds both a Workplace and a Position.

The Workplace is part of the Position.

The Position is part of an Organizational Unit.

The Organizational Unit is allocated to a particular Cost Center.

The Position describes a Job.

The Job describes one or more Tasks.

A Task describes a special case of a Position.

FIG. 6.3
Part of an Enterprise
Data Model.

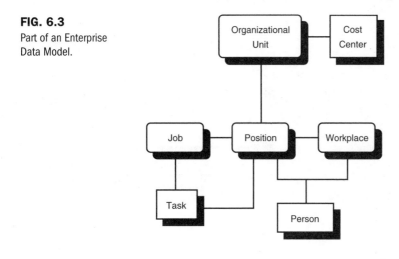

There is a system of graphical symbols that are used by the R/3 System to display different views of the Enterprise Data Model. The different views emphasize the relationships between the objects of the model.

Exploring the Enterprise Data Model

The SAP R/3 System provides a comprehensive suite of standard business functions ready to be set into action. The R/3 Reference Model is a master plan of the whole system that you can copy and edit until it corresponds to the way you intend to do business. At this stage it deserves the title of "Enterprise Data Model."

But this model is no toy. The EDM is a complex structure with many constituents. They are all equally important.

The Data Attributes of an Event

In the language of SAP system design, the data object recognized as an event is able to store an unlimited amount of data. This enables SAP R/3 to withhold posting action until the intended transaction has been tested for validity, no matter how complicated the data processing needed to prove it. However, this data cannot be readily accessed unless it is recorded in a systematic manner and uniformly across all events.

The data fields of an event master record are clustered as "Attributes." And each attribute cluster is assigned a set of standard data field titles which can be extended and developed during customizing, if necessary.

Event Attribute One

The following fields are located in Attribute One:

Name of the event

Identifier code

Synonymous names for this event, aliases

Full designation of the event which places it in the software context

Description or definition of the event

Author of the event specification

Origin of the event

The following data fields are available in the event master to indicate the originating source of the control and substantive information associated with the event:

Outside of company

In-house

Outside of system

Within system

System-interdependent

Event Attribute Two

Additional characteristics of the event are stored in Attribute Two in order to specify the type of the event, the classification of the event in terms of its logical function, and the function of the event in the context of an event-driven process chain.

Type of Event   The assembly of critical information that constitutes an event can be generated in one of three ways that serve to define the type of the event as follows:

>   Interactively generated event
>
>   Automatically generated event
>
>   Manually generated event

Classification of an Event   The status of an event as part of an event-driven process chain is used to classify it.

Trigger   If the event is able to initiate an event-driven process chain at any time the specified data becomes critical, then it is classified as a trigger event.

Secondary Condition   If the event is not itself a trigger but an intermediate or secondary criterion cluster of data, it is classified as a secondary condition. This type of event represents the situation in which additional data may have to be consulted before an event-driven process chain can reach its conclusion.

State   An event that acts as a buffer or collating store for the results from a number of processes can be classified as a state. A state can be referenced by perhaps many different event-driven process chains.

Functional Purpose of an Event   In the context of an event-driven process chain, the beginning and end items are clearly of especial importance because they constitute the occasions for input information and output results to be available to the rest of the system. Events are therefore categorized according to their function as follows:

>   Start event
>
>   Finish event
>
>   Start or finish event
>
>   Internal process event which may be subject to monitoring for special purposes, but which will not normally be apparent to the user of the system

Event Attribute Three

The third attribute cluster of an event carries the data concerned with time. It will be consulted by the system on a routine basis to determine whether the event has to be set to trigger the associated event-driven process chain.

Time of Occurrence   The system will need to identify which events have been scheduled for a fixed time or a schedule of times. This attribute value can be Known or Unknown.

Frequency of Event If the event is scheduled to recur, then the details will be recorded as follows:

Times per year

Times per month

Times per week

Times per day

The Data Attributes of a Function

The standard structure of the data associated with a function is as clusters of data elements named as three attributes.

Function Attribute One

The following fields are located in Function Attribute One:

Name of the function

Identifier code

Synonymous names for this function, aliases

Full designation of the function that places it in the software context

Description or definition of the function

Author of the function specification

Source information

System attributes including the transaction code and the release level

Function Attribute Two

The way the function is used and its classification as a standard business program or a function written specifically for the customer is recorded in Function Attribute Two.

Functional Assignment The assignment of a function in terms of its functional use is categorized as follows:

Outside of company

In-house

Outside of system

Within system

Optional function

Mandatory function

Classification of the Function   The system recognizes the following types of function by a code in the function master record:

> Standard system function
>
> Customer-specific additional system function
>
> External system function

Function Attribute Three

The third function attribute cluster is devoted to data concerning the processing type and frequency. There is also a record maintained in the function master of the time needed for the function to acquire the data needed to specify the task to be performed and the time needed to actually process the data to complete it. The system costs of processing are accumulated in this attribute.

Processing Type of the Function   The type of processing entailed by the function will determine the system resources to which it is assigned. The processing types are specified as follows:

> Interactive
>
> Automatic
>
> Manual
>
> Central
>
> Local

Frequency of Processing   The actual times of processing may be used to accumulate frequency data as follows:

> Times per year
>
> Times per month
>
> Times per week
>
> Times per day

Duration of Processing   The learning or data acquisition time is recorded as a moving average to indicate the time taken for the function to acquire all the data sources and documents which will be needed to perform the function.

The actual processing time is also recorded as a moving average of the time taken to process the data once it has been assembled from its sources.

Costs of Processing   The costs of calling this function can be accumulated on a moving average basis and evaluated in financial terms or on the basis of system processing costs expressed in resource usage units.

The Data Attributes of a Process

A process taking part in an event-driven process chain can be assigned a very large number of data elements. They are clustered into two attributes.

Process Attribute One

The following fields are located in Process Attribute One:

Name of the process

Identifier code

Synonymous names for this process, aliases

Full designation of the process that places it in the software context

Description or definition of the process

Author of the process specification

Process Assignment   A process can be assigned to a single organizational unit or to an entire system. The details are stored under the following headings:

Organizational unit

System assignment to application, module, transaction

Required input information

Generated output information

Start event identification

End event identification

Process links

Processing Changes   There will be changes in the organization in which a process is carried on. The details of these processing changes are recorded in the process master record under the following headings:

Organizations involved in the changes

Frequency with which the organization is changed

Systems and media affected by the changes

Frequency with which the system or medium is changed

Information Statistics   The information storage requirements generated by the operation of a process can be a source of major costs. These requirements are recorded on the process master in terms of the following groups:

Information storage within the system

Information storage outside the system

Information storage requirements which are not supported by information technology methods and equipment

Process Attribute Two

Additional information about the process is stored in the master in Attribute Cluster Two. The theme is processing statistics.

Duration of the Process   The following data objects are stored in the process master:

Learning time

Processing time

Transmission time

Wait time

Entry time

Output time

Process Quantity Structures   The process master stores data structures to record the quantities of material or information processed, and also the quantities transmitted.

Process Costs   The following process costs are cumulated:

Overall costs

Personnel costs

Machine costs

Material costs

Data Transmission   Statistics are recorded for the following classes of data transmission entailed by the process:

IT-supported, online

IT-supported, batch

Manual

Transmission Medium   The distribution of data transmission across the following media and methods is recorded for the process:

Network

Data processing list

Written documents and forms

Card file

Oral data transmission

This chapter has pointed to some of the necessary complexity of data and the thoroughness with which data in the SAP R/3 System is stored and managed.

Part

II

Ch

6

EDM Documentation Components

The main source of EDM information is the online SAP R/3 System itself. The examples of EDM documentation in this book are adapted from the book, *SAP Enterprise Data Model, Materials Management, Release 2.2, System R/3.*

The documentation for the SAP-EDM in the Materials Management Application Area comprises the following elements:

- A listing of the architecture areas into which the entity type records are divided
- A text for each architecture area that outlines the business significance of the entity types located in it
- A structured information section for each entity type

Business Aspects of the Materials Architecture Area

The architecture area MATERIAL contains general information relating to the material.

Through a dividing up (classification) of materials into different material types (for example, raw material, semi-finished product), basic features of a material are characterized and the manner in which a material is handled in the enterprise is specified. The industry sector (for example, chemicals, machine construction) to which a material belongs also has an influence on the manner in which it is handled in the enterprise.

For a material, different units of measurement can be valid, whereby for each unit of measurement a conversion factor is defined for its conversion into the base unit of measurement. For identification of the material, European Article Numbers that are dependent upon the unit of measurement can exist for the material.

For a material, information is kept with regard to purchasing, design and engineering, and storage. Plant-specific features of a material are recorded in the plant material. In order to form production units for a plant material that display the smallest possible differences in quality, a plant material can be divided into batches.

Structured Information for an Entity Type

The materials management application area of the SAP-EDM contains some entity types that are of general significance in addition to the entity types particular to materials management. The following example refers to the entity type "Material," which is used to format all individual material master records:

Entity Type

1027

Description

> Material

Definition

> A Material is a tangible or intangible good that is an object of the business activity.

Comment

> A Material is bought and sold, used, consumed, or manufactured during production.

Example

> Tangible good: object, substance (gas, powder, and so on)
>
> Intangible good: service, right, patent

This basic layout is adopted for all the entity types in the Enterprise Data Model documentation.

Specialization Types

The specialization types of any entity type will be numbered from 0001, but they will have different interpretations according to the entity type of which they generate variants.

In the current example, Entity type 1027, Material, there are two standard specialization types and three standard specializations using the first of these types.

Specialization types 0002, 0004, and 0005 are available for definition during customizing.

> 0001 Material Use—Specialization according to the manner in which the material is used.
>
> 0003 External Use of Material—Specialization according to the manner in which the material is externally used.

Standard Specialization (1)

> From 1027 Material
>
> To 1031 Material—purchasing
>
> Specialization type 0001 Material Use

The following is a typical interpretation: Entity type 1031 is used for material in the purchasing process. The attributes of Entity type 1027 will be inherited by Entity type 1031. There will be additional attributes to store the data particular to the purchasing specialization, which is characterized by the use to be made of the material.

Standard Specialization (2)

From 1027 Material

To 1034 Material—engineering and design

Specialization type 0001 Material Use

Standard Specialization (3)

From 1027 Material

To 1036 Material—storage

Specialization type 0001 Material Use

Relationships Between Entity Types

The relationship between entity types is determined as part of the specification of these types. The role of a relationship is normally Role 1, which indicates a specific cardinality.

Relationship may be interpreted as a means of navigating from one entity type to another.

The cardinality of a relationship is taken from the following list:

1:CM Referential

1:CM Aggregating

1:CM Hierarchical

C:CM Conditional Referential

C:CM Conditional Aggregating

C:CM Temporary Referential

1:M Aggregating

1:M Hierarchical

The interpretation of the role and the cardinality is illustrated in the arrowed upstream and downstream sections of the relationship information structure.

Relationship (1)

From 1001 Client*

To 1027 Material

Role 1 Cardinality 1:CM Hierarchical

Downstream (⇒) Relationships ⇒   For a Client* there can be several Material(s).

Upstream (⇒) Relationships⇒   A Material is allocated to exactly one Client*.

Relationship (2)

From 1015 Material type

To 1027 Material

Role 1 Cardinality 1:CM Referential

Downstream (➟) Relationships   A Material type can classify several Material(s).

Upstream (➟) Relationships   Each Material is classified by exactly one Material type.

Relationship (3)

From 1021 Industry sector

To 1027 Material

Role 1 Cardinality 1:CM Referential

Downstream (➟) Relationships   To an Industry sector several Material(s) can be allocated.

Upstream (➟) Relationships   A Material belongs to exactly one Industry sector.

Relationship (4)

From 5386 Catalog—hazardous material

To 1027 Material

Role 1 Cardinality C:CM Conditional Referential

Downstream (➟) Relationships   In a Catalog—hazardous material several Material(s) can occur.

Upstream (➟) Relationships   A Material can relate to a Catalog—Hazardous material.

Relationship (5)

From 6020 Division

To 1027 Material

Role 1 Cardinality C:CM Temporary Referential

Downstream (➟) Relationships   A Division can be allocated to several Material(s).

Upstream (➟) Relationships   A Material can relate to a Division.

Other Features of EDM Documentation

Although the data structure of an entry in the EDM documentation for an entity type is shared for all types, there are some fields that only appear where relevant.

Starred Name Client*

The unique uppermost organizational level is coded as the client level and title Client* to distinguish it from possible uses of the word "client" to refer to a customer in some sectors of industry.

Time Dependency Annotation

Some entity types are used for aggregating data over a defined period of time. For example, Entity type 4017, "Cost accounting area", is time dependent and the time unit is business year. If it is relevant, a time dependency annotation is displayed under the entity type name, together with the time unit. "Goods issue—quantity" is time dependent and the unit is a point in time.

How to Interpret the EDM Documentation

The R/3 Reference Model can show you what is available in the SAP R/3 Basis system and any applications you have installed and configured with it. The EDM Enterprise Data Model is built from components in the R/3 Reference Model, but the result will be an extensive elaboration of it.

When your SAP R/3 System is just sitting quietly, with no traffic, no transaction processing, no routine database backup in progress, no software maintenance under way; this is the time when your business information is all held in storage. Everything of value—in terms of information about your products, your processes, your suppliers, your staff, your liquidity—is just binary digits in some storage medium. Your enterprise is represented by a collection of data.

You may like to follow through the thinking that put this information in this database system. You may like to consider how your system will find it again and make sense of it as soon as anyone tries to conduct a transaction.

Dividing the Data Model for Clarity

At the level of system operating code, the software of SAP R/3 is fully integrated, although there is a gradual evolution of the software through successive releases. This evolution is in the direction of separating functional modules that can be used in various different ways according to the system in which they are embedded.

However, the ideas are not affected by this evolution in the way the SAP R/3 products are marketed.

A full enterprise data model of a large implementation would comprise many thousands of elements. To appreciate all their interconnections would be beyond the comprehension of any one consultant, and this breadth of understanding is certainly not needed by the users and their managers.

In documentation and in presentation, the EDM is divided into parts. This discussion will focus on the SAP Enterprise Data Model where it relates to the MM-Materials Management application Release 2.2. Necessarily, the model overlaps with financial and control functions, and you may well require it to be closely related to the HR-Human Resources application if you have this installed and configured in your implementation.

Displaying an EDM

SAP-SERM is the technical term used for a standard graphical display format that is used to view an enterprise data model shown as a structured entity-relationship model. The visual appearance of your model can be controlled by the presentation system you are using. However, the logical relationships in the model will be preserved, no matter which display conventions you have available.

Parallel presentation media include CD-ROM demonstrations and textbook compilations of the EDM fundamentals.

If you are using an online presentation system to explore the EDM, you will have the advantage of seeing the details of your company model rather than the master or paradigm formulations that are used to shape the specific elements of your own structures.

Area Architecture

The entities of your EDM are taken from master molds provided in the SAP R/3 System. They copy the masters because your system has been programmed to handle only data that is formed according one of the master formats. These patterns are termed "entity types". You will find that there is a suitable entity type for virtually any item of business information you will ever need to store or process.

These entity types are located in areas in your applications. The names of these areas will probably be familiar business terms that you will recognize. However, the SAP use of a business term may hold some surprises. The literature and the help texts may slip easily between business meanings and software meanings of the same term.

For example, "Material" is the name of an architecture area in the EDM. The word can also refer to a parcel in your warehouse. It can also refer to a physical substance such as stainless steel. The word is used to denote the code number of the item, whether it is a package or a constituent. The word can denote a book of instructions. You could even find people included in a list of materials.

Part
II

Ch
6

An Ordering Principle for Entity Types

Individual entity types can be ordered according to the degree in which they are existence dependent. This concept points to the fact that some business entities are very complex and do not lead simple lives. An office is like a manufacturing plant because it can be used to add value to "things," mainly documents, passing through it. The office can exist even if there is no business going on in it. Of course, its existence is dependent on some organization's owning it and paying for its rent and upkeep; but, by and large, it is independent of whatever else exists in your enterprise or elsewhere.

By contrast, a business document such as a goods receipt has no existence of its own. You could think of a blank goods receipt form: no items, no supplier, no storage instructions, no destination. A real goods receipt that would be accepted by your data processing system needs a vendor who is recognized by the system and at least one item that mentions a material that is accepted as an entity for which this vendor is an approved supplier. So the goods receipt has high existence dependency.

The more an entity type is dependent upon other entity types, the further it is positioned to the right of an ordering of entity types on the basis of their degree of existence dependency. You could ask to see this list displayed as a graph with the right side of the graph depicting the higher values of this characteristic. However, you can run into visual difficulties if you select too many items to fit your screen.

Connections Between Areas

Assigning entity types to architecture areas that have been given familiar business names is a simplification. Some aspects tend to get left out of the picture. In particular, it may not be apparent just how many cross-connections there are in an integrated system that provides online accounting of value movements for a complex system of materials and warehousing.

One method of revealing interconnections is to set up interfaces. You could arrange them so that all traffic from one part of your system came and went through exactly one gateway. If you are looking for virus infections, this might be a good idea. But the EDM method is to set up entity types that relate to more than one architecture area.

Articulated Entity Types   An articulated transportation vehicle, a truck or a lorry with a trailer, is made up of at least two parts joined by a linking structure. Entity types can be articulated.

Entity type 2242 is

> "Goods receipt—value—posting—profit/loss—costs"

Specialization   The units of an articulated train of entity types are often generated by the process of specialization.

Entity type 2203 is "Goods receipt—value—posting—profit/loss".

Entity type 2042 is "Goods receipt—value—posting—profit/loss—costs".

Entity type 2042 is termed a specialization of Entity type 2203. The difference between them is the type of profit-and-loss account to which the posting takes place.

The documentation of Entity type 2203 will show that there is one specialization type allowed for this entity. Specialization type 0001 is the type of profit-and-loss account.

The conclusion is that if you want to attach business meaning to a data element, then you will have to use the correct entity type or entity type specialization.

Processes in a Data Model

In the ordered and stable world of business data processing, activities begin only when signaled. The signal is an event which is on the list of events for that process. A process ignores any events not on its list.

The process may have variants. It may have a little subtlety built in so that if there is more than one signal on the list, the process will adjust what it does according to which signal it recognized.

Typing

Every variant needs its own signal. Types are used as shorthand to classify event components. A type is a name of a set of elements. These elements can all be processed in the same way once they are identified with a type name. This is stereotyping.

Events

In this context, a signal is defined as an "event". A system recognizes events by frequently looking out for them. It scans all the places where important information could be lurking. It will be able to recognize types and similar group definitions. If the information forms a recognizable pattern, if it makes sense, and if this pattern is on the list, then the process will become active.

There is no limit to the complexity of a pattern. If your system has an event master record that specifies which data elements are to be scanned and which values will be taken as significant, then this event pattern can be linked to a specific standard business function that has already been programmed. Of course, your system has thousands of event masters, and you can add to them and combine them in ever-increasing complexity.

A process can be defined as a series of actions that change things. What things get changed and how this is done will be a matter for the particular process. What is stored in the database is the event that is to be taken as a signal for the process to begin. You will also expect there to be at least one event that will be recognized as the occasion for the process to come to an end.

Part
II

Ch
6

Event-Driven Process Chains

When you associate an event with a process, you create an "Event-Driven Process." If you have set up another event to terminate the process, and if you have a second process that is triggered by the termination of the first, then you are well on the way to building an EPC, an event-driven process chain.

Entity Types as Significant Events

The many facets of an entity type, its specializations, and its relationships with other entity types, all contribute to the rich possibilities of setting up significant data patterns as the trigger events for your business processes. There has to be an event for every process and an event to show that it has completed its work.

The EDM system of entity types is an economical way of storing data so that there is no danger of separating the stored information from its business significance. If you have information in a standard entity type, then your system will be able to understand how to process it and to tell you what it means using the formal language of the enterprise data model, its entity types, and its event-driven process chains.

Existence Dependency of Entity Types

Entity types are like master formats that can be copied and filled with specific data to create an instance of the entity. Some entity types can exist without any relationship to any entity other than the client code. All entity types have to belong to the client code that stands for the highest corporate level of your enterprise.

Some entity types rely on other entities. A purchase order cannot exist unless it contains a reference to an item that can be purchased. The entity type "Purchase order" has a relatively high degree of existence dependency.

SAP R/3 is delivered with built-in specifications for a large number of entity types, sufficient to create all the business documents and internal communications needed to run your enterprise.

Master data is held in entity types of low existence dependency. Flow data is held in entity types of highest existence dependency. There is an intermediate "higher" category.

Architectural Areas with Entity Types of Low Existence Dependency

The architecture areas with low existence dependency tend to refer to the basic structure and processes of your specific company. These areas are often termed master data areas because their contents are seldom changed.

Person

The interpretation of a person entity type will be to associate a master record with a natural person with whom your company has made a contract to create goods and services within your enterprise. There can be entity types for various categories, such as previously or currently employed.

Hazardous Material

This area includes entity types for storing data about hazardous substances and their handling in different regions of legal force.

Material

General information relating to a material is stored in the area. For example, design and engineering information, purchasing and storage details, and European Article Numbers are held here.

Storage Area

The architecture area named "Storage Area" contains the entity types that identify the specific structures of your warehouse system, such as the types of physical storage racks and containers, and the virtual units of materials that might be managed as if they were co-located. Some safety procedures are assigned to groups of storage bins that need not be in the same physical area.

Plant

The plant is the unit of the enterprise specializing in production or in otherwise adding to the value of material. A specific plant may be divided into plant storage areas so as to differentiate stocks of materials within the plant. For example, you may carry out some processing for a customer and some for your own purposes such as replenishing your inventory.

Material Valuation Area

The entity types in the material valuation area include masters that you can use to set up certain plant areas to be valuated using certain prices. A different set of pricing procedures may apply to the same materials assigned elsewhere. The valuation areas can be conceptual or virtual; they need not be co-extensive with physical layout areas.

Material Valuation Type

The entities in this area can be used to group materials independently of the areas in which they are stored. You may find it useful to use types such as "Internally manufactured" and "Externally manufactured" so that the materials so designated can be handled or valuated differently.

Purchase Order Acceptance/Fulfillment Confirmation Structure

This area contains entity types that can be arranged in sequence to track the confidence you have in the reliability of the date of delivery of some materials. For example, the delivery date that has been confirmed by acknowledgment of your purchase order is less reliable than the date given in a shipping confirmation. A better estimate of when the materials will be available for use can be given at successive stages in the sequence of fulfillment confirmations.

Vendor Evaluation Criteria

Price, quality, delivery, and service are the cornerstones of vendor evaluation, and they are recorded in a range of entity types held in this area. The scoring system will be stored as a set of subcriteria down to the smallest entity that is scored in the evaluation procedure used by your purchasing organization.

Condition Rule

The condition rule architecture area contains entity types for storing the set of rules used for the determination of final prices in connection with sales and procurement transactions.

Purchasing Organization

The procurement of goods and services for one or more plants, and the negotiation of general conditions of purchase with a vendor are matters for the purchasing organization. A buyer group carries out the purchasing operations using the conditions set up by the purchasing organization.

Sales and Distribution Organization

Entity types in this area represent the sales and distribution organizational units, such as divisions responsible for profits on sales materials.

Legal/Logistic Area

Entity types in this area identify the geographical or virtual areas that share legal or logistic frameworks.

Logistics Information Structure

The entity types of the logistics information structure carry the formulae and grouping rules by which business facts can be summarized as ratios. The values calculated from these procedures are stored in the Transaction Figures—Logistics architecture area.

Task

An entity type in the task area will specify the actions that are to be carried out to achieve a specific business objective.

Fixed Asset

A fixed asset and the changes in the value of it over time are represented as a data structure using entity types from this area. An object, a right, or any other entity of economic value that is permanently available for possible use by your enterprise is recorded as a complex fixed asset. A complex fixed asset records the changes in value over time of all the fixed assets of which it is made.

Asset Valuation Chart

This area of entity types provides for structures to store the requirements for meeting the statutory rules for valuation and the valuation conventions of your enterprise. You can have a store of asset valuation charts from which the company code determines the choice. Each company code can use a different asset valuation chart if necessary. Each chart may be as complex as the needs of the company code that uses it.

Account Determination

This area offers entities to arrange for material subsidiary ledger accounting in which a finance account is assigned, according to the posting type, to a material valuation class. This class may be used to group materials so that their accounts are all posted to the same general ledger accounts. Each group may be posted to different accounts according to the material valuation area.

Payment Rule

The payment rule architecture area stores entity types for rules or terms of payment. These terms specify periods of time within which settlement for the delivery of goods and services will attract cash discounts. A term of payment group contains similar terms.

Business Year Division

This area contains specifications for dividing your business year into periods. An entity called "Business year division—period" contains a defined time period within a business year division.

Time

The time architecture area contains time units. These data objects comprise a point in time or a time interval with appropriate units, together with a note of the business significance such as "Delivery date" or "Accounting period".

Language

The language used to communicate between the SAP system and the user is stored as an entity in this area. Several languages may be available.

Currency

Entity types for each currency are held in this area as are entity types storing the conversion procedures from one to another.

Unit of Measurement

The variables that are stored for data objects may be open to scaling. This area includes entity types for the units.

Business Partner

If there is a natural person or a legal entity that has the status of a person, and your company has a business interest in this person, then you may use a business partner entity type to store data about this interest. If you have a high volume of transactions with one person, you may establish a business partner master record for them. If you have many customers about whom you do not wish to hold very much information, you may have them managed as a collective business partner. This architecture area includes entity types to differentiate the type of a business partner as, for example, customer or vendor. You may also differentiate business partners by their "role" as receiver of goods, debtor, creditor, and so on.

If you need to store information about a vendor that is specific to your purchasing organization, you can do this in the entity type "Purchasing organization vendor".

If there is information about a vendor that is relevant to a particular material, you can store it in the purchasing information entity for this material.

Business Partner Structure

You may need to classify your business partners by using the entity types in this area. For example, a vendor grouping is a specification of how vendors shall be grouped so that the same calculation rule may be used for each.

Cost Accounting Area

The company code is normally the cost accounting area, but you may use a cost accounting area entity to assign objects of interest in other ways for reporting and analysis.

Business Area

Internal reporting is carried out for business areas. These may not necessarily be coextensive with the statutory reporting areas represented by the company codes. A derived business area may comprise any combination of the accounting entities that normally contribute to the separate company code accounting reports.

Company Code

An enterprise is legally defined in terms of financial accounting according to the separate sets of financial documents that are created each financial year and made available for public scrutiny. The financial documents are the balance sheet and the profit-and-loss statement.

In the SAP R/3 System, the client is a unique entity type that prevents accounts from one enterprise being attributed to another. But under the single client there must be one or more company codes. A company code is an entity type that is used to identify a legally independent unit that prepares its own balance sheet and the profit-and-loss statement. The scope of a company code need not correspond to any physical or organizational segment of the enterprise. Any transaction will be posted to the correct set of accounts by referencing the assigned company code.

However, it is customary to use a different company code for each country or legal region so that the appropriate tax calculation rules and accounting conventions may be applied.

Although the enterprise may hold more than one chart of accounts, only one is assigned for any specific company code.

Consolidation is the process of generating an enterprise-wide financial report by combining the financial documents of two or more company codes belonging to the same client.

Client

The architecture area "Client" or "Client*" contains the data structures to represent the central organizational unit of an enterprise. There are entity types to hold various views of the organizational structure. The main entity types in this area define an independent business system to produce or procure and distribute goods and services. There will be entity types to differentiate logistics, accounting, and human resources management information.

A small enterprise may be represented by a client that is coextensive with a single company code. A large enterprise may comprise a client and several company code entities.

Cost Origin

The entity types in this area are used to differentiate between as many different reasons for cost accruals as are required for the analysis of your company. These entities can record and value the costs on a continuous basis from the transaction data.

Cost Type

Costs may be posted to cost origins or to units according to the rules set out in the entity types of this architecture area.

Account Structure

This area contains the entity types needed to form the data structures you need to be able to record and trace the changes of value that result from accounting transactions.

Value changes are recorded as attributable to only one value category, such as receivables from sales or services, expenses for raw materials, or employee expenses. Each value change may carry the information that identifies the objects from which it was generated.

Exactly how costs may be posted is determined by a chart of accounts held in the account structure architecture area. The items in this chart may refer to profit and loss categories or expense and revenue categories in finance. The chart may also contain items such as cost or sales revenue entity types which are used in cost accounting and profitability analysis.

Thus, a transaction value change posted for profit and loss purposes may update simultaneously the transaction figures in finance and the transaction figures in cost accounting.

Ledger Updating Rule

This architecture area contains entity types to store the updating rules that could be used to determine which accounting transaction figures are to be updated for which ledgers. The choice of which set of rules to use is controlled by the transaction type.

Ledger

A ledger records value or quantity movements in accounting. The general ledger required for legal accounting can be supplemented by subsidiary ledgers which may differentiate value movements according to cost objects which are not necessarily identified in the general ledger. A consolidation ledger will be maintained at the company code level in order to allow consolidation at the client level.

Architectural Areas with Entity Types of Higher Existence Dependency

The intermediate group of architecture areas contain entity types that tend to change, but relatively slowly, and which depend on the existence of a few other entity types.

Material Requirement

The entity types required to represent the requirements for plant materials separate the following groups:

- Independent requirements are pre-planned anonymously or against a customer order and will contribute to final products or salable intermediate products.

- Dependent requirements are for intermediate products or raw materials. They usually arise from explosions of bills of material at the planning stage.

- Material reservations identify plant materials for a certain point of time. The user can reserve materials. A business transaction such as a production order or purchase order(subcontracting) can set aside material as a reservation.

- Forecast requirements for materials can be generated by the various forecasting procedures.

Production Order

This architecture area includes entity types to store the networks of sequences of individual operations that constitute ordered production runs.

Warehouse Stock

Each material may be assigned a "quant," which is defined as the smallest measurable unit of the material in a storage bin that can be used in a transfer order item. Entity types in this area allow warehouse stock to be managed by the batch and on the basis of valuation type. The data object recording the contents of a storage bin can reference individual customers or the particular vendors.

Plant Stock

Entity types are available to managed stock at the plant level and at plant storage area level. Stocks can be identified as special stocks such as consignment stock or provided material. Inventory management may be conducted on the basis of batches of materials and differentiated according to valuation types.

Transaction Figure—Material

This area includes the entity type "material valuation area—material" which identifies how a material is assigned to a valuation area. Within a material valuation area a material is valuated at a certain price. Changes to the stock are posted as values to update the "material valuation— transaction figures" data objects and the general ledger transaction figures. The transaction figures record the total value, the quantity, and the moving average or standard price. These values are recorded per period and may also be modified according to the material valuation type of the material.

Purchase Requisition

Entity types for a purchase requisition have to store a request to the purchasing department for them to procure materials or services. Purchase requisitions for internal procurement are differentiated from those for external procurement. A stock transfer must be ordered within the company for internal procurement. For external procurement, an outline agreement with a vendor must be concluded, or a vendor must be requested to deliver a material.

Vendor Inquiry

This architecture area provides entity types used to invite vendors to submit a quotation. These invitations comprise identifications of the materials or services and may include schedule lines that give directions as to the delivery destinations and scheduled delivery dates. The buyer group responsible will also be identified.

Vendor Quotation

In reply to a vendor inquiry, a vendor quotation will mention the items and the schedule lines. Specific conditions attached to items and general conditions such as discounts are provided for as entity types in this architecture area.

Purchase Order

The architecture area for purchase orders includes entity types to differentiate requests by a purchasing organization to a plant or to a vendor to deliver materials or render services. A plant belonging to an enterprise can be requested by a stock transfer purchase order. A vendor receives a purchase order.

The vendor can be requested to replenish consignment stores, or to render services as a subcontractor. He can deliver material to a third party, or deliver material to be provided for a customer order.

The schedule lines for a purchase order item can specify delivery quantities and dates. These dates or alternative delivery dates can be confirmed in the purchase order acceptance/ fulfillment confirmation. This confirmation can be an order acknowledgment or a shipping notification.

The purchase order can include conditions valid for individual items or for the order as a whole.

Purchasing Outline Agreement

This architecture area provides entity types to store details of long-term agreements with a plant or vendor. If the materials or services are to be delivered according to fixed conditions, a purchasing scheduling agreement will be used. If there are no schedule lines, the purchasing contract will be fulfilled by purchase orders.

Procurement Information

The quotation history, the purchase order price history, business volumes, and delivery codes are held in entity types from this architecture area. Each purchasing organization can store this information separately.

Source lists comprise details of possible or preferred means for the procurement of all the materials and services of interest. Procurement quota records show the quantity specifications in a period of time, for each material for each procurement type. Shipping notification data objects show the delivery dates assured by the vendor. Each purchasing information entity type can store a vendor evaluation for each material he can supply.

Condition

A condition is a fixed agreement granted according to certain influencing factors. The fixed agreement typically concerns prices, surcharges, discounts, bonuses, and so on. The influencing factors may comprise some combination of identified customer, specific material, customer group, for example. The factor may be graduated according to the purchase quantity.

Customer Order

Entity types in this area allow records to be kept of the contractual arrangements between a sales organization and a customer in the matter of the delivery dates of materials or services in defined quantities and at defined prices.

Sales

This architecture area provides the entity types to record the business transactions between the sales organization and the customer insofar as these transactions occur within the sales department. "Order—sales" is the name of the entity type that stores a request or a quotation for the performance of services for a customer. Such services can include customer inquiry, customer quotation, customer order, customer complaint order. If the order—sales pertains to delivery, it will include one or more schedule lines to partition the order according to delivery date and delivery quantities.

Transaction Figures—Logistic

Entity types in this area summarize by accounting period information assembled from logistics objects and work centers.

Transaction Figure—Fixed Asset

A fixed asset account is defined for each fixed asset. Postings to this account show the changes in the balance sheet value of this asset and are correlated with the business year. These postings can update "finance account—transaction figures" entities at the same time.

Transaction Figure—Cost Type

Entity types for the costs for objects relevant to cost accounting are found in this architecture area. The name "controlling object—costs" refers to the entity for which costs are to be recorded and differentiated in accord with the chart of accounts. The controlling object will be a cost center, an order, a project, or an object set up for the purpose of collating a particular category of costs. Separate data objects allow further subdivision and differentiation for the purpose of cost accounting.

Transaction Figures—Finance

Entity types in this architecture area are structures for recording value movements that will be compiled for the financial documents, the balance sheet, and the profit-and-loss statement. For example, entity types are used to set up separate debit or credit accounts under each company coded for each debtor or creditor. Ledgers additional to the general ledger are updated at the same time using entity types from this area.

Architectural Areas with Entity Types of Highest Existence Dependency

The architecture areas that contain entity types for transient or flow data objects are dependent on many other entity types and tend to change relatively rapidly.

Shipping

The entity type "Customer delivery" is used to specify the combination of sales materials that are delivered together. This entity records the shipping of material and/or the rendering of services as well as the return of materials by a customer.

Stock Movement

Entity types such as "Stock movement" record the transfer of quants within a warehouse complex from a starting storage bin to a destination storage bin.

Goods Receipt

The movement of goods to or from a vendor or a plant is represented as a goods receipt using entity types from this area. Changes in quantity caused by a goods receipt are recorded in materials management. A goods receipt can comprise several items relating to different plant materials and thus give rise to postings to different company codes according to the ownership of the plants involved. The inward movement of a fixed asset does not cause a change of any stock of material.

Goods Issue

A customer or an internal recipient may take part in a goods issue. Changes in quantity caused by a goods issue are recorded in materials management. For each goods issue, there is a change in the stock of materials. Material returned by a customer because of a complaint will increase stock although it may be recorded on a goods issue.

Creditor Invoice

A payable due to a creditor is represented by a creditor invoice. A receivable due from a creditor in the case, for instance, of a return delivery can also be recorded in a creditor invoice.

When a creditor submits an external demand for payment it is recorded as a creditor invoice with items which each represent either exactly one purchase order item or exactly one goods receipt item.

The entity type "creditor invoice—performance" is used to handle payables and receivables across company codes.

Creditor Payment

Credit subsidiary ledger accounting requires entity types to represent a payment to a creditor, or a payment from a creditor in the form of a credit memo.

Inventory

Stocktaking based on quantity for the material of an enterprise is recorded in entity type "Inventory". "Inventory—value" is used to store the book stock balance resulting from the stocktaking. The changes in the value of stock are posted in the current assets account, and also to the expense or revenue accounts according to the results of the inventory.

Price Change

The valuation of the stock of a material in the current assets account is updated when there is a price change. The value of the stock is calculated from the valuation price and the total quantity of the stock.

Cost Settlement

A "controlling object—costs" can be relieved of costs that were previously collected on it by a cost settlement, which is a transfer of value. The cost settlement can produce assets as capitalization, or transfer the cost to other objects.

Purchase Order History

The purchase order history records the quantity and value postings resulting from a purchase order item. The data structure includes entity types for goods and invoice receipts for a purchase order, and there are objects to store details of the payment transactions with the vendor.

Posting

This architecture area contains entity types used to represent the postings typical of accounting transactions. In particular, an entity type "Posting" documents the transaction figure that is updated by the business process of posting.

The collected postings documents all the value changes that have occurred. Each posting represents exactly one accounting transaction with regard to a value category, which means that exactly one "company code—general ledger account" is involved.

Using an Entity-Relationship Model

The enterprise data model is a meta-document. It is a text about something else, in this instance, the data layouts and processes of your computing system. It is also capable of being presented graphically. What use can you make of it?

If you have a map of a piece of terrain, and you know how to interpret the symbols, then you have some chance of being able to find your way from one place on the map to another. Perhaps this is overstating your capabilities. With a map you understood, you could trace routes with your finger and talk about traveling. Actually moving would require something else. And it would be no bad thing if you knew how to turn the map around so that North on the chart really did point to the North Pole.

Entity-relationship diagrams are rather like maps. They show you that there are connections between things. They do not necessarily tell you what these things are nor how to get from one to another.

The arrows indicate parts of an EDM where the relationships between entities are stated in plain language. The following annotations are from the documentation for Entity type 1015, Material type.

➠

In a CLIENT* there can be several Material types.

➠

A Material type belongs to exactly one Client*.

Entity Relationships in Purchasing

As an example to illustrate the way entities are linked via specializations and relationships, Entity type 1027 holds information about a Material:

- Entity type 1031, Material—purchasing, identifies a material for which "Purchasing Information" is recorded such as dunning data, tolerance data.
- Entity type 1006, Plant material, contains plant-specific features of a material.
- Entity type 1045, Plant material—purchasing, points out that information relevant to purchasing this material is recorded at the plant level.
- Entity type 5021, Purchase order item, contains a quantity of material or service to be ordered.

There are several specializations of the purchase order item entity type which indicate how the costs are to be accounted for:

- Entity type 5022, Purchase order item—subcontracting
- Entity type 5024, Purchase order item—stock transfer

- Entity type 5025, Purchase order item—third party delivery
- Entity type 5026, Purchase order item—provision of material by customer
- Entity type 5027, Purchase order item—consignment

Materials Grouping for Storage

The next example shows how entity types may be assigned to ensure an orderly format of different types of information. Entity type 1036, Material—storage, identifies a material for which the manner of storage has been determined in terms of container requirements, temperature and storage conditions. Each of these requirements may be specified for a classified group of materials:

- Entity type 1070, Material grouping, is the master for "classification viewpoint" specializations that represent the reason for grouping the materials or services.
- Entity type 1072, Material Grouping—storage condition, allows materials for which the same storage conditions are valid to be grouped together when picking plant storage areas.
- Entity type 1074, Material Grouping—temperature condition.
- Entity type 1075, Material Grouping—container requirements.

Units of Measurement

Entity type 1080, Material—unit of measurement, when instantiated, contains the factor for converting the unit of measurement of a specific material into the base unit in which inventory management takes place. The gross weight is calculated as the sum of the net weight, which is base units times conversion factor, and the appropriate packaging.

Entity type 9035, Unit of measurement, is a unit that can be used for the scaling of the variable of a data object. This object can be an activity type, an output connected with an activity, or a tangible material. Instantiations of Entity type 9035 include the following:

Piece	Meter
Kilogram	Liter
Second	Minute
Hour	Day
Week	Month
Year	

Business Partners

Entity type 1057, Business partner, is a legal or natural person or group of interest to your business. The following specializations are established:

- Entity type 1058, Individual business partner
- Entity type 1059, Collective business partner
- Entity type 2016, Creditor
- Entity type 5047, Vendor
- Entity type 5365, Order recipient
- Entity type 5366, Supplier of goods
- Entity type 5367, Invoicing party
- Entity type 6001, Customer
- Entity type 6155, Ordering party
- Entity type 6156, Ship-to party

Business partners may be classified using Entity type 1066, Business partner type, to differentiate the main classes of business partner such as Customers, Vendors, and so on.

Plant Material

Entity type 1027, Material, has an "Aggregating" relationship to Entity type 1006, Plant material, which allows a plant to be identified with several materials.

Entity type 1006, Plant material, stores the plant-specific features of a particular material. The following specializations of Plant material are established:

- Entity type 1029, Plant material—forecast
- Entity type 1032, Plant material—material requirements planning
- Entity type 1035, Plant material—production
- Entity type 1037, Plant material—quality assurance
- Entity type 1045, Plant material—purchasing

This chapter has illustrated how entity types are related to each other. These relationships allow their instantiations to inherit the data along the same relationship pathways if necessary.

Viewing an Information Model

The SAP R/3 Reference Model and the SAP-SERM structured entity-relationship model are filtered views or interpretations of the R/3 itself. When the full range of applications have been installed and configured to carry out the data processing for an extensive worldwide enterprise, it is not easy to know what to look at and what to look for if you want to understand how the system works.

It is apparent from the complexity of the data attribute structures that there are very many data elements to be stored in the system. Consistency of data structure and usage is ensured by using, as a standard reference, a suite of data structures which are stored centrally.

From the point of view of the user, the system contains all the information that is available. What is more difficult to appreciate is the extent and variety of this information, and the infinite flexibility of the systems available to retrieve it.

The SAP approach is to offer the user five avenues by which the extensive SAP database may be approached. Each avenue of approach affords a different view of the data structures and their contents. The standard SAP object orientation is maintained throughout. It is essential to efficient internal program logic.

Because they all originate in the same database, these five views are dovetailed. They are over-lapping partial views, each of which is logically consistent because of the shared basis and consistent use of data structures and processing disciplines.

The five views of the R/3 Reference Model are as follows:

The Process View interprets the R/3 Reference Model as an integrated network of event driven process chains and thus relates directly to the operation of your R/3 system.

The Data View sees the R/3 Reference Model as clusters of aggregated data structures which can be represented through the SAP R/3 Analyzer as data objects using their names and "header" data to navigate with the aid of graphical displays. These same data structures can also be viewed down to the detailed level that is required for in-house programming developments using the ABAP/4 programming language.

The Information Flow View concentrates on the necessary flow of information between event driven process chains. It can be used in the early stage of system design when the details of the functions have yet to be specified. In the information flow view, it is not necessary to say how or when the information is captured and transmitted.

The Function View provides a summary display or listing of the complete array of func-tions, which are active in a specific implementation of the R/3 system.

The Organization View is used to show the semantic relationships between the various organizational units that you have chosen to represent your company as a functioning enterprise supported by the R/3 system. A master organization view is held in the R/3 system which depicts the organizational structure of the system itself so that you can compare your specific organizational structure with the master to check that the hierar-chical relationships correspond. Should you wish to establish an organizational structure that cannot be modeled using the standard R/3 Reference Model components, there is a provision to add to these modeling components during customizing.

These views are discussed in more detail in subsequent sections, beginning with the process view because of its emphasis on event-driven process chain logic. But first, it is necessary to explicate the graphical symbology that is used for all SAP displays and views of the R/3 Refer-ence Model and the Enterprise Data Model.

Part

II

Ch

6

The Formal Graphics of EPC Modeling

The aim of the Reference Model is to be precise about the events to which the R/3 system can and will respond, and about the actions that will take place as a consequence. To express this model entirely in the form of a spoken language would run the risk of losing much of this precision, not only in the process of translating the model for use in different countries of the world, but also in the interpretation by those who speak the language in which it is expressed. Each reader has a particular educational background which enables him or her to understand his or her native tongue by recognizing symbols that can be combined to become words or concept icons which can then be combined in groups to express actions, relationships, and ideas.

The computer will not take this vagueness. It must be told when a number is to be treated as an amount, which currency is to be used, and so on. If the system is to issue a warning if a customer order will exceed the amount of credit allowed, then the system will have to know what this amount is, and which items in the order must be used to compute it.

So the system must work from defined events that it can recognize, and it must have the ability to carry out a series of processes, each of which may be a sequence which will be triggered or not according to precise conditions detected when specific events occur.

And to enable programmers and system managers, consultants, and heads of departments to communicate with precision, across national language barriers when necessary, there has to be a logically formal system of symbols and relationships for this purpose.

A convenient way of sharing ideas about this formal system of symbology is to present it in graphical format.

The exact format or style of the symbols is obviously not the critical factor, but the way they are used and interpreted do have to conform to the defined logic.

Event

The R/3 system defines an event as a set of values for which it has a predefined action which it will initiate if this set of values occurs. The location of these values in the records of the system is part of the definition of the event, and so are the specific amounts or other data elements which will be treated as significant if they occur in these defined locations.

For example, if the total amount on the sales order document that is being processed is going to be the cause of a warning message being sent to the operator, then the system must know that the credit limit for this customer is recorded in a specific field in the master data records for this customer. The system has been set to check all sales orders against available credit.

In logical language, this example situation can be expressed as follows:

> IF the current document is a sales order,
>
> AND IF this current customer has a credit limit,
>
> AND IF the value of the sales order total is greater than the value of the customer's credit limit,
>
> THEN issue a warning to the user who is entering the sales order.

The warning is an action that happens when the system recognizes a significant event. In this example, the event is made up of three components:

> The document being entered has to be a sales order.

> The customer has to be one subject to a credit limit.

> There has to be an arithmetic relationship between two numbers, namely the order total and the customer's credit limit.

The warning is an action that takes place because the appropriate triggering conditions have occurred and because the system has been provided with a warning function. This warning function will have several constituent processes which will probably include at least the following actions:

> The system will log the event and timestamp it to record the fact that this customer placed an order which exceeded his credit limit.

> The system will display a standard text which will include fields to receive the actual values—in this case, the credit limit and the amount of the excess.

> There will be a suggestion or proposal to the operator concerning what should be done, if anything, to get authorization for the extra credit or block the order pending further investigation.

Although this is a very simple example, there are clearly many elements in the process chain that are driven by the event of a customer about to exceed his credit limit.

The Standard Symbol for an Event   The trigger for an event-driven process chain is defined in terms of a set of specific data elements and the critical values or ranges of values that will generate consequent activities on the part of the system. Figure 6.4 shows the shape that is used to depict an event on charts of event-driven process chains.

FIG. 6.4
Graphical symbol for an event.

Generated Event   Each of the activities in an event-driven process chain will bring into being a set of logical conditions that may include the set of values that constitute the critical triggering event for another event-driven process chain. This subsequent event is referred to as a generated event.

In our example, the logging of the over-credit event is triggered by a generated event which includes the result of the arithmetic comparison. If the difference is one way, the warning function is triggered; if it is in the other direction, the warning function is not triggered.

Function

In mathematical or logical terms, a function brings about a transformation from an initial state to a target state. For example, an inverse function could be defined as that which changes a plus sign (+) into a minus sign (-). It would also be expected to transform a minus sign (-) into a plus sign (+). Another example would be a currency conversion function.

The transformation effected by a function can be expressed in the conditional form. For example, the inverse function can be specified as follows:

If the sign is (+), then substitute the sign (-).

If the sign is (-), then substitute the sign (+).

In this example, the inverse function would be followed by a chain of other processes if it were called in an accounting situation. And it would be called only if one of certain events occurred which met the conditions for triggering it.

The purpose of a function is to do something. It is activated by one of a set of events, and it can operate on information gathered from any sources. Which items of data are processed can be determined by the function itself. Alternatively, the objects on which the function is going to work can be indicated or passed to it in the function call which is triggered by the significant event.

The Standard Symbol for a Function   The symbol for a function is rectangular with rounded corners and may be connected by flow lines emanating from any convenient part of it. Figure 6.5 illustrates this symbol.

FIG. 6.5
Graphical symbol for a function.

Logical Operators

There has to be a convention for representing the fact that a process chain may only be driven by a particular set of circumstances. Three logical operators suffice: AND, XOR, and OR.

AND   The conjunction of events is shown by the AND symbol, which is a circle containing an inverted V shape. It is interpreted as meaning that all the inputs to the symbol have to be TRUE for the output to occur. Figure 6.6 shows the symbol for AND (Conjunction).

FIG. 6.6
Graphical symbol for AND (Conjunction).

Exclusive OR (XOR)   The exclusive OR (XOR) is interpreted as requiring one, but not both, of its inputs to be TRUE for the output to occur. Figure 6.7 shows the XOR symbol.

FIG. 6.7
Graphical symbol for
Exclusive OR.

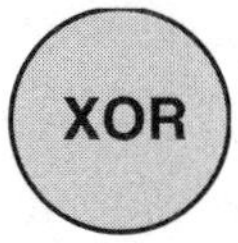

Either or Both (Don't Care)   The Don't Care circled V symbol represents the situation where either of the inputs will suffice on its own, or both may be TRUE, to allow an output. See Figure 6.8.

FIG. 6.8
Graphical symbol for
Either or Both (Don't
Care).

Control Flow

Control flow may be a matter of time or sequence ordering. The dotted line with an arrow-head shows how one event depends on a function, or one function depends on an event. See Figure 6.9.

FIG. 6.9
Graphical symbol for
control flow.

The dotted arrow is not used to represent the flow of information such as the details of a purchase order. The control arrow merely indicates that two elements of a graphical model are necessarily joined by a control connection which is able to carry one binary digit which can be interpreted as TRUE or FALSE, YES or NO.

This signal may, in fact, pass along a communication link which also carries large quantities of information. If so, this channel may appear on the enterprise model using the full line arrow symbol.

Process Pointer

The purpose of the process pointer is to show where the next process in a chain is to be found. Figure 6.10 shows a process pointer symbol.

Part

II

Ch

6

FIG. 6.10

Graphical symbol for a process pointer.

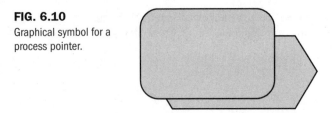

Organizational Unit

The ellipse is used for an organizational unit. It represents the element used in the company organizational structure. It may be a department or a section or a person. You may also define organizational units in terms of the material groups they process or the markets they serve. Figure 6.11 shows the symbol for an organizational unit.

FIG. 6.11

Graphical symbol for an organizational unit.

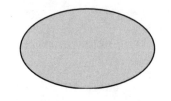

Information or Material or Resource Object

The real-world objects such as information packages, materials, and resource objects such as energy or services may have to be represented in the event-driven process chain model. A plain rectangle with sharp corners is the standard symbol. See Figure 6.12 for the symbol for an object.

FIG. 6.12

Graphical symbol for information or material or resource object.

Information or Material Flow

The flow of information is usually to read, change, or write data. This arrow symbol may also be used to show the movement of material. Figure 6.13 depicts the type of arrows used for the flow of information or material.

FIG. 6.13
Graphical symbols for information or material flow.

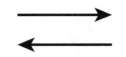

Resource or Organizational Unit Assignment

A continuous line without arrowheads is used to indicate which unit or staff resource is processed by a function. Figure 6.14 illustrates how a plain line may have to make several right-angled turns to depict how a function is associated with a resource including personnel.

FIG. 6.14
Graphical symbols for resource or organizational unit assignment or attachment.

Combining Events and Functions

In order to draw a true and useful picture of how your company carries out its business operations, the graphical symbols have to be combined. An event is a combination of logic and data that has been defined as the trigger for the initiation of one or more functions. You can build a model of any complexity by combining a fairly small number of symbols in various ways which are illustrated in the next few sections.

Two Events May Trigger a Function

A programmed business function may be designed to handle many different kinds of events. Some of these events may be exclusive; others may occur in conjunction with each other. These differences in the logic of the event-driven process chain are shown in the diagrams by the way the various symbols are arranged.

Either of Two Events   Figure 6.15 shows the situation where either one or the other of two events is sufficient to trigger the function. In this illustration, there is no possibility that both of the events could occur together.

Part

II

Ch

6

FIG. 6.15
Either of two events may trigger a function, but not both.

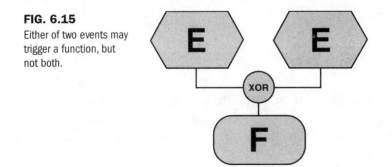

Both Events   If a particular function needs several events to occur before it can start to run, there are two ways of setting it out in the graphical model:

■ Define an event so as to include all the conditions and critical values of the data which are necessary for the function to be triggered.

■ Define the trigger to be a combination of events which have already been defined for other purposes.

Figure 6.16 shows the situation where there are two essential events that have to occur in conjunction for the function to be initiated.

FIG. 6.16
Both events must occur to trigger the function.

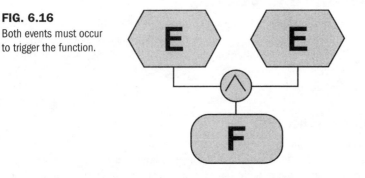

One or More of the Events   If a function has been designed to cope with several events, in any combination, the trigger can be defined as one or more events from a list or set of possibilities. The function will run if any event in the set occurs, regardless of how many others may also occur. See Figure 6.17 for a simple illustration of this situation.

FIG. 6.17
At least one of the events must occur to trigger the function.

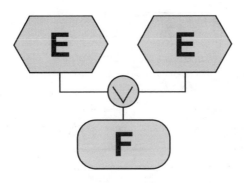

A Function May Generate Two Events

It will be very rare for the operation of a function to generate just a single event. At the very least, there will be one event if the function operates successfully and another if a problem is encountered. However, an EPC has to be shown at a selected level of detail. The user will be able to instruct the system to leave out details or include them so as to make the graphical display as helpful as possible.

Figure 6.18 shows part of a model where the function is depicted as being the generator of one or the other of two events, but not both. Figure 6.19 shows a function that generates both of two events every time it runs. Figure 6.20 depicts a function that will generate one or more events according to the results of the computation that goes on as part of the function.

FIG. 6.18
The function generates either of two events, but not both.

FIG. 6.19
The function generates both events.

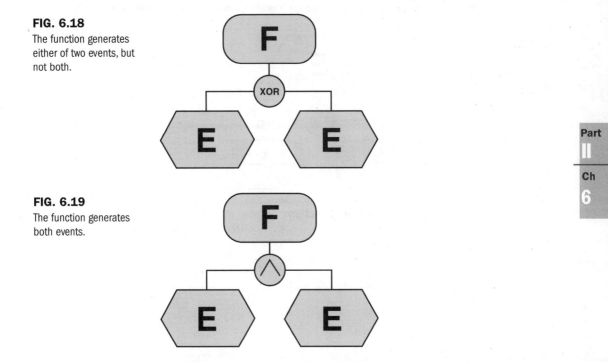

FIG. 6.20

The function generates one or more of the events.

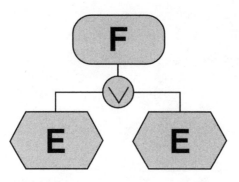

An Event May Trigger More Than One Function

The interpretation of data according to predefined criteria is what goes to define an event in an SAP model of your company. When the computer has decided that a particular combination of data has become a critical event, several different functions may be called into action automatically.

An Event May Not Be Ambiguous   The SAP definition of an event is as the reliable trigger for one or more events. There cannot be any doubt as to which event is triggered. Therefore, the diagram in Figure 6.21 that uses the XOR symbol is not allowed because it does not show how each function has a distinct triggering event or combination of events. An EPC diagram cannot include a symbol to show that either one or both events will occur because this would be equivalent to saying that the event is ambiguous about which function to trigger.

FIG. 6.21

An event may not trigger either of two or more events.

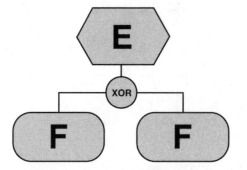

An Event May Trigger Two or More Functions   If your model needs to show that an event will cause the running of two or more functions, the AND symbol is used as illustrated in Figure 6.22.

FIG. 6.22
An event can initiate
more than one
function.

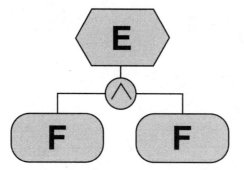

An Event May Not Be Indecisive   The diagram in Figure 6.23 is not allowed because it would suggest that either of the two functions could be triggered. An event is defined as the necessary and sufficient collection of data for the triggering of a specific function. If there are several functions which occur in response to an event, then they must all occur. An event may not be indecisive in identifying which business functions shall perform.

FIG. 6.23
An event must select
reliably which function
to trigger.

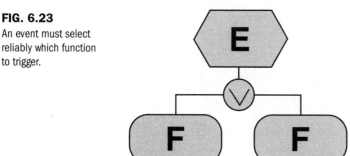

Two Functions May Generate the Same Event

A critical arrangement of data can arise from more than one situation. There are three logical possibilities, all of which are legal in EPC modeling.

One, and only one, of the functions generates the event. It may be the case that an event, which is critical for something else, can be caused by a variety of functions. The first of the two functions to operate will generate this event in the situation shown in Figure 6.24.

Part

II

Ch

6

FIG. 6.24

Either of two functions may generate the event, but not both.

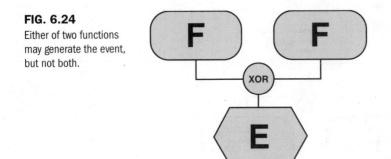

All Functions Must Operate to Generate the Event One of the uses of an event is to register the moment when a certain set of functions have all operated successfully. Figure 6.25 shows the situation where two functions have to have finished before the event is generated.

Either Alone or Both Functions Together Will Generate the Event If any one or more than one of a group of functions will suffice to generate an event, you can depict the logic as in Figure 6.26.

FIG. 6.25

Both functions have to operate in order to generate the event.

FIG. 6.26

One or more functions have to operate in order to generate the event.

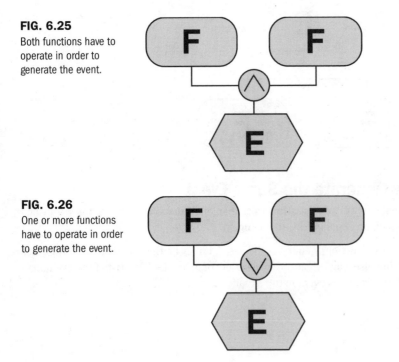

Process View

The dynamics of an information system are best seen from the process view because the objects of scrutiny are the significant occasions, defined in terms of events, which will inevitably prompt the R/3 system into action in the form of one or more event-driven process chains.

Lean Event-Driven Process Chains

There are too many events and processes associated with the typical user transaction to make a useful presentation to the user or the system developer. The ABAP/4 programmer will know how to get down to the level of detail he or she needs, but for many purposes, a summary format is more useful. This is provided as a system of lean or sparse displays of event-driven process chains, which show the essential relationships in each of the five views and can offer a display of reasonable size and complexity to the user. Drilling down for extra detail is always possible by selecting the item of interest on the display and using the special function keys.

Event-Driven Process Chain Example

To illustrate the semantics of event-driven process chain methods of specifying how business is recorded in order to be transferred to a computer support system, a simple scenario is described in text and in graphical terms.

Text Process Description   Goods arrive and are checked. If they are satisfactory, then they are passed to production. If they are not, then they are either rejected or blocked pending further inspection.

Graphical Process Description   Each event-driven process chain has to begin with at least one event and be completed by at least one final or finish event. The main constituents of an event-driven process chain are passive components, which are events, and active components, which are the functions that do something. The control flow connections between these events and functions are shown as dotted arrows, which may be branched at logical operators shown as circles bearing the appropriate logical symbol to signify AND, Exclusive OR, or Don't Care.

Plain continuous lines without arrows indicate associated organizational elements, such as the department or work center responsible for the function. Continuous line arrows show the flow of information, documents, or material. Figure 6.27 shows part of an event-driven process chain seen in the form of a lean EPC which depicts only the main events and functions, and their essential relationships.

Part
II

Ch
6

FIG. 6.27

Example model of a lean event-driven process chain.

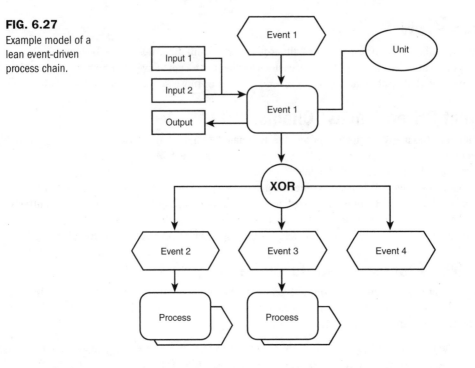

The example is a lean event-driven process chain because there are many finer details hidden in order to make the overall structure of the business function clear.

If you place your cursor on an element in an event-driven process chain (see Figure 6.28), and call for help using a special function key, then there will be displayed a window pointing to the element and containing the detailed reference document that may be scrolled and bookmarked as required. The reference document may be a more detailed view of the chart or a textual document of notes and procedural instructions. These documents will be developed and annotated as the system implementation proceeds.

When the particular functions are identified by the graphical element labels, the generalized form of the event-driven process chain becomes particular and will be stored by the system as a unique graphical object. This will gradually build up to the EDM enterprise data model of your company. Figure 6.29 illustrates how a fragment of this model might look when it takes account of the specific work centers and process flows in a target company.

FIG. 6.28
A specific event-driven
process chain.

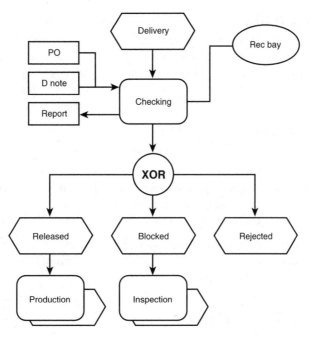

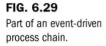

FIG. 6.29
Part of an event-driven
process chain.

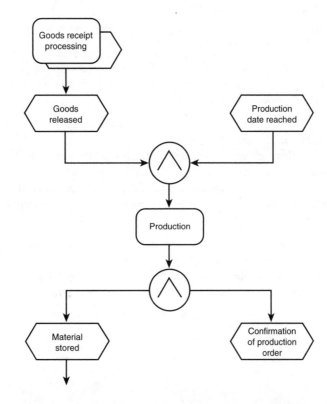

Part
II

Ch
6

Choosing Key Events

The formal method of depicting the processes of business in terms of event-driven process chains which can be supported by software depends very much on the ability of the implementers to choose the right significant events to become the triggers for the key functions. In the previous fragment of an event-driven process chain, there are two significant events which initiate production, but only if they occur in conjunction:

- Goods released for production.
- The date for production has been reached.

In the same example, there are two significant events which mark the end of the production function: Material is stored after production processing, and the financial system is informed by a confirmation of the production order. Both of these events should be depicted in the chart of the business process because they will each be needed for subsequent activities.

If the event-driven process chain is not initiated by a carefully chosen event set, or if it does not terminate with events which will take part in other event-driven process chains, then the power of the method will not be fully realized.

Information Flow View

Every event-driven process chain depends on information being input to the function through the data objects of the triggering events. There will be additional inputs of information if the chain is a complex one made up of a structure of event-driven process chains, each with its own data held in the critical events.

And because the purposes of the function will include the generation of events that carry items of information that will cause other event-driven process chains to activate, then every function can be seen to generate output information.

If you had the full details of an event-driven process chain, then you could work out the effective input and output information flow across the function. However, at the early stage in business system implementation, the exact details of the component event-driven process chains may not be known. In such cases, it may be helpful to plot the structure of the business in terms of information flows, knowing that the SAP R/3 System will be able to provide the precise standard business software when the time comes to develop and elaborate the implementation.

The R/3 Reference Model provides a powerful facility to portray automatically the existing and necessary information flows between the standard business functions at the application and functional area levels. Figure 6.30 depicts the information flows that are to be expected between the functions and for which R/3 standard business programs have been developed.

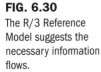

FIG. 6.30
The R/3 Reference
Model suggests the
necessary information
flows.

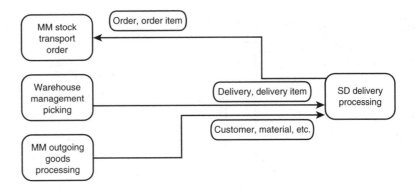

Data View

Although the operation of event-driven process chains creates and changes the information stored in the individual data objects of the system as a result of the functions initiated, there are also certain relationships which exist between data objects, independent of any processing that may occur.

For example, a plant may "own" a production capacity because it is responsible for the machinery and personnel that can provide it. A warehouse, which is treated as a plant, can be assigned certain materials, quite independently of any functional relationships that may exist when this material is used for production or sales.

These operational relationships between the data objects of the system are stored in the form of information objects which may be seen by calling for the data cluster view of the R/3 Reference Model. Figure 6.31 shows how the necessary data objects are clustered together to form the data structure which, in this illustration, represents a type of material located in a specific plant in your company.

In this fragment of a data cluster view, the Client owns the Plant which is the responsible owner of the Plant material. The Client is also the owner of data objects representing the types of material used in the company and the definition of Industry sector which is specific to the industry or perhaps defined purely for the convenience of this company.

The Material data object has to be related to the Client, to the Material type, and be placed in the appropriate Industry sector.

The Client may own several plants, each of which may hold stocks of the same material. Therefore, there has to be a data cluster of records in the database which represent the conjunction of plant and material to be labeled in this example as Plant material. An item of material from one plant is not necessarily treated as identical to the same item from another.

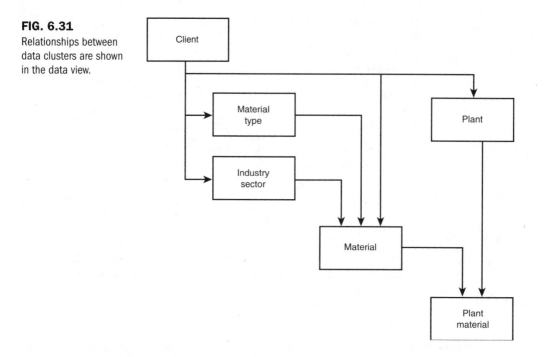

FIG. 6.31

Relationships between data clusters are shown in the data view.

There will, of course, be many other data input relationships for each of the information blocks shown on this data cluster view. And there will also be many additional outgoing relationships to data structures which need the information represented, in this example, by the blocks labeled Material type, Industry sector, Material, Plant, and Plant material.

For the purposes of program development, the fine details of data objects have to be made available from the R/3 Reference Model. However, for the purposes of customizing and analyzing your business with the aid of the R/3 Reference Model and the SAP R/3 Analyzer, the data level that is most appropriate will usually be an aggregated data structure in which the objects are displayed at the summary level which is referred to as the data cluster.

A continuous range of data cluster levels is available from level 0, Entry Level, down to the level of the finest detail as required for software development. These levels correspond to the function view levels discussed in the next section.

At any stage, it is possible to point to a charted element and use the special function keys to drill down for more detailed information.

Function View

The function view of the R/3 Reference Model is able to show how the functions are subordinated to each other in the form of a function tree. Four levels have been found to be useful.

Function View Level 0

This view displays applications, such as MM-Materials Management, or HR-Human Resources, as single entities. Your implementation may have several applications in the form of an integrated business system.

Function View Level 1

This view shows the functional areas covered by each application as the blocks on the organization chart or its equivalent in listing format.

Function View Level 2

This view reveals the principal functions that are needed to support each functional area, such as Invoice Verification in the materials area.

Function View Level 3

This view displays the variations within each function. These will be recognized by the user as requiring a slightly different method of processing. For example, third party order processing is slightly different from standard order processing.

Function View Level 4 and the levels below are not usually regarded as part of the functional view because they are the province of the system development teams rather than of concern to the user or the implementer of a standard business software system.

Organization View

The R/3 Reference Model contains a model of the organizational system on which it is based. Although there are many variations of company organization which can be replicated using the components and relationships provided as standard in the R/3 system, it is also possible to design custom-built organizational structures if the standard elements are not sufficient.

Figure 6.32 shows the organization view of part of the R/3 Reference Model. This model can be used to form the basis for the elaboration of your company organization view of the reference model by replicating the entities, or "blocks," at each level until the model corresponds to the organizational structure of your company.

FIG. 6.32

The structure of the R/3 Reference Model can be used as a pattern.

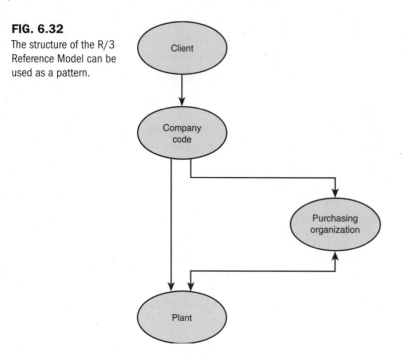

The graphical displays of the model are amenable to a wide variety of presentation style and annotation possibilities. Figure 6.33 shows the standard graphical presentation of part of the reference model. It is being elaborated by copying and editing the component graphical structures so as to build an EDM enterprise data model of a specific company. You could use this technique to show your organization as it is now, or as you would like it to be when you have completed the process of business process reengineering.

The Concept of a Business Framework

A framework is a device for holding things in place. The SAP Business Framework is a conceptual organizer that has the job of holding SAP R/3 components in place so that you can see what is available and how to use it. It is much more than just a list of modules. The business framework puts all the parts in relationship to each other. The theme of this relationship is ease of use because good software will not give you benefits unless you can use it properly and have it working quickly.

FIG. 6.33
The organizational structure of your company will be in accord with the R/3 model.

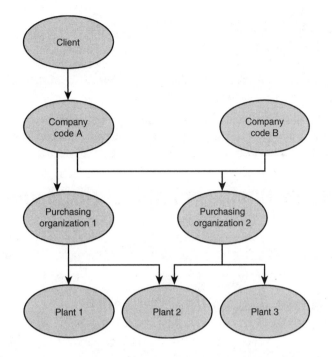

This section will remind you that the SAP R/3 Business Framework includes effective and easy-to-use tools and methods for building and updating a modern business system:

- The Business Framework is the methodology of making all components fit seamlessly together the first time.
- The Business Engineer is for all SAP R/3 implementations.
- Network-enabled systems can be built from existing components.
- Productive SAP R/3 Systems can be reconfigured and updated without disruption.
- Third party systems can be integrated with SAP R/3.

Open Architecture

Software that is fully tested and known to be effective in many different situations is attractive if you can get it to work in your situation. It must be open to receive messages and to send back its results.

Software is open if it can be accessed by other software using published communication protocols. Software is closed if it is not accessible by any of the standard protocols. Of course, you may be a user who does not have the requisite authorization to use a module.

Part

II

Ch

6

Mapping Business Logic

If you intend to look in the business framework with a view to developing your business, you will expect to see the logic of your kind of business reflected there. For example, you want to recognize the technical terms of your industry. The processes of your daily work ought to be recognized in the presentation of the software.

There are limitless possibilities for programming computers to serve your company, but you want to identify a reliable and efficient package of software that can be speedily implemented. You will perhaps select SAP R/3 Basis and several R/3 applications.

A Structure of Business Engineering Tools

The inner core of SAP R/3 implementations could be regarded as the operating system of the individual computers. However, the policy of SAP R/3 software development is to ensure portability by designing the data processing components to be independent of all aspects of the underlying hardware systems.

The BEW Business Engineering Workbench

The purpose of the SAP R/3 Business Engineer is to help you configure an implementation by selecting the parts you need and putting them all together quickly to yield a robust, flexible, and efficient business system.

The Business Engineer is an integration of the R/3 Reference Model, the R/3 Analyzer, and the ABAP/4 Development Workbench. The BEW Business Engineering Workbench gives you the full toolkit to exploit the open Business Framework architecture.

There are two notable additions to the business process reengineering toolset that are provided by the Business Engineer:

- Components and sub-systems may be integrated with the core SAP R/3 System as they become available after SAP certification. It is not necessary to adhere to the formalities of the release cycle in which the entire system is converted to the updated software.

- The Business Engineer can organize third party applications so that they become integrated with SAP R/3.

This important contribution to flexibility and rapid implementation is made possible because of a wide range of robust messaging technologies which can bridge the communication and control gaps between systems and installations that might otherwise be incompatible. SAP ALE, Application Link Enabling, and SAP Business Workflow are examples. The widespread use of business objects comprising data and processing components is another reason why contemporary business systems can be quickly implemented in spite of their complexity.

For example, your company might wish to choose the following SAP applications to be preconfigured and customized by the Business Engineer and thus become components of your Business Framework:

- HR-Human Resources
- PDM-Product Data Management
- Treasury
- ATP, Available-to-Promise Server
- Reporting Server

The business framework concept has been developed by successive releases of SAP R/3 from a marketing idea to a fully-equipped environment for supporting continuous business development through reengineering.

Runtime and Development Environments

The next layer above the hardware operating systems can be titled "Runtime Environment". In this context, the environment is the set of business objects that could be accessed and the control commands that would be accepted if properly formed. The environment is basically the sets of menus and the functions that you can initiate from them. In practice, the environment will also include some help and safety measures that only appear if you generate an error.

The runtime environment has to have been built, and the tool for doing this is the ABAP/4 Development Workbench. This workbench is an integrated set of tools which serve to generate a "Development Environment". This is defined as the set of functions you can call and the commands needed to initiate them. Obviously, the programmers must be able to carry out functions that would not be permitted in the runtime environment. For example, they must post data to the database to test their work, but they are not allowed to post data to the live production database which would increase their salary, for instance. This can only be done by an authorized user in the runtime environment.

On the other hand, users in the runtime environment must not be allowed to make any alterations to the software. This happens only in the development environment. Alterations to the standard business software can have far-reaching effects in an integrated system. New releases of a software function are not allowed until the full testing and proving processes have been completed.

The way that you can alter how SAP R/3 works in your implementation is by customizing the components and by controlling the workflow sequences of your facilities.

One of the aims of the Business Engineer product family is to give you the ability to reshape your business data processing quickly and without disruption. Therefore, it takes advantage of the development environment of the ABAP/4 Development Workbench and allows you to reshape your software configuration from the runtime environment. The business engineer will make sure that nothing you do will break the close integration of the SAP R/3 System and its applications.

Part
II

Ch
6

Elements of the Development Environment

One of the big mistakes made by designers of all kinds is to ignore what is already available. The engineer fails to look in enough catalogues to find what he needs, so he designs one from scratch. The programmer cannot remember where or how she wrote a function previously so she writes a new one. Both examples can contribute to a storehouse of useful items that differ from each other perhaps only in their part numbers and names—the very things that cause them to be classified and hence stored in different locations.

The R/3 Repository is a warehouse of data objects ranging from simple data elements to complex business objects with their associated software procedures. The common R/3 database includes the R/3 Business Object Repository.

To find things in a warehouse you need either experience or a good inventory, and a good inventory is characterized by having an indexing system that really does include the names and code words that you will be likely to use when you need to find something.

The R/3 Classification system is this index to the R/3 Repository.

Object Browsers and Navigation

The business framework can be explored by looking in the Repository on an element basis using the terms of the R/3 Classification. It can be scanned at the level of business objects. And it can be thoroughly navigated by a range of third party tools such as Business Navigator.

ABAP/4 Processor

If you have access to the ABAP/4 processor, you will be able to use this high level programming language to construct new or modified SAP R/3 components.

The software engineer has a catalogue, and it is a serious matter to reinvent software that is already in it. There are two components:

- ABAP/4 Dictionary, which can show you all the key words of the language and your software, and what they mean. This will also show you the functions already programmed that you might wish to call.

- Data Modeler, which can show you the format, range of accepted values, and relationships of every data object in your system.

The programmer needs an ABAP/4 Editor and his supervisor will certainly need comprehensive reporting facilities to see how the work is going and where the software elements are used throughout the system.

To speed the construction of screens and dialogs with the users, the Development Workbench provides Screen Painter and Menu Painter. These tools suggest the displays and arrange the associated processing under the supervision of the programmer.

As a programmer, you will also need tools for the following operations:

- Testing
- Tracing
- Debugging
- Performance Tuning

These facilities are provided through the BEW Business Engineering Workbench.

The BEW itself is a complicated system and is therefore provided with a Workbench Organizer that can conduct project management on the software development projects.

Finally, the Development Workbench needs a system for transporting the new software to the production system. The Transport System is a product that controls the transfer and documents any events in this process.

The Framework of Multi-Tier Client-Server Architecture

SAP R/3 software is designed to be independent of the underlying technical system of hardware and operating system. It achieves this independence by being organized in three levels.

Presentation Level Your SAPGUI specializes in presenting dialogs so that you may enter your data and choices to carry out your work. Printing is another output or presentation level function.

Your presentation device could be running in any of the following environments:

- Windows 3.x
- Windows 95
- Windows NT
- MacOS
- OSF/Motif
- OS/2 Presentation Manager

Application Level When your interaction with a presentation device is concluded with a successful transaction. The information is posted to a particular application, and perhaps copied to several others. You place an order for a material by communicating with the MM Materials Management application. Ripples from this transaction will affect the financial components and probably your inventory modules.

This activity is conducted at the application level, largely by business objects that are optimized for the purpose; the vendor documents are good examples.

Your application server could be running on any of the major UNIX operating systems, on AS/400 systems, or on Windows NT.

Part

II

Ch

6

Database Level   Nothing could happen in your transaction if you could not access the database. Your list of approved vendors is there, for example, so are the safety instructions for handling the material you have ordered. Your authorization needs the database: and the results of your activities will cause changes in many places in this database.

Your database could be running on any of the following systems:

- IBM DB2/6000 for AIX
- IBM DB2/400 for AS/400
- Informix Online
- Microsoft SQL Server
- Oracle
- Software AG Adabas D

One of the advantages of being able to use so many systems in your SAP R/3 installation is that you may use the best device for each job and replace them individually as required.

There are many different ways of configuring a system. You may decide to implement each layer on a different system, for example, or you may combine layers in various ways.

Network-Centered Computing with Objects

Effective network-centric applications are compact for quick delivery over a network. Small size makes it practical to maintain the applications centrally. Users work with a set of features that is no larger than they need. There are no superfluous options. Being modular, the network-centric applications can be downloaded only to the users that have need of them.

The applets can connect to each other and to legacy systems such as spreadsheets and corporate databases. The communication process need be no more difficult than using a Web browser, which will become a standard skill.

Customers, business partners, suppliers, and managers can all have controlled access to the same processes and information which is current. Their separate hardware and operating systems will all be able to run the Web browsers and such inclusions as the Java Virtual Machine. A business application written entirely in Java will work on any machine without editing.

Customizing to Fit Your Company

The SAP R/3 Business Engineer is a programming interface which can select R/3 functions and build them into business systems.

The SAP Business Engineer provides a graphical view of the supply chain in action through dynamic business processes that drive the company.

Configured, Inspected, and Tested Before Installation

A particular advantage of the Business Engineer programming interface lies in the fact that R/3 processes can be used and tested before you install an R/3 system. Typical transaction data can be processed and displayed on screens that have been customized for your specific situation. You can make alterations before implementation. You can also use the same interface to make alterations to the processing and the reporting after the system has gone live.

Dynamic and Continuous Business Reengineering

By controlling your processing sequences with the SAP Business Workflow, perhaps via an intuitive graphical display, you can automate and timetable the execution of related activities across application boundaries, components, and organizational units.

Recommended for All R/3 Implementations

The Business Engineer has become the recommended mode of designing and building a focused implementation of the R/3 system. When the system is in productive operation, the same interface will handle system maintenance because it can select and de-select R/3 applications and modules and authorize settings and formats specific to the user—and all this at the graphical flow diagram level if required.

The function of the Business Engineer is to serve as a business system Implementation Assistant. You can see which elements of R/3 you will need and the Implementation Management Guide will show you how to put them to work using your data and your way of doing business.

The graphical modeling displays can be used to control the Business Engineer, or you can work with tabular data if you prefer.

Tools to Update the Data Objects

Any editor can be used to insert your particular terminology and other information. You then reload the changed information to the R/3 Repository. Advanced assistants such as the ARIS Toolset, IntelliCorp's Live Model for R/3, and Visio's Business Modeler can be used.

Configure to Order

The Business Engineer supports the SAP Configure-to-Order initiative and some automatic custom R/3 configuration. For example, R/3 can be customized on the basis of components and procedures, and specific user interfaces can be generated from standard settings, for example, to create transaction dialogs for a particular Industry Solution.

Continuous Customization

Interactive process optimization, and the addition of new processes or components to live R/3 applications would be examples of continuous customization. The Business Engineer will keep track of the changes and allow testing and simulation before releasing any newly customized element.

From Here...

■ How is SAP R/3 marketed and implemented?

See Chapter 1, "Implementing Integrated Materials Management."

■ How can SAP R/3 improve the efficiency of buying goods and services?

See Chapter 2, "Understanding Materials Purchasing."

■ How can MM make my store's departments more effective?

See Chapter 4, "Understanding Inventory and Warehouse Management."

CHAPTER 7

Analyzing Materials Information

In this chapter

- How can I glean information from my materials purchasing records?
- What are going to be the demands on my information system if I want materials information analyzed?
- What kinds of analysis come pre-programmed?
- How can I find out materials information for myself?

In the center of SAP R/3 is a powerful suite of data analysis programs that can operate on any data that has been arranged according to the format standards of SAP master records. The MM-IC Inventory Controlling component includes additional functions for inventory analysis. In materials management, there are two sets of records of particular interest: purchasing and inventory.

Purchasing Analysis Options

The large volume of purchase documents and master records to be found in most systems running the MM-Materials Management module necessitates a powerful yet flexible suite of functions to display to the user just what is wanted for the immediate purpose, and to leave out what is not wanted.

Purchasing managers have to keep track of all their purchase orders and all their purchasing organizations. They must also be continually aware of their vendor population and newcomers to it that they have not yet used.

Analysis of Purchasing Documents

The following search specifications are typical of the needs of the purchasing managers:

- List the purchase orders issued to the selected vendor in the specified period.
- Which outstanding purchase orders have resulted in goods delivered to date?
- What proportion of deliveries are only partial?
- Does this vendor have a history of incomplete deliveries?
- List all purchase orders issued by this particular purchasing group during this specific time period.
- List the requisitions for this material from any or all of the specified group(s) of vendors.
- List all archived purchasing info records for this material for this plant.

Discerning Trends

If there are trends in the requirements of your company, your purchasing managers must notice them in time to plan their purchasing schedules. You will probably want to see these trends in graphical form or tabulated as summaries to reveal the significant movements in the data. For example:

- What is the trend in the monthly average value of purchase orders issued by this particular buying group?
- Display the purchase order history of the selected material item.

Analysis of Materials Accounting

In accord with the aim of adding value throughout the process chains of your business, you will want to be able to see if there are any opportunities for doing so in the management and accounting of your materials activities. Here are some examples:

- Check the receipts against the orders and list items with discrepancies.
- Check receipts against invoices and list items with discrepancies.
- Tabulate value of orders with discrepancies against the total value from each vendor.

Vendor Performance Analysis

Faults in your materials can interfere with your manufacturing and may be passed on to your customers with a consequent harm to your reputation and to your cost-effectiveness. Late deliveries can have similar effects. Early deliveries can overload your warehousing and handling capacities. Are your suppliers getting better or worse in keeping to delivery schedules? Complete the following and review your answers:

- Separately identify the suppliers of all items identified as faulty during manufacturing and as reported by customers.
- Rank the industry sectors of the vendors against delivery performance, early and late.
- Plot the distribution of delivery time discrepancies over a specified period for the indicated transportation contractors.

Components of the Logistics Information System

The information systems are clearly central to efficient controlling of materials management. There are particular display functions optimized for the purchasing functions as the PURCHIS-Purchasing Information System, and for the inventory management system under the title of MM-IC Inventory Controlling. These elements can be integrated as the MM-IS Information System.

The aim of an information system is to select only the pertinent information and then to present it in ways that increase the probability of correct decisions being made by those who view it.

There are two types of error associated with information presented to the user for a decision:

- Error one is to offer the user a choice of items that do not mean anything, or mean something to the viewer that was unintended by the system designer.
- Error two is to omit from the list of options some of the important possibilities, which can include such options as "Do Nothing" and "None of the Above Is a Sensible Choice."

The PURCHIS-Purchasing Information System maintains its own database and can perform several important analysis procedures on it. For example, it can produce an analysis of vendors and of purchasing group activities. It can publish its results in terms of some 30 performance measures, such as the number of purchase orders in the period.

Not only can the PURCHIS present data in a wide variety of list and graphical formats, it can also assemble the data using the widest range of search strategies.

It is characteristic of SAP R/3 standard business programs that the reports can be tailored to suit the needs of the viewers. For example, those who need detail can see it and those who need an overview can get it, both from the same analysis.

The method uses a set of standard evaluation structures, which can be supplemented by the user on the basis of edited copies of the standards, if convenient. A data dictionary has to be identified, on which the evaluation structure will call in order to assemble the data it needs. A system document file containing purchasing documents would be a convenient type of data dictionary for many purposes.

The PURCHIS-Purchasing Information System is part of the LO-LIS Logistics Information System and shares many of its routines with the SD-IS Sales and Distribution Information System.

The Inventory Controlling System, which is also part of the Logistics Information System, is designed to reduce the information held in the inventory management system to a few informative performance measures that show you which areas of this part of your business offer opportunities for improvement.

Standard Information Structures

The basis of analysis using the PURCHIS methodology is the information structure, which comprises data objects and performance measures associated with a time unit or period. For example, an information structure can be defined for a weekly period, comprising the following data objects:

- Purchasing group
- Vendor

The performance measures to be gathered on this information structure may include:

- Invoice value
- Net order value
- Number of order items
- Number of deliveries

The standard PURCHIS component is provided with three information structures containing more than 30 meaningful performance measures for all the analyses relevant to purchasing, grouped in thematic clusters.

Update rules are predefined for every field in the information structures, and you can change the rules if you wish. The updating of these statistical files can take place in synchrony with interactive processing or as a separate update processing run.

You can also define your own information structures by selecting objects and performance measures from lists and using the "pickup" technique to copy them to a display or printing format of your own design.

Standard Analytical Reports

The standard analyses cover the statistical information that you might need for the following organizational entities:

- Purchasing groups
- Vendors
- Material groups
- Materials

The scope of the data used for these compilations can be restricted interactively by applying selection criteria. Any item of interest in the display of results can be selected online and become the focus for the "drill-down" technique. The drill-down function will retrace the sequence of layers in the information hierarchy that was used to compile the value in the report you selected in the first instance.

At every level of a drill-down search, you can call for graphical and list displays and apply any of the following functions:

- Totals
- ABC analysis
- Classification to the SAP R/3 scheme
- Dual classification
- Ranking lists
- Planned versus actual comparisons
- Net order value frequency analysis
- Forecasting

Detailed information can be sought at any level from the associated vendor master records, material master records, and purchasing documents.

Totals

Totals analysis will let you see the number and total value of existing purchase orders, or whatever data structure you have selected, for the compilation of data.

ABC Analysis

The ABC analysis concept refers to groupings of data objects according to the relative importance of one of the values held in a specified data element of all of these objects.

For example, you can rank-order all vendors in terms of their contribution to the total order value in the period of scrutiny. You can then specify that the A vendors will be those who together account for the first 70 percent of the order value; the B vendors will be those who together contribute the next 20 percent of the total order value; and the C vendors will be the remainder in the rank-ordered list, because they have individually contributed least and together contribute only 10 percent of the total order value for the period. The number of vendors in each of the A, B, and C groups will be in itself an interesting result of the ABC analysis.

There are four different strategies of this kind available for structuring ABC analysis, and they can be conducted using planned or actual values of the performance measure in question. The four standard sets of percentage values for the ABC analyses can be modified at customizing.

R/3 Classification

The classification function, which is an integral part of the R/3 System, provides a standard method for grouping together several data objects specified by a range of one of their values. For example, you could ask to see an analysis of all production cost centers with company codes A to D and F. The members of this group are then examined with regard to one or more of the other performance data elements in their records, such as the number of work calendar days lost to production and the total value of output in the period.

Dual Classification

If you are interested in the way in which two sets of data co-vary, you can use the dual classification function to reveal the relationship between the two performance measures and to demonstrate it in graphical or list format, using any of the materials or vendor data fields.

Ranking Lists

To use a ranking method, you have to first choose a data field on which the ordering shall take place. For example, you may rank your materials in terms of the total value of the stock of that item on your inventory.

You can choose which way to sequence the list: highest first or lowest first.

Although the ranking method is very useful if you have many materials, it does not necessarily show the magnitude of the differences between successive items in the ranked ordering. For instance, item one may be twice the value of item two. You need to look at the key values after you have generated a display of the items in rank order.

Planned and Actual Comparison

It is often helpful to see how the planned values compare to the actual results. The same information structures will accept planned and actual values, with the full facilities of the flexible display functions on hand to make clear the relationships in the data.

In this context, the technique of simulating future possibilities can be enacted using copies of the analyses, each conducted on a different set of hypothetical parameters. The simulation that has the best outcome can then be designated as the official plan.

Using a Comparison Period

Analysis in comparison with a reference period is designed to show how a composite value has changed over time or across data objects, such as a comparison between this period last year and the current period for the total value purchased by each of the purchasing organizations in the company.

Net Order Value Frequency Analysis

Frequency analysis shows which order values occur most often in each purchasing organization and can be used, for example, to negotiate a better discount based on an immediate discount for large orders rather than an end-of-year volume rebate.

Forecasting

A forecast is an estimation of the future values of a time series. Materials requirements will be a set of forecasts, one for each material needed.

There are several choices of which forecast model to use: constant model, trend model, seasonal model, or seasonal trend model. In the SAP System, a forecast is carried out by a first-order exponential smoothing procedure (Winter's procedure).

Forecast-based planning is an automatic reorder point planning procedure in which the forecast requirements are taken into account.

Preparing the Analysis Sequence

The PURCHIS component can be primed to execute user-defined analyses specified by settings on the following dimensions:

- Number of periods to be analyzed
- Performance measures to be displayed
- The standard structure to be followed when the user calls for a drill-down sequence
- The format and layout of the displayed or printed reports

Information Systems Requirements

If you need the answers to the various questions in order to make better use of your materials supply chains, then your database system must be able to cope.

High Volumes of Transactions

Your Operational Systems for ordering, purchasing, and warehousing must be able to accept high volumes of transactions. Depending on your industry sector and your company's place in it, your system will have to take in, store, and efficiently retrieve detailed data.

Current Period Queries

Current period information is something you will need immediately. Your staff will get asked questions during the course of their interactions with vendors and customers, so they must be able to launch efficient queries at your database and get rapid replies that are immediately useful.

Predictable Reports

There will be predictable information demands such as period reports, although the time scale for these reports is moving from quarterly to monthly to daily, and to virtually continuous reporting in some industries. Telephone sales, for example, are dependent upon accurate knowledge of what is in stock and available to promise. When it can be delivered could be a deciding factor.

Anticipating Analysis Requirements

Some information processing demands will be focused on specific operational activities. If you are seeking a vendor suitable for placing an order for some materials, then you will need a list of vendors of exactly those materials. In this instance, the report of vendors sorted by each material of interest should be associated with the order creation activity because you will expect your buyers to need such information. To put this requirement another way, the business object "purchase order" should include the search procedures for vendors of each material identified on the order. A specific buyer may not need this report because there is a single and constant source of supply for some material. But should the regular supplier be unable to deliver, your buyer will need to come up with sensible alternatives very quickly because there may have to be an extended series of transactions to set up the substitute supply chain.

Diverse Patterns of Demand

Your information system has to cope with variable volumes of transactions according to the scope of your queries and requests for standard reports. The system must be able to provide you with summaries and aggregates of data. It must be able to look at data from the past. It must be able to compute reasonable forecasts and apply them to future time periods, taking into account any additional data, such as anticipated new requirements.

It must handle ad hoc unpredictable queries and analytical exploratory activities.

Analysis for Inventory Controlling

The essence of inventory controlling is to make a plan that attempts to anticipate the requirements for all the materials for the planning periods out to the extent of the planning horizon, to compare the planned with the actual, and to make effective and timely adjustments to the replenishment arrangements so that no shortages occur. This is a difficult assignment, and there are some guidelines about keeping safety stocks on hand in case of unforeseen material requirements or unscheduled late deliveries.

If your company has a large inventory with many different materials, the problem is one of sampling the data. Here the MM-Materials Management system can help a great deal through its MM-IC Inventory Controlling component.

Firstly, it can demonstrate to you which materials and subassemblies ought to be monitored for such reasons as the following:

- High capital lock-up while in storage or production.
- The materials needed are purchased or stored in quantities that are not efficient purchasing or storage units.
- Materials are stocked in excess of a reasonable coverage requirement, bearing in mind their expected consumption.
- Materials are seldom withdrawn from inventory and might be better purchased only for specific orders.

Once you have used the system to detect possible opportunities for improvements to your stock control processes, the MM system is able to accept any modifications and execute the new procedures reliably thereafter.

Optimization in Inventory Controlling

The inventory controller may be authorized to adjust the safety stock levels and may be able to influence the purchasing lot size. The MM-IC Inventory Controlling component will enable this controller to reduce stock by a specific amount through the automatic distribution of the target savings to the material stocks that are most sensitive. The controller can choose which materials to monitor on account of their values or the costs of storing and handling them. There can also be some worthwhile lessons to be learned from a study of fluctuations in inventory that could be directed at improving the synchronization of goods issues and receipts.

Meaningful Performance Measures

The MM-Inventory Controlling component has been able to concentrate the most important analysis data into six composite performance measures:

- Consumption value using ABC analysis
- Stock value
- Dead stock
- Range of coverage
- Slow-moving items
- Inventory turnover

The results of these compilations can be studied in two- and three-dimensional graphics and replicated in detailed checklists for closer examination. Any displayed aggregate value can be subjected to the drill-down procedure to reveal the data elements used to compute it.

Objects to Analyze

The standard data structures of the SAP R/3 System are designed to be analyzed at any level. Every materials analysis can be carried out using the data aggregated to any particular level down to the plant level, which is the lowest used for material master records. This means that you can see what is happening at any of the following levels in the organizational hierarchy:

- All plants, cumulated in a specified sequence
- Sales organization level
- Purchasing organization level
- Plant by plant

There are two types of analysis:

- Total analysis
- Ranking list analysis

Total analysis allows a completely flexible definition by the user of the way the data records are to be collated and the measures that are to be computed. How the results are to be related to operational units and to materials are also matters under complete control of the user.

Ranking list analysis prepares the data in the form of rank orderings of the records according to the values specified by the user. They may be grouped, as in ABC analysis, or narrowed by the exclusion of very high and very low values. The scope is flexible with respect to the accounting periods so that the inventory controller can focus the analytical procedures according to such factors as seasonal market movements or delivery reliability.

Standard Analysis for Inventory Controlling

Each of the standard analysis procedures can be carried out at different organizational levels. You can arrange for the scope of your inquiry to range over companies, over departments, over individual storage locations, or whatever meets your needs.

Scoping the Inventory Analysis

The following data objects may be the target for your analysis:

- All Plants Cumulative
- Sales Organization
- Purchasing Organization
- Plant

Building a Set of Items for Analysis

When you have found the type of information you require, you will be able to use it to call for an aggregate of similar information items. "Other purchase orders for this material that were delivered by this shipping agency," for instance. Related items could be requested: "All assemblies in which this item is a part."

When you are satisfied that you have collected all the items for analysis, you can call for one of the standard reports or trend forecasts.

Total Analysis of the Materials

The scope of a totals analysis will be all the materials in a given storage area or set of areas. However, you can limit the target to a particular range of material identification numbers. If you are using an ABC analysis, you can also specify the material type.

The time period for a total analysis is freely adjustable.

Ranking List Analysis

Ranking begins with grouping and the threshold values for membership of these groups have to be established. The area of data to be covered by these groups can be defined by the following methods:

- Range of material numbers
- Specified material group
- Specified material type

If your target object for analysis is a plant, you can further narrow the area by specifying additional parameters such as:

- ABC indicator
- Purchasing group
- MRP controller

The scope of the analysis can be further restricted by specifying either of the following:

- Value of the materials
- Number of materials counted in a rank ordering of them by value from either high or low

You are free to adjust the period over which the analysis will be performed.

Displaying Analysis Results

The results of your analysis can be grouped according to various classification parameters. You can set your own upper and lower limits for membership of the classes for the following performance measures:

- Range of coverage (estimated number of days stock on the inventory)
- Slow-moving items
- Inventory turnover

The MM system automatically calculates the class boundaries for the following performance measures:

- Stock value
- Dead stock

The list display is the default format, but an equivalent graphic is readily called by a standard function. The graphic display options include pie-charts, columnar frequency charts, and dual classification charts that are shown in 3-D format.

For example, you may wish to show how long your stock is expected to last. If you have divided your stock by an ABC analysis into high-, medium-, and low-valued materials, you could have these two dimensions combined to give you a 3-D picture in the "hollow-room" layout.

User-Specific Analysis

If you do not see precisely the report or analysis specification that you require, you should look more carefully because the materials management area has been thoroughly used by SAP R/3 and what you need has probably been required by many others before you. However, you may not wish to look again.

Unique Report Design

You can design a report to suit your requirement for a particular analysis of some or all of your materials. This report will then be available for you to call using the name you assigned to it when you specified it.

Interactive Analysis

The interactive method of finding information is to use the "Drill-Down" option that is available from your SAPGUI. In this technique, you first select with your cursor a displayed menu item, field, or point on a graph. For example, you could point to a material on a materials list.

Depending on how your user interface is configured, you can then point or use keys or buttons to initiate a drill-down operation.

You will then see a new screen or overlay window in which the object you chose with your cursor will be displayed again. This time the display will comprise "deeper" details about the object of your choice.

If these details are not quite what you required, you can return to the previous display and try again. Perhaps the details include an item of interest. If so, you can point to it and drill down again.

If you continue drilling down on successive displays, you will arrive at the smallest data object in the database. You can always go back up your trail and branch off to pursue a different drill-down route.

Drill-Down Analysis Path

The R/3 drill-down function relies on the database including a specification of the analysis path to be followed by successive selections from the options presented. A drill-down path record has to be created for each type of situation.

In the standard materials path, a material number from a list is the first choice to be made.

You will then be offered the following two options:

- Graphs
- Tables

Displaying Graph Data

The following types of graphs can be displayed with the data correct to the latest update, which will probably be no more than one day old:

- Cumulative receipts and issues
- Material issues
- Material receipts
- Stock level

Displaying Info Table Data

The items on an info table are themselves open to one further drill-down operation resulting in the corresponding material document from which the data summary is derived. The following displays are standard:

- Stock movements
- Cumulative stock movements
- Stock overview, which is created by the Inventory Management stock overview function

Part

II

Ch

7

Exploring the Logistics Information System

Logistics is the technology of getting the right things to where they are needed on time.

LO-Logistics is an SAP application in which sales and distribution, materials management, production, quality management, plant maintenance, and elements of project management are integrated by the R/3 System into flexible, universal process chains. One of the components is the LO-LIS Logistics Information System.

The SAP integrated logistics system is focused on managing production from purchasing through sales and distribution. It will embrace many of the profit-generating activities of your company and, therefore, be of vital interest to the enterprise controllers.

The LO-LIS Logistics Information System includes components that collate information from each of the applications that are installed and configured in your implementation, such as SD-Sales and Distribution, PP-Production Planning, MM-Materials Management, PM-Plant Maintenance, and QM-Quality Management.

The basic concept of logistics is a simple one of making sure that everything is in the right place when it is needed. Once upon a time, at least in the large organizations, this meant having a number of work processes in which the labor required was divided between as many people as necessary. You had to employ enough to produce the volume of work required; but also a range of people with specialized skills. Nobody could be expected to have all the different skills required in rapidly developing industries, because there had not been time enough for each apprentice to learn every aspect of his or her trade.

There was another human resource factor. If many fresh people had to be taken on and set to work without much training, then the jobs had to be divided into tasks that could be mastered quickly, provided each person had to master only one task.

Logistics in this context meant making sure that there was a reservoir of work pieces at each stage so that nobody need be idle. Hard manual work was gradually reduced by providing power-assisted tools. Then parts of the work became automated as the machines were provided with the sensing devices that could at first inform the operator and then replace him in the task of keeping that part of the process under control. As the cost of the machinery increased, it also became more important, at least to the profitability of the company, to ensure that each machine was utilized up to or close to its full capacity. This entailed more measurement and calculation, but it did boost profitability.

In parallel with this automation of work processes, the art of quality measurement and control developed, because it became apparent that the cost of re-working faulty products could be considerable—to say nothing of the loss of markets if the product acquired a reputation for uncertain quality.

Again in parallel with the other developments, the cost of holding stock started to be questioned. How large should the reservoirs be at each activity in the production network? When is it cheaper to put up with some idle time rather than carry excessive quantities of stock? At one time the answer would be a matter of anticipating demand: making a plan of stocks and activities that should cope with the expected demand.

These planning skills are still much in demand. Some materials have to be brought into the logistics chain well ahead of processing. If they can be bought in a favorable market and held without too much expense, the logistics chain may be able to add considerable value to them before the production activities begin. The same line of reasoning applies to every link in the production network: how and where can the logistic chain add value?

The logic is the same with products that carry a considerable body of knowledge, whether it is added in the form of a book or in the form of a particular tangible construction. For example, an electronic circuit makes the work piece much more valuable once it is installed.

Even with a simple product that does not appear to carry a payload of knowledge, it is possible to add value by the judicious use of information. If the salesperson takes the trouble to find out which product comes closest to meeting the exact needs of the customer, the sale of this item will carry more value to the customer than if he purchased second best.

So it has come to pass that the measurement and control of quality has been extended to cover not only the production processes, but also the activities that come before and after. Logistics has now come to mean making sure that the right things are in the right place at the right time, including accurate and pertinent information. The scope extends from production planning and control, through materials management, plant maintenance, and quality management, to sales and distribution.

Nothing could add more value than the right person in the right place at the right time. Even (or especially) human resources have to be brought into the logistics chain and treated to human resource planning, controlling, and inevitably quality management.

The Components of the R/3 Integrated Logistics System

There are some R/3 standard business functions that are identified with the logistics functions at a general level; the rest are located in the individual applications. The exact configuration of the logistics elements will depend on the extent to which you wish to build an enterprise control function in addition to a central information collating facility.

Core Logistics Applications   The SAP R/3 System is delivered with the core applications installed and integrated at the code level. Which functions you configure will be a matter for negotiation. The needs of your company may have to be balanced against the costs of configuring all the necessary elements. The following applications would need to be installed and configured to provide a comprehensive logistics system:

- SD Sales and Distribution
- PP Production Planning and Control
- MM Materials Management
- PM Plant Maintenance
- QM Quality Management
- HR Human Resources

Logistics General Components The following components are available as part of the Logistics General module:

- LO-MD Logistics Master Data
- LO-PR Forecast
- LO-VC Variant Configuration
- LO-ECH Engineering Change Management
- LO-LIS Logistics Information System

Computer Integrated Manufacturing

The LO-CIM component is available for production control from the logistics system. There are many production control devices from a wide range of suppliers that can be accessed by the SAP R/3 interfaces. The following systems are examples of linked devices used as part of the LO-CIM component:

- DASS Plant Control System, which interfaces to SAP R2 Control Station Technology
- Digital Corporation PDAS Process Data Acquisition System
- Hewlett-Packard RTAP Real Time Application Platform

The effect of integrating the logistics facilities with the production operations is to allow your system to make modifications to your workflows, which take account of the information coming from your sources. This can constitute "fine tuning" of your business.

For example, you could set up control procedures with logical rules that take account of the different needs of your specific customers within the context of your total mix of operations. Alternatively, you could adjust your workflows according to the industry classification of your customer groups.

Because the standard business processes of SAP R/3 invariably post quantities and values simultaneously, your logistics management and financial accounting can be synchronized absolutely.

Engineering Change Management

The R/3 System manages engineering changes as a central basic data function that is applied automatically to the following data objects:

- Materials
- Documents
- Bills of Materials
- Task Lists

Each change is dated and assigned a standard reason selected automatically or manually. Documents recording changes can be sorted by number, date, or reason. Any number of similar objects can be changed using one change number. For example, engineering change management is facilitated by mass changes to bills of material.

The monitoring of engineering changes can be carried out from the Logistics Application through the LO-ECH Engineering Change Management component. The integrated engineering change management functions allow you to track the complete history of changes to a bill of material.

Maintaining the Logistics Information System

The following key features of the LO-LIS component provide you with a fast and objective decision support system to help business planning and forecasting:

- Online support aids
- Pre-defined LIS performance measures to give you fast and objective data
- Flexible information system that you can adjust to suit your reporting needs
- Integrated and interactive graphics to manipulate your data using the familiar SAPGUI techniques, such as drill-down

Exception Reporting

The principle behind exception reporting is that you do not need to be told when everything is going well. A routine weekly or monthly report takes time to peruse. Why not let the system just signal to you if anything strange happens?

This is how LIS handles very large volumes of data without generating very large volumes of reports.

Triggered Reporting

The economy of the LIS is achieved by setting up performance measures that can be primed to trigger exception reports. If the critical values are exceeded, then you get to see where and how.

Separate LIS Database

The information used in logistics is generated from data created in the various applications, but this information is maintained in a separate LIS database for the following reasons:

- A dedicated database is quicker for supporting analysis online.
- Historical operational data can be accessed for comparison.
- A dedicated LIS database can be arranged to suit the needs of its users.

You can decide which performance measures are to be compiled for the LIS database and how the data is to be stored.

Sources of Data for the LIS

Online transaction data can be automatically routed to the LIS, but you can limit your storage requirements by defining restrictions. For example, you may decide to monitor transactions only if they are with customers whose moving average order value puts them in the top 15 percent.

In the SD Sales and Distribution application of SAP R/3, there is the SIS Sales Information System that includes the most important performance measures and reports as standard. Your LIS can select any of these measures or reports without further adjustment. If you have configured any other applications, you will have immediate access to their performance measures and pre-configured reports.

Updating the LIS Database

The LIS database is updated automatically by certain events in the online transaction system. For instance, order value and order quantity will be updated each time a sales order is confirmed.

The LIS updating can be carried out as a background task in real time, or the data can be copied online and saved for asynchronous updating to make better use of times when the system load is low. The choice between these two methods can be defined for each information structure separately.

LIS Information Structures

When you are setting up the rules for your logistics data monitoring operations, you have to build information structures by selecting from three groups of data objects, all of which have been previously established in your main R/3 repository:

- Reporting objects
- Reporting periods
- Performance measures

Reporting Objects

An information structure for the LIS database comprises at least one reporting object, a reporting period, and a performance measure. For example, you could declare your interest by creating an information structure called "work center" that embraced the data objects "customer," "sales organization," and "distribution channel."

The result would be that your LIS would collect instances of transactions and distribute them appropriately across your structure so that you could examine the performance of each of your work centers. The advantage of doing this in your LIS is that you can set up work centers, or any other information structures, that do not have to correspond to any department or plant arrangements in your company. In our example, you could specify "virtual work centers" in order to concentrate on certain aspects of your business.

Reporting Periods

The reporting period chosen for your LIS information structure could be one of the predefined time periods such as daily, weekly, or monthly. You can also define your own time period and select it for your LIS structure. For example, you could define a time period made up of a certain number of working days so as to exclude the dates when your facilities are closed for public holidays or planned maintenance shut-downs. This information would be obtained from the appropriate plant calendars that your company had defined and stored previously.

Predefined Performance Measures

There are over 250 performance measures and ratios already defined in the LIS module. You can find them using the R/3 Classification system. They include the following measures that are particularly important in managing materials:

- Inventory turnover
- Purchase order values
- Internal order values
- Value of incoming sales
- Value of returned products
- Customer order quantity
- Customer order value
- Target order quantity
- Target order value

You can select any of the relevant performance measures for the reporting objects in your LIS information structures.

User-Defined Performance Measures

If the performance measurement that you require is not already defined in the LIS system, you can create it by nominating any combination of the data objects that R/3 uses in online business transaction processing. Any mathematical or logical formula can be used to build the performance measure you need. Of course, you can save these definitions and make them available throughout your implementation.

Part

II

Ch

7

Using the LIS Standard Functions

If you want to get reports about your inventory or your warehousing operations, you can call for them from the MM Materials Management application. If you want to have a broader picture of your enterprise, the Logistics Information System will provide it by opening access to the sales and production applications and their data.

Standard Reporting from the LIS

The pre-designed standard reports in the LIS assume you will probably want to collect your data from anywhere in your implementation. They offer you a variety of roll-up and summary levels so that you can monitor aggregated information in the most useful ways.

For example, you may decide to move across your collated data at the roll-up level of the plant. You could examine the average value of the inventories across a region partitioned according to industry sector. If you found that one warehouse was holding a very large value of stock, you could drill down on this data object to see if you could find out why.

Most of the kinds of analysis and reporting that you will need will be available by selecting a combination of predefined standard information structures and performance measures already specified in the LIS database.

Reporting Pathways

The sequence of steps that you could take to arrive at a result can be likened to a path. Follow this path to get to the information you want. A predefined LIS standard report contains such a pathway.

If you prefer to find out what you want to know by interacting online with your LIS, you can adopt the standard SAPGUI technique of pointing to objects and using the function keys or mouse clicks to direct your path to the information you need.

What many users do is to call a standard LIS report and then move about within it by, for example, drilling down a customer analysis by material and then by period to find the value of one material sold in one period.

At any stage the following analysis and display functions will be intelligently applied to the data you are working with:

- Totals curve
- Classification
- Dual classification
- Comparison of planned versus actual
- ABC analysis

Filtering Tactics

There are two aspects to a filter: what you catch in the filter and what passes through. You can take out the exceptions to avoid distorting the broad picture. You can take out the normal values to isolate unusual values, which might suggest places or processes where you might be able to make some improvements or prevent an irritation.

The LIS offers the following tactics for shaping your data before and after analysis:

- Interactive selection of measures, picking one at a time to assemble a collection ready for further processing
- Having the system rank order your items of interest and then picking out a number or proportion of items from the top or bottom of the list
- Plotting Pareto charts to show which of your products arranged in rank order account for 90 percent of your sales, for example
- Computing, or depicting graphically, pairs of differences such as planned and actual values for the same item or period
- Sorting records on the basis of one or more fields
- Plotting a histogram to compare frequencies
- Performing correlation analysis to detect how far one factor co-varies in tune with another
- Setting up two-dimensional ranking, for example, to show business volume against the number of incoming orders so that the customers who generate many small orders can be identified

LIS Predefined Analyses

The reports and evaluations that users are most likely to need already exist as information structures in the LIS. The following are examples:

- Sales: incoming orders, delivered quantities, invoiced values
- Inventory: inventory value, turnover, range of coverage, dead stock
- Purchasing: total order value at a supplier, on-time delivery performance

LIS Presentation Graphics

Standard business charting tools can be accessed from the LIS. If you have a particular interest in scheduling situations, the LIS can display Gantt charts to depict the duration of overlapping activities on a common time scale.

The LIS can draw input-output diagrams based on entity-relationship data.

Part
II

Ch
7

LIS Report Writer Functionality

The report writer is used in the LIS to modify and format a comprehensive report that you have generated to suit your company's requirements. It may well be based on a standard LIS report, although it could use one of the reporting structures you have developed and installed to supplement the predefined reports.

You will be able to choose from a range of report layout types to create the basis for your design. You can use the report writer functions to modify the detailed layout parameters such as colors, fonts, backgrounds, and frame arrangement.

Critical Performance Early Warnings

The purpose of the LIS early warning facilities is to draw attention to parts of a report. You choose the items to be tested for critical values and you decide how you want the standard display to be changed to alert the user to the critical elements. You can have the system display a warning message and apply format changes to the display. You can also arrange for the criterion performance measures to be displayed only if they become critical.

The LIS will allow you to run periodic or event-driven reports in the background and send you an e-mail only if a warning situation goes critical.

Threshold Value Warnings   If you have defined a warning for a threshold value, the system will issue a warning when the critical performance measure moves above or below the warning-level.

Trend Warnings   If you have indicated that you are interested in a trend, the system will use a stochastic trend model on historical data to compute a value for the trend. You can specify the critical value that will trigger a warning.

LIS Planning Functions

There are two principal objectives for the planning functions of the LIS:

- To plan target data such as sales quantities
- To plan target values for performance measures

The full suite of R/3 stochastic modeling and forecasting capabilities is accessible from the LIS so that you can set up automatic forecast generating procedures. You can also enter planned or target values manually or import them from an external system.

From the LIS, you can plan target values for stock levels and inventory turnover. If your MM application has been integrated with your production system, you could prepare targets for manufacturing lead times.

Once you have established target values, you can use them as reference points against which to judge the actual figures. You may then set up these comparison computations as the basis for early warning actions.

If your system is using the SOP Sales and Operations Planning component, you can access its data from your LIS. The mechanisms exist in R/3 to close the loop by using the results of operations to influence automatically the planning of future business activities.

As a component of the EIS Executive Information System, the Logistics Information System will be a contributor to any information warehousing initiatives in your enterprise. You may be interested in collecting information from a broad range of sources in order to discern patterns upon which you might base future strategic business decisions.

There is a wide variety of configurable interfaces available for linking the SAP R/3 LIS to certified third-party software products. For example, the following operational units can submit data online:

- Mobile data entry devices
- CAD
- Warehouse control systems
- DASS Plant Control System, which interfaces to SAP R2 Control Station Technology
- Digital Corporation PDAS Process Data Acquisition System
- Hewlett-Packard RTAP Real Time Application Platform
- Repetitive manufacturing order-less production
- Electronic Kanban and just-in-time ordering systems
- Plant maintenance ordering based on counter readings
- Service management from service agreement through equipment maintenance
- Interactive planning table and control station systems at all planning levels
- Variant configuration sub-systems from sales through production
- Assembly order planning and control
- Progress reporting, cash management, and forecasting in project management

The LIS Logistic Information System has the functionality to act as the center of an integrated and diverse multi-level system monitored by exception reporting.

From Here...

- What controls can I exercise over the way my purchasing department places orders?

  See Chapter 2, "Understanding Materials Purchasing."

- How can stock replenishment be automated?

  See Chapter 3, "Understanding Material Requirements Planning."

- What is the best way to marshal thousands of stock items?

  See Chapter 4, "Understanding Inventory and Warehouse Management."

Utilizing Reports and Interfaces

In this chapter

- How to improve custom ABAP reports
- How to use direct upload for new materials
- How to identify fields for specifying batch upload programs

The purpose of this chapter is to introduce some basic programming and analysis techniques with particular emphasis on examples from the MM module. The nature of the ABAP/4 programming environment means that these techniques will also be useful for developers working in other modules as well.

The chapter is written for beginner programmers and configuration consultants involved in specifying code for customization. It is assumed that the reader has a basic understanding of the ABAP/4 programming language but little experience of actually developing programs.

Using Reports

Reports can be used for a variety of purposes including providing management information to know what is going on in the business or for controlling activities, seeking errors, and so on. SAP has standard reports, but it is also possible to write custom reports using ABAP programs.

Reports can be run online with outputs going to either the screen or printers. They are frequently scheduled for running in batch. When running reports users should be aware of the processing capacity that large reports can use. Consideration should also be given to the amount of data made available online before archiving.

Creating Custom Reports

Attending an ABAP course on programming reports is a good introduction to the language. This section moves on from those basics to discuss some of the practicalities of specifying and writing reports.

Specifying Tables and Fields   When an analyst designs a custom report one of the first tasks is to identify the database tables or views where the information is actually stored for the report's SELECT statements.

The analyst knows that the data is stored somewhere because it can be viewed on screen or output in another report, but because SAP is built from hundreds of interdependent database tables locating a specific field can be difficult. This is because the same field name may be used in many different tables.

This section outlines some techniques that can be used to help identify the relevant table and field. It is not comprehensive but provides a good starting point. In some cases a value can only be determined by stepping through code and identifying relevant function calls or data manipulation.

Technical Info   When data required for a report is available in a screen field then this is the first step taken by an analyst. The technical information available for every screen field identifies the field name and table, view, or structure from which it is taken.

This screen is accessible when the cursor is on the field by pressing F1 Help. From the Help screen, press F9 Technical Info. Technical information for the material field in Display Material: Initial Screen (transaction MM03) is shown in Figure 8.1.

FIG. 8.1
The relevant field and table name are shown in the field data section.

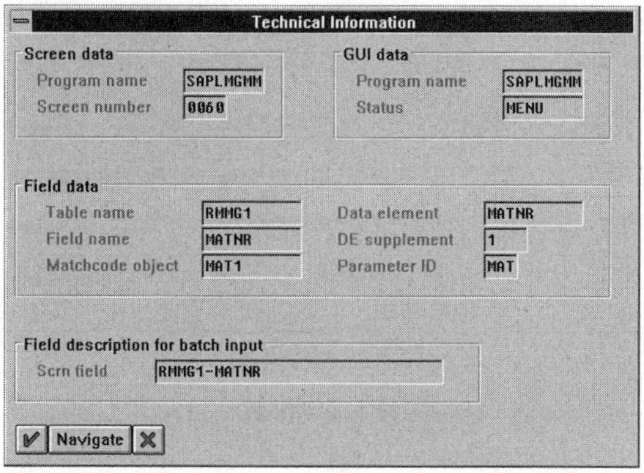

Some fields are displayed directly from the underlying table and in these cases no further investigation is required. The report can be built directly from the table/field combination shown in the technical information. The type of table can be determined from the data dictionary.

Otherwise, the table name actually refers to a structure from the data dictionary, which is blank until populated by a program during screen processing. There is no direct relationship between the screen field and the source table, and in the worst case it is necessary to determine the source of the data by working through the underlying code.

Because this can be quite time consuming there are some other approaches to try first. Some of these are discussed in the following sections.

ABAP/4 Data Dictionary   The data dictionary (transaction SE11) lists all the tables and fields on which SAP is built with data types, descriptions, and some relationships to other tables.

It is accessed from Tools/ABAP/4 Workbench, Development/ABAP/4 Dictionary. Enter the table name in the Object name field and press F7 Display.

In the example (refer to Figure 8.1), the table named is RMMG1. However, when this is displayed using the data dictionary it is identified as a structure (see Figure 8.2).

FIG. 8.2

A sample ABAP/4 dictionary structure.

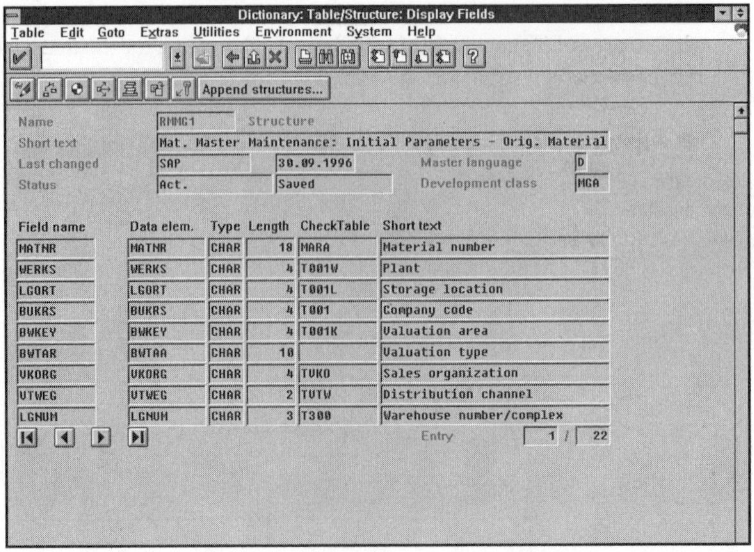

In this case, however, the MATNR field in the structure includes an entry in the check table column—MARA. MARA is a transparent table and, therefore, suitable for reporting.

Alternatively, a matchcode object is also available for the field—MAT1 (as in Figure 8.1). The data dictionary can display matchcode objects as well (see Figure 8.3).

FIG. 8.3

An ABAP/4 matchcode object.

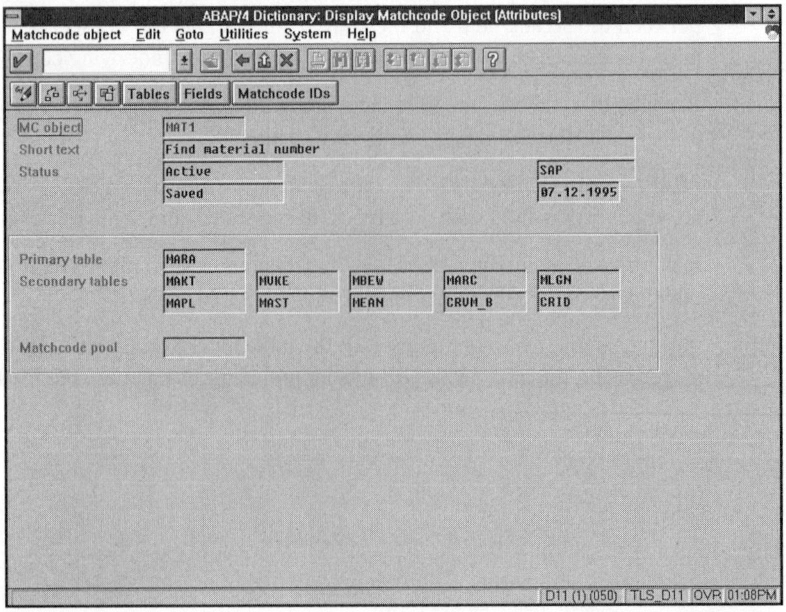

The primary table for MAT1 is MARA—the transparent table required by the report in this example. The match code object also contains a number of secondary tables, which may be useful for other fields required for the report.

SQL Trace   If the required information is not available in a screen field or from the data dictionary, then the SQL trace can provide valuable information about tables.

The SQL trace report for a transaction details every database operation, including select, insert, modify, and delete commands. Useful information includes the names of tables referenced, keys used for record selection, and the numbers of matching records.

When specifying reports, the SQL trace output can help identify source tables and their relationships with one another. The required field can be found by searching the tables listed in the trace using the data dictionary.

If the trace is long, then it is useful to know which tables actually contain the target field before searching them all. A full list of tables can be generated using the Repository Infosys described in the next section.

To generate an SQL trace report, the following steps must be performed:

1. Switch the trace on.

   Select System/Utilities/SQL trace (transaction ST05).

   Press Trace on. Press OK.

2. Execute the required transaction or report to the point the required data is displayed.

   Use the transaction code or menu path to go to the transaction.

   Work through the transaction until the required field is displayed. To minimize the amount of analysis data generated by the trace, it is best to reach the field by the most direct route.

3. Switch the trace off.

   Return the SQL trace (Step 1) and press Trace off.

4. List the trace.

   Press List trace. All traces for a particular date are appended. By entering a start time, information from traces earlier in the day can be suppressed.

The SQL trace contains a column listing table names. The information generated in or by a transaction must be derived from fields in these tables. This considerably narrows the task of locating the field.

If there are a large number of entries it may be useful to save the trace to a local file and process it using other tools (such as spreadsheets or databases) to filter out repeated references to tables.

Tables for Field Name   Although the SQL trace identifies the tables from which a field is derived, it is a time consuming process to search through each relevant table in the data dictionary. It may be that the SQL trace produces so much information that manually locating a field is still not realistic.

The Repository Infosys provides a search facility to locate all tables containing a particular field. This is very powerful when the range of possible tables can be limited, for example, by using the SQL trace output.

To search through the tables for a particular field the following steps should be performed:

1. The Repository Infosys is accessed from the ABAP/4 Dictionary (SE11) by selecting Environment/Repository Infosys from the menu (SE85).
2. Select Views or Tables from the list of Fields objects.
3. Enter the field name as displayed in the Technical Info screen.
4. Press All selections to display further options and check the required table types. Usually transparent tables will be sufficient.

The selection options can be used to narrow the search further.

Two options lend themselves: a multiple selection with all the likely looking tables from the SQL trace, or a mask selecting just the tables for the application area. For material management the mask is M* because materials tables commence with M. Configuration tables (containing no transactional or master data) commence with T.

Tables for Program   The Object Browser (transaction SE80) can be used to list all the tables used in a program.

Enter the program name as listed in technical information under screen data and click display. In the example (refer to Figure 8.1), the program name is SAPLMGMM. The Dictionary Structures branch of the program tree lists all the relevant tables and, helpfully, their names.

Writing Reports   Reports provide the window through which users at all levels view their organization, and the quality of custom reporting directly impacts the effectiveness of employees as they attempt to use the information now potentially available.

Custom reporting provides a unique opportunity for organizations to gain an advantage over competitors using the same application by making better use of the wealth of information stored.

This section outlines techniques for enhancing the functionality and presentation of basic reports. Although the emphasis is placed on the MM module, the techniques can be applied to other SAP modules as well.

> *Report Basics*—A trivial report listing materials of each type is shown later. It illustrates some basic principles of business reporting.

Generation Data—Information about the source of the report is included to facilitate subsequent queries from people reading it. This includes details about the person responsible (user id), the date and time that the report is produced, and information about the source system and client.

Selection Criteria—The selection options used to generate the report are output on the first page. Without these, someone reading the report may make incorrect assumptions about the completeness of the data.

Completion Indicator—The last line of the report should indicate that the end has been reached. This is necessary to help detect that pages are missing.

Sample Report ZMARA000 Sample report ZMARA000 show a trivial report listing materials and their type. It illustrates the basic elements which should be part of any business report. In subsequent sections, the report will be modified to illustrate how color, formatting, and drill-down functionality can be added.

Listing 8.1 shows the code to generate report ZMARA000.

Listing 8.1 The code to generate report ZMARA000.

```
REPORT ZMARA000
  NO STANDARD PAGE HEADING.
*-------------------------------------------------------------------
* Program:      Zmara000
* Description:  Count number of materials of each type
*               Incorporates essential parts of a business report
*-------------------------------------------------------------------
* Modification History
* Date         Programmer      Action
* 05.08.1997   P. Chapman      Created
*-------------------------------------------------------------------
*--> Global definitions
TABLES:
  MARAV,                     " Material Master: General Data
  T134T.                     " Material Type Descriptions
DATA:
*... Internal table for selected material records
  BEGIN OF T_MARAV OCCURS 5,
    MTART LIKE MARAV-MTART,
    COUNT TYPE I,
    MTBEZ LIKE T134T-MTBEZ,
  END OF T_MARAV,
  TOTAL_COUNT TYPE I.
*--> Selection screen
SELECT-OPTIONS:
  S_MTART FOR MARAV-MTART                   " material type
    MEMORY ID MTA
    OBLIGATORY,
  S_MATNR FOR MARAV-MATNR                   " material number
    MEMORY ID MAT.
```

continues

Listing 8.1 Continued

```
*--> Main processing
START-OF-SELECTION.
  PERFORM DATA_EXTRACT.
END-OF-SELECTION.
  PERFORM DATA_REPORT.
TOP-OF-PAGE.
  PERFORM REPORT_HEADING.
*&---------------------------------------------------------------------*
*&      Form   DATA_EXTRACT
*&---------------------------------------------------------------------*
*        Populate t_marav with selected marav records                  *
*----------------------------------------------------------------------*
FORM DATA_EXTRACT.
*... Count number of materials of each type
  SELECT MTART COUNT( * )
    INTO TABLE T_MARAV
    FROM MARAV
    WHERE MATNR IN S_MATNR AND        " material number
          MTART IN S_MTART            " material type
    GROUP BY MTART.
*... Update table with material type descriptions
  LOOP AT T_MARAV.
    SELECT SINGLE MTBEZ                   " Material type
      INTO T_MARAV-MTBEZ
      FROM T134T                          " Material type descriptions
      WHERE SPRAS = SY-LANGU AND
            MTART = T_MARAV-MTART.
    CHECK SY-SUBRC EQ 0.
    MODIFY T_MARAV.
  ENDLOOP.
ENDFORM.                     " DATA_EXTRACT
*&---------------------------------------------------------------------*
*&      Form   DATA_REPORT
*&---------------------------------------------------------------------*
*        Output material data in table t_marav                         *
*----------------------------------------------------------------------*
FORM DATA_REPORT.
  LOOP AT T_MARAV.
    PERFORM REPORT_DETAIL.
    ADD T_MARAV-COUNT TO TOTAL_COUNT.
  ENDLOOP.
  PERFORM REPORT_END.
ENDFORM.                     " DATA_REPORT
*&---------------------------------------------------------------------*
*&      Form   REPORT_HEADING
*&---------------------------------------------------------------------*
*        Output column headings for report                             *
*----------------------------------------------------------------------*
FORM REPORT_HEADING.
  IF SY-PAGNO = 1.
    PERFORM REPORT_OPTIONS.
  ENDIF.
```

```
*... Incorporate the following fields into a page heading:
*     sy-datum    Date
*     sy-uzeit    Time
*     sy-repid    Report name
*     sy-uname    User
*     sy-sysid    Server
*     sy-mandt    Client
*     sy-title    Report description
*     sy-pagno    Page number
*... Column headings
  WRITE:
  /(4)   'Type'(100),
   (25)  'Description'(110),
   (10)  'Count'(120) RIGHT-JUSTIFIED.
  SKIP.
ENDFORM.                      " REPORT_HEADING
*&---------------------------------------------------------------------*
*&      Form  REPORT_DETAIL
*&---------------------------------------------------------------------*
*       Output report detail from table t_marav
*----------------------------------------------------------------------*
FORM REPORT_DETAIL.
  WRITE: /
    T_MARAV-MTART UNDER TEXT-100,
    T_MARAV-MTBEZ UNDER TEXT-110,
    T_MARAV-COUNT UNDER TEXT-120.
ENDFORM.                      " REPORT_DETAIL
*&---------------------------------------------------------------------*
*&      Form  REPORT_END
*&---------------------------------------------------------------------*
*       Output end-of-report message                                   *
*----------------------------------------------------------------------*
FORM REPORT_END.
  SKIP.
  WRITE: /
    'Total'(130),
    TOTAL_COUNT UNDER TEXT-120 RIGHT-JUSTIFIED.
  SKIP 2.
  WRITE / '*** End of Report ***'(999).
ENDFORM.                      " REPORT_END
*&---------------------------------------------------------------------*
*&      Form  REPORT_OPTIONS
*&---------------------------------------------------------------------*
*       Print selection options using standard function call           *
*----------------------------------------------------------------------*
FORM REPORT_OPTIONS.
  DATA:
    T_SELOPTS LIKE RSPARAMS OCCURS 0,
    MAIN_PROGRAM LIKE SY-REPID.
*... Get the selection options
  main_program = sy-repid.
  call function 'RS_REFRESH_FROM_SELECTOPTIONS'
          EXPORTING
               CURR_REPORT = MAIN_PROGRAM
```

continues

Listing 8.1 Continued

```
        tables
            selection_table = t_selopts.
*... Output the selection options
  FORMAT COLOR COL_BACKGROUND INTENSIFIED OFF.
  CALL FUNCTION 'RS_LIST_SELECTION_TABLE'
    EXPORTING
        REPORT       = MAIN_PROGRAM
        SELTEXT      = 'X'
    TABLES
        SEL_TAB      = T_SELOPTS.
endform.
```

Colors and Formatting   Presentation is a key factor in a user's perception of a system. Even delays seem shorter when they are presented well, for example, with a dynamic progress indicator.

It takes only a small amount of extra effort to format custom reports and the improvement in perceived user-friendliness makes the effort very worthwhile.

SAP provides standard colors for different elements of reports in Table 8.1.

Table 8.1   Standard Color Options

Option	Element	Description
COL_BACKGROUND	Background	GUI-specific
COL_HEADING	Headers	grayish blue
COL_NORMAL	List body	bright gray
COL_TOTAL	Totals	yellow
COL_KEY	Key columns	bluish green
COL_POSITIVE	Positive	green
COL_NEGATIVE	Negative	red
COL_GROUP	Control levels	violet

Additionally, an intensified flag can be set on or off.

The color commands—FORMAT, COLOR, and INTENSIFIED—are illustrated in the sample report ZMARA010 (see Listing 8.2).

Colors should be used wherever possible to enhance the readability of a report by grouping related concepts. For example, one color for headings, another for totals and summaries, and so on.

The SAP GUI interface automatically interprets line characters and displays them three dimensionally. As well as improving the look of a report, using lines can help identify data grouping and relationships.

The line commands—SY-VLINE and ULINE—are illustrated in the sample report ZMARA010 (see Listing 8.2).

Creating Sample Report ZMARA010   Sample report ZMARA010 shows how the report ZMARA000 from the previous section can be improved by the addition of colors and line formatting.

Listing 8.2 shows the code to generate report ZMARA010.

Listing 8.2 The code to generate report ZMARA010.

```
REPORT ZMARA010
  NO STANDARD PAGE HEADING.
*-------------------------------------------------------------------
* Program:     ZMARA010
* Description: Count number of materials of each type
*              Incorporates formatting
*-------------------------------------------------------------------
* Modification History
* Date        Programmer      Action
* 05.08.1997  P. Chapman      Created
*-------------------------------------------------------------------
*--> Global definitions
TABLES:
  MARAV,                " Material Master: General Data
  T134T.                " Material Type Descriptions
DATA:
*... Internal table for selected material records
  BEGIN OF T_MARAV OCCURS 5,
    MTART LIKE MARAV-MTART,
    COUNT TYPE I,
    MTBEZ LIKE T134T-MTBEZ,
  END OF T_MARAV,
  TOTAL_COUNT TYPE I,
*... Control flag for alternating detail line colour          "E1
  COLOR_FLAG.                                                 "E1
*--> Selection screen
SELECT-OPTIONS:
  S_MTART FOR MARAV-MTART             " material type
    MEMORY ID MTA
    OBLIGATORY,
  S_MATNR FOR MARAV-MATNR             " material number
    MEMORY ID MAT.
*--> Main processing
START-OF-SELECTION.
  PERFORM DATA_EXTRACT.
END-OF-SELECTION.
  PERFORM DATA_REPORT.
```

continues

Listing 8.2 Continued

```
TOP-OF-PAGE.
  PERFORM REPORT_HEADING.
*&---------------------------------------------------------------*
*&      Form  DATA_EXTRACT
*&---------------------------------------------------------------*
*         Populate t_marav with selected marav records           *
*----------------------------------------------------------------*
FORM DATA_EXTRACT.
*... Update progress indicator                                  "E1
CALL FUNCTION 'SAPGUI_PROGRESS_INDICATOR'                       "E1
     EXPORTING                                                  "E1
          PERCENTAGE = 10                                       "E1
          TEXT      = 'Analysing Materials Table'(210).         "E1
*... Count number of materials of each type
  SELECT MTART COUNT( * )
    INTO TABLE T_MARAV
    FROM MARAV
    WHERE MATNR IN S_MATNR AND     " material number
          MTART IN S_MTART         " material type
    GROUP BY MTART.
*... Update progress indicator                                  "E1
CALL FUNCTION 'SAPGUI_PROGRESS_INDICATOR'                       "E1
     EXPORTING                                                  "E1
          PERCENTAGE = 75                                       "E1
          TEXT      = 'Updating Descriptions'(220).             "E1
*... Update table with material type descriptions
  LOOP AT T_MARAV.
    SELECT SINGLE MTBEZ              " Material type
      INTO T_MARAV-MTBEZ
      FROM T134T                     " Material type descriptions
      WHERE SPRAS = SY-LANGU AND
            MTART = T_MARAV-MTART.
    CHECK SY-SUBRC EQ 0.
    MODIFY T_MARAV.
  ENDLOOP.
ENDFORM.                  " DATA_EXTRACT
*&---------------------------------------------------------------*
*&      Form  DATA_REPORT
*&---------------------------------------------------------------*
*       Output material data in table t_marav
*----------------------------------------------------------------*
FORM DATA_REPORT.
  LOOP AT T_MARAV.
    PERFORM REPORT_DETAIL.
    ADD T_MARAV-COUNT TO TOTAL_COUNT.
  ENDLOOP.
  PERFORM REPORT_END.
ENDFORM.                  " DATA_REPORT
*&---------------------------------------------------------------*
*&      Form  REPORT_HEADING
*&---------------------------------------------------------------*
*       Output column headings for report                       *
*----------------------------------------------------------------*
FORM REPORT_HEADING.
```

```
       IF SY-PAGNO = 1.
         PERFORM REPORT_OPTIONS.
       ENDIF.
*... Incorporate the following fields into a page heading:
*     sy-datum    Date
*     sy-uzeit    Time
*     sy-repid    Report name
*     sy-uname    User
*     sy-sysid    Server
*     sy-mandt    Client
*     sy-title    Report description
*     sy-pagno    Page number
*... Column headings
     FORMAT COLOR COL_HEADING INTENSIFIED ON.                   "E1
     ULINE.                                                     "E1
     WRITE: /                              SY-VLINE,            "E1
       (4)  'Type'(100),                   SY-VLINE,            "E1
       (25) 'Description'(110),            SY-VLINE,            "E1
       (11) 'Count'(120) RIGHT-JUSTIFIED,  SY-VLINE.           "E1
     ULINE.
ENDFORM.                     " REPORT_HEADING
*&---------------------------------------------------------------------*
*&      Form  REPORT_DETAIL
*&---------------------------------------------------------------------*
*       Output report detail from table t_marav
*---------------------------------------------------------------------*
FORM REPORT_DETAIL.
*... Alternating line colours                                  "E1
     FORMAT COLOR COL_NORMAL.                                  "E1
     IF COLOR_FLAG IS INITIAL.                                 "E1
       FORMAT INTENSIFIED ON. COLOR_FLAG = 'X'.                "E1
     ELSE.                                                     "E1
       FORMAT INTENSIFIED OFF. CLEAR COLOR_FLAG.               "E1
     ENDIF.                                                    "E1
     WRITE: /                              SY-VLINE,           "E1
       T_MARAV-MTART UNDER TEXT-100,       SY-VLINE,           "E1
       T_MARAV-MTBEZ UNDER TEXT-110,       SY-VLINE,           "E1
       T_MARAV-COUNT UNDER TEXT-120,       SY-VLINE.           "E1
ENDFORM.                     " REPORT_DETAIL
*&---------------------------------------------------------------------*
*&      Form  REPORT_END
*&---------------------------------------------------------------------*
*       Output end-of-report message                                  *
*---------------------------------------------------------------------*
FORM REPORT_END.
     ULINE.
     FORMAT COLOR COL_TOTAL INTENSIFIED OFF.                   "E1
     WRITE: /                              SY-VLINE,           "E1
       'Total'(130),
       TOTAL_COUNT UNDER TEXT-120 RIGHT-JUSTIFIED,  SY-VLINE.  "E1
     ULINE.                                                    "E1
     FORMAT COLOR COL_BACKGROUND.                              "E1
     SKIP 2.
     WRITE / '*** End of Report ***'(999).
ENDFORM.                     " REPORT_END
```

continues

Listing 8.2 Continued

```
*&-----------------------------------------------------------------*
*&      Form  REPORT_OPTIONS
*&-----------------------------------------------------------------*
*          Print selection options using standard function call    *
*-----------------------------------------------------------------*
FORM REPORT_OPTIONS.
  DATA:
    T_SELOPTS LIKE RSPARAMS OCCURS 0,
    MAIN_PROGRAM LIKE SY-REPID.
*... Get the selection options
  main_program = sy-repid.
  call function 'RS_REFRESH_FROM_SELECTOPTIONS'
         EXPORTING
            CURR_REPORT = MAIN_PROGRAM
         tables
            selection_table = t_selopts.
*... Output the selection options
  FORMAT COLOR COL_BACKGROUND INTENSIFIED OFF.
  CALL FUNCTION 'RS_LIST_SELECTION_TABLE'
     EXPORTING
          REPORT      = MAIN_PROGRAM
          SELTEXT     = 'X'
     TABLES
          SEL_TAB     = T_SELOPTS.
  endform.
```

Drill Down Users of legacy systems often print out entire reports when only a small section is actually required. Even if it is possible to limit the output, users may find the process too complicated or simply not know in advance which part will be required.

Online reporting actively discourages this by presenting an initial summary report, which contains enough detail to identify areas requiring further attention.

The required detail behind a summary line can then be displayed by drilling down on that line. Just the relevant detailed output can then be printed or mailed to other users if required.

Two alternative approaches are available when designing a drill-down report:

- Reporting can be completely performed by a single program
- Independent report programs can be written and then called from one another with the appropriate selection values

The advantage of the latter approach is that users can go directly to a particular detail report if they already know the area they are interested in.

On the other hand, using separate programs can be less efficient if the same selections must be performed again for each level of detail as the user drills down.

For both alternatives, the following sections describe the tasks that must be performed.

Detect That the User Has Clicked on Something ABAP/4 provides an AT LINE-SELECTION event. When the user double-clicks on any part of the report the code in this event is executed.

Determine What Is Selected When the AT LINE-SELECTION event is triggered, the contents of the line are stored in the system variable SY-LISEL exactly as displayed on screen.

If the user clicked on a specific field, this can be determined using the command:

```
GET CURSOR FIELD fld.
```

If the field corresponds to the material number field, the actual value can be extracted using the command:

```
READ CURRENT LINE FIELD VALUE fld INTO var.
```

Perform Drill-Down Processing If another report program is used to generate the drill-down report, the SUBMIT should be used with the AND RETURN variant to return control to the calling report:

```
SUBMIT ZMM01DT1 WITH S_MTART IN R_MTART AND RETURN.
```

Alternatively, if the drill-down report is included in the main report program, then the following should be taken into account:

- Any output from write statements after the AT LINE-SELECTION command will be displayed as the drill-down report.
- Page handling for drill-down reports is provided by the TOP-OF-PAGE DURING LINE-SELECTION command.
- The drill-down level can be ascertained from the SY-LSIND system variable. The first drill-down number is 1, incrementing for each subsequent drill down.
- Use a CASE SY-LSIND structure in the AT LINE-SELECTION event to branch to the appropriate processing when more than one drill-down level is provided.

Creating Sample Report ZMARA020 Sample report ZMARA020 shows how drill down functionality can be added to report ZMARA000 (refer to Listing 8.1) using the commands described in this section. Clicking on a material type lists the materials in that type by executing report ZMARA021, described in the next section.

Listing 8.3 shows the code used to generate report ZMARA020.

Listing 8.3 The code to generate report ZMARA020.

```
REPORT ZMARA020
  NO STANDARD PAGE HEADING.
*------------------------------------------------------------------
* Program:     Zmara020
* Description: Count number of materials of each type
*              Incorporates drill down
*------------------------------------------------------------------
* Modification History
```

continues

Listing 8.3 Continued

```
* Date        Programmer    Action
* 05.08.1997  P. Chapman    Created
*-------------------------------------------------------------------
*--> Global definitions
TABLES:
  MARAV,                    " Material Master: General Data
  T134T.                    " Material Type Descriptions
DATA:
*... Internal table for selected material records
  BEGIN OF T_MARAV OCCURS 5,
    MTART LIKE MARAV-MTART,
    COUNT TYPE I,
    MTBEZ LIKE T134T-MTBEZ,
  END OF T_MARAV,
  TOTAL_COUNT TYPE I.
*--> Selection screen
SELECT-OPTIONS:
  S_MTART FOR MARAV-MTART              " material type
    MEMORY ID MTA
    OBLIGATORY,
  S_MATNR FOR MARAV-MATNR             " material number
    MEMORY ID MAT.
*--> Drill down processing                              "E2
AT LINE-SELECTION.                                      "E2
  DATA: MTART LIKE MARAV-MTART.                         "E2
  READ CURRENT LINE FIELD VALUE T_MARAV-MTART INTO MTART.  "E2
  CHECK NOT MTART IS INITIAL.                           "E2
  SUBMIT ZMARA021 WITH S_MTART = MTART AND RETURN.      "E2
*--> Main processing
START-OF-SELECTION.
  PERFORM DATA_EXTRACT.
END-OF-SELECTION.
  PERFORM DATA_REPORT.
TOP-OF-PAGE.
  PERFORM REPORT_HEADING.
*&------------------------------------------------------------------*
*&      Form   DATA_EXTRACT
*&------------------------------------------------------------------*
*        Populate t_marav with selected marav records              *
*-------------------------------------------------------------------*
FORM DATA_EXTRACT.
*... Count number of materials of each type
  SELECT MTART COUNT( * )
    INTO TABLE T_MARAV
    FROM MARAV
    WHERE MATNR IN S_MATNR AND      " material number
          MTART IN S_MTART          " material type
    GROUP BY MTART.
*... Update table with material type descriptions
  LOOP AT T_MARAV.
    SELECT SINGLE MTBEZ              " Material type
      INTO T_MARAV-MTBEZ
```

```
        FROM T134T                             " Material type descriptions
        WHERE SPRAS = SY-LANGU AND
              MTART = T_MARAV-MTART.
      CHECK SY-SUBRC EQ 0.
      MODIFY T_MARAV.
    ENDLOOP.
ENDFORM.                        " DATA_EXTRACT
*&---------------------------------------------------------------------*
*&      Form  DATA_REPORT
*&---------------------------------------------------------------------*
*       Output material data in table t_marav
*----------------------------------------------------------------------*
FORM DATA_REPORT.
  LOOP AT T_MARAV.
    PERFORM REPORT_DETAIL.
    ADD T_MARAV-COUNT TO TOTAL_COUNT.
  ENDLOOP.
  PERFORM REPORT_END.
ENDFORM.                        " DATA_REPORT
*&---------------------------------------------------------------------*
*&      Form  REPORT_HEADING
*&---------------------------------------------------------------------*
*       Output column headings for report                              *
*----------------------------------------------------------------------*
FORM REPORT_HEADING.
  IF SY-PAGNO = 1.
    PERFORM REPORT_OPTIONS.
  ENDIF.
*... Incorporate the following fields into a page heading:
*     sy-datum    Date
*     sy-uzeit    Time
*     sy-repid    Report name
*     sy-uname    User
*     sy-sysid    Server
*     sy-mandt    Client
*     sy-title    Report description
*     sy-pagno    Page number
*... Column headings
  WRITE:
   /(4)  'Type'(100),
    (25) 'Description'(110),
    (10) 'Count'(120) RIGHT-JUSTIFIED.
  SKIP.
ENDFORM.                        " REPORT_HEADING
*&---------------------------------------------------------------------*
*&      Form  REPORT_DETAIL
*&---------------------------------------------------------------------*
*       Output report detail from table t_marav
*----------------------------------------------------------------------*
FORM REPORT_DETAIL.
  WRITE: /
    T_MARAV-MTART UNDER TEXT-100,
    T_MARAV-MTBEZ UNDER TEXT-110,
    T_MARAV-COUNT UNDER TEXT-120.
ENDFORM.                        " REPORT_DETAIL
```

continues

Listing 8.3 Continued

```
*&-----------------------------------------------------------------*
*&        Form   REPORT_END
*&-----------------------------------------------------------------*
*         Output end-of-report message                             *
*.----------------------------------------------------------------*
FORM REPORT_END.
  SKIP.
  WRITE: /
    'Total'(130),
    TOTAL_COUNT UNDER TEXT-120 RIGHT-JUSTIFIED.
  SKIP 2.
  WRITE / '*** End of Report ***'(999).
ENDFORM.                     " REPORT_END
*&-----------------------------------------------------------------*
*&        Form   REPORT_OPTIONS
*&-----------------------------------------------------------------*
*         Print selection options using standard function call     *
*-----------------------------------------------------------------*
FORM REPORT_OPTIONS.
  DATA:
    T_SELOPTS LIKE RSPARAMS OCCURS 0,
    MAIN_PROGRAM LIKE SY-REPID.
*... Get the selection options
  main_program = sy-repid.
  call function 'RS_REFRESH_FROM_SELECTOPTIONS'
         EXPORTING
             CURR_REPORT = MAIN_PROGRAM
         tables
             selection_table = t_selopts.
*... Output the selection options
  FORMAT COLOR COL_BACKGROUND INTENSIFIED OFF.
  CALL FUNCTION 'RS_LIST_SELECTION_TABLE'
     EXPORTING
             REPORT        = MAIN_PROGRAM
             SELTEXT       = 'X'
     TABLES
             SEL_TAB       = T_SELOPTS.
  endform.
```

Drill to Transaction   This enhancement will encourage users to use reports online rather than on paper. It allows the user to go directly from the report detail to a relevant transaction for more detail or for processing.

The following steps must be performed to enable a report to drill down processing to a transaction:

1. Identify the transaction. First, it is necessary to determine the transaction code for the drill-down transaction. In the example, the Display Material transaction is used—transaction code MM03.

2. Identify parameter IDs for first screen. Usually the fields on a first screen are associated with parameter IDs. These store the most recent value entered so it can be defaulted when the field is next required, in the same transaction or a different one.

   The PID can be determined by going to technical info for the field. From transaction MM01, click the selection field and press F1 Help. Press F9 Technical Info. The three character parameter ID is displayed for field MATNR—MAT.

3. Detect that the user has clicked on something (see "Perform Drill-Down Processing").

4. Determine what is selected (see "Perform Drill-Down Processing").

5. Populate the PID. Once the required material number has been stored in a variable— matnr in the example—it is saved in the corresponding process id:

   ```
   SET PARAMETER ID 'MAT' FIELD matnr.
   ```

6. Call the transaction. This is performed by using standard SAP keywords in the context shown below:

   ```
   CALL TRANSACTION 'MM03' AND SKIP FIRST SCREEN.
   ```

7. Finally, the transaction is executed. When the user finishes with the transaction (by pressing F3 Back), the report will be displayed again.

Creating Sample Report ZMARA021   Sample report ZMARA021 illustrates the use of the Call Transaction function described in this section to drill down from a report to an SAP transaction. The report itself lists materials for a specified type. Clicking on the material goes directly to the display material transaction MM03.

Listing 8.4 shows the code used to generate report ZMARA021.

Listing 8.4 The code to generate report ZMARA021.

```
NO STANDARD PAGE HEADING.


*-------------------------------------------------------------------------
* Program:     ZMARA021
* Description: List materials in each material type
*              Incorporates drill to transaction
*-------------------------------------------------------------------------
* Modification History
* Date         Programmer      Action
* 05.08.1997   P. Chapman      Created
*-------------------------------------------------------------------------


*--> Global definitions
TABLES:
  MARAV.                     " Material Master: General Data

DATA:

*... Internal table for selected material records
  BEGIN OF T_MARAV OCCURS 5,
```

continues

Listing 8.4 Continued

```
      MTART LIKE MARAV-MTART,
      MATNR LIKE MARAV-MATNR,
      MAKTX LIKE MARAV-MAKTX,
    END OF T_MARAV.

*--> Selection screen
SELECT-OPTIONS:

  S_MTART FOR MARAV-MTART                " material type
    MEMORY ID MTA
    OBLIGATORY,

  S_MATNR FOR MARAV-MATNR                " material number
    MEMORY ID MAT.

*--> Drill to transaction processing
AT LINE-SELECTION.                                          "E3
  DATA: MATNR LIKE MARAV-MATNR.                             "E3
  READ CURRENT LINE FIELD VALUE T_MARAV-MATNR INTO MATNR.   "E3
  CHECK NOT MATNR IS INITIAL.                               "E3
  SET PARAMETER ID 'MAT' FIELD MATNR.                       "E3
  CALL TRANSACTION 'MM03' AND SKIP FIRST SCREEN.            "E3

*--> Main processing
START-OF-SELECTION.
  PERFORM DATA_EXTRACT.

END-OF-SELECTION.
  PERFORM DATA_REPORT.

TOP-OF-PAGE.
  PERFORM REPORT_HEADING.

*&---------------------------------------------------------------------*
*&      Form  DATA_EXTRACT
*&---------------------------------------------------------------------*
*       Populate t_marav with selected marav records                   *
*----------------------------------------------------------------------*
FORM DATA_EXTRACT.

*... Count number of materials of each type
  SELECT MTART MATNR MAKTX
    INTO CORRESPONDING FIELDS OF TABLE T_MARAV
    FROM MARAV
    WHERE MATNR IN S_MATNR AND       " material number
          MTART IN S_MTART.          " material type

ENDFORM.                      " DATA_EXTRACT

*&---------------------------------------------------------------------*
*&      Form  DATA_REPORT
*&---------------------------------------------------------------------*
*       Output material data in table t_marav
```

```
*-------------------------------------------------------------------*
FORM DATA_REPORT.

  LOOP AT T_MARAV.
    PERFORM REPORT_DETAIL.
  ENDLOOP.

  PERFORM REPORT_END.

ENDFORM.                          " DATA_REPORT

*&------------------------------------------------------------------*
*&      Form  REPORT_HEADING
*&------------------------------------------------------------------*
*       Output column headings for report                          *
*-------------------------------------------------------------------*
FORM REPORT_HEADING.

  IF SY-PAGNO = 1.
    PERFORM REPORT_OPTIONS.
  ENDIF.


*... Incorporate the following fields into a page heading:
*      sy-datum     Date
*      sy-uzeit     Time
*      sy-repid     Report name
*      sy-uname     User
*      sy-sysid     Server
*      sy-mandt     Client
*      sy-title     Report description
*      sy-pagno     Page number

*... Column headings
  WRITE:
   /(4)  'Type'(100),
    (18) 'Material'(110),
    (25) 'Description'(120).
  ULINE.

ENDFORM.                          " REPORT_HEADING

*&------------------------------------------------------------------*
*&      Form  REPORT_DETAIL
*&------------------------------------------------------------------*
*       Output report detail from table t_marav                    *
*-------------------------------------------------------------------*
FORM REPORT_DETAIL.

  WRITE: /
    T_MARAV-MTART UNDER TEXT-100,
    T_MARAV-MATNR UNDER TEXT-110,
    T_MARAV-MAKTX UNDER TEXT-120.

ENDFORM.                          " REPORT_DETAIL
```

continues

Listing 8.4 Continued

```
*&---------------------------------------------------------------*
*&      Form   REPORT_END
*&---------------------------------------------------------------*
*          Output end-of-report message                          *
*----------------------------------------------------------------*
FORM REPORT_END.
  ULINE.

  SKIP 2.
  WRITE / '*** End of Report ***'(999).

ENDFORM.                        " REPORT_END

*&---------------------------------------------------------------*
*&      Form   REPORT_OPTIONS
*&---------------------------------------------------------------*
*          Print selection options using standard function call  *
*----------------------------------------------------------------*
FORM REPORT_OPTIONS.

  DATA:
    T_SELOPTS LIKE RSPARAMS OCCURS 0,
    MAIN_PROGRAM LIKE SY-REPID.

*... Get the selection options
  main_program = sy-repid.
  call function 'RS_REFRESH_FROM_SELECTOPTIONS'
          EXPORTING
              CURR_REPORT = MAIN_PROGRAM
          tables
              selection_table = t_selopts.

*... Output the selection options
  FORMAT COLOR COL_BACKGROUND INTENSIFIED OFF.

  CALL FUNCTION 'RS_LIST_SELECTION_TABLE'
     EXPORTING
          REPORT        = MAIN_PROGRAM
          SELTEXT       = 'X'
     TABLES
          SEL_TAB       = T_SELOPTS.

  endform.
```

Using Interfaces

Interfaces are needed to transfer data to and from other systems that are used alongside SAP.

This section addresses the steps required for a typical material master upload while avoiding details that will vary depending on the source database or SAP release in use. There are vagaries to the process that may necessitate a period of continuous improvement before settling on a final approach. It is particularly important to rigorously test the process before moving into the production environment.

There are two approaches to loading materials data into SAP: Batch Input or Direct Input. Non material master data, which cannot be uploaded using direct input, can be transferred using the traditional batch approach. Both techniques are described in the following sections.

Direct Input

Direct Input loads material master data directly into SAP tables, instead of performing the usual online screen processing in the background. This is much faster than the alternative batch input processing but is available only for material master data.

The following activities must be carried out to successfully perform a direct uploaded:

- Create a database containing the cleaned up legacy data to be uploaded
- Convert the data to a format suitable for the direct upload program
- Configure SAP for the upload file
- Perform the upload

These activities are described in more detail in the following sections.

Source Database

The first task is to collect all the material data for the upload into a single place. Even in the event that the legacy material data has attained a high degree of integrity, it is usually beneficial to generate a source database distinct from the legacy production environments to facilitate tight project control.

Centralizing the material master in this way can effectively focus the business on the need to uniquely identify each material in use. Even if gathering information from distributed systems proves relatively straightforward, filtering out duplication requires the co-operation of everyone involved.

The source database can be maintained on a powerful PC. A product such as Microsoft Access provides an ideal platform if the person responsible is an expert user.

The actual structure of the source database is not critical and will reflect the process required to collect and clean up the data from legacy systems rather than the required output format.

Creating the Upload File

Information from the source database must be exported to a specially formatted text file (the upload file) before it can be loaded into SAP.

The structure of each line in the file varies. Every material in the file will commence with a header line. The structure of subsequent lines for the material will depend on the type of information to be uploaded.

The first character of the line specifies the record structure. The available upload structures are listed in the source code for program RMMMBIMX. In release 30F, they are listed in Table 8.2.

Table 8.2 Upload Structure

Record	Type	Description
BGR00	'0'	Batch input session data
BMM00	'1'	Material Number and views
BMMH1	'2'	Main data
BMMH2	'3'	Country tax data
BMMH3	'4'	Forecast values
BMMH4	'5'	Consumption values
BMMH5	'6'	Descriptions
BMMH6	'7'	Units of measure
BMMH7	'8'	Long texts
BMMH8	'9'	Referential EANs

Text files containing nested structures and variable width fields are very difficult to create using common PC spreadsheet or database applications. Although it is possible to create such a file using PC software, SAP is much better suited to the task. This is because the upload structures are already available in SAP with the required field widths and types, and SAP performance will be superior.

If the data is stored using Microsoft Access, for example, then each Access table should be downloaded using tab-separated text files (for example) and then formatted into the required upload file using a custom written ABAP/4 program.

On projects where a large number of different upload structures will be required, it is worth developing a generic upload utility and training users to configure it to their own needs. This gives data owners more control over their data and reduces the risk of bugs appearing unexpectedly in isolated upload programs at a critical point in the project.

Configuring for the Upload

The first task is to make the upload file accessible to SAP. The new upload file must be assigned to an SAP logical filename. Each logical filename references a physical file, but may include dependencies such as the host or client. The Basis team should be involved in configuring the appropriate logical filename. RMDATIND defaults to MATERIAL_MASTER_BTCI as the logical file.

When the logical filename has been successfully created it is possible to create variants for report RMDATIND. Two variants should be set up: a test variant with the "Check data but do not update" option selected, and an actual variant where the option is not checked.

The upload file format can be easily tested by executing RMDATIND with the test variant. This should be performed with a small subset of the upload file.

For production uploads, SAP provides transaction BMV0 to control the execution of RMDATIND. It allows RMDATIND to be safely restarted in the case of an abnormal termination—a necessity because tables are updated directly without the usual error handling. This is why SAP advises against using RMDATIND to upload data in a production system.

A new job is defined in BMV0 specifying the report RMDATIND and the actual variant. If the upload is to be tested in BMV0, then a second job can be created specifying the test variant. After a job has been executed progress is indicated by "traffic lights:" Green indicates success, orange in progress and red that failures have occurred.

Batch Input

Although direct input provides superior performance for loading specific material master data, any uploads or processing that cannot be defined using the BMMH fields will be implemented using batch input structures. This is the case for all MM transactional data.

At its most basic, a batch input structure is a table that describes the actions of an operator keying in data.

An internal table is generated describing the screen flow and the contents of each field in the screen. This table is then used to execute a transaction directly (call transaction) or to build a batch session that can be processed using Batch Input (transaction SM35). Batch input provides more control over the upload process but involves the user in additional steps.

A batch input structure contains the fields in Table 8.3.

Table 8.3   *BDCDATA*

Field Name	Data Type	Length	Description
PROGRAM	CHAR	8	BDC module pool
DYNPRO	NUMC	4	BDC Screen number
DYNBEGIN	CHAR	1	BDC dynpro start
FNAM	CHAR	35	BDC Field name
FVAL	CHAR	132	BDC Field value

By creating an internal BDCDATA table with the correct values, the processing for an entire transaction can be simulated.

For example, a BDC session that automatically creates the quality view for a material commences by specifying the material number in the create material transaction (MM01).

To perform this processing in a BDC table, it is necessary to know the following information for the screen:

- Program name and screen number
- Table and field name for every field to be populated
- OK code, which is the command selected to continue from the screen; for example, save (F11) or back (F3)

In this example, the program name and screen number can be determined by selecting the transaction (MM01) and then choosing System/Status... from the menu.

Alternatively, selecting a field, pressing F1 and then clicking Technical Info will display a popup box with the required screen data—program name and screen number (refer to Figure 8.1). This is essential for popup boxes when the main menu is not accessible.

The row in the BDCDATA table to specify the screen is as follows:

Program	Dynpro	Dynbegin	Fnam	Fval
SAPLMGMM	60	X		

Note that the Fnam and Fval fields are left blank because they are not relevant when specifying a new SAP screen.

The first field to be populated is the material number. The screen field containing the material number can be determined by selecting the material number field and pressing F1, then clicking Technical Info.

If the material number entry is 1000, then the entry in the BDC table is

Program	Dynpro	Dynbegin	Fnam	Fval
			RMMG1 - MATNR	1000

Note that the Program, Dynpro, and Dynbegin fields are left blank because they are not relevant when specifying a field and value.

This is repeated for each field on the screen, which must be manually populated.

Finally, the OK code must be determined. Any code that can be entered in the command field (below the main menu line) can be specified for the OK code. Possibilities are listed in Table 8.4.

Table 8.4 OK Code Possibilities

Function	Key	Code	Example
Default	ENTER	/0	/0
Function Keys	Fn	/n	/6
Function Code	xxxx	xxxx	SCHL

The function key can be determined from the popup menu (right mouse button) or from the tag text. The OK code is simply the function key number (add 12 to n for SHIFT+Fn functions) preceded by /.

The function code is determined by pressing F1 while a menu option is highlighted—do not release the mouse button before pressing F1. A help box is displayed containing the function key code of up to four characters.

The OK code can be tested by typing it into the command field and pressing Enter.

In this example, Enter would be pressed after keying in the material number—OK code /0.

Program	Dynpro	Dynbegin	Fnam	Fval
			BDC_OKCODE	/0

Note that the Program, Dynpro, and Dynbegin fields are left blank because they are not relevant when specifying a field and value.

If a button must be selected, then this is specified using the BDC_CURSOR field. Each button is assigned a field name, which can be seen using the screen painter (SE51) and viewing the field list for the screen. Buttons are Ftype Push.

Program	Dynpro	Dynbegin	Fnam	Fval
			BDC_CURSOR	SPOP-OPTION1

Note that the Program, Dynpro, and Dynbegin fields are left blank because they are not relevant when specifying a field and value.

The complete BDCDATA table entries for specifying the first screen of transaction MM01, selecting material 1000, and pressing Enter is

Program	Dynpro	Dynbegin	Fnam	Fval
SAPLMGMM	60	X		
			RMMG1-MATNR	1000
			BDC_OKCODE	/0

Implementing BDC Processing

This section provides code samples for implementing the BDC processing described previously.

Most of the effort involved in writing BDC sessions is in determining correct screen flows. The actual program code is simple and repetitive and is used to populate the BDCDATA table correctly and submit it to SAP for processing.

The following sections contain the core routines used to build all batch processing programs. They can be placed in an Include report and used by all programmers on a project.

Writing Useful BDC Procedures   Two procedures can be written that are particularly useful for populating BDC tables. They are as follows:

Add Screen—This procedure adds a row to the internal BDC table with the program and screen number for a new screen. Sample code:

```
form bdc_dynpro using program dynpro.
clear bdcdata.
  bdcdata-program = program.
  bdcdata-dynpro  = dynpro.
  bdcdata-dynbegin = 'X'.
  append bdcdata.
endform.
```

Add Field—This procedure adds a row to the internal BDC table with the field name and a value for the field. It can also be used to populate the OK code or BDC cursor. Sample code:

```
form bdc_field using fnam fval.
  clear bdcdata.
  if fval ne nodata.
    bdcdata-fnam = fnam.
    bdcdata-fval = fval.
  endif.
  append bdcdata.
endform.
```

Populating BDC Fields for a Screen   Using these procedures in the program, the table entries for the previous example could be created using the following code extract:

```
data: bdcdata like bdcdata occurs 5.
perform bdc_dynpro using 'SAPLMGMM' '60'.
perform bdc_field using 'RMMG1-MATNR' '1000'.
perform bdc_field using 'BDC_OKCODE' '/0'.
```

Processing the Completed BDC Transaction   The completed BDC transaction can be processed immediately or later using a batch session.

To process the transaction immediately, use the call transaction command as illustrated in the example:

```
CALL TRANSACTION 'MM01' USING BDCDATA
MODE 'N'
UPDATE 'A'.
```

Alternatively, or if an error occurs in the call transaction, a batch session can be generated and processed at a later time.

Use the BDC_OPEN_GROUP function to open a group of transactions when it is certain that at least one will be processed:

```
call function 'BDC_OPEN_GROUP'
     exporting
           client              = sy-mandt
           group               = group
           holddate            = holddate
           keep                = keep
           user                = user.
```

Loop through each transaction, generating a new BDCDATA table for each one and adding it to the BDC group using BDC_INSERT. Do not forget to refresh BDCDATA after each call:

```
call function 'BDC_INSERT'
  exporting
       tcode           = 'MM01'
  tables
       dynprotab       = bdcdata
  exceptions
       internal_error  = 1
       not_open        = 2
       queue_error     = 3
       tcode_invalid   = 4
       others          = 5.
```

When all transactions have been inserted into the group, close it using BDC_CLOSE_GROUP:

```
call function 'BDC_CLOSE_GROUP'.
```

The resulting output can be processed using transaction SM35. This also logs the progress of each session as it is executed and shows the screen flow for each transaction (if processed in the foreground).

The terms interface and upload are used here interchangeably because the principles are the same for both operations. An interface is simply an upload performed at regular intervals, although it should incorporate handling to ensure that files cannot be accidentally loaded out of sequence.

From Here...

■ How are the various components put together?

See Chapter 6, "Understanding the SAP R/3 Business Engineer."

■ How can you find out details about your stocks of materials?

See Chapter 7, "Analyzing Materials Information."

■ How are networked systems built?

See Chapter 9, "Understanding Network Computing."

Understanding Network Computing

In this chapter

- Why extend your enterprise as a network?
- Are the technologies available to network safely and profitably?
- Why involve materials management in networking?
- How has networking been used in materials management?
- How will networking develop in the immediate future?

Network computing is a form of distributed computing where applications and data reside on a network, and users can access resources anywhere on the network, not just on their own PCs. The annual expense for a typical desktop computer running a standard set of business productivity applications is believed to be $8,000 to $12,000. Much of this is spent on support, training, and maintenance. Updating the software, for instance, entails re-loading each PC.

SAP R/3 has always been thought of as a layered system: outside is the presentation and user interface; below this resides the application layer in which the processing takes place; and in the core is the database and its processors. The layered concept is implemented to allow as much processing power and data storage capacity to be assigned to each layer as the volume and type of traffic demands. New processors can be brought in as the load increases. This dynamic and largely automatic control allows the system to be scaled up to handle larger numbers of users and also to execute more complicated processing where this is required.

The Attractions of Business on the Internet

The development of network software is proceeding rapidly because the mechanisms are available and there are many advantages. The attractions, or at least the potentials, are distributed between consumer-to-business, business-to-business, and within-business applications.

This is because network software provides the following features:

- Easy to use around the world, at any time.
- Easy access to information that is relevant at a pace and complexity under the control of the reader.
- A low-cost marketing channel with wide market exposure and considerable penetration.
- The same familiar interface can access a variety of services in depth, if required.
- Inquiries are answered immediately.
- Inquirer can be asked intelligent questions because previously-collected information about the inquirer can be taken into consideration, either automatically or by the operator.
- Moving images with sound can be under the control of the viewer to demonstrate the product and discover which aspects interest the prospective purchaser.
- Increased revenue may arise from a low cost of sales.
- The Internet may have become the preferred source of information on all matters for some sectors of the market.
- Simple cut-and-paste can be used to compile e-mail purchase orders and to request other services.

Although it does seem that the network in all its forms is going to play an increasing part in business, it will no doubt take some time to become the preferred medium for the public. The telephone is ubiquitous, but not all purchases are carried out by its use. However, the benefits of networking for business-to-business communication are rapidly becoming apparent.

Electronic Commerce in Supply Chain Improvement

As a product is developed from raw materials to the point of consumption and possibly disposal, the links in this supply chain are traversed with variable efficiency. For example, the storage of goods in a warehouse against unknown future orders, must often be counted as an inefficiency that has to be weighed against the possible consequences of having to purchase at an unfavorable point in the market for materials or resources.

Electronic commerce can be regarded as a system of sending messages quickly and often automatically. This system has to be available globally. It has to justify the cost of installing the equipment, training the users, and persuading the management and user community to exploit the messaging system rather than try to bypass it.

Electronic commerce has to carry the details to support the following important classes of message:

- The customer wants, expects, and demands detailed understanding by the supplier of what is required. This is in contrast to the catalog approach of letting the customer know what is available and refusing all variants.

- The customer has electronic access to all vendors who are prepared to make the relatively small investment required to advertise their products on a worldwide basis.

- The customer expects a product to comply with his local regulations and specifications.

- The customer expects to be able to order the latest version of every item.

- The customer expects to access one point of contact for all requirements.

Effective supply chain management requires rapid and up-to-date analysis of order patterns, product flows, and the state of inventories. Electronic commerce is essential if this information is to be gathered and collated in time to contribute to sensible decision-making.

Tracking Materials

Some industries have always kept track of batches and their origins because of the possible legal and commercial consequences of being unable to say where a particular material originated and the processes it has subsequently undergone. Increasingly, it is prudent to track most materials and their processes because vital clues to the significant opportunities for improving profitability may be found in data routinely collected—about waiting times and stock discrepancies, for example.

Serialized parts management in the aviation industry is available as an SAP standard solution for the R/2 system. It provides the following functionality for parts that have to retain their serial numbers:

- Material requirements planning allocation

- Maintenance order cycle

- Measurement of usage by time in service, counted events, and time since previous inspection

- Configuration management in the aircraft so that the location of each serialized part may be determined
- Tracking of parts though conditions, such as serviceable or unsuitable for service, through to disposal details
- Tracking and valuation of all parts throughout the various conditions
- Compilation of part history through maintenance and usage episodes
- Overall cost processing
- Management of repair orders for individual parts
- Maintenance of equipment owned by a customer
- Sales of equipment owned by a customer

Manufacturer Part Number Management

The existence of a range of approved suppliers of parts that have to be maintained as serialized parts poses the problem of correlating the part numbers of interchangeable components supplied by different manufacturers. This function is serviced by an integrated component in the SAP R/2 System in association with serialized part management.

Customer Electronic Commerce with R/3

The implementation of local networks based on mainframe computers and dedicated communications has a relatively long history. Client/server configurations allowed distributed computing whereby the user at a workstation or simple terminal could be connected, not only to databases, but also to additional computing power to process the data. In simple terms, the concept entailed accessing a system through a terminal dedicated for this purpose. The extent and complexity of the system often are not apparent to the individual user, nor need they be in most applications.

However, there are very real limitations on the number of terminals that can be operating at the same time. SAP R/3 and R/2 are able to adjust the allocation of computing resources to the workload on a dynamic basis, and the provision of procedures to cope with equipment and communication channel malfunctions is well understood.

Apart from automated banking terminals, the direct conduct of commercial business by individual users is not yet widespread, but the SAP R/3 range of standard business software is anticipating a change.

Electronic Data Interchange

Electronic Data Interchange, or EDI, is the standard and the communication link that enables the direct exchange of information by electronic signal processing without modulating the information so as to be acceptable to voice telephone equipment. The EDI equipment is fast and reliable. It has become essential to the conduct of business for many companies, their customers, and suppliers.

With the fast exchange of data, the clerical processes have become largely automated by using systems that report only if there are exceptions or problems with the commercial transactions or the rules under which they have been automated.

The very speed of EDI enables goods to be tracked throughout their passage from manufacture through warehousing to delivery. The traditional slow-moving material requirements planning can be conducted in real time and the decisions communicated without delay to the key suppliers. And because an effective management process can be in place, the need has diminished for stocks of materials and reservoirs of work waiting for clerical processing. Jobs inevitably disappear. Costs diminish. Out-of-hours working becomes standard. Plant utilization can be increased, including computing plant.

Part
II

Ch
9

Components for Internet and Intranet Use

There are two ways of developing your business system via a network. You can open links to a public or private network and then restrict certain operations to users who have been identified as authorized individuals. Sales orders might be acceptable from those with sufficient credit; information inquiries might be limited to representatives of registered companies. The other way of developing your business is to initiate coded messages on a network that are understood only by their intended recipient. A command to a warehouse to dispatch an item would have to be coded. Several different types of component are needed to do business over the networks.

Browsers

Netscape Navigator and Microsoft Internet Explorer are two browsers that can be used to present screens and transmit data to a user who is at the end of a low-bandwidth Internet channel. If you open a location, you will see a display that will be maintained by a distant computer, which selects the display according to the details you entered when you specified the location. If your terminal is connected to a computer that does not have the location you are seeking, then it will try another computer, and so on until the searching is fruitful, exhausted, or timed out.

The job of a browser is to put together the responses from the location so that the user is not aware of the complexity of the selection and delivery processes, although the delay in response may suggest that the mechanism is by no means straightforward.

Browsers are often given away free to those who rent a telephone line. Their operation is becoming familiar to an increasing number of people. They can be made to operate in just about any language. They can be mounted in very modest computing and display devices.

Web Servers

A Web server is a computing resource assigned to the job of connecting Web clients with the database or other service that has been requested. The server can be a standard software package such as the Microsoft Internet Information Server or the Netscape Enterprise Server.

Internet Transaction Server

The SAP R/3 Internet Transaction Server (ITS) connects Internet Application Components and the Web server. It presents information in Web page format, which can be accessed by employees, customers, and other users via a browser. The ITS manages network transactions and supports Java.

SAP Automation

SAP Automation is a programming interface. It allows Internet Application Components and other third-party application components to automate the interaction with R/3. It also integrates R/3 with new technologies such as COM/DCOM, OMG CORBA, and Java, as well as with external applications such as IVR (Interactive Voice Response) applications and forms-based interfaces.

Internet Application Components

SAP Internet Application Components (IACs) are easy-to-use software modules that customers can use to perform specific business tasks and operations across the Internet and intranets. SAP has available 25 IACs and 10 Employee Self-Service Application Components for the HR-Human Resources application.

Business Application Programming Interfaces

The work unit of SAP systems is the transaction, and so it is for Electronic Commerce. The components available for electronic commerce are software units that can be carried in a range of operating systems and hardware devices. The concept is to make them available for use by any system that has received the SAP certification.

Business Application Programming Interfaces (BAPIs) are open, object-oriented interfaces based on SAP business objects. The BAPI defines how a business application will respond to a transaction.

In essence, the application receives a message through a BAPI, which sets up the procedures for dealing with the data that also arrives at the BAPI. For example, a BAPI to a Human Resources database server may be configured to recognize a request for a person who has particular qualifications and who is also available to carry out a task, such as process a sales order. The server finds such a person, if possible, and returns the details to the system or to the person who initiated the request.

Several hundred BAPIs have been defined across all R/3 business application areas. They integrate IACs and core R/3 system functions and reside in the application server layer. Both SAP and independent developers can use the BAPIs to build Internet and intranet solutions using R/3 and other business applications. BAPIs are Microsoft COM/DCOM compliant and OMG CORBA compatible.

Customer-Driven Production by IAC

An IAC, Internet Application Component, is a standard business interface that is specifically designed to operate with the Internet or with an intranet. It is a characteristic of SAP R/3 Internet Application Components that they are isolated from the kernel of the R/3 system. They can be seen as separate components that can be developed and adapted without requiring any change in the main R/3 system.

In particular, the way an Internet Application Component reacts is determined when the Internet Web page is designed. Full multimedia facilities can be available, and the very style of the interchange between user and system is to build on the idea that the whole supply chain is responding without delay to the requests and requirements of the user. Both goods and information are handled in the style of a production process in which the customer is source of the prime information.

Online Facilities

The following titles indicate the range of services that have been rapidly elaborated using the SAP R/3 Internet Application Components and their supporting Business Application Programming Interfaces. Some of them are available as loosely coupled systems using the ALE, Application Link Enabling, protocol:

- Product Catalog with facilities to service Interactive Requests
- Employment Opportunities with reporting to users on their Application Status
- KANBAN stock control logic and reporting from the SAP Available-to-Promise server
- Service Notification
- Sales Order Creation with reporting on Sales Order Status
- Measurement and Counter Readings from production plant and laboratory systems
- Quality Notification and Quality Certificates
- Consignment Stocks Status
- Project Data Confirmation
- Collective Release of Purchase Requisitions and Purchase Orders
- Who is Who staff listing and Integrated Inbox
- Internal Activity Allocation and Workflow Status
- Internal Price List, Requirement Request, and Requirement Request Status
- Asset Management

Electronic Commerce and Security

The variety of processes and the very large numbers of users who will have access to a networked electric commerce system inevitably raises queries about the privacy of personal data and the restriction of commercially sensitive information. Malicious damage to databases and other forms of hacking are real threats.

It must be reasonable to expect that the more people can access your business information system, the more people can use it for fraudulent purposes. If you download a file of text, or view a picture, or watch a movie sequence, you are allowing a complex file to pass into your system. Within this file there can reside some kind of virus that can immediately or subsequently affect your data. If you are operating a thin client, your download can be very extensive indeed.

There are two issues: gaining access to private personal information and gaining access to restricted commercial information. Illegal and malicious activities can follow from either of these processes.

You can set up firewall procedures to protect your systems. You can code your transmissions. You can make sure that your management controls are updated to match the developments in fraudulent techniques. And of these, probably the most important is to make sure that your staff and your business partners with access to your systems are all aware of the ways in which damage can be done and are prepared to keep on using the protective measures that have been provided.

Firewalls are interfaces that only allow the transmission of information and commands that have been authorized and their sources verified. Encryption is the process of transforming a data stream according to a code that can be used by the recipient to restore the stream to its original structure. The complexity of encryption procedures has to be increased as code-breakers acquire the capability to de-code private data. Yet there has to be international cooperation because commerce is conducted on a global basis and requires secure communication.

The SAP R/3 business interfaces and Internet components are designed to be able to implement the SET (Secure Electronic Transaction) standard that is under development by the Internet Engineering Task Force.

SAP R/3 Year 2000 Compliance

All releases of R/3 are compliant. No migration or upgrade is required for R/3 users. All date fields are four bytes, as are all related record layouts, screen layouts, matchcodes (secondary indexes), and data dictionary definitions.

Certification Tests

Year 2000 certification tests have been conducted on fields, transactions, and reports, by using hundreds of consultants and developers who entered predefined and arbitrary data to verify software quality. Using the SAP R/3 CATT (Computer-Aided Testing Tool), many of these tests were repeated with various system dates in the range of years from several years before to several years after 2000.

Date Change Across Data Interfaces

Third-party data interfaces may present dates in two-digit format, but the SAP system will automatically convert a two-digit year into the proper four-digit number, so there is no impact. The input of data simulates data entry from a keyboard so existing programs that process keyboard data entry correctly will interpret and automatically convert two-digit year dates to the proper four-digit number.

Continuous Process Improvement Capabilities

If a business is to make best use of the possibilities of electronic commerce, it is essential that the workflow through business processes should be amenable to adjustment to be in a position to benefit from any change or anticipated change in the market conditions. An installed and configured SAP R/3 implementation must be capable of improvement without disruption.

Developments in Application Interfaces

The Business Framework architecture includes two types of Business Application Programming Interface. The earlier type is used to access SAP and third-party applications from the R/3 Basis core. The most recent type of BAPI resides in the application where it can process workflow instructions which, in effect, re-configure the complex of business processes. It is used to enable customer organizations to apply new process-control logic and to change the presentation logic to correspond. This is achieved without disrupting business, but, of course, under the strict discipline of change management wherein all adjustments are held in abeyance until the release date when their introduction is recorded in the change management documentation. For example, a production company might adjust its logic from an emphasis on process control to a distribution logic if the production plant became part of a different enterprise.

Engineering Change Management

The occurrence of a change of specification or process recipe is recognized as a significant event by the ECM (Engineering Change Management) function. An ECM document is generated automatically and the total series of such documents can be inspected in order to determine how a product evolved.

The ECM function can also be called into play from the MM application when the specification of an inventoried item is recognized as different from the stock already held and perhaps from the stock ordered.

Internet Transaction Server

Fundamental to R/3 Release 3.1 and 4.0 is the R/3 Internet Architecture, which allows the system to be scaled up to serve very large numbers of users via the SAP Internet Transaction Server, which runs on Window NT 4.0.

The next generation of Internet servers will be running at many times the speed of the current devices, but there will be much more traffic on the Net. There are several developments at the research stage with SAP that, if adopted as standards, will facilitate the setting up of systems that can accommodate literally millions of users online.

Thin Clients

If your processor does not have the code to do what you require, it can be made to download this code from a central repository. You may not be allowed to alter it, and when you next download it, there may have been some updates carried out centrally. This thin client working is standard in SAP installations.

If your processor is an NC (Network Computer) or perhaps a NetPC (Network Personal Computer), then you may be operating from a screen that is entirely driven by code that has come to you from afar. The Java language is designed to run on almost any kind of computing device. It builds a Java Virtual Machine, which will then respond appropriately to Java Application Elements, "applets," which will present you with such items as display windows and active forms into which you are invited to enter data or choose an option.

The attraction of the thin client is the small bandwidth it needs in order to communicate with its host. An intranet within a company or the Internet worldwide could be the link even if there has to be a tone-modulated stage using an analog telephone line.

There are not enough high performance workstations and advanced PC devices to provide terminals for all the people who would like to communicate over the Internet. Thin client technology enables them to use whatever computing devices can be made available. The user console may be just a television display and a set of response buttons.

SAP R/3 Release 3.1 Java User Interface

The Java Virtual Machine can be deployed into virtually any presentation device. The SAP R/3 Java User Interface can then be transmitted to any of these devices, which can then be allowed access to R/3.

The essential feature of the SAP Java BAPIs is that they use standard business objects and, therefore, provide a way of operating with standardized business content and logic without reference to the specific terminal device used for access.

Effective network applications, in whatever language, have to be compact for quick delivery over a network link. The small size of Java components makes it practical to maintain the applications centrally. Users work with a set of features that is no larger than they need. There are no superfluous options. Being modular, the network-centric applications can be downloaded only to the users who have need for them.

The applets and other modular units can connect to each other and to legacy systems such as spreadsheets and corporate databases. The communication process need be no more difficult than using a Web browser, which is becoming a standard user skill.

Customers, business partners, suppliers, and managers can all have authorized access to the same processes and information that is current. Their separate hardware and operating systems will all be able to run the Web browsers and such inclusions as the Java Virtual Machine. A business application written entirely in Java is intended to work on any machine without editing.

PP-CBP Constraint-Based Planner

If there are two systems that are linked by reciprocal messaging interfaces, there is the potential for conflict and circular processes in which the demand for action is passed back and forth. The R/3 PP-CBP Constraint-Based Planner carries out planning and scheduling material requirements and capacity requirements in real time. The application includes a real time Due Date Quoting capability as an option within the ATP (available to promise) server.

Intelligent planning and scheduling for global supply chain management across both inter-enterprise and intra-enterprise supply chains is embedded in SAP R/3 Release 4.0 to give fast, advance warning of impending constraints in their supply chain plan. These potential trouble spots can be published to the relevant part of the company or network of business partners. The intelligent planner will automatically suggest ways of removing the constraints.

Self-Service Applications

SAP has always made use of development partners in order to accelerate the introduction of products that meet the SAP certification standards. Some of the more recent partner applications illustrate the widening range of business applications that has become apparent as the potential market is opened by the introduction of reliable network standards.

There is a rapidly increasing range of possibilities for a user to log into a self-service system to get information and take commercial actions under control of the authorization regime.

For example, an engineer can decide to consider replacing a component defined on the engineering drawing on the screen. If the materials management system is able to recognize the part in question from the indication given by the design engineer, there will be a set of relevant documents defined automatically by the R/3 Classification system. From this set, the engineer can select the specification of the part and have this information directed into an inquiry format, which can be presented to some or all of the vendors that the system will automatically identify because they are able to supply a part that meets the specification. The engineer might relax some aspects of the specification until there is a manageable list of possible substitute components.

If this engineer is so authorized, he or she can seek quotations from the suitable vendors. These could well be returned via EDI (Electronic Data Interchange). The engineer may then accept a quotation and initiate a purchase order for a sample again via EDI. There would be a set of EDI exchanges, largely automatic, with a bank to provide credit for the purchase, and an invoice to the engineer's department.

The next message could be a delivery date and a detailed drawing of the replacement part, which the engineer may use to modify the technical drawing from which the sequence began. The payment could be through EDI and the whole sequence conducted rapidly because there is almost no waiting in queues. Probably the slowest process will be the physical delivery of the part.

EARS (European Administration Resources System)

Another example of self-service business data processing is provided by the EDS computer programming outsourcing service company. It has implemented an SAP R/3 staff administration system that allows responsibility for decision-making to be selectively delegated down to local level. Staff can conduct online everything of an administrative nature, such as purchase orders, travel arrangements, and expenses claims.

Automating Marketing and Sales Force Administration

The widespread interest in remote working and networking to mobile terminals is expected to make a very large impact on the work of marketing and sales departments. Computer telephony and laptop terminals are now deemed essential by many companies who have recognized that the sales and marketing arena has tended to lag the back office functions and manufacturing facilities in the matter of adding value by providing rapid and relevant business data processing. The importance of changing sales staff attitudes to new technologies has not gone unrecognized by the training services consultancies.

Two aspects of sales and marketing can be discerned: the use of the Internet for advertising and providing product information and the use of a restricted part of the Internet or a dedicated intranet to link sales staff. Both of these functions can be available 24 hours a day and on a worldwide basis.

Using Push Technology

Where a network is in place, a user can send identical messages to some or all of the other users. An extension of this idea is to dispatch an electronic magazine or catalog that is transmitted as a Web site in which the initial page contains "hot links" that can be clicked in order to view the page referenced by the link. The Unilver organization uses this push technology to transmit corporate information to staff.

There are many extensions to the push technology at the research stage with the aim of building a central agency that can transmit to any connected terminal the exact functionality required by the user of that terminal at that time. Almost no software is stored permanently at the user's installation. The self-service concept is thus extended from passive information taken from a catalog to active program elements provided automatically depending on need from a central repository.

Trends in Consumer-Led Supply Chain Technology

The effects of improving the efficiency of the supply chain can be seen fairly clearly in the retail sector of industry where the following effects have been discerned in the enterprises that have implemented such measures as sales-based ordering or sales-influenced inventory control:

- Stock levels reduced by a quarter without affecting customer service.
- Supply chain inventory down to a coverage of around three weeks.

These kinds of benefits are being enjoyed as a result of relatively simple, automatic EDI for repetitive ordering of materials in bulk. If your products are complex assemblies and your raw materials comprise very large numbers of different technical parts, then there has to be a corresponding quantum increase in the complexity of any improvements you make to the supply chain.

SAP R/3 Business Objects

An object in the language of OO (Object-Oriented) programming is an entity that carries a data element that signifies the state it is in, such as OFF or ON, and some method by which this state can be changed. There may be more than one method of changing an object's state, and it may have more than two states. What matters to the user is what else happens or could happen if an object was made to change its state. For example, an object that had the function of recognizing when a purchase order had arrived could also have been given the functions of initiating such other actions as checking the stock availability and the customer's credit status.

You could imagine a more complicated business object that had the function of finding not only the best supplier for the goods required but also other potential customers for these goods. Such a business object might behave very much like a free marketer. It could be allowed to search widely for both customers and suppliers. You may also wish to endow it with rules for choosing the best buy in the context of the pool of customers available. You may also wish it to use the profitability of each potential trading activity as one of the factors to be taken into account when deciding on the best course of action. It might be prudent to set limits to the scope of this free marketer business object and have a human assessor called into the functionality when these limits are approached.

This example would not be too creative in many industrial contexts. There will be purchasing staff and marketing staff and sales staff carrying out elements of this complex function. What a standard business object could add would be the routine widening of search horizons because the information-gathering process will not entail extra human time.

Now suppose the suppliers identified by our marketer business object were themselves alert to the fact that a requirement for their type of product was being put out to competitive tender. They might well have a similar type of business object, which could find the best way of meeting the requirement. And so the marketer business object could find itself being used over and over again; each re-incarnation using different particular details; but each utilizing the standard business process that had to be programmed to work as efficiently as possible as a business object.

Using the Business Object Repository

The BOR (Business Object Repository) is a database that holds reusable standard business processes that can be called upon to build a specific implementation quickly. This is an extension of the SAP process of building standard business software elements that can be customized to suit their circumstances, but only within limits that are set so that the functional integrity of the program is not compromised. In particular, an SAP R/3 Business Object cannot be altered in such a way that it is no longer compatible with the rest of any R/3 implementation. It will always remain a fully-integrated component.

The concept of a business object is central to the design philosophy of SAP software. Each SAP standard business process is programmed in ABAP/4 code. These highly reliable software components are not open to alteration by the user organization. However, the actions they take can be controlled by the information stored, perhaps dynamically, in the tables associated with them. Because the code of a business object is alterable only by the SAP-authorized programmers, the system of business objects works reliably together. What the implementation engineers have to do is to charge the control tables with the data required to service the client organization. Now these control tables are themselves made according to master data specifications, which are business objects in their own right, because they are able to prevent unsuitable data from getting into their storage locations.

Thus, the total collection of business objects, whether single data records or complex modules of data and procedures, constitutes the SAP R/3 System. If you examine any one of these objects, you will be made aware of the functions it performs and the controls that will be exercised over the information it will accept. The set of business objects is, therefore, a dynamic system documentation. Whatever you need to know is always available as part of the business object itself.

The way to access this documentation is by means of an API (Application Programming Interface). For example, you could invoke an API that will present the application documentation on your GUI (Graphical User Interface). If you are working with SAP R/3 Release 3.1 or 4.0, this GUI could be presented to you across the Internet and displayed on your portable PC or whatever terminal device could operate as a virtual machine for Java applets. If you had a business process modeling tool with a suitable API to your R/3 application, then you could see the system documentation in the form of graphical and other displays according to how you had configured your modeling tool. Should you be operating with an SAP or third-party business process re-engineering tool, then you will probably have a suitable API to look at the structure of your SAP R/3 application. Over 1,000 SAP Business API components have been created.

Structure of the Object Repository

So that you may access the contents of the R/3 Business Object Repository in an orderly and efficient manner, its contents are identified by its purpose.

Application Programming Interfaces:

- Process Models
- Function Models
- Data Models
- SAP Business Objects
- Object Models with Data and Connections

Other Repository Contents:

- Data Object Definitions
- Screen Specifications
- Program Objects Needed for Developments to R/3 Basis
- BOR, SAP Business Object Repository

The BOR (Business Object Repository) was introduced in SAP R/3 Release 3.0 to manage the data, transactions, and events in an R/3 implementation as an integrated set of SAP Business Objects. Each of these objects gives access to processes and data that are structured according to specific data models, which themselves are part of the enterprise data model. Thus, by design, an SAP Business Object will only deal with data that conforms to the correct structure as defined by the EDM (Enterprise Data Model). Therefore, any other application or external system that has to interact with this object will be able to interpret data and condition it to be acceptable to the model.

The SAP Business Object is a component that is built from the first to integrate seamlessly with the rest of an R/3 implementation.

At runtime, the coding and location of the business object are identified by the registration element, which is defined as part of the definition of object types in the Business Object Repository. The client never knows the registered location of the object. The client may be accessing the business object via a distributed system, perhaps using the Internet, but the business object merely receives a request via the BOR and reports the results back to the client along the same route.

Another opportunity afforded by the inclusion of the Business Object Repository is the facility to allow an individual client to create a company-specific business object, which is created as a subtype of a standard SAP Business Object. It, therefore, inherits all the attributes, methods, and events that are essential if the object is to integrate with the rest of the R/3 implementation. The client can then edit the data definitions and store the company-specific business object under its own name. The runtime component of the BOR is then simply instructed to use the new business object in place of the master that is supplied with the system.

The BOR is equipped to respond to SAP-RFC (Remote Function Calls) from outside R/3, perhaps from an R/2 or a third-party system, for example. There are interfaces currently available to comply with standards such as OMG's (Object Management Group) CORBA and Microsoft's COM/DCOM.

Release 3.0 contained 170 SAP Business Objects in the Business Object Repository. Release 3.1 includes almost 1,000 different business objects designed to the high SAP standards. Release 4.0 will contain many more.

SAP R/3 Business Workflow

From the user's point of view, a workflow system may present itself as a list of work items to be accomplished. The display medium may be the user's inbox in the integrated mail system. Double-clicking an item will automatically start the necessary application and load the data.

The source of a workflow item may be an event that is triggered by a change of status of a document info record, a production order, or even a change master record.

The specific user who receives the work item may have been chosen from a predefined distribution list or work sequence. If you have installed and configured the Human Resources application, the recipient of a workflow item may have been chosen on the basis of such factors as:

- The person is available for work now or soon.
- The person has the qualifications and experience necessary for the work item.
- The person is authorized to perform this task.

Thus, the workflow principle can be applied to the adaptive sequencing of any kind of document-based tasks as well as to the sequencing of other types of activity.

The SAP R/3 Workflow component is designed to operate across applications to provide a dynamic method of sequencing and re-sequencing the tasks performed by your system according to the needs of the work to be done at the time. One example is where your materials have to be assembled in various configurations according to the customer order being processed.

The workflow product has been extended to allow your system to sequence tasks performed by distributed networked manufacturing or processing plant, which may include third-party systems. The SAP concept is to be able to integrate seamlessly with "best of breed" systems from any of the approved suppliers.

For example, Documentum has built on standard DMS (Document Management Systems) and ArchiveLink technologies to develop a technology to handle most formats such as images, word processing documents, spreadsheets, HTML Web pages, archives, and CAD drawings. The capability to access both SAP and non-SAP documents is included.

Requirements for Extended Document Management

A document is most useful if it is known to be the most up-to-date version possible. This entails having documents managed by a central function that is operating strict ECM disciplines to ensure that any alterations to material items are recorded in the associated documents. Any alterations to documents are apparent to the users who are using them because they concern a material or technical specification, for example, in connection with a customer order.

Personnel who have the required authorization may need to call up all types of technical and commercial documents at any time. It is the function of the R/3 Document Management System to provide this service.

A document created perhaps by an external application, such as a word processor or CAD installation, is associated with a document info record that carries administrative information and details of the origin of the original document. This document info record is subject to status control so that any viewer will see whether it is a draft, a provisional edition, or a document released for use in production. The stages of status control are named and arranged during the customizing of your system. You may have several versions of a document at different status levels.

If your company is using the BOM (Bill of Materials) function, you can links documents with this facility to set up a hierarchy of documents and sub-documents that may be arranged to coincide with the assemblies and subassemblies of your inventoried items.

A document info record may be used to link the original document to a routing as an item on the PRT (Production Resources and Tools) list.

At any stage, you can find a relevant document or set of documents by using any of the standard search facilities:

- Search by group names in the classification
- Search by parameters known or expected to be part of the target documents
- Search by matchcodes that were assigned as a documentation policy for the important classes of documents in your company
- Search through the document hierarchy generated through the BOM function

Product Data Management

The SAP R/3 PDM (Product Data Management) functions can integrate with the following components, which are available in Release 3.0 of R/3:

- Document management
- ECM (Engineering Change Management)
- SAP R/3 Classification
- CAD integration
- PS (Project System)
- Product configuration
- Product structure browser

These standard functions can be configured by the user and stored for subsequent use.

PDM Workflow Template

The standard SAP R/3 System contains a workflow template that can set up the PDM environment in association with the ECM (Engineering Change Management) facilities. A central data control department first establishes an ECR (Engineering Change Record) that determines which data objects are to come within its scope. The workflow is used to inform the relevant specialist departments about the intended change. When all the scrutinizers are satisfied with the proposed change or a specified deadline is reached, the central data control department is automatically informed by workflow so that a decision to release the changed document may be taken. The ECR is upgraded to an ECO (Engineering Change Order) that commands the specialist departments, via workflow, to make the change. The ECM process terminates when the change is released for use in MRP and Production.

SAP R/3 Release 4.0 enhances these functions and integrates them fully to provide the PDM application, which is also available as a stand-alone system. The PDM application is designed to provide not only an efficient and comprehensive product data management facility as an integral part of your SAP R/3 installation, but also to offer seamless linkage to other product information systems, which you may have in place already or wish to install because they have been specifically optimized for your sector of industry.

Networked Workflow

Standard Web browsers, Microsoft Exchange, Lotus Notes, and custom applications can use R/3 Workflow Wizards to automate workflow design and, thus, control the workflow via a network. Workflow status reports are made available in HTML format. The WMC (Workflow Management Coalition) is an integrated implementation that includes the 52 published Workflow Application Programming Interfaces and provides the following components:

- Session Manager
- Distribution Architect
- Reference Model
- CATT Testing
- Organization Architect
- IMG Implementation Management Guide

Executing Workflow Templates

Workflow templates can be executed and may serve as a guide for a company's own development. The individual steps of workflow templates are pre-defined as standard tasks. They contain a task description, linkage to the application logic through business objects, and prepared linkage to the company organization structure.

The business object repository delivered in R/3 includes predefined key fields, attributes, methods, and the events associated with the business objects Workflow Definitions made from standard tasks can easily be combined and changed at any time using the graphical editor.

Configuring R/3 with Specialized Subsystems

Distribution, logistics, and manufacturing are each served by business software systems that have been developed specifically for each of these business areas. There are several specialist software suppliers that can claim to have developed an optimized solution for each of these areas. These area applications do not necessarily integrate with each other or with a central financial and controlling core.

By contrast, the SAP organization and similar enterprise management suppliers can offer business functions that are fully integrated and able to be optimized for each particular area.

A third possibility is to use a tailor-made specialist system for a specific business function for which it is optimized, and address it by one of the distributed network technologies.

Supply Chain in Context

The main links of a supply chain are as follows:

- Customers
- Purchasing
- Production
- Sales and Distribution

These main links will be associated with the controlling functional areas such as:

- Finance
- Balance Sheet and the Profit-and-Loss Statement
- Capital
- Cost Control

If you are thinking of the wider environment in which your enterprise operates, then you will want to add some links to your supply chain, such as:

- The vendor market for your purchases
- The customer market for your sales
- The plant and machinery available to your enterprise
- The human resources available to your company, both staff and contractors
- The market for the human resources you might need
- The market for the human resources you already have and might lose

Business information has many sources. You will perhaps build some of them into your supply chain concept:

- Marketing information about potential and actual customers
- Marketing information about potential and actual competitors
- Customer requirements forecasting
- Sales force feedback information and suggestions
- Manufacturing staff feedback information and suggestions

Forecasting Business Configurations

One way of conducting a forecast is to look at data collected in the past and try to extrapolate on the basis of logical or statistical tendencies what you have been able to deduce or infer. These forecasts can be supported by mathematical techniques, but they can also be manipulated or illuminated by intelligent guesswork. For instance, you could predict that an increasing market share for your company would continue unabated for the next few years. If you knew that a considerable research budget had been allocated to ensure this, then you might be justified in such a forecast. However, if you had a product planning scheme, and a few ideas on how the wishes of your future customers might develop, then you could bend your forecast to try to take advantage of your foresight.

Here are some guesses that have turned out to be highly profitable for those companies that were prudent enough to set up their supply chains to add maximum value under the anticipated conditions:

- There will be an ever closer connection between a product and the services offered with it. For example, a consumer product will include intelligible user instructions and addresses of local service providers. A purchase order may initiate a customer management sequence that continues until the customer is known to be fully satisfied.
- Customers will be recognized as soon as they declare their name or post code. The responding company representative will have immediate access to the customer history and the notes made on previous contacts.
- Products will be individually configured, combined, and packaged to meet the requirements of the individual customer.
- Delivery will be at the convenience of the customer and within a narrow time frame agreed to in advance.
- The profitability of customer service provisions will be computed routinely.
- Production will be in lot sizes according to customer requirements, or in batches of customer requirements.
- Processes will be automated and linked in automatic workflow systems that modulate standard bills of material and standard routings to meet the customer requirements and make best use of the available resources.

- Lead times will be reduced.
- Production networks may extend worldwide and there will be close linkage between companies throughout the supply chain.

Automated Transportation Developments

One network that is often necessary in the materials sector occurs in the management of transportation contractors as carriers between vendors, warehouse, production plant, distribution storage, and customers. Other members of such networks are forwarding agents and service agents. Although several companies may be involved, the complex is virtually an integrated business system if all the elements are more or less continuously connected by EDI, by an intranet, or by the Internet.

SAP R/3 facilities are available to provide connection via BAPI (Business Application Programming Interfaces) to specialized subsystems that can be provided by third-party vendors or by distributed SAP applications. In the transportation of discrete materials sector, the following services can be provided on an automated, self-service basis:

- Shipment planning and optimization
- Freight rate calculation
- Shipment papers
- Loading and weighing
- Shipment tracking
- Standard financial services such as invoicing and settlement

For the transportation of bulk materials, the SAP R/3 IS-OIL (Industry Solution for Oil) provides the detailed functionality necessary to automate as much as possible of the bulk transportation process.

Vehicle Definition   The IS-OIL application is able to define a vehicle as a composite of one or more transport units. A unit can be a tractor, locomotive, a truck, a trailer, or a rail car for a train. A marine vessel may be treated as a vehicle with a particular pattern of constraints. Pipelines may be defined in a similar fashion.

A defined vehicle is constrained by weight and volume, and it has an availability that depends on its location and the shift situation of its crew.

Shipment Scheduling   Scheduling has the task of selecting delivery note documents representing delivery requirements. The aim is to make best use of the transportation plant, which can be a road vehicle, a ship, an aircraft, or a continuous flow system such as a pipeline or conveyor. Other factors will be the customer, destination, route, planned delivery time, customer delivery priority, special delivery, and handling conditions.

At the same time as deliveries are being assembled into delivery rounds or shipments, the vehicles or other transportation modes have to be selected on the basis of such factors as their availability, the transportation planning point responsible, and the loading capacities available.

There has to be a check that the assigned vessels or vehicles are suitable for the products proposed in the delivery notes. The vehicles have to be checked for any constraints imposed by the customer's delivery location, which may be unable to accept deliveries larger or heavier than a certain specification.

Dynamic maintenance of schedules is often essential because customer requirements may be added to or deleted from shipments at any stage.

A similar robust system of assigning transportation crew and substitutes is called for.

Shipment Loading   The automated transportation solution entails capturing data concerning the actual quantities loaded into each compartment of the vehicle or vessel. Conversion of loaded quantities into industry standard and alternate units of measure is expected.

It may happen that a vessel or vehicle is not completely empty prior to loading because not all of a previous shipment was off-loaded. These "prior-to-load" quantities have to be tracked through whatever routes are traversed by the vehicle in which they are being carried.

If your materials are shipped in discrete units, you may have installed rack meters that record their passage into and out of particular storage or transportation units.

If some of your materials are defined by bills of materials, then your shipment loading data capture may have to include records of the quantities loaded for the separate materials of the BOM.

Rebranding is the process of recording and notifying interested parties of the fact that, although a cataloged and inventoried sales product is no longer available, a substitute product is available. There may have to be consequent adjustments of the inventory and the valuation of these rebranded items.

The ownership of stock in transit remains with the delivering plant until the delivery is confirmed by a receipt at the customer. The stock can be conceptually assigned from the delivering store location to an in-transit store location for the plant while its delivery is awaiting confirmation by the customer.

Delivery Confirmation   In addition to recording delivery, it may be necessary to track a delivery that is being diverted to a "ship-to" customer different from that specified in the shipment.

Product may be returned to stock after a shipment. This has to be recorded in the inventory and in the accounts.

There may be transport gains or losses that can be detected by comparing the quantity loaded with the quantity delivered. The "left-on-vehicle" quantity has to be tracked and proposed as the quantity on the vehicle when it is presented for loading the next shipment.

The vehicles themselves may have meters, which can be automatically ready by the materials management system.

BDRP (Bulk Delivery Requirements Planning) is a component intended to use a customer's current and forecast product usage to create orders and plan shipments automatically so that transportation bottlenecks and product shortage and overstocking may be minimized.

Developing the Controlling Role of the Customer

You could claim that the customer has always had the dominant role in business. "The customer is always right" has been a declared policy in some companies. The mail order business has always used a paper-based catalog to invite orders. Under these circumstances, customers can order anything they require—provided it is in the current catalog. What is new as the result of the introduction of more complex communication systems is the possibility of the customer having the supplier put together a custom delivery in the way that a tailor makes a suit for an individual customer.

Unlike the tailor, the modern manufacturing and assembly plant may not be open to detailed instructions from the customer as to exactly what shall be purchased. But if the manufacturing plant can be made a slave of the assembly plant, and if the assembly plant can be under the control of the network of customers, then the role of the customer can begin to approach the status of production controller.

If you have had experience of being in control of production, you will appreciate some of the problems. It may not be economical to manufacture individual items or very small batches. It may be best to wait for a backlog of orders to build up. So it can happen that a customer who orders from a catalog or from an exhibition believing that the products are in stock will find that the order is not delivered immediately, or even after the promised delay.

However, the higher the degree of automation in the manufacturing process, the more likely it is that the individual processes can be controlled by a workflow system that allows variants to be produced economically. If the whole logistics chain is focused on the customer, then the associated data processing may indeed be used to satisfy and retain the customer.

From Here...

- How does SAP R/3 support precise control of materials from the ordering stage?

  See Chapter 3, "Understanding Material Requirements Planning."

- What do I have to do to associate my manufacturing data processing systems with materials management?

  See Chapter 5, "Integrating MM."

- What can SAP provide to help me build the best system for managing my company so as to keep it lean but efficient?

  See Chapter 6, "Understanding the SAP R/3 Business Engineer."

CHAPTER 10

MM Education and Training

In this chapter

- How to raise awareness of the training issues and draw up a sound policy for your department
- How to recognize the key training activities
- How to structure a well-integrated program using a checklist as a guide
- How to set out a plan of the courses showing the balance between classroom, workshop, seminars, and computer-based training

Managing Change

The largest audience for information on Materials Management training will inevitably come from the manufacturing sector. However, as the module comes with the purchase of the system, other industries will find that they are able to use some of the functions to a greater or lesser extent.

In a complex manufacturing or processing environment, the flow of materials lies at the very heart of the business. A substantial amount of time and money would have already been invested in existing systems and practices. The introduction of SAP will change the way that the business is done. The challenge, in educational terms, is to identify the valuable skills that already exist in the workforce and utilize them in the changeover process. The difficulty is to maintain the core business while the implementation takes place using the skill base on which the business depends. It is rather like reading a map, while driving—not without its risks.

Understanding the Challenges

Successful implementation of the MM module will ensure that the company improves operations and provides improved LEVEL OF service to its customers. Commitment to these goals is a critical factor. The risks lie not so much in the technology as in the human issues; people won't accept a new idea unless they've had some part in its development or unless they feel they'll benefit from it personally. Getting people to accept new ideas is part of the educational challenge.

SAP is designed to help people do a better job—a job they can be proud of, a job providing a real sense of accomplishment. Employees seek recognition and personal benefits and an assurance that their contribution adds value to the business.

Users who are familiar with an existing system are often able to arrive at answers quickly without having to go through all the formal steps. They may have routines memorized; they may know who must sign forms and where to distribute them. This knowledge makes for a comfortable way of life in which employees perform job functions efficiently without having to refer to manuals or ask for help. They have probably developed shortcuts, which they understand but that provide only very limited benefit.

The introduction of a new system requires new forms, new procedures, and new disciplines. New systems may require changes in the reporting structure, changes in job roles and functions, such as changing from expediting to planning.

This change can be threatening because users may feel that their existing skills have lost value. The commitment of management to learning within a company needs to be stressed constantly.

Knowing the Key Points of Principle

The key messages for MM Module users to appreciate during education and training are:

- The MM module is all about getting the right parts to the right place at the right time at the lowest cost, with minimum movement.

- The more inventory there is, the more flexible the operation; this naturally requires more company investment but in the early stages of implementation it can pay. If the business can weather a temporary rise in stock levels, the users can begin to hone the system to meet their needs and demonstrate newly acquired skills.

- The project team must not lose sight of the core purpose of the business; materials and processes still need to be monitored carefully as staff are released for training.

- Education and training form part of the staff development on an ongoing basis, not just for the new systems implementation.

- Education provides background and contextual input—why users do things in the broader picture.

- Training is very specific—what SAP does, how it does it, and what the user must do to support the operations of the business.

So, the situation facing the Materials Manager will be how to keep the business running smoothly while the managers and end users learn about the system and master new skills. It is useful at this stage to start some basic planning.

The first step will be to assess the existing levels of skills and knowledge in the department. If existing roles do not require computer skills, there could be some ominous-looking gaps. However, if it is a question of training to simply input small amounts of data, then the gaps might not seem so daunting. The second step will be to prioritize the needs. This in itself is a good exercise for the project team and the trainees. It focuses on the essentials.

The next big question is: Am I educating or training? If you are educating, what methods will you use? If training, what skills and techniques are you trying to impart? In this third stage of initial planning, it is the method of learning that is the key question.

Finally, having thought about what, when, and how, it is wise to be very clear from the outset just who in the organization will be verifying the training. To whom are you accountable? If the answer to this is no one individual but a team of interested parties, then it is even more important to gain consensus on what constitutes an acceptable level of competence.

This initial planning will probably raise more questions than it answers; this is no bad thing as it helps to shape a shared approach to learning and hopefully a shared commitment.

Realizing the Impact on Business

Understanding the impact that integrating systems and altering job responsibilities can have on a business is an important part of working with the challenges to come.

Education starts by explaining the challenges and changes in an honest and open manner in the context of the business. There are three basic areas that ought to be addressed by managers and educators early in the program of education:

- The disappearance of existing systems
- The responsibilities of teamwork in an integrated system environment
- Understanding the key success measures for each new role

Perhaps the most significant challenge for many people comes as the company prepares to abandon most or all of its old systems. The knowledge, understanding, and mastery of these systems suddenly become redundant information. Anyone associated with training and education needs to be aware of the sense of vulnerability this can generate in the workforce.

Understanding what is entailed in the new roles will be a priority to the staff and the job of explaining this, with clarity, cannot be fudged by managers.

Understanding the impact of group responsibility as an integrated system as comprehensive as SAP is implemented will also be a challenge. Timely and accurate entry of data will be of paramount importance as errors in one area ripple throughout the whole system. It will herald the end of inward-looking isolated departments and encourage an open process-oriented way of working.

The third challenge is one for the managers and depends on how well the two preceding ideas are understood. It requires a clear description of the new roles and responsibilities and the key success factors associated with them. This opens up the way the business is conducted and in many cases changes the reporting structures, performance monitoring requirements, and management practices.

Commitment of Management   The impact of changing integrated systems is like replacing the nervous system of a body and will clearly raise anxieties at all levels.

Staff will look for sound leadership. There are obvious advantages to building a project team using a representative cross-section of managers from key user areas. Departmental training needs can be monitored and shared.

The importance of a clear comprehensive education and training program timed to address the need for new competencies is vital, particularly because the materials management function is at the heart of the business. Frequently, education and training and the generation of related documentation involve far more time and effort than the project team might expect early in the project.

Achieving consensus and commitment, and setting the right momentum early in the project will address these issues.

Job Roles, Responsibilities, and Standards   Staff job content will change: Their roles may remain the same if the system is being overlaid on the current organization, but how they achieve results will be different.

A manager responsible for end-user training in the oil industry gave a simple but very human example. The integrated system had done away with the need for a goods-inward clerk, armed with clipboard and manifest, checking off the delivery schedule. The goods arrived with their destination in the warehouse already planned.

The goods-inward clerk was happily relocated to the shipping department, where for the first time in his life he was required to use a computer. The warehouse manager needed to consider retraining his team to receive goods using new codes and procedures.

In a manufacturing or processing environment the demands on staff to perform different roles may be far more dramatic than in a financial environment, where the level of IT knowledge may be higher.

As the working world of people changes, the threat of job loss and anxiety over their performance in their new roles raise stress at all levels in the company.

If the introduction of an integrated system has a big impact on the business, a well-planned approach to corporate learning can greatly improve staff morale by their active participation.

Staff will need to be fully trained on the new procedures and will need extensive documentation to support their activities. These analysis, documentation, and training skills may need to be brought in.

Companies need to be sure that they do not lose their ISO9000 accreditation. All new procedures need to be verified as complying with ISO9000.

Structuring a Program

In structuring a company program, it is important not to reinvent the wheel. SAP and other suppliers have some excellent courses that may be cost effective for the project needs.The following section discusses SAP courses and gives detailed advice on designing in-house courses.

Using SAP Courses

SAP courses are ideal for project team members to obtain an understanding of SAP functionality. End users need to receive education and training appropriate to their environment.

Timing of attendance is all-important. A candidate returning to his work environment needs to be given the opportunity to make use of newly acquired skills. This can be done in several ways:

- Contribute to project activities
- Deliver a presentation to colleagues
- Access demonstration SAP database and work through examples
- Create discussion papers for policy development
- Highlight specific areas of concern for the project team

The point of giving structured follow-up work is to reinforce the content of the course and to make the information accessible to colleagues.

There are further benefits in attending public courses. Staff will meet others from similar industries that are likely to be at different stages of the project cycle to exchange war stories. It is to be hoped that these will be of a positive nature and raise morale.

Designing In-house Courses

No public courses exist to meet the needs of each individual company. The project will need to devise, plan, and deliver courses with the assistance of key users. If they do not have the time or specific skills to do this, then they ought to be prepared to use the services of a training consultant, who could carry out a needs analysis, devise a plan, and create the material.

At this stage, the contentious issue of the cost of training arises. Quality training can be seen to be an expensive overhead, but it is not half as expensive as a poorly trained work force and error-ridden data.

Whether you choose imported or home grown, it is useful to have some idea about what characterizes quality training.

Specific industries can extend this by incorporating their own unique industry requirements or features (for example, safety standards, confidentiality, hygiene, and so on).

Setting Goals To be successful, an education program must have clear goals. Ideally, they would be as follows:

- To communicate and educate at all stages, particularly in the early stages
- To gain early user acceptance
- To generate high motivation
- To aim for a shared understanding of the language and function of the system
- To demonstrate a commitment to team learning in vertical groups as well as in departments
- To allow users to identify their own success and that of the system
- To understand the skills users need in order to make the system work and help users acquire them
- To celebrate success and progress

If the above appears overly optimistic, consider the alternative scenarios:

- Confusion and perceived job insecurity arising from rumors
- User resistance
- Poor motivation
- Interdepartmental struggles and ambiguous communication
- Users' not understanding the purpose of the system
- Users' ignoring the system or using it badly, corrupting or losing data

Even if this is an exaggeration, it illustrates the point that although training isn't cheap, a lack of it is very expensive indeed.

Quality Training Once you have set some high-reaching goals for the trainers, consider what goes into designing quality training. Ask: What will be needed to achieve these goals? Quality training can be defined as the efficient acquisition of the knowledge, skills, and attitudes necessary to achieve and sustain specific goals.

An effective training plan should do the following:

- State the learning objectives—these should be the long-term changes in the knowledge, behavior, and skills you expect of users.

- Record and make known to the learner the success criteria used to assess learning. For example:

  A learning objective could be: The user needs to understand that the system allows for the planned movement of materials on a specific date, such as a reservation.

  The success criteria would be: The user is able to select the correct screen and create a reservation, listing materials by date.

  The terms "task" and "outcome" may be preferred. The important thing is that it must be clear to all parties concerned what is being taught and what *is* being learned.

- Consider the methods that will result in learning. Such methods may include computer-based learning, workshops, tutor-led sessions, consultant presentations, reading and video assignments, or practice with the system. If there are optional teaching methods, consider the candidates' preferred style of learning.

- Define the objectives before selecting a teaching method.

- Use documentation that is as good as you can possibly afford—working with well-constructed training materials will help develop the skills of less-experienced members of the project team who are called upon to carry out training.

  If the learning objectives or groups of learning objectives are written into the phased project planning, along with descriptors, roles, deliverables, and accountability, it is possible to deliver the training on a just-in-time basis. The training schedule must not be written in isolation from the project plan because timing is all-important. Deliver the course at a time when the project cycle will allow the user to learn, rehearse, then apply knowledge in a meaningful situation. It does wonders for morale.

Remembering the Adult Learner   There are other factors to take into account when dealing with adult learners (such as users who may be set in their ways) in the workplace:

- Motivation—The learner must be inspired to change behavior, to respond to instruction, and to accept what is being taught.

- Content—The learning objectives must be presented in the context of what the learner already knows and understands.

- Structure—The learning must be sequenced to provide repetition, practice, and feedback on the results of exercises. Such structure reinforces newly acquired knowledge and skills and transfers them to real-world applications.

- Meaningfulness and relevance—The learner sees and accepts the purpose of the education as personally relevant.

- Immediate usefulness—The learning should be applied immediately, before it is forgotten.

- Excitement—The structure usually stimulates through participation. Physically doing things keeps a marginally attentive learner interested.

A key to successful change management is to overcome fears that will inhibit learning at all levels. By eliminating fear or apathy, you can develop an atmosphere that will create support for your manufacturing system. You can then make everyone want to succeed by using the system and by using it properly. This will happen if the time and effort are invested to ensure that all employees do the following:

- Understand, accept, and believe that the system will be personally beneficial, that their jobs will be better, that each department and the entire company will function more efficiently, and that resorting to informal methods to circumvent the system is self-defeating and must be prevented.

- Achieve some degree of reward and prestige by demonstrating that they have learned how to use the system correctly.

View the implementation of SAP as a challenge and an opportunity, not a painful problem. Each person should profit from the system, should grow professionally, and should feel of increased worth to the company and receive increased respect from it in return.

Managing Expectations

The expected benefits from the MM module may include the following:

- Stock reduction
- Reduced purchasing costs per item
- Improved service levels of material to the appropriate operation
- Reduced costs of reporting
- Reduced clerical cost and the elimination of duplication
- Reduced headcount
- Reduction of movement costs
- Reduced cost of running old systems and associated hardware and software maintenance costs
- Increased visibility

Management needs to explain why these benefits are required and how these benefits can be achieved. This is crucial, as it justifies the replacement of old familiar systems.

Fear of the system is usually caused because the end users do not see what is in it for them; if they can see the personal benefits, they will more likely contribute to it.

Know that the possibilities of reduced headcount will inevitably cause high anxiety and will demand some sensitive handling when developing education and training messages.

If you keep these things in mind and address them openly, and continually explain how individuals will personally benefit from the implementation, a higher level of commitment will be realized.

Developing Detailed Education and Training Plans

So far, the ground rules for training and education have been covered. The detail in an education and training plan will vary considerably. So many factors influence it: the nature of the business, the level of existing expertise, the size of the budget, the need for speed—no two companies will be alike.

An integrated education and training program needs to be synchronized with other module-implementation plans. SAP is usually implemented in many different locations with different products; it is therefore important to have a structured approach.

The following sequenced checklist may help members of a project team, users, or managers address some of the key communication, education, and training activities to be included in a program.

Show appreciation of the environment:

- Understand the overall implementation plans and timings
- Assess the company's communication policies
- Review user requirements
- Assess all areas of the business change, such as reengineering and business renewal
- Assess the executive and management commitment levels to change
- Fully appreciate the past track record of implementations
- Assess the competencies of staff at all levels

Develop an education and training strategy:

- Prepare alternative approaches, a variety of teaching styles: one on one, workshops, modeling, self-paced, computer-based learning
- Recommend an approach showing advantages and disadvantages of each alternative
- Secure top-level executive commitment
- Use the senior levels of management to launch the overall program

Launch the program:

- Announce overall plans in project newsletter or similar medium
- Address staff concerns as they arise
- Overall education program commences, such as background understandings of project, understanding of integration issues, best practice implementation

Assess role definition and the level of expertise:

- Work with the project team during MM configuration and develop lists of tasks and procedures (SAP and non-SAP) that will be performed by the various units
- The overall education and training program is developed to support change-management activities, such as courses and how much job-release time is required by various units

- When roles have been defined, these will be allocated to the new or existing positions in the departments where the MM functionality is being implemented
- Level of expertise needs to be defined for new employees to ensure that their training requirements do not delay implementation

Identification of the trainers:

- Trainers are identified from key users
- Training prepared for key users who will have to sign off policies, proposed systems operation, and converted data for system implementation
- ISO9000 continued accreditation verified for new procedures
- Trainers are trained on how to train
- Trainers develop education and training material

Define your competencies:

- Competency measurement program is developed to assess the effectiveness of training and users
- Existing staff are assessed for existing competencies and appropriate courses developed to improve competencies (for example, PC use capabilities prior to starting the full MM education and training)
- Individuals are identified for the various positions in the new/existing organization

Develop training schedules:

- Locate and verify training facilities and equipment
- Detailed training schedules are developed for individuals

When going live:

- Education and training program for company commences
- Staff and trainers are assessed prior to the system's going live

Post-implementation support:

- Post-implementation support program is designed to ensure that, following education and training sessions, support is provided
- Refresher education and training are provided after going live
- Follow-on and ongoing training programs ensure that the staff use the system correctly and that they follow ISO9000 standards
- Induction procedures for training new starters are formalized
- Education and training programs are adopted by the company training department

All of the preceding will involve detail tasks of the Project Team and users. It is important for the accountability to move between the participants and that the project plan provides this visibility—in other words, who is delaying whom.

Scope of Education and Training

Having outlined the possible training opportunities within the project cycle, it is useful to have an idea of the range of courses that may be applied to meet the business training needs. It is possible to opt for off-the-shelf material or professionally produced courses. However, the project team must be prepared to be creative and design training if the need arises. The following checklist suggests a range of courses generally on offer.

Overview Courses:

- Executive overview
- SAP integration course
- Team building
- MM introduction for users

Functional courses:

- Material requirements planning
- Purchasing
- Inventory management
- Goods receiving
- Warehouse management
- Invoice verification
- Logistics information system
- MM conditions
- Self-paced learning programs

Policy, role, and responsibilities:

- Policy development and sign-off procedures
- Introduction to implementation plans
- Role of key users to support configuration, customizing, and implementation
- Defining roles and responsibilities
- Role of Purchasing Manager
- Role of Inventory Manager
- Role of Planner
- Competency assessment

Walk-throughs and demonstrations:

- Business cycle simulation
- Purchasing cycle
- Inventory control

- Planning
- Policy control
- Performance measures

Implementation:

- Policy definition and control
- Data structuring, classification, and conversion
- Data conversion and sign-off procedures
- Performance measure

Post-implementation support:

- Help Desk procedures
- Issue management
- Responding to user requests

MM Module Education and Training Planning Example

With so many activities traversing so many departments, especially when considering the MM module, it is useful to put the overall plan on one piece of paper. It addresses that eternal problem of keeping all parties informed. The table at the end of this section, "MM Module Education and Training Course Planner," provides an example of a training manager's overview.

MM Training from a Consultant's Perspective

To understand some of the significant issues surrounding SAP training, it is worth listening to the voice of experience. The following is a composite view of a group of people who have worked with SAP for many years as users, trainers, and consultants.

In the initial stages, it helps if the reasons for opting for a system change generally, and SAP in particular, is shared with the workforce. Many companies change their core business over a period of time, change direction, or find that existing systems simply will not cope. It ought to be clearly explained to the workforce how cost benefits can be achieved in realistic timescales.

The SAP system now runs on Windows 95, is compatible with other best-of-breed mainframes, and is built ready-to-go.

An expert could configure a basic system in a matter of days; however, it would be of little use because from the top to the bottom of the company, staff have to change their routines and learn a new way of working. This takes time and costs money. It has been suggested that the ratio of software costs to hardware costs to consultancy works out to be about 1:1:3. So, the required commitment to this level of investment should be understood from the outset.

In order to benefit from this level of spending and potentially reduce these costs, it makes sense to focus on the transfer of skills.

There are four learning zones, each requiring a unique and clear training approach. They are technical, application, management, and change-management skills.

Utilizing Technical Skills

The candidates for this learning zone would be the employees who are going to be involved at the database-management end—programmers with background knowledge of commercial applications. ABAP, UNIX, and BASIS skills and sound knowledge of the existing company computer networks would be a prerequisite. These are the people who are going to configure and maintain the technical end of SAP.

Their education would start at the SAP Training Headquarters, using computer-based learning techniques and continue in the workplace under the initial guidance of consultants or in-house trainers.

Utilizing Application Skills

SAP is one piece of software that can be adapted to an infinite variety of businesses. It goes without saying that the company needs staff with the skills to structure the software so that it fits the industry: oil, sugar, medical, financial, and so on. A company implementing SAP will have legacy applications and staff with a sound knowledge of the functions they perform; these staff should attend SAP applications training as a first step.

Key users with sound business acumen and thorough understanding of the existing applications will need their skills enhanced so that they can not only operate after a satisfactory implementation, but support and use SAP creatively, continuously molding it to fit their own business.

Utilizing Management Skills

Skills at the managerial level need to be enhanced to confront the issues that will arise as a result of systems change. They have to be apprised of the business risks as well as the opportunities; they need to know what to retain and what to let go, and how to formalize company policies. The SAP integration course provides a good grounding in the impact of features, functions, and policies in an integrated business-systems environment.

Utilizing Change-Management Skills

It is clear that any training needs associated with the implementation of the SAP Materials Management module will cut across all business departments. Ideally, representatives should be involved at the selection stage; they will then form the basis of the project team.

Change-management skills are being sought increasingly. The human issues are now becoming more and more important; as the technology becomes more familiar, the need to derive a competitive edge from its use will rely on the human element.

The Change Manager needs to work with the Board to develop a transformation program that encompasses all aspects of change.

Companies that have developed a successful implementation and the consultants who have supported them will be valued for the education and training that they are able to pass on. This will further raise the profile of SAP training.

From Here...

■ How are the various components put together?

See Chapter 6, "Understanding the SAP R/3 Business Engineer."

■ How can you find out details about your stocks of materials?

See Chapter 7, "Analyzing Materials Information."

■ How are networked systems built?

See Chapter 9, "Understanding Network Computing."

Stage	Education and Training Courses	Executive Management	Inventory Management	Purchasing Management	Distribution	Sales	Production	Finance	Works Engineering	Information Systems	Planners	Buyers	Storemen
	Prior to starting project - SAP Integration courses	S	S	S	S	S	S	S	S	S			
	During feasibility study - SAP courses on:												
	* MM introduction for users		S	S	S	S	S	S	S	S			
	* Policy development and sign off procedures		W	W	W					W			
	* Introduction to implementation plans		W	W	W					W			
	* Team Building		W	W	W					W			
	Selecting software and Conceptual Design -												
	Functional Courses on:												
	* Material Requirements Planning		S	S	S					S			
	* Purchasing		S	S	S					S			
	* Inventory Management		S	S	S					S			
	* Goods Receiving		S	S	S					S			
	* Warehouse Management		S	S	S					S			
	* Invoice verification		S	S	S			S		S			
	* Logistics Information System		S	S	S	S				S			
	* MM Conditions		S	S	S					S			
	* SAP and other self-paced learning programs		S	S	S					S			
	Detail design, Policy Definition and Data Conversion -												
	Policy, Role and Responsibilities Courses/ Workshops on:												
	* Policy development and sign off procedures		W	W	W					W	W	W	W
	* Introduction to implementation plans		W	W	W					W	W	W	W
	* Role of Key Users to support configuration, customizing and implementation		W	W	W					W	W	W	W
	* Defining roles and responsibilities		W	W	W					W	W	W	W
	* Role of Purchasing Manager		W	W	W					W	W	W	W
	* Role of Inventory Manager		W	W	W					W	W	W	W
	* Role of Planner		W	W	W					W	W	W	W
	* Competency assessment		W	W	W					W	W	W	W
	* Policy definition and control		W	W	W					W	W	W	W
	* Data structuring, classification and conversion		W	W	W					W	W	W	W
	* Data conversion and sign off procedures		W	W	W					W	W	W	W
	* Performance Measures	W	W	W	W	W	W	W	W	W	W	W	W
	System/ solution demonstration - Walk Throughs												
	and Demonstrations:												
	* Business Cycle	D/W	D/W	D/W	D/W	D/W	D/W	D/W	D/W	D/W	D/W	D/W	D/W
	* Purchasing Cycle	D/W	D/W	D/W	D/W	D/W	D/W	D/W	D/W	D/W	D/W	D/W	D/W
	* Inventory Control	D/W	D/W	D/W	D/W	D/W	D/W	D/W	D/W	D/W	D/W	D/W	D/W
	* Planning	D/W	D/W	D/W	D/W	D/W	D/W	D/W	D/W	D/W	D/W	D/W	D/W
	* Policy control	D/W	D/W	D/W	D/W	D/W	D/W	D/W	D/W	D/W	D/W	D/W	D/W
	* Performance Measures	D/W	D/W	D/W	D/W	D/W	D/W	D/W	D/W	D/W	D/W	D/W	D/W
	* Help Desk Procedures		D/W	D/W	D/W					D/W	D/W	D/W	D/W
	* Issue Management		D/W	D/W	D/W					D/W	D/W	D/W	D/W
	* Responding to user requests		D/W	D/W	D/W					D/W	D/W	D/W	D/W

Legend:
S=Seminar   W=Workshop   D/W=Demo/Workshop

Part II

Ch 10

Stage / Education and Training Courses	Management & Project Team									Key Users		
	Executive Management	Inventory Management	Purchasing Management	Distribution	Sales	Production	Finance	Works Engineering	Information Systems	Planners	Buyers	Storemen
Best Practice and Contextual Training - Policy, Role and Responsibilities:												
* Policy development and sign off procedures	W	W	W	W	W	W	W	W	W	W	W	W
* Introduction to implementation plans	W	W	W	W	W	W	W	W	W	W	W	W
* Role of Key Users to support configuration, customizing and implementation		W	W	W					W	W	W	W
* Defining roles and responsibilities	W	W	W	W	W	W	W	W	W	W	W	W
* Role of Purchasing Manager		S	S	S					S	S	S	S
* Role of Inventory Manager		S	S	S					S	S	S	S
* Role of Planner		S	S	S					S	S	S	S
* Competency assessment		W	W	W					W	W	W	W
* Policy definition and control		W	W	W					W	W	W	W
* Data structuring, classification and conversion		S	S	S					S	S	S	S
* Data conversion and sign off procedures		W	W	W					W	W	W	W
* Performance Measure	S	S	S	S	S	S	S	S	S	S	S	S
Job training - Functional and Procedural Courses:												
* Material Requirements Planning		C	C	C					C	C	C	C
* Purchasing		C	C	C					C	C	C	C
* Inventory Management		C	C	C					C	C	C	C
* Goods Receiving		C	C	C					C	C	C	C
* Warehouse Management		C	C	C					C	C	C	C
* Invoice verification		C	C	C					C	C	C	C
* Logistics Information System		C	C	C					C	C	C	C
* MM Conditions		C	C	C					C	C	C	C
* Self paced learning programs		CBT	CBT	CBT					CBT	CBT	CBT	CBT
Follow up, Refresher and New start Training - Overview Courses on:												
* Executive overview	S	S	S	S	S	S	S	S	S	S	S	S
* SAP Integration course	S	S	S	S	S	S	S	S	S	S	S	S
* MM introduction for users		S	S	S					S	S	S	S
* Material Requirements Planning		S	S	S					S	S	S	S
* Purchasing		S	S	S					S	S	S	S
* Inventory Management		S	S	S					S	S	S	S
* Goods Receiving		S	S	S					S	S	S	S
* Warehouse Management		S	S	S					S	S	S	S
* Logistics Information System		S	S	S					S	S	S	S
* Role of Purchasing Manager		S	S	S						S	S	S
* Role of Inventory Manager		S	S	S						S	S	S
* Role of Planner		S	S	S						S	S	S
* Competency assessment		S	S	S						S	S	S
* Policy definition and control	S	S	S	S	S	S	S	S	S	S	S	S
* Data structuring, classification and conversion		S	S	S						S	S	S
* Performance Measure	S	S	S	S	S	S	S	S	S	S	S	S
* Help Desk Procedures		W	W	W					W	W	W	W
* Issue Management		W	W	W					W	W	W	W
* Responding to user requests		W	W	W					W	W	W	W

Legend:
S=Seminar   W=Workshop   D/W=Demo/Workshop   C=Classroom

Appendix

A   MM—A Consultant's Perspective   385

MM—A Consultant's Perspective

In this appendix

- Implementing Successfully
- Consumption-Based Planning
- Purchasing
- Inventory Management
- Valuation and Account Assignment
- Warehouse Management
- Invoice Verification
- From Here…

The Materials Management (MM) module in SAP is the engine room of all the other logistic modules, providing as it does, the tools for managing a company's purchasing activities, material stocks, and hence a significant part of its assets. It would be hard to imagine a logistics-driven SAP implementation that did not use all or some of the functionality that MM offers.

Having participated in a number of SAP implementations involving the MM module, there are always a number of issues involving the understanding and integration of MM in SAP that appear time and time again, regardless of the industry sector that the client is operating in. These arise not because of any shortcomings with the software, but rather that implementing SAP forces a company to critically re-examine the way its business processes are carried out, not just in the area of materials management, but in the logistics supply chain as a whole. It is almost certain that an implementation of SAP that seeks to superimpose existing business processes and practices on the software is not going to be as successful as one that critically compares and contrasts its operations with the functionality and logical business flows that SAP has to offer and, most important of all, is prepared to change the way it operates. To my mind, one of the main benefits of SAP is that it is often a catalyst for change within an organization, and recognition of this is one big step toward a successful MM and SAP implementation project.

Implementing Successfully

So what are some of the factors that need to be faced when implementing MM, and which can mean the difference between a successful and not-so-successful project? The main thing is to ensure that the project is not considered by management to be just a replacement of an aging computer system by another more modern one, and that the client's project team has the right skills set. Ideally for MM, this would mean that there are several senior members of the project team that have spent a number of years working in line management within the logistics umbrella. Their knowledge and understanding of the needs of the company's operations will go a long way to ensuring that the software is configured to support today's and, just as importantly, tomorrow's business requirements.

Having decided to implement MM, the next step is to set the scope of the implementation. In other words, are you going to implement it all in one go, or have a phased approach consisting of two or more distinct projects? It is important that the scope is decided and agreed on at the start of the project, as so-called scope creep can lead to delays and greater than budgeted costs. In MM, things like "Vendor Evaluation" and "Warehouse Management" are often areas that are tackled as a second phase project.

One of the first tasks that will have to be faced in an MM or any other module implementation is the configuring or mapping of the business organization into SAP. In MM, this means determining the Company Code/Plant and Purchasing Organization relationships. Once that is done, together with addressing the cross-module issues such as business partners and classification, you arrive, within the IMG guide, at Materials Management.

So what is MM and what does it consist of? In the IMG guide, MM is broken down into the following headings:

- Consumption-Based Planning
- Purchasing
- Inventory Management
- Valuation and Account Assignment
- Warehouse Management
- Invoice Verification

It is interesting to look at each of these in turn, from the point of view of some of the issues that may arise during the implementation.

Consumption-Based Planning

This area of MM deals with the strategies available to support the planning and replenishment of material stocks, based primarily on using historical usage as a basis for determining future requirements. While techniques such as re-order point and forecast-based planning are perfectly adequate for many businesses, for others these may not be appropriate. However, if they were to look a little wider within the Production Planning (PP) module, they would find a host of other deterministic strategies that might be more appropriate for their business needs—even though one may not be a manufacturing company or intend to use SAP to manage their manufacturing activities. The point here is that a strictly modular view of SAP may lead to missed opportunities, and one must always keep in mind the integration of the software, a theme I will pick up on again and again in this appendix.

Purchasing

Having personally spent many years working in the procurement field, I can say with some justification that MM offers a very powerful set of tools for managing a company's purchasing requirements. That being said, there are some issues that occur time and time again in this area.

One of the first decisions that needs to be made relates to how the purchasing function is to be set up or mapped into SAP. There are no hard and fast rules here, as no two companies are exactly the same. However, the approach to take is to first ensure that the project team thoroughly understands what a Purchasing Organization and a Purchasing Group mean in SAP, particularly in the context of master data maintenance and performing purchasing activities. Getting it right in the early stages of the project will help to ensure a successful project delivered on time. Getting it wrong can mean that additional project resources will be needed to correct it later in the project life cycle.

Perhaps one of the areas that can consume a lot of project resources and time is the setting up of the release strategies for requisitions. A release strategy in SAP is a definition of the rules that determine the levels of authorization needed to approve the purchase of an item. The aim here should be to keep it as simple as possible, and also to question, if necessary, whether MRP-generated requisitions need to be subject to a final authorization (release), or should this be part of managing your demand correctly at a higher level within the supply chain.

Purchasing document number ranges often leads to differences of opinion during an implementation. This is because a number range or interval is set at the document type level, and is independent of any organizational structures such as plants and purchasing organizations. As such, all the plants within a company will use the same number range for the same document type (for example, a purchase order). Reporting facilities in SAP mean that it is not necessary to have specific number ranges and, hence, document types for each plant. This keeps things simpler and less confusing to the business users.

Inventory Management

This area of MM deals with the management of stock and stock transactions (movements), and is integrated with many other modules such as SD, PP, and FI. Many projects have difficulties being implemented as their employees are not prepared for the stock disciplines that SAP imposes. Unless you have configured SAP to allow negative stocks—which should only be done if absolutely necessary for operational reasons—stock transactions need to be carried out in the order in which they physically happen and as they happen. Failure to comprehend this can lead to a loss of confidence in SAP by the user community, which may see it as an inflexible computer system. It is well worth trying to assess a company's inventory accuracy (and BOM accuracy) at the beginning of the project to determine the likely impact that these new stock disciplines will have.

Often, deciding whether to use batch management can be difficult. Although for some industries, such as chemical or pharmaceutical, the answer is quite straightforward, for others it is not so clear cut. Batch managing materials can require extra resources and impose even stronger stock disciplines as the material and batch number have to be declared for every stock movement. Although it is technically possible to switch batch management on for a material in the future, in practice, this will involve a significant amount of work in a live SAP environment. In deciding whether to batch manage a material, you should bear in mind not only the needs of the business today, but also the possible future requirements, such as in the area of environmental legislation and so on. A possible solution could be to switch batch management on for a material and use a "generic" batch number until such time as you need full batch traceability.

Valuation and Account Assignment

This part of MM is where the integration to FI is focused, providing as it does the assignment from a financial viewpoint of all the different stock movements to the specified GL accounts. Configuring this from scratch can be a daunting task, and it is often easier to use the appropriate standard chart of accounts and account assignments that SAP offers as a demonstration model to the finance project team members. This will facilitate their understanding of the process and allow them to map their own company accounts to the stock movements. Keep in mind that no stock transactions involving financial transactions can take place without this determination having been configured and put in place. This is true regardless of whether FI is to be implemented or not.

Difficulties can occur if a company has already implemented FI and now plans to implement MM. Depending on the knowledge and future vision that was given to the integration of FI with MM, this can be a simple task, or, at worse, a major problem of mutually incompatible configuration requirements.

Warehouse Management

Although this falls in the area of MM, Warehouse Management (or WM, as it is often called) can be considered as an almost standalone module in its own right. It deals with the management of stock down to a level of identification at an individual bin or pallet location in the warehouse. Thought of only in this respect, a lot of implementations have gone for solutions whereby SAP interfaces into a standalone warehousing software package that has probably been designed for specific warehousing requirements. However, SAP has provided increasingly more functionality within WM, particularly in the way it integrates with other SAP modules. This should be taken into consideration when deciding whether to use it at all, or possibly in the future. A personal experience of this came when working on a project that included a PP implementation that required automated handling of the back flushing of materials used in the manufacturing process. This could only be achieved to the client's satisfaction by using material staging for production—a facility found within WM.

One major criticism of WM is that it demands a large number of computer transactions to drive it. Although this is true, it can lead a company to introduce automatic data collection systems, such as bar coding, to support WM if they are not already in place. Often, the proposed implementation of WM can provide the cost justification for this.

Invoice Verification

The question often asked is "Why is this in MM and not in FI?" The answer is that it deals with the final part of the procurement chain, prior to handing the supplier's invoice over to FI for final payment. Thus, all that invoice verification does is match the purchase order to the corresponding invoice, and pass it to FI for payment ensuring the quantities and value match. Just because this falls within MM does not mean that it can't or shouldn't be done by the bought ledger department.

Make sure that things such as invoice tolerances and authorization limits are addressed and resolved well before you go live and not at the last possible moment. On the subject of leaving things to the last minute, do consider the design and layout requirements for printed documents in sufficient time, so that they can be in place—and preprinted, if required—well before the system is implemented.

From Here...

This is a personal view of MM, in which I have discussed some, but by no means all, of the issues that I have experienced when working on implementation projects. Although no two projects are the same, it is also true to say that no business is totally unique and that all businesses have similar problems to overcome.

Finally, in my opinion, the best MM consultant is one who can work with—and convince the client to work with—the best business practices that SAP embraces. If you are going to configure SAP, do it by exception.

Good luck with your MM implementation.

Note to the reader: The views expressed in this appendix are entirely personal and are not necessarily those of the other contributors to this book.

Index

A

ABAP/4 data dictionary, 284, 315

ABAP/4 Editor, 284

ABC analysis, 21
analytical reports, 293
inventory analysis scope, 142
purchasing reports, 60

Access, upload structure, 336

According to User Entry storage, 163

account assignment, 389
cost object, 104
purchase orders, 57

account assignment category, 14

account determination area, architectural area, 249

account groups, 14
master data, 189
vendor data concept, 50

account structure, architectural area, 252

accounting
accruals, 64
intercompany, 68
materials receipt, 13
chart of accounts, 13
goods, 13
material valuation, 13
transactions, 13
relating to MM, 172

accounting procedures, material valuation, 153
balance sheet, 153

cash discounts, 153
delivery costs, 153
index LIFO, 156
LIFO valuation, 154
quantity LIFO, 154
split valuation, 153
stock layer methods, 155

Accounts Payable, Financial Accounting, 64

Accounts Receivable, Financial Accounting, 64

Accounts Receivable component, 182

accruals
accounting, 64
percentage method, 80
plan/actual method, 80
target/actual method, 80

Activity-Based Accounting module
activity simulation, 86
Order and Project Accounting module, 92
process cost rates, 91
services costing, 90
subprocesses, 91

Activity-Based Cost Accounting module, 73, 85
activity planning, 86
activity rates, 90
activity types, 85
allocation bases, 85
charging variances, 89
cost center variances, 88
cost planning, 87-88
political prices, 87

actual costing, 81

Add Field procedure, 340

Add Screen procedure, 340

Addition to Stock Already in a Bin storage, 163

agreements, outline
contracts, 58
scheduling, 58-59

analysis
ABC, 21
information systems
requirements, 296
inventory, 142
scope, 142
inventory control, 296
displaying results, 300
drill-down path, 301
objects, 298
optimization, 297
ranking list analysis, 299
scoping, 298
set of items, 299
total of material, 299
user-specific, 300
LIS filters, 309
critical performance, 310
predefined, 309
presentation graphics, 309
report writer functionality, 310
product cost accounting, 107
purchase order values, 60
ABC analysis, 60
comparison period, 60
display options, 60
frequency analysis, 60
totals, 60

analysis sequence, 295

analytical reports, 293
ABC analysis, 293
comparison period, 295
dual classification, 294
forecasting, 295
net order value frequency
analysis, 295
planned/actual comparison, 294
R/3 classification, 294
ranking lists, 294
totals, 293

AND operator, 264

AND RETURN variant, 327

APIs, BOR (Business Object Repository), 357

applications, self-service, 353-354
automating sales/marketing, 354
EARS, 354

architectural areas
connections between
articulated entity types, 244
specialization, 244
higher existence dependency
conditions, 255
customer orders, 255
material requirement,
252-254
plant stock, 253
production order, 253
purchase order, 254
purchase requisition, 253
purchasing outline
agreement, 254
sales, 255
transaction figures-cost type,
255
transaction figures-finance,
256
transaction figures-fixed
asset, 255
transaction figures-logistic,
255
transaction figures-material,
253
vendor inquiry, 254
vendor quotation, 254
warehouse stock, 253
highest existence dependency
cost settlement, 257
creditor invoice, 256
creditor payment, 257
goods issue, 256
goods receipt, 256
inventory, 257
posting, 257

price change, 257
purchase order history, 257
shipping, 256
stock movement, 256
low existence dependency, 246
account determination, 249
account structure, 252
asset valuation chart, 249
business area, 250
business partner, 250
business partner structure,
250
business year division, 249
client, 251
company code, 251
condition rule, 248
cost accounting, 250
cost origin, 251
cost type, 251
currency, 250
fixed asset, 249
hazardous, 247
language, 249
ledger, 252
ledger updating rule, 252
legal/logistic area, 248
logistics info structure, 248
material, 247
material valuation area, 247
material valuation type, 247
payment rule, 249
person, 247
plant, 247
purchasing organization,
248
sales/distribution
organization, 248
storage area, 247
task area, 248
time, 249
unit of measure, 250
vendor evaluation criterion,
248

area architecture, 243
connections between, 244
ordering principle, 244

ASAP, 29

assembly, MRP, 118

assessment, cost distribution, 83

Asset Accounting, integrating Order and Project Accounting, 99

asset valuation chart, architectural area, 249

AT LINE-SELECTION event, 327

ATP Server, PDM, 186

Attribute One, 232

Attribute Three, 233
event frequency, 234
time of occurence, 233

Attribute Two, 233
event type, 233
secondary condition, 233
state, 233
trigger, 233
functional purpose, 233

automated purchase order component, 56

automated transportation, 363-365
delivery confirmation, 364-365
shipment loading, 364
shipment scheduling, 363-364
vehicle definition, 363

automatic reorder point planning, 121

B

backflushing, 103

balance sheets, accounting procedures, 153

BAPIs (Business Application Programming Interfaces), 348-351
Internet Application
Component, 349
Web-enabled workflow, 186

base unit of measurement, 15, 212

Basis System, 22

batch data inventory management, 137
data structure, 137
goods movement, 138

batch input, interfaces, 337-339

batch management displays, goods movement control, 135

batches
material types, 40
R/3 data structure policy, 213

BDC processing, interfaces, 340
completed BDC transaction,
340
populating for screen, 340

BDC_OPEN_GROUP function, 341

BDCDATA tables, 339
internal, 337

BEW (Business Engineering Workbench), 23, 282

bill of material, *see* **BOM**

Bill of Materials Explosion, 123

bins, searches, 162

block storage, 163

blocked invoices, releasing
automatic blocking release, 175
canceling individual blocking reasons, 175
invalid blocking reason, 175
terms of payment, 175

blocking reasons, 175
canceling, 175

BOM (bill of material), 43, 123
assembling with R/3 classification, 45
display and drill-down, 45
engineering change of management, 45
header, 43
items, 43-44
maintaining, 44
master data, 192
types of, 44

BOR (Business Object Repository), 356-358
APIs, 357
structure, 356-358

browsers, 347

bulk materials, production orders, 137

business, departments of, 11
head office, 12
material, 12-13
plant, 12
subsidiaries, 12

Business Application Programming Interfaces, *see* **BAPIs**

business area, 110
architectural area, 250

Business Engineer
architectural areas
higher existence dependency, 252-256

highest existence dependency, 256-257
low existence dependency, 246-252
BEW, 282
business partners, 260
common database, 208
customizing, 286-287
configure-to-order, 287
preinstallation, 287
R/3 implementations, 287
reengineering, 287
development environment, 284
ABAP/4 processor, 284
client/server architecture, 285
network-centered computing, 286
object browsers, 284
Enterprise Data Model
area architecture, 243
Attribute One, 232
Attribute Three, 233
Attribute Two, 233
data model processes, 245
documentation, 242
documentation components, 238
entity types relationships, 240
event data attributes, 232
Function Attribute One, 234
Function Attribute Three, 235
Function Attribute Two, 234
function attributes, 234
materials architecture area, 238
Process Attribute One, 236
Process Attribute Two, 237
process attributes, 236
structured information, 238
entity-relationship model, 223, 258
data architecture, 228
displaying entity relationships, 226
Enterprise Data Model, 229-231
purchasing, 258
semantic data modeling, 223-225
EPC modeling, 262
control flow, 265
organizational units, 266
event-driven process chains, 217
design priciples, 218
events, 262

function, 264
information flow, 266
information models, 218-219
logical operators, 264
objects, 220
process pointer, 265
resource object, 266
existence dependency, 246-257
information model, 260
material master record, 209
materials grouping for storage, 259
plant material, 260
plant structure, 206
defining client, 206-207
defining company code, 207
defining plant, 208
defining purchasing group, 207
defining purchasing organization, 207
defining storage location, 208
R/3 data structure policy, 209
batches, 213
European article numbers, 212
general data, 209
industry sectors, 212
material control functions, 211
MRP/purchasing data, 210
quants, 213
storage area, 212
storage location level, 211
units of measure, 212
R/3 Reference Model, 216
customizing, 217
data object structure, 216
enterprise model, 217
materials data records, 213
runtime environment, 283
sematic model, 214
diagrams as, 215
interpreting, 214
stimulus response theory, 221-222
s-r chains, 222
system responses, 222
units of measure, 259
vendor masters, 213

Business Engineering Workbench (BEW), 23, 282

business functions
sets, 27
Warehouse Management component, 158

Business Object Repository,
see **BOR**

business objects, 355-358
altering, 356
BOR, 356-358
documentation, 356

business partner networking, 185

business partners, architectural area, 250

business planning
control, 72
controlling area concept, 73
cost/profit controlling, 72
cost accounting methods, 72

business segments, 114

business software, role of tables, 28

business transactions, 24
types
complaints, 194
cross-company sales, 195
customer consignment stock, 194
inquiries and quotations, 193
production to order, 193
rush order, 193
sales orders, 193-194
scheduling agreements/ contracts, 193
stock transfers, 194
third-party deal, 194

Business Workflow, Web-enabled workflow, 186

business year division area, architectural area, 249

C

capital spending orders, 94, 99

carriers, master data, 189

CAS Sales Support
activity types, 196
customer master data, 195

cash discounts
accounting procedures, 153-154
excluding items, 178
gross posting, 178
net posting, 178

catalogs, QM, 148-149

chart of accounts, 13

classification function, analytical reports, 294

client area, architectural area, 251

clients, 110
Enterprise Data Model, 230
plant structure, 206
testing client, 207
training client, 207
thin, 352

CO-Controlling module, 62
stock by value, 131

code listings
ZMARA000 sample report, 319
ZMARA010 sample report, 323
ZMARA020 sample report, 327
ZMARA021 sample report, 331

commands
GET CURSOR FIELD fld., 327
READ CURRENT LINE FIELD VALUE, fld INTO var., 327
TOP-OF-PAGE DURING LINE-SELECTION, 327

commerce partners
CBP Contraint-Based Planner, 184
networked workflow, 184
workflow templates, 185

Company Code, 110
architectural area, 251
defining, 207
Enterprise Data Model, 230

comparison periods, purchasing reports, 60

competitors, master data, 196
companies, 196
products, 196

complaint processing
credit memo requests, 202
debit memo requests, 202
master data, 194
returns, 202

Completion Indicator, 319

Componentisation project, 29

components, *see* **modules**

condition rule, architectural area, 248

conditions, architectural area, 255

configurable BOM, 44

Configure-to-Order initiative, 287

configuring for upload, interfaces, 336

confirmation option, transfer requirement documents, 161

consignment, 21

consignment material, 21
customer, 138
vendors, 138

consignment processing, 165

consignment stock, 21

constant consumption model, 126

Constraint-Based Planner (CBP), 184

consultants, 386
consumption-based planning, 387
education and training, 378
application skills, 379
management skills, 379
technical skills, 379
implementation issues, 386
inventory management issues, 388
invoice verification issues, 389
purchasing issues, 387
valuation/account assignment, 389
warehouse management issues, 389

consumption
goods receipts, 133
planning based, 387
R/3 data structure policy, 211

consumption-based planning, 120

contact person, master data, 189

contacts, master data, 195

continuous flow production, 103

continuous inventory management, 122

control charts, production, 148

control data flow, routes, 111

control flow, 265

control functions, material types, 39
alternative units of measure, 39
industry sector, 39

R/3 data structure policy, 211
standard units of measure, 39

controller, materials controlling, 62

controlling area, 73, 110

controlling functions, 62

Controlling module, 71, 75
control data flow routes, 111
cost element parameters, 79
integrating with Financial
   Accounting module, 75-76
   planning/decision support,
      76
   R/3 apps, 78
   reporting, 77
   value-adding process, 76
price fluctuations, 80

corporate headquarters, 12

cost accounting, methods, 72

cost accounting area, architectural area, 250

cost center
area controlling, 74
Human Resources, 202

Cost Center Accounting module, 73, 81
actual costing, 81
cost distribution, 82
   assessment, 83
   planning procedures, 83
   surcharge calculation, 83

cost centers, 81
activity planning, 86
activity rates, 90
charging variances, 89
cost planning, 87-88
political prices, 87
process cost rates, 91
services costing, 90
subprocesses, 91
transfer postings, 135
variances, 88

cost distribution, 82
assessment, 83
planning procedures, 83
surcharge calculation, 83

cost element accounting, 73
accruals, 80
parameters, 79
price variances, 80
principles, 78
reporting, 80

Cost Element Accounting module, order settlement, 97

cost objects
account assignment device, 104
area controlling, 74
costing, 105
value-adding process, 76

Cost of Sales Accounting module, profitability analysis, 108

Cost of Sales Accounting Using Actual Costs, 109

cost origin area, architectural area, 251

cost settlement, architectural area, 257

cost type, architectural area, 251

costing
cost object, 105
unit, planning/simulation, 107

costing requirements, 101

credit memo requests, complaint processing, 202

creditor invoice, architectural area, 256

creditory payment, architectural area, 257

Cross Application, 28

cross-company sales, master data, 195

currency
architectural area, 250
converting, 70
Financial Accounting, 70
   exchange, 71
   transactions, 70

current period queries, information systems requirements, 296

customer consignment stock, master data, 194

customer material info records, master data, 192

customer orders, architectural area, 255

customer special stocks, 40

customer-driven production, 183

customer-order BOM, 44

customers
master data, 195
special stock, inventory
   management, 138

customizing
Business Engineer, 286-287
   configure-to-order, 287
   colors/formatting, 322
   drill down, 326-327
   drill to transaction, 330
   preinstallation, 287
   R/3 implementations, 287
   reengineering, 287
   reference model, 217
   reports, 314
   sample report ZMARA000,
      319
   sample report ZMARA010,
      323
   tables/fields, 314-318
   writing, 318
inventory types, 140
ZMARA020 sample report,
   327
ZMARA021 sample report,
   331
units of measure, alternatives,
   40

Customizing component, materials management, 37

D

DASS Plant Control System, 304

data architecture, 228
areas, 228
existence dependency, 228
structured models, 228

data dictionary, 315

data entry, goods movement control, 135

data environment, purchasing info records, 41

data model, processes, 245
event-driven process chains,
   246
events, 245
significant events, 246
typing, 245

Data Modeler, 284

data objects
business departments, 11
enterprise model, 217
inventory analaysis, 142
maintaining basic data, 14
sets, 27
structure, 216

data structure, batch data, 137

data structure policy, 209
general data, 209
MRP/purchasing data, 210
plant-specific, 210
sales-specific, 211
valuation, 210
warehouse management, 210

Data View, 261, 277

databases, Business Engineer, 208

date required, 16

dates, converting, 351

debit memo requests, complaint processing, 202

decentralized shipping, 201

decentralized warehouse management, 168

delivery costs, 16
accounting procedures, 153

delivery date, 17

delivery management, shipping, 198
output documents, 199
pick list, 199
shipping elements, 199
status update, 199

delivery note, transfer requirement documents, 161

delivery schedules, 17, 59

delivery time, reorder point planning, 120

delivery units, stock removal, 164

demands, information systems requirements, 296

departments (business), 11
head office, 12
material, 12
classification, 12
plant, 12
subsidiaries, 12
vendor data concept, 49

design, user interface, 22
Dynpro, 23
SAPGUI, 22

development environment, 284
ABAP/4 processor, 284
client/server architecture, 285
network-centered computing, 286
object browsers, 284

Development Workbench, 285

deviation charts, 148

diagrams, as semantic models, 215
entities, 215

Dictionary Structures branch, 318

direct input, interfaces, 335

display options, purchasing reports, 60

distribution
cost, 82
QM, 148

distribution channels, 188

document header fields, 25

document items, 43

document line item detail fields, 25

Document Management System, 358-359
search facilities, 359

document principle, 24

documentation
EDM, 242
displaying EDM, 243
dividing data model, 242
transactions, 24
document header fields, 25
document line item detail fields, 25
document principle, 24

documents
material purchasing, 54
Product Data Management, 186
purchasing
analyzing, 59
materials information systems, 290
simulation, 177
automatic creation of tax items, 177
cash discount, clearing, 178
cash discounts at invoice posting, 178
standard terms of payment, 178

down payments, material invoice verification, 179

downstream relationships, 240

drill down, custom reports, 326
drill-down processing, 327
to transactions, 330
user actions, 327
user selections, 327

drilling down
interactive analysis, 301
inventory control, analysis path, 301

Dynpro, 23

E

EARS (European Administration Resources System), 354

ECM (Engineering Change Management), 351

EDI (Electronic Data Interchange), 346-347

education
challenges of, 368
consultant's perspective, 378
application skills, 379
management skills, 379
technical skills, 379
detailed plans, 375-376
impact on business, 369
job roles, 370
management commitment, 370
key points of principle, 368
MM module, 378
program structure
adult learners, 373
expectations, 374
in-house courses, 372
quality training, 372
SAP courses, 371
setting goals, 372
scope of, 377-378

effective price, 17

Either or Both (Don't Care) operator, 265

electronic commerce, 345-346
BAPIs, 348, 351
Constraint-Based Planner, 353
ECM, 351
improvement capabilities, 351
Internet Transaction Server, 351
Java User Interface, 352-353
security, 349-350
encryption, 350
firewalls, 350
thin clients, 352

Electronic Data Interchange (EDI), Sales and Distribution module, 187

Employee Substitution component, 203

encryption, 350

Engineering Change Management (ECM), 304, 351
BOM, 45

Enterprise Data Model, 217
area architecture, 243
as reference model, 217
Attribute One, 232
Attribute Two, 233
event type, 233
business departments, 11
data model processes, 245
event-driven process chains, 246
events, 245
significant events, 246
typing, 245
documentation
interpreting, 242
starred name client, 242
documentation components, 238
entity types, 230
existence dependency, 246-257
relationships, 240
entity-relationship model, 229
event attribute three, 233
event frequency, 234
time of occurence, 233
event data attributes, 232
existence dependency, 228
Function Attribute One, 234
Function Attribute Three, 235
processing costs, 235
processing duration, 235
processing frequency, 235
processing type, 235
Function Attribute Two, 234
functional assignment, 234
function attributes, 234
materials architecture area, 238
organizational structure, 230
Process Attribute One, 236
information statistics, 236
process assignment, 236
processing changes, 236
Process Attribute Two, 237
data transmission, 237
process duration, 237
process costs, 237
process quantity structures, 237
transmission medium, 237
process attributes, 236
relationships, 231
structure, 110
structured information, 238-239

entities
complex families, 225
Enterprise Data Model, entity types, 230
relationships between, 225
data architecture, 228
displaying, 226
semantic models, 215
types
business partners, 260
chart of accounts, 13
existence dependency, 246
goods receipt, 13
head office, 12
higher existence dependency, 252-256
highest existence dependency, 256-257
information model, 260
low existence dependency, 246-252
material classification, 12
material valuation, 13
materials grouping, 259
ordering principle, 244
plant material, 260
plant stock, 12
plants, 12
purchasing, 258
relationships, 240
significant events, 246
structured information, 238
subsidiaries, 12
transactions, 13
units of measure, 259

entity-relationship model, 223, 258
data architecture, 228
areas, 228
structured models, 228
displaying, 226
Enterprise Data Model, 229
entity types, 230
organizational structure, 230
relationships, 231
semantic data modeling, 223
entities as complex families, 225
entity relationships, 225
entity types, 223
entity types specializations, 224
info inheritance, 224

entity-relationships, purchasing, 258

entries, recurring, 26

EPC modeling, 262
control flow, 265

events, 262
generated, 263
standard symbol, 263
function, 264
information flow, 266
logical operators, 264
organizational units, 266
process pointer, 265
resource object, 266

Euro functions, 185

European Administration Resources System (EARS), 354

European article numbers, R/3 data structure policy, 212

European Monetary Union (EMU), 185

event attribute one, 232

event attribute three, 233
event frequency, 234
time of occurrence, 233

event attribute two, 233
event type, 233
secondary condition, 233
state, 233
trigger, 233
functional purpose, 233

event data attributes, 232

event-driven process chains, 217
design principles, 218
information models, 218
info models, 219
task models, 219
unit models, 219
objects, 220
process view, 273
stimulus response theory, 221-222
s-r chains, 222
system responses, 222

event-related stocks, 41

events, combining with functions, 267
function triggers, 269
two events, 267

exception reporting, 305

exchange rate, 20

Exclusive OR (XOR) operator, 265

Executive Information system,
LIS planning functions, 311
reporting in Controlling module, 77

existence dependency, 228
  entity types, 246-257
  higher degree flow data, 229
  highest degree, 229
  low degree master data, 229

external procurement, 17

F

family trees, 218

FI, *see* Financial Accounting module

FI-AR (Accounts Receivable component), 182

FI-GLX Extended General Ledger, set concept, 27

fields, custom, 314
  ABAP/4 data dictionary, 315
  SQL trace, 317
  tables for field name, 318
  tables for program, 318
  technical info, 314

FIFO, stock removal, 164

filters, LIS, 309
  cirtical performance, 310
  predefined analysis, 309
  presentation graphics, 309
  report writer functionality, 310

final delivery, 17

Financial Accounting Extended General Ledger, ledger-based period accounting, 116

Financial Accounting module, 57, 63
  account assignment, 389
  components, 63
    currency, 70
    currency exchange, 71
    currency in transactions, 70
    data checks, 64-65
    General Ledger, 66
    General Ledger transactions, 66
    intercompany accounting, 68
    intercompany payments, 69
    intercompany purchases, 69
    international taxation, 67
    language differences, 69
    taxation functions, 67
    vendor payments, 69
    year-end closing, 67
  credit memo requests, 202
  debit memo requests, 202

document principle, 24
goods issue, 200
integrating with Controlling module, 75-76
  planning/decision support, 76
  R/3 apps, 78
  reporting, 77
  value-adding process, 76
materials invoice processing, 175
returns, 202
stock by value, 131
valuation, 389

Financial Controlling, 63

financial management, materials management, concepts, 63

firewalls, 350

fixed asset, architectural area, 249

fixed asset accounts, 255

Fixed Bin storage, 163

forecast models, 16
  monitoring validity, 127

forecast trend model, 126

forecast-based planning, 120

forecasting
  analytical reports, 295
  LIS planning functions, 310

forecasting business configurations, 362-363

forecasts, 16
  reprocessing, 127

foreign currency, entering invoices, 179

formatting reports, 322

framework, 280
  mapping business logic, 282
  open architecture, 281

frequency analysis, purchasing reports, 60

Function Attribute One, 234

Function Attribute Three, 235
  processing costs, 235
  processing duration, 235
  processing frequency, 235
  processing type, 235

Function Attribute Two, 234
  functional assignment, 234

Function View, 261
  level 0, 279

level 1, 279
level 2, 279
level 3, 279

functional controlling systems, compared to operational controlling systems, 72

functions
  BCD_OPEN_GROUP, 341
  combining with events, 267
    function triggers, 269
    two events, 267
  controlling, 62
  LIS
    reporting pathways, 308
    standard reporting, 308
  MM
    consignment, 21
    consignment material, 21
    consignment stock, 21
    multiple account assignment, 21
    order, 21
  sets, 27
  taxation, 67

G

GAAP (generally accepted accounting procedures), 13
  data checks, 64

Gantt charts, 309

general data, 190

General Ledger, 63
  Controlling module, 75
  cost elements, 79
  functions
    financial health monitoring, 66
    results for year, 66
  profitability reports, 117
  transaction data, 111
  value flow, 75

General Ledger module, 65

Generally Accepted Accounting Principles (GAAP)
  Generation Data, 319
  revenue element accounting, 112

GET CURSOR FIELD fld. command, 327

GI-General Ledger account, stock by value, 131

GLX Extended General Ledger, 71

goods issues
architectural area, 256
Shipping module, 200
transfer requirement
documents, 161

goods movement control, 132
data entry, 135
goods issues, 134
batch management displays, 135
storage location display, 135
material planning, 134
dynamic availability
checking, 134
reservations, 134
purchase orders, 132-133
withdrawals, 135

goods receipt, 13, 19
architectural area, 256
cash discounts, 178
inspection procedures
details planning, 146
inspection stock, 146
quality certificates, 146
supply relationship, 147
usage, 147
invoices with references, 176
material movements, 166
posting lowest value
determination, 157
subcontractors, MM special
functions, 167
transfer requirement
documents, 160

goods receipt blocked stock, 19

graphics, presentation, LIS, 309

graphs, inventory control analysis, 301

gross posting, 178

gross price, 20

grouping material, 15

GUI, 22
line characters, 323

H

hazardous entity type, 247
head office department, 12
headers, BOM, 43

history logs, inventory bins, 140

Human Resources Enterprise Data Model, 202-203

Human Resources records, master data, 189

I

IACs (Internet Application Components), 348
services enhanced, 349

IMG guide, MM, 387

implementing MM, 386-387

index LIFO, accounting procedures, 156

indicators (inventory), 140

industry sectors, 39
master data, 190
R/3 data structure policy, 212

Industry Solutions, configurations, 30

information flow, symbol, 266

Information Flow View, 261, 276

information inheritance, 224

information models, 218
info models, 219
task models, 219
unit models, 219
viewing, 260

information statistics, 236

information structures, 292
LIS, 306
predefined performance
measures, 307
reporting objects, 306
reporting periods, 307
user-defined performance
measures, 307

information systems requirements
analysis requirements, 296
current period queries, 296
patterns of demand, 296
predictable reports, 296
transaction volume, 295

inheritance of information, 224

input valuation, product cost accounting, 106

inspection lots, functions of, 145

inspection planning
instruction, 149
inventory management, 149
QMIS, 150
usage decision, 150

inspection stock, goods receipt, 146

INT-International module, tax items, 177

integrating with MM
accounting, 172
materials invoice verification, 172

interactive analysis, 300

interfaces, 22, 334
batch input, 337-339
BDC processing, 340
completed BDC transaction, 340
populating for screen, 340
configuring for upload, 336
design, 22
Dynpro, 23
SAPGUI, 22
direct input, 335
Java User Interface, 352-353
sessions, 23
R/3 Session Manager, 23
source database, 335
upload file, 335

interim receiver accounts, 136

International Demonstration and Education system, 185

international taxation, 67

Internet
BAPIs, 348, 351
browsers, 347
business applications
advantages, 344
EDI, 346-347
part number management, 346
tracking materials, 345-346
electronic commerce, 345-346
improvement capabilities, 351
security, 349-350
IACs, 348-349
services enhanced, 349
ITS, 348
SAP Automation, 348
Web servers, 347

Internet Application Components, see IACs

Internet Transaction Server, 351

inventory analysis
Inventory Controlling component, 290
Logistics Information system, 292

inventory control
analysis, 296
    displaying results, 300
    ranking list analysis, 299
    scoping, 298
    set of items, 299
    total of material, 299
architectural area, 257
drill-down path
    graph data, 301
    info table data, 301
optimization, 297
    objects, 298
    performance measures, 297
user-specific analysis
    interactive analysis, 300
    report design, 300

Inventory Controlling component (IC), 141, 297

inventory management, 19, 388
analysis scope
    ABC analysis, 142
    anaysis period, 142
    material numbers, 142
    material types, 142
batch data, 137
    data structure, 137
    goods movement, 138
benefits, 130-131
    stock by quantity, 131
    stock by value, 131
continuous, 122
decentralized warehouse management, 168
goods movement control, 132
    material planning, 134
    purchase orders, 132-133
goods receipt, 19
goods receipt blocked stock, 19
inspection planning, 149
    instruction, 149
    QMIS, 150
    usage decision, 150
Inventory Management module, interim storage record, 140
ISO 9000, 142
lowest value determination, 157
    goods receipt posting, 157

material planning
    dynamic availability checking, 134
    goods issues, 134-135
    reservations, 134
material value, 150
    accounting procedures, 153-156
    categories, 151
    classes, 151
    criteria, 152
    lowest value determination, 156
    perspectives, 156-157
    types, 152
    valuation structures, 151
MM special functions, 165
    consignment processing, 165
    goods receipt, 167
    material movements, 166
    special stocks, 166
    stock transfers, 167
    subcontracting, 166
    vendor special stocks, 167
performance measures, 141
physical, 138-139
    inventory analysis, 141
    inventory types, 140
    sampling, 139
procurement, automatic notification, 146
QM functions
    catalogs, 148-149
    central, 143
    comprehensive, 143
    integrating, 145-148
    internal, 144-145
search strategies, 162
    bin type, 162
    storage bin type, 163
    storage type, 162
special stock, 138
    customer, 138
    vendor, 138
stock placement strategies, 163
stock removal strategies, 163
    assigning, 164
    FIFO, 164
    large delivery units, 164
    LIFO, 164
    partial quantities, 164
    quantity, 164
    storage unit functions, 165
    storage unit management, 164
storage location, 19
transfer postings, 135
    consumption, 136

one-step stock transfer, 136
quality inspection stock, 137
stock transfer reservations, 136
two-step stock transfer, 136
transfer requirement
documents, 159-160
    confirmation option, 161
    goods for delivery note, 161
    goods issue, 161
    goods receipt, 160
    inventory differences, 162
    transfer order processing, 162
    stock transfers, 161
Warehouse Management component, 158
    storage bin type, 159
    storage section, 159
    storage type, 159
    warehouse number, 159

inventory management data, master data, 191

Inventory Management module (IM), 140

invoice receipts
materials invoice verification, canceling by credit memo, 179
posting, 176
tax items, 177

invoice verification (MM-IV), 20, 32, 389
exchange rate, 20
gross price, 20
net price, 20
stock, 20
stock material, 20
unplanned costs, 181

invoices
blocked, releasing, 175
foreign currency, 179
incorrect
    automatic invoice blocking, 175
    defining tolerances, 174
    overwriting variances, 174
manual entry, 26
materials invoice verification, different accounts, 179
materials verification, 172
original sources, 173
posting, adjusting times before, 177
purchase orders, 173
    multiple order references, 173
    references, 173
    related information, 174

purchasing analysis, 291
without references, 176
ISO 9000
inventory management, 142
QM, 145
issuing plant, 15
ITS (Internet Transaction Server), 348

J - L

Java, 352
Java User Interface, 352-353
Job entity type, 231
key figures, profitability analysis, 115
key points of principles, 368
languages
architectural area, 249
Financial Accounting module, 69
last-in-first-out (LIFO) evaluation procedure, 151
ledger updating rule, architectural area, 252
ledger-based period accounting
profit center level, 116
profitability reports, 117
ledgers, architectural area, 252
legal/logistic area, architectural area, 248
LIFO
index, 156
stock removal, 164
LIFO valuation, accounting procedures, 154
LIS (Logistics Informatoin System)
database, 305-306
filters, 309
critical performance, 310
predefined analysis, 309
presentation graphics, 309
report writer functionality, 310
information structures, 292, 306
predefined performance measures, 307
reporting objects, 306
reporting periods, 307

user-defined performance measures, 307
inventory analysis, 291
planning functions, 310-311
standard functions
reporting pathways, 308
standard reporting, 308
LO-CIM component, 304
LO-ECH Engineering Change Management component, 305
loading point, 188
local networks, customer-driven production, 183
logical operators, 264
logical relationships, entities, 216
Logistics application, QM functions, 143
Logistics General module, components, 304
logistics info structure, architectural area, 248
Logistics Information System (LO), 302-303
components
core, 303
general, 304
engineering change management, 304
LO-CIM, 304
maintaining, 305
exception reporting, 305
LIS data sources, 306
LIS database, 305-306
triggered reporting, 305
lot-sizing
optimum, 124
periodic, 124
procedures, 123
restrictions, 124
static, 124
lots, batches, 40
lowest value determination
material valuation, 156
posting results, 157

M

make-to-order company, 102
management structures, controlling area concept, 73
manual document entry,

transactions, 26
recurring entries, 26
set concept, 27
marketing trends in SAP R/3, 29
Master Data (SD-MD), 188
account groups, 189
carrier and supplier, 189
contact person, 189
HR-Human Resources Records, 189
Materials Management masters, 190
master data
BOM, 192
business transactions
complaints, 194
cross-company sales, 195
customer consignment stock, 194
inquiries and quotations, 193
production to order, 193
rush order, 193
sales orders, 193-194
scheduling agreements/contracts, 193
stock transfer transactions, 194
third-party deal, 194
competitors, 196
companies, 196
products, 196
contacts, 195
customer material info records, 192
existence dependency, 246
material status, 192
partners/personnel, 195
sales activities, 196
stock inquiries, 192
master pricing conditions, 47
master records
cost centers, 81
inspection planning, 149
materials purchasing, 37
vendor, 213
material data records, R/3 data structure policy, 213
material department, 12
classification, 12
plant stock, 12
material forecasts, models, 126
constant consumption, 126
forecast trend, 126

monitoring validity, 127
reprocessing, 127
seasonal fluctuation, 126
seasonal trend, 127

material groups, 15

material master, 118
industry sector, 39

**material master record,
departmental access, 209**

material masters, 15

**material planning, inventory
management, 134**
dynamic availability checking,
134
reservations, 134

material purchasing
BOM, 43
assembling with R/3
classification, 45
display and drill-down, 45
engineering change of
management, 45
header, 43
items, 43-44
maintaining, 44
types of, 44
info records, 41
central control function, 43
creating, 42
data environment, 41
structure, 42
material types, 38
batches, 40
control functions, 39-40
special stocks, 40
operations, 53
document structure, 54
documents, 54
requisitions, 54
supply sources, 55
outline purchase agreements,
58
scheduling, 58-59
types of contracts, 58
purchase orders, 56
account assignment, 57
buyer options, 57
documents, 57
purchase requisition, 56
references, 56
quotation procedure, 56
requisitions
buyer-generated, 55
release strategy, 55
supply sources
alternative pricing plans, 53
automatic vendor evaluation,
51

sub-criteria, 52
vendor evaluations,
displaying, 52
vendor net price simulation,
52
vendors for specific
material, 50-51
vendor data concept, 47
account groups, 50
once-only vendors, 48
user departments, 49
vendor master records, 49

**Material Requirements
Planning, 118**
Activity-Based Cost Accounting
module, 85
activity planning, 86
activity simulation, 86
activity types, 85
charging variances, 89
cost center variances, 88
planning, 87
political prices, 87
Asset Accounting module, 99
business planning and control,
72
controlling
automatic reorder point
planning, 121
automatic replenishment,
121
automatic steps in MRP run,
122
continuous inventory
management, 122
inventory management, 121
storage location, 122
Controlling module, 71
Cost Center Accounting
module, 81
actual costing, 81
Cost Center module, cost
distribution, 82
cost element accounting
principles, 78
accruals, 80
parameters, 79
price variances, 80
data at plant level, 210
plant-specific, 210
sales-specific, 211
valuation, 210
warehouse management,
210
defining material, 118
assembly, 118
material master, 118

Financial Accounting module
currency, 70
currency exchange, 71
data checking, 63-64
General Ledger functions,
66
General Ledger
transactions, 66
intercompany accounting,
68
intercompany payments, 69
intercompany purchases, 69
international taxation, 67
language differences, 69
taxation functions, 67
vendor payments, 69
year-end closing, 67
forecast, 16
material group, 119
material type, 119
net change planning, 119
Order and Project Accounting
module
capital spending orders, 99
cost accounting
transactions, 96
open items, 95
order classification, 94
order data formats, 93
order planning, 94
order settlement, 97
order summary evaluations,
98
settlement rules, 97
status management, 93
unit costing, 95
procurement by exception, 34
product cost accounting, 100
cost object, 104
input valuation, 106
quantity structures, 101
techniques, 102
valuation methods, 106
Profit Center Accounting
module, 116-118
ledger-based period
accounting, 116
Profitability Analysis module,
108
fixed cost absorption, 109
results
display formats, 125
MRP list, 125
run exception reporting, 125
stock/requirements list, 125
revenue element accounting,
112
estimate elements, 113
posting data, 112

material requirements planning, results, 125

material types, 15, 38
batches, 40
control functions, 39
alternative units of measure, 39
industry sector, 39
standard units of measure, 39
master data, 190
special stocks, 40

Material Valuation, 13, 19, 35
price control, 20
price unit, 20
valuation area, 20
valuation category, 20

material valuation area, architectural area, 247

material valuation type, architectural area, 247

material value, 150
accounting procedures, 153
balance sheet, 153
cash discounts, 153
delivery costs, 153
index LIFO, 156
LIFO valuation, 154
quantity LIFO, 154
split valuation, 153
stock layer methods, 155
criteria, 152
stock changes, 152
lowest value determination, 156
perspectives, 156
linked procedures, 157
lowest value by market price, 156
lowest value by movement rate, 157
lowest value by range of coverage, 157
valuation structures, 151
categories, 151
classes, 151
types, 152

materials, semantic models, 214

materials architecture area, 252-254
business aspects, 238

materials controlling
business logic, 62
controlling functions, 62
financial management, 63

materials delivery cost accounting, 180

materials grouping, 259

materials information systems, purchasing, 290
discerning trends, 290
documents, 290
materials accounting, 291
vendor performance, 291

materials invoice processing, accounting functions
goods receipt references, 176
invoice receipts, 176
invoices without references, 176
release transactions, 175

materials invoice verification
additional costs after transactions, 179
assigning invoices to different accounts, 179
down payments, 179
foreign currency, 179
invoice receipts, canceling by credit memo, 179
relating to MM, 172
text notes, 180

Materials Management
customizing, 37
divisions, 14
ABC analysis, 21
inventory management, 19
invoice verification, 20
maintaining basic data, 14
material valuation, 19
materials requirements planning, 16
purchasing, 16-19
purchasing document category, 18
special functions, 21
warehouse management, 20
event flow, 11
material types, 38
price list modules, 30
inventory management (MM-IM), 31
invoice verification (MM-IV), 32
master data (MM-BD), 30
purchasing (MM-PUR), 31
purchasing information system (MM-IS), 31
requirements planning (PP-MRP), 30
warehouse management (MM-WM), 31

routings, 183
sets, 27
special functions, 165
consignment processing, 165
goods receipt, 167
material movements, 166
special stocks, 166
stock transfers, 167
subcontracting, 166
vendor special stocks, 167

Materials Management masters, master data, 190

materials master records
data attributes, 37
materials purchasing, 36

materials masters, alterations, 38

materials procurement
inquiry QM, 145
purchasing QM, 146
vendor inspection, 146
vendor selection QM, 146

materials purchasing
master records, 37
materials master records, 36
procurement by exception, 34-36
procurement procedures, 45-46
maintaining conditions, 47
price determination, 46
pricing conditions, 46
reports
analyzing documents, 59
values, 60

materials receipt, 13
chart of accounts, 13
goods, 13
material valuation, 13
transactions, 13

materials references, purchase orders, 173

MATNR field, 316

MM-Material Management, *see* **Materials Management**

models, semantic data modeling, 223

moderate lowest value principle, 156

modules
Componentisation project, 29
materials purchasing, procurement by exception, 34-36

price list, 30
 inventory management
  (MM-IM), 31
 invoice verification (MM-
  IV), 32
 master data (MM-BD), 30
 purchasing (MM-PUR), 31
 purchasing information
  system (MM-IS), 31
 requirements planning (PP-
  MRP), 30
 warehouse management
  (MM-WM), 31
movement rate, 157
**moving average price (MAP)
 control, planned delivery cost,
 180**
MRP, *see* **Material
 Requirements Planning**
MRP list, 125
**multiple account assignment,
 21**
multiple BOM, 44

N

net change planning, 119
**net order value frequency
 analysis, 295**
net posting, 178
net price, 20
net price simulation, 52
**net requirements calculation,
 121**
network computing
 advantages, 344
 BAPIs, 348, 351
 browsers, 347
 Constraint-Based Planner, 353
 ECM, 351
 EDI, 346-347
 electronic commerce, 345-346
  improvement capabilities,
   351
  security, 349-350
 IACs, 348-349
 Internet Transaction Server,
  348, 351
 Java User Interface, 352-353
 online facilities, 349
 part number management, 346
 push technology, 354
 SAP Automation, 348

self-service applications, 353-354
 automatic sales/marketing,
  354
 automating sales/
  marketing, 354
 EARS, 354
supply chain technology, 355
thin clients, 352
tracking materials, 345-346
Web servers, 347
workflow, 360-361
 specialized subsystems, 361
 templates, 360-361
**networked workflow, commerce
 partners, 184**
**networking, business partner,
 185**
Next Empty Bin storage, 163
nonstock items, 43

O

**object types, Human Resources
 Enterprise Data Model, 202**
objects
 business, 355-358
  altering, 356
  BOR, 356-358
  documentation, 356
 event-driven process chains,
  220
 inventory control, 298
one-time vendor, 17
**online reporting, drill down,
 326**
Open FI, 181
Operating Concern, 110
**operational controlling systems,
 compared to functional
 controlling systems, 72**
**operations, material
 purchasing, 53**
 document structure, 54
 documents, 54
 requisitions, 54
 supply sources, 55
order, 21
 area controlling, 74
**Order and Project Accounting
 module, 73, 92**
 capital spending orders, 99
 cost accounting transactions, 96
 integrating Asset Accounting,

  99
 open items, 95
 order classification, 94
 order data formats, 93
 order evaluations, 98
 order planning, 94
 order settlement, 97
 order status management, 93
 settlement rules, 97
 unit costing, 95
order data formats, 93
order master, 93
order price unit, 15
order units, 15
orders
 capital spending, 99
 classification by content, 94
 cost accounting transactions, 96
 evaluations, 98
 open items, 95
 planning, 94
 settlement, 97
 settlement rules, 97
 status management, 93
 unit costing, 95
Organization View, 261
organizational digraphs, 219
organizational levels, 15
organizational structure, 110
**Organizational Unit entity type,
 230**
organizational units
 Human Resources, 203
 symbol, 266
organizational view, 279
**outline purchase agreements,
 58**
 scheduling, 58
  benefits, 59
  vendor delivery, 59
 types of contracts, 58

P

Pareto charts, 309
partners, master data, 195
**pathways, LIS standard
 functions, 308**
**payment rule area, architectural
 area, 249**
payments, intercompany, 69

PDAS Process Data Acquisition System, 304

PDM (Product Data Management), 359
workflow template, 360

performance
inventory control, 297
inventory management, 141

performance measures, LIS information structures
predefined, 307
user-defined, 307

person entity type, 247

Personal Accounts, 63

Personal Sub-ledgers, 64

personnel, master data, 195

physical inventory, 138-139
inventory analysis, 141
inventory types, 140
indicators, 140
posting differences, 140
sampling, 139

pick lists, 199

planned delivery costs, 180
entering, 181
purchase order, 180

planning, forecast-based, 295

planning functions, LIS, 310-311

Planning phase, ISO 9000, 143

plant department, 12

plant stock, 12

plant structure, 206
defining client, 206
testing client, 207
training client, 207
defining company code, 207
defining plant, 208
defining purchasing group, 207
defining purchasing organization, 207
defining storage location, 208

plant-specific data, 191

plants, 187
architectural area, 247
defining, 208
Enterprise Data Model, 230
issuing, 15
material, entity types, 260
ranking list analysis, 299
stock, architectural area, 253

PM (Plant Maintenance), 143
QM functions, 143

political prices, 87

Position entity type, 230

postings
architectural area, 257
clearing
excluding items, 178
gross, 178
net, 178
inventory management, 135
consumption, 136
one-step stock transfer, 136
quality inspection stock, 137
stock transfer reservations, 136
two-step stock transfer, 136
preliminary documents, 177

PP-CBP Constraint-Based Planner, 353

preliminary document entry, document simulation, 177
automatic creation of tax items, 177
cash discount, clearing, 178
cash discounts at invoice posting, 178
standard terms of payment, 178

preliminary documents, 177

price change, architectural area, 257

price comparison list, 17

price control, 20
price determination
procurement, 46
valuation criteria, 152

price index, LIFO index, 156

price list modules
inventory management (MM-IM), 31
invoice verification (MM-IV), 32
master data (MM-BD), 30
MM, 30
purchasing (MM-PUR), 31
purchasing information system (MM-IS), 31
requirements planning (PP-MRP), 30
warehouse management (MM-WM), 31

price unit, 20

pricing conditions, 17

probabilistic risk-taking, 35

Process Attribute One, 236
information statistics, 236
process assignment, 236
processing changes, 236

Process Attribute Two, 237
data transmission, 237
process costs, 237
process duration, 237
process quantity structures, 237
transmission medium, 237

process cost rates, 91

process pointer, 265

Process View, 261

process view, event-driven process chains, 273

procurement
by exception, 34-36
inventory management, automatic notification, 151
materials purchasing, 45-46
maintaining conditions, 47
price determination, 46
pricing conditions, 46
source of supply, 19

procurement lead time, 16

procurement types, 16

product cost accounting, 100
analysis/reporting, 107
cost object
account assignment device, 104
costing, 105
costing requirements, 101
input valuation, 106
product costing, 102
order costing, 103
unit costing, 103
quantity structures, 101
continuous flow, 102
make-to-order, 102
make-to-stock, 102
unit costing, planning/simulation, 107
valuation methods, 106

Product Cost Accounting module, unit costing, 103

product costing, 102
order costing, 103
unit costing, 103

Product Data Management (PDM), 186

production
  continuous flow, 103
  costs, planning/decision
    support, 76
  customer-driven, 183
  LO-CIM component, 304
  master data, 193
  QM, 147

production lots, batches, 40

**production order area,
  architectural area, 253**

production orders, 94
  bulk materials, 137

**Production phase, ISO 9000,
  143**

production planning (PP), 182
  routings, 182
  work centers, 182

**Production Planning
  application, QM functions,
  147**

**Production Planning format,
  BOM, 44**

**production resources and tools
  (PRT), 147**

Profit Center, 110

**Profit Center Accounting
  module, 108, 116**
  ledger-based period accounting
    profit center level, 116
    profitability reports, 117
  profitability analysis, 110

profit centers, 116

**profit planning, Profitability
  Analysis module, 116**

profitability, calculating, 114
  business segments, 114
  key figures, 115

profitability analysis, 62, 73
  Operating Concern, 110
  posting revenue data, 112

Profitability Analysis module
  business segments, 114
  calculating, 114
    business segments, 114
    key figures, 115
  compared to Profit Center
    Analysis, 108
  Cost of Sales Accounting Using
    Actual Costs, 109
  fixed cost absorption
    accounting, 109

  planning
    profits, 116
    revenue, 116
    sales, 116

**profitability reports, ledger-
  based period accounting, 117**

progressive implementation, 72

projects, area controlling, 74

**provisional values, material
  planning, 134**

**purchase info records, pricing,
  46**

**purchase order history,
  architectural area, 257**

purchase orders, 17
  architectural area, 254
  central control function, 43
  data object, 217
  generating, 56
    account assignment, 57
    buyer options, 57
    documents, 57
    references, 56
    requisitions, 56
  goods receipts, 132-133
    contingencies, 133
  materials invoices, 173
    multiple order references,
      173
    references, 173
    related information, 174
  operations, 53
  planned delivery costs, 180
  pricing, 46

purchase requisitions, 17
  architectural area, 253

purchasing, 16, 387
  analysis
    analysis sequence, 295
    analytical reports, 293
    information systems
      requirements, 295
    Logistics Information
      System, 291
  architectural area, 248
  date required, 16
  delivery costs, 16
  delivery date, 17
  delivery schedule, 17
  effective price, 17
  entity relationships, 258
  external procurement, 17
  final delivery, 17
  intercompany, Financial
    Accounting module, 69

  materials information systems,
    290
    discerning trends, 290
    documents, 290
    materials accounting, 291
    vendor performance, 291
  one-time vendor, 17
  order price history, 17
  outline agreement, architectural
    area, 254
  price comparison list, 17
  pricing conditions, 17
  purchase order, 17
  purchase requisition, 17
  purchasing document, 17
  purchasing document category,
    18
  purchasing document type,
    17-18
  purchasing group, 18
  purchasing info record, 18
  purchasing organization, 18
  purchasing value key, 18
  QM functions, 146
  quantity contract, 18
  rejection letter, 18
  release point, 18
  release strategy, 18
  scheduling agreement, 18
  source list, 19
  source of supply, 19
  third-party deals, 194
  value contract, 19
  vendors, 19
  volume-based rebate, 19

purchasing document, 17

**purchasing document category,
  18**

**purchasing document type,
  17-18**

purchasing group, 18
  defining, 207

purchasing info records, 18, 41
  central control function, 43
  creating, 42
  data environment, 41
  structure, 42

**purchasing information system
  (MM-IS), 31**

purchasing organization, 18
  defining, 207

purchasing reports
  analyzing documents, 59
  values, 60
    ABC analysis, 60
    comparison period, 60

display options, 60
frequency analysis, 60
totals, 60
purchasing value key, 18
PURCHIS component, analysis sequence, 295
PURCHIS-Purchasing Information System, 291
push technology, 354

Q

QM, catalogs, 148-149
QM functions
control charts, 148
goods receipt inspection
details planning, 146
quality certificates, 146
supply relationship, 147
usage, 147
integrating, 145
materials procurement, 145
internal, 144
quality control, 145
quality inspection management, 144
quality planning, 144
inventory management
central, 143
comprehensive, 143
materials procurement
inquiry QM, 145
purchasing QM, 146
production, 147
sales/distribution, 148
vendor inspection, 146
vendor selection QM, 146
QMIS (Quality Management Information System), 145
quality control, 145
quality certificates, goods receipt, 146
quality control, QM functions, 145
quality inspection, 137
consigment materials, 166
quality inspection indicator, goods receipts, 133
quality inspection management, 144
quantity contract, 18
quantity structures, 101
continuous flow, 102

make-to-order, 102
make-to-stock, 102
quants, R/3 data structure policy, 213
quota system, supply sources, 51
quotas, arrangements, 123
quotation procedure, 56

R

R/3
Classification System, BOM, 45
Controlling module, integrating with, 78
data structure policy, 209
batches, 213
European article numbers, 212
general data, 209
industry sectors, 212
material control functions, 211
material data records, 213
MRP/purchasing data, 210
quants, 213
storage area, 212
storage location level, 211
units of measure, 212
reference model, 216
customizing, 217
data object structure, 216
enterprise model, 217
Session Manager, 23
ranking list analysis, 142, 299
READ CURRENT LINE FIELD VALUE fld INTO var. command, 327
reasons, blocking, 175
recurring entries, 26
Reference Model, EPC modeling, 262
control flow, 265
events, 262
function, 264
information flow, 266
logical operators, 264
organizational units, 266
process pointer, 265
resource object, 266
reference model (R/3), 216
customizing, 217
data object structure, 216
enterprise model, 217

rejection letters, 18
release point, 18
release strategy, 18, 55
reorder point planning, 120
delivery time, 120
safety stock, 120
Report Basics, 318
report writer, LIS, 310
reporting
cost element accounting, 80
product cost accounting, 107
reporting periods, LIS information structures, 307
reports, 314
analytical, 293
ABC analysis, 293
comparison period, 295
dual classification, 294
forecasting, 295
net order value frequency analysis, 295
planned/actual comparison, 294
R/3 classification, 294
ranking lists, 294
totals, 293
Controlling module, 77
custom, 314
colors/formatting, 322
drill down, 326-327
drill to transaction, 330
sample report ZMARA000, 319
sample report ZMARA010, 323
tables/fields, 314-318
writing, 318
ZMARA020 sample report, 327
ZMARA021 sample report, 331
information systems requirements, 296
LIS standard functions, 308
Repository Infosys, table fields, 318
requirement tracking number, 16
requisitions
buyer-generated, 55
material purchasing, 54
referencing, 56
release strategies, 55

reservations
material planning, 134
transfer postings, 136

resource object, symbol, 266

returnable packaging material
customer, 138
vendors, 138

returns, complaint processing, 202

revenue element accounting
estimate elements, 113
posting data, 112

revenue planning, Profitability Analysis module, 116

revenues, profit centers, 117

RMDATIND, 337

routings
allocating materials to, 183
production planning, 182

RTAP Real Time Application Platform, 304

run exception reporting, MRP, 125

Runtime Environment, 283

rush order, master data, 193

S

s-r chains, 222

safety stock, reorder point planning, 120

sales
activities, master data, 196
architectural area, 255
inventory management, 130
QM, 148

Sales and Distribution module
activity types, 197
invoice verification, 32
partners/personnel, 195
plant-specific data, 191

sales area, 188

sales area specific data, 191

sales divisions, 188

sales group, 188

Sales Information System (SD-IS), 187

sales office, 188

sales order stock, customer, 138

sales orders, 94
master data, 193-194

sales organization, 188

sales planning, Profitability Analysis module, 116

sales/distribution, architectural area, 248

salesperson, 188

sampling, physical inventory, 139

SAP Automation, 348

SAP courses, 371

SAPGUI, 22
interactive analysis, 300

scheduling agreements, master data, 193

SD-IS Sales Information System, 187

SD-MD Master Data, 188
account groups, 189
carrier and supplier, 189
contact person, 189
HR-Human Resources Records, 189
Materials Management masters, 190

SD-Sales and Distribution, 186-188

SD-SHP Shipping module, 197

search strategies, warehouse management, 162
bin type, 162
storage bin type, 163
storage type, 162

seasonal fluctuation model, 126

seasonal trend model, 127

sectors, master data, 190

security, electronic commerce, 349-350
encryption, 350
firewalls, 350

Selection Criteria, 319

self-service applications, 353-354
automating sales/marketing, 354
EARS, 354

semantic models, 214
diagrams as, 215
entities, 215
interpreting, 214

servers
ITS, 348
Web, 347

sessions, user interface, 23
R/3 Session Manager, 23

set concept, 27

settlement rules, 97

shelf section storage, 163

shipping
architectural area, 256
criteria for automatic, 198

shipping elements, 199

Shipping module, 197
complaint processing
credit memo requests, 202
debit memo requests, 202
returns, 202
decentralized shipping, 201
delivery management, 198
output documents, 199
pick list, 199
shipping elements, 199
status update, 199
goods issue, 200
shipping work list, 197-198
Warehouse Management system, 200

shipping point, 188

simple BOM, 44

source database, interfaces, 335

source lists, 19
supply sources, 51

source of supply, 19

special functions
inventory management, 138
customer, 138
vendor, 138
MM, 165
consignment processing, 165
goods receipt, 167
material movements, 166
special stocks, 166
stock transfers, 167
subcontracting, 166
vendor special stocks, 167

special stocks, material types, 40

specializations, entity types, 224

split valuation, accounting procedures, 153

SQL trace, 317

standing orders, 94

starred named client, 242

statistical orders, 94

status management, orders, 93

stimulus response theory, event-driven process chain methods, 221-222
  s-r chains, 222
  system responses, 222

stock, 12, 20
  architecural areas, 253
  consumption-based planning, 387
  forecast-based planning, 120
  inventory management
    by quantity, 131
    by value, 131
  master data, 192
  material planning
    dynamic availability checking, 134
    reservations, 134
  one-step transfer, 136
  physical inventory, 138-139
    inventory analysis, 141
    inventory types, 140
    sampling, 139
  placement, 163
  removal, 163
    assigning, 164
    FIFO, 164
    large delivery units, 164
    LIFO, 164
    partial quantities, 164
    quantity, 164
    storage unit functions, 165
    storage unit management, 164
  special, inventory management, 138
  transfer postings, 135
  transfers, MM special functions, 167
  two-step transfer, 136
  valuation, 152

stock items, 43

stock layer valuations, accounting procedures, 155

stock material, 20

stock movement type, architectural area, 256

stocks
  batches, 40
  consignment processing, 166

special, 40
transactions, master data, 194
transfer requirement documents, 161

storage, materials grouping, 259

Storage Area architecture area, 247

storage areas, R/3 data structure policy, 212

storage bins
  inventory types, 140
  searches, 163
  Warehouse Management, 159

storage locations, 19
  defining, 208
  displaying, goods movement control, 135
  goods receipts, 133
  master data, 191
  MRP, 122
  R/3 data structure policy, 211
    consumption data, 211
    forecast data, 211
    storage location, 211
    storage location level, 211
    MRP/purchasing data, 210
    general data, 209

storage sections, Warehouse Management, 159

storage types
  searches, 162
  Warehouse Management, 159

storage unit functions, stock removal, 165

storage unit management, stock removal, 164

strict lowest value principle, 156

structured entity-relationship model, 260

structures
  data object, 216
  organizational, 110
  plants, 206
    defining client, 206-207
    defining company code, 207
    defining plant, 208
    defining purchasing group, 207
    defining purchasing organization, 207
    defining storage location, 208

R/3 data structure policy, 209
  batches, 213
  European aricle numbers, 212
  industry sectors, 212
  material control functions, 211
  material data records, 213
  storage area, 212
  units of measure, 212
  quants, 213
upload, 335

subcontracting, MM special functions, 166

subitems, 44

subsidiary companies, 12

suppliers, master data, 189

supply chain technology, 355

supply chains, 361-365
  customer roles, 365
  forecasting, 362-363
  transportation, 363-365
    delivery confirmation, 364-365
    shipment loading, 364
    shipment scheduling, 363-364
    vehicle definition, 363

supply relationship, goods receipt, 147

supply sources
  material purchasing, 55
  sub-criteria, 52
  vendors
    alternative pricing plans, 53
    automatic evaluation, 51
    displaying evaluations, 52
    for specific material, 50-51
    net price simulation, 52

surcharges, calculations, 83

system inventory records, 140

T

table data, inventory control analysis, 301

tables
  custom reports, 314
    ABAP/4 data dictionary, 315
    SQL trace, 317
    tables for field name, 318
    tables for program, 318
    technical info, 314
  standard components, 27
    role of tables, 28

task area, architectural area, 248

Task entity type, 231

task models, 219

tax items, creating, 177

taxation
  functions, 67
  international, 67

text files, upload structure, 336

text items, 44

thin clients, 352

third-party deals, master data, 194

threshold values, 310

time area, architectural area, 249

time dependency annotation, 242

time periods, LIS information structures, 307

tolerances, invoices, 174

TOP-OF-PAGE DURING LINE-SELECTION command, 327

training
  challenges of, 368
  consultant's perspective, 378
    application skills, 379
    management skills, 379
    technical skills, 379
  detailed plans, 375-376
  impact on business, 369
    job roles, 370
    management commitment, 370
  key points of principles, 368
  MM module, 378
  program structure
    adult learners, 373
    expectations, 374
    in-house courses, 372
    quality training, 372
    SAP courses, 371
    setting goals, 372
  scope of, 377-378

transaction figure area, architectural area, 253

transaction figures-cost type, architectural area, 255

transaction figures-finance, architectural area, 256

transaction figures-fixed asset, architectural area, 255

transaction figures-logistic, architectural area, 255

transactions, 13, 24
  account assignment category, 14
  automatic documentation, 24
    document header fields, 25
    document line item detail fields, 25
    document principle, 24
  BDC, 340
  blocked invoices, 175
  custom reports, drill down, 330
  Financial Accounting, currency, 70
  General Ledger, 66
  information systems requirements, 295
  LIS database, 306
  manual document entry, 26
    recurring entries, 26
    set concept, 27
  materials invoice verification, addtional costs, 179
  Receivables Account, 65
  Warehouse Management component, 158
  withdrawals, 135

transfer order processing, transfer requirement documents, 162

transfer orders, goods receipt, 160

transfer requirement documents
  inventory management, 159-160
    confirmation option, 161
    inventory differences, 162
    goods for delivery note, 161
    goods issue, 161
    goods receipt, 160
    stock transfers, 161
  transfer order processing, 162

transport orders, stock, 167

transportation
  complaint processing
    credit memo requests, 202
    debit memo requests, 202
    returns, 202
  decentralized shipping, 201
  delivery management, 198
    output documents, 199
    pick list, 199
    shipping elements, 199
    status update, 199
  goods issue, 200

shipping work list, 197-198
Warehouse Management system, 200

transportation (automated), 363-365
  delivery confirmation, 364-365
  shipment loading, 364
  shipment scheduling, 363-364
  vehicle definition, 363

trends
  LIS warnings, 310
  purchasing, materials information systems, 290

triggered reporting, 305

U

unit costing, planning/simulation, 107

unit of issue, 16

unit of measures, 14-16
  architectural area, 250
  control functions
    alternatives, 39
    standard, 39
  goods receipts, 133
  R/3 data structure policy, 212

upload files, interfaces, 335

upload structure, 336

upstream relationships, 240

Usage phase, ISO 9000, 143

user departments, vendor data concept, 49

user interface, 22
  design, 22
    Dynpro, 23
    SAPGUI, 22
  sessions, 23
    R/3 Session Manager, 23

V

validity periods, 81

valuation, 389
  MRP/purchasing data, 210

valuation area, 20

valuation category, 20

valuation methods, product cost accounting, 106

valuation structures, 151
  categories, 151
  classes, 151
  types, 152
value contract, 19
value flow, General Ledger, 75
value-adding process, cost objects, 76
variable-sized items, 43
variant BOM, 44
vendor data concept, material purchasing, 47
  account groups, 50
  once-only vendors, 48
  user departments, 49
  vendor master records, 49
Vendor Evaluation component, 52
vendor master records, 49
  terms of payment, 178
vendor masters, 213
vendor special stocks, 40
vendors, 19
  buyer options, 57
  down payments, 179
  evaluation criterion, architectural area, 248
  industry sectors, 39
  inquiries, architectural area, 254
  material invoice verification, 172
  payments, alternative recipient, 69
  procurement procedures, 45
  purchasing, materials information systems, 291
  purchasing info records, 41
  quotation procedure, 56
  quotations, architectural area, 254
  selection QM, 146
  special stocks
    inventory management, 138
    MM special functions, 167
views
  data, 277
  function, 279
  information flow, 276
  organizational, 279
  process, 273
volume, units of measure, 212
volume-based rebate, 19

W

warehouse management, 20, 389
  decentralized, 168
  inventory management, 130
  MRP/purchasing data, 210
  stock placement strategies, 163
  stock removal strategies, 163
    assigning, 164
    delivery units, 164
    FIFO, 164
    LIFO, 164
    partial quantities, 164
    quantity, 164
    storage unit functions, 165
    storage unit management, 164
Warehouse Management module (MM-WM), 31, 132, 158, 200
  decentralized shipping, 201
  storage bin, 159
  storage bin type, 159
  storage location, displaying, 135
  storage section, 159
  storage type, 159
  warehouse number, 159
warehouse master record, 159
warehouses
  quants, 213
  stock, architectural area, 253
  storage areas, 213
Web servers, 347
Web-enabled workflow management, 186
WMC (Workflow Management Coalition), 184, 360
work centers
  production planning, 182
  routing, 183
work lists, shipping, 197-198
Workflow Management Coalition (WMC), 184, 360
workflow system, 358-360
  Document Management System, 358-359
    search facilities, 359
  networked, 360-361
    specialized subsystems, 361
    templates, 360-361
  PDM (Product Data Management), 359
    template, 360

workflow templates, commerce partners, 185
Workflow Wizards, 184
Workplace entity type, 230
writing reports, 318

X - Z

year 2000 compliance, 350
  certification tests, 350
ZAMARA000 sample report, 319
ZAMARA010 sample report, 323
ZMARA020 sample report, 327
ZMARA021 sample report, 331

Complete and Return this Card
for a *FREE* Computer Book Catalog

Thank you for purchasing this book! You have purchased a superior computer book written expressly for your needs. To continue to provide the kind of up-to-date, pertinent coverage you've come to expect from us, we need to hear from you. Please take a minute to complete and return this self-addressed, postage-paid form. In return, we'll send you a free catalog of all our computer books on topics ranging from word processing to programming and the internet.

Mr. ☐   Mrs. ☐   Ms. ☐   Dr. ☐

Name (first) ☐☐☐☐☐☐☐☐☐☐   (M.I.) ☐   (last) ☐☐☐☐☐☐☐☐☐☐☐☐☐☐☐☐

Address ☐☐☐☐☐☐☐☐☐☐☐☐☐☐☐☐☐☐☐☐☐☐☐☐☐☐☐☐☐☐☐☐☐

☐☐☐☐☐☐☐☐☐☐☐☐☐☐☐☐☐☐☐☐☐☐☐☐☐☐☐☐☐☐☐☐☐

City ☐☐☐☐☐☐☐☐☐☐☐☐☐☐   State ☐☐   Zip ☐☐☐☐☐   ☐☐☐☐

Phone ☐☐☐   ☐☐☐   ☐☐☐☐   Fax ☐☐☐   ☐☐☐   ☐☐☐☐

Company Name ☐☐☐☐☐☐☐☐☐☐☐☐☐☐☐☐☐☐☐☐☐☐☐☐☐☐☐☐☐☐

E-mail address ☐☐☐☐☐☐☐☐☐☐☐☐☐☐☐☐☐☐☐☐☐☐☐☐☐☐☐☐☐☐

1. Please check at least (3) influencing factors for purchasing this book.

Front or back cover information on book .... ☐
Special approach to the content .... ☐
Completeness of content .... ☐
Author's reputation .... ☐
Publisher's reputation .... ☐
Book cover design or layout .... ☐
Index or table of contents of book .... ☐
Price of book .... ☐
Special effects, graphics, illustrations .... ☐
Other (Please specify): _____ ☐

2. How did you first learn about this book?

Saw in Macmillan Computer Publishing catalog .... ☐
Recommended by store personnel .... ☐
Saw the book on bookshelf at store .... ☐
Recommended by a friend .... ☐
Received advertisement in the mail .... ☐
Saw an advertisement in: _____ ☐
Read book review in: _____ ☐
Other (Please specify): _____ ☐

3. How many computer books have you purchased in the last six months?

This book only .... ☐   3 to 5 books .... ☐
2 books.................. ☐   More than 5 .... ☐

4. Where did you purchase this book?

Bookstore .... ☐
Computer Store .... ☐
Consumer Electronics Store .... ☐
Department Store .... ☐
Office Club .... ☐
Warehouse Club .... ☐
Mail Order .... ☐
Direct from Publisher .... ☐
Internet site .... ☐
Other (Please specify): _____ ☐

5. How long have you been using a computer?

☐ Less than 6 months   ☐ 6 months to a year
☐ 1 to 3 years   ☐ More than 3 years

6. What is your level of experience with personal computers and with the subject of this book?

	With PCs	With subject of book
New	☐	☐
Casual	☐	☐
Accomplished	☐	☐
Expert	☐	☐

Source Code ISBN: 0-0000-0000-0

7. Which of the following best describes your job title?

Administrative Assistant .... ☐
Coordinator .... ☐
Manager/Supervisor .... ☐
Director .... ☐
Vice President .... ☐
President/CEO/COO .... ☐
Lawyer/Doctor/Medical Professional ..... ☐
Teacher/Educator/Trainer .... ☐
Engineer/Technician .... ☐
Consultant .... ☐
Not employed/Student/Retired .... ☐
Other (Please specify): _____ ☐

8. Which of the following best describes the area of the company your job title falls under?

Accounting .... ☐
Engineering .... ☐
Manufacturing .... ☐
Operations .... ☐
Marketing .... ☐
Sales .... ☐
Other (Please specify): _____ ☐

9. What is your age?

Under 20 .... ☐
21-29 .... ☐
30-39 .... ☐
40-49 .... ☐
50-59 .... ☐
60-over .... ☐

10. Are you:

Male .... ☐
Female .... ☐

11. Which computer publications do you read regularly? (Please list)

_____
_____
_____
_____
_____
_____
_____
_____
_____
_____

Comments: _____
_____
_____

Fold here and scotch-tape to mail

Check out Que® Books on the World Wide Web
http://www.quecorp.com

As the biggest software release in computer history, Windows 95 continues to redefine the computer industry. Click here for the latest info on our Windows 95 books

Make computing quick and easy with these products designed exclusively for new and casual users

Examine the latest releases in word processing, spreadsheets, operating systems, and suites

Desktop Applications & Operating Systems

que®

new Users

what's new?

Que's Publishing Areas

Windows 95

Internet And New Technologies

The Internet, The World Wide Web, CompuServe®, America Online®, Prodigy®—it's a world of ever-changing information. Don't get left behind!

Find out about new additions to our site, new bestsellers and hot topics

Calendar of Events

DEVELOPER AND EXPERT USERS

ZD ZIFF-DAVIS PRESS

Que's Top 10 Titles

Macintosh & Desktop Publishing

In-depth information on high-end topics: find the best reference books for databases, programming, networking, and client/server technologies

A recent addition to Que, Ziff-Davis Press publishes the highly-successful *How It Works* and *How to Use* series of books, as well as *PC Learning Labs Teaches* and *PC Magazine* series of book/disc packages

Stay on the cutting edge of Macintosh® technologies and visual communications

Find out which titles are making headlines

With 6 separate publishing groups, Que develops products for many specific market segments and areas of computer technology. Explore our Web Site and you'll find information on best-selling titles, newly published titles, upcoming products, authors, and much more.

- Stay informed on the latest industry trends and products available
- Visit our online bookstore for the latest information and editions
- Download software from Que's library of the best shareware and freeware

que® Copyright © 1997, Macmillan Computer Publishing-USA, A Viacom Company

MACMILLAN COMPUTER PUBLISHING USA

A VIACOM COMPANY

Technical ---- **Support:**

If you need assistance with the information in this book or with a CD/Disk accompanying the book, please access the Knowledge Base on our Web site at **http://www.superlibrary.com/general/support**. Our most Frequently Asked Questions are answered there. If you do not find the answer to your questions on our Web site, you may contact Macmillan Technical Support **(317) 581-3833** or e-mail us at **support@mcp.com**.

Why Join the ASAP team?

We are a fast growing dynamic group of companies operating globally in an exciting new virtual environment. We have the simple aim to be the best at what we do. We therefore look to recruit the best people on either contract or permanent basis

If you are any of the following, we would like to hear from you.

1. Highly Skilled and Experienced SAP Consultant.

You will have been working with SAP systems for many years and will be a project manager or consultant of standing in the industry. If you are willing to assist in the training and development and perhaps recruitment of your team, then we will be able to offer you exceptional financial rewards and the opportunity of developing the career of your choice.

2. Skilled in Another Area and Looking to Cross Train

You may be a computer expert or a business person with expertise in a particular area, perhaps, logistics, finance, distribution or H.R. etc., and/or with a particular industry knowledge. If you are committed to working with SAP systems in the long term, we will be able to offer you SAP cross training and vital experience. You must have a proven track record in your field and must be prepared to defer financial advancement whilst training and gaining experience. If you have the commitment and the skill you will in time be able to receive from us the high financial rewards and career development choice above.

3. A Person who has worked in a functional job

for an End User Company and who has been involved in all aspects of an SAP project from initial scoping to implementation and post implementation support.

You will have an excellent understanding of the industry or business function you are in. You are likely to have a good degree, ambition, drive, flexibility and the potential to become a top SAP consultant. You will thrive on the prospect of travel and living and working in other countries, jetting off around the world at short notice and working as part of a highly motivated and productive team. You must be committed to a long term career working with SAP. We will be able to offer you an interesting and rewarding career, giving you training and experience in a number of different roles. If you can prove yourself, you can expect rapid career development, with excellent financial rewards. Your only limit is your ability and your aspirations.

How To Contact Us

ASAP World Consultancy, ASAP House, PO Box 4463,
Henley on Thames, Oxfordshire RG9 6YN, UK
Tel:+44 (0)1491 414411 Fax: +44 (0)1491 414411

ASAP - 24 Hour - Virtual Office - New York, USA
Voice Mail: (212) 253 4180 Fax: (212) 253 4180

E-Mail: info@asap-consultancy.co.uk

Web site: http://www.asap-consultancy.co.uk/index.htm

A S A P
WORLD CONSULTANCY™

ASAP Worldwide

Enterprise Applications Resourcing & Recruitment

The company established in July 1997 has ambitious plans to become the world's largest global recruitment company specialising entirely in "the placement of permanent, temporary and contract staff who will be engaged in the implementation, support, training and documentation of systems known as enterprise applications". These include: SAP, BAAN, Peoplesoft, Oracle Applications, System Software Associates, Computer Associates, JD Edwards, Markam, JBA etc.

The company benefits from:

- Detailed knowledge of the market, its requirements and dynamics.

- Use of one of the world's most advanced recruitment systems.

- Access to large databases of candidates.

- A global approach to the staffing problems of a global market.

- Unique and innovative solutions for solving the staffing problems of a high growth market.

- A commitment to offer clients and candidates a professional, efficient and high quality service that is second to none.

- A commitment to the continual development of the services that we offer.

- Reciprocal partnership arrangements with other recruitment companies worldwide.

Services to companies looking for staff

Permanent, Contract & Temporary Recruitment

ASAP Worldwide has a deep understanding of the enterprise application resourcing market, its requirements and dynamics. Whether your requirement is for a single individual or a team of hundreds, we offer the best practices and standards of service you would expect from one of the world's most professional recruitment companies to solve your staffing requirements.

In such a high growth market where the right people are at a premium, it takes a very different approach to find and place candidates. We offer a unique range of services to companies of all sizes and in all sectors worldwide. We leave no stone unturned in our search for candidates and we have unique techniques for selecting the very best candidates to offer you. We offer originality and innovation that make us stand out from the crowd.

Service to people looking for work

We believe that there is far more to our work than simply trying to fill job vacancies. We believe that we are providing a service of equal value to both employers and candidates looking for work. We are genuinely interested in your personal and career development and we undertake to try our very best to find you the work that best meets your requirements. Because of the size of our network, we are able to offer a truly global service, so whatever part of the world you would like to work in, whatever the type of employer and whatever the type of work you would like, we believe that we are better placed to give you what you want.

Send us a copy of your C.V./resumé and receive a free copy of our "Career Development Programme" booklet, designed to help you advance your SAP career.

How to contact us:

ASAP Worldwide
PO Box 4463 Henley on Thames
Oxfordshire RG9 6YN UK
Tel: +44 (0)1491 414411
Fax: +44 (0)1491 414412

ASAP Worldwide - 24 Hour - Virtual Office - New York, USA
Voice Mail: (212) 253 4180 Fax: (212) 253 4180

E-Mail: enquiry@asap-consultancy.co.uk

Web site: http://www.asap-consultancy.co.uk

A S A P
WORLDWIDE™